Illustrious Daughters of the Land

Timeless Stories of Struggle, Resilience and Inspiration

Illustrious Daughters of the Land

Timeless Stories of Struggle, Resilience and Inspiration

Written by
Dr. Iti Samanta

Translated by
Jugal Kishore Mishra
Debamitra Mishra

BLACK EAGLE BOOKS
Dublin, USA | Bhubaneswar, India

BLACK EAGLE BOOKS
USA address:
7464 Wisdom Lane
Dublin, OH 43016

India address:
E/312, Trident Galaxy, Kalinga Nagar,
Bhubaneswar-751003, Odisha, India

E-mail: info@blackeaglebooks.org
Website: www.blackeaglebooks.org

First International Edition Published by
Black Eagle Books, 2025

ILLUSTRIOUS DAUGHTERS OF THE LAND
Timeless Stories of Struggle, Resilience and Inspiration

Written by **Dr. Iti Samanta**

Translated by **Jugal Kishore Mishra** | **Debamitra Mishra**

Odia original copyright © **Dr. Iti Samanta**
Translation copyright © Jugal Kishore Mishra, Debamitra Mishra

All rights reserved. No part of this publication may be reproduced, stored in a retrieval system, or transmitted, in any form or by any means, electronic, mechanical, photocopying, recording or otherwise without the prior permission of the publisher.

Cover Concept & Design:
Himanshu Shekhar Khatua & **Shreejit Abhishek**

Interior Design: Ezy's Publication

ISBN- 978-1-64560-720-5 (Paperback)
Library of Congress Control Number: 2025947747

Printed in India

Abstract

This book pays tribute to the lives, voices, and legacies of Indian women-women who have walked diverse paths, often uncelebrated and relegated to the margins of history. Drawn from the rich and intricate shades of India's cultural, historical, and social landscape, these stories highlight the strength, spirit, remarkable resilience and silent struggles of women who have, in countless ways, shaped the nation's destiny.

Over three years, the author undertook a fascinating journey through archives, literature, oral histories, and regional narratives to rediscover and reimagine these women's stories. Some of them were leaders and reformers, some artists, and thinkers, while many were ordinary women leading extraordinary lives in the quiet corners of homes and communities. From myths to modernity, and the pages of history to the margins of memory, these women are brought vividly to life through thoughtful interpretation and literary reflection.

This work is not merely a collection of biographies; it is a meditation on Indian womanhood. It explores the duties, responsibilities, dreams, and sacrifices that have defined and shaped women's lives in India throughout the ages. It captures their enduring quest for dignity, respect, and equality in a patriarchal world, as well as the many ways they have resisted, redefined, and triumphed over adversity.

In each story, one finds a spark of courage, intellect, compassion, and rebellion. Together, these sparks from a luminous flame that continues to illuminate the path generations to come would follow. The book invites readers to remember, reflect on, and honour the countless Indian women, whose stories deserve to be told, celebrated, and passed on.

Introduction

Women, and their stories.

The words are few, yet they hold entire worlds within them. Within these simple phrases lies a universe of meaning: her actions, her responsibilities, her dreams, her sacrifices, her mind and spirit, her land and role, her affection and love-all underscored by her dignity and self-worth.

Her words resonate with her rights, freedoms, aspirations, individuality, desires, and her long, arduous journey in the pursuit of equality in a world shaped by men. Through it all, she has carried the torch of culture, grace, wisdom, and quiet strength. Her manners, her steps, her thoughts-each a subtle revolution. The light she carries does not flicker; it illuminates the path for coming generations, a flame that burns from age to age, until the end of time.

I have always felt a deep connection to women's lives and narratives. My journey has never been about finding a singular story but rather about uncovering perspectives-perspectives that not only empower a woman's own life but also uplift her family, her community, and the generations that follow. Each woman's story offers a new way forward for all of us.

In my quest for these stories, I have explored the pages of history, traversed various mediums, and crossed geographical and cultural boundaries. The women whose stories are shared in this book have been discovered through diverse sources, each a testament to the courage and resilience embedded in their lives.

The deeper I searched, the more captivated I became. Their strength, their silence, their voices, their actions-all spoke volumes. These women redefined struggle and redefined duty. They never forgot their responsibilities, no matter how difficult their lives. And yet, their stories remain largely untold, under-discussed, and sometimes even forgotten.

The COVID-19 pandemic swept across the world like a silent storm, leaving deep scars on the fabric of human life. It stole loved ones from our embrace, stripped livelihoods away, and robbed even the simplest rhythm of daily living. Above all, it dimmed the eternal flame of hope. Yet, within its shadowed corridors, there were also glimmers of unexpected light. People unearthed hidden strengths, stumbled upon new possibilities, and began to see life through a different lens. It was in the heart of this strange and transformative time that I met these extraordinary women; not in person, but through the power of their stories. Each one carried within her courage, the steadfast beat of resilience, and the glow of hope. Their journeys stirred something deep within me, compelling me to breathe life into them once more, in my own words and my own language; so that their spirit may travel beyond the page and inspire countless women in our society.

This book is the result of three years of relentless pursuit-to find them, to learn about them, to see them through the lens of my own experience, and to transform those encounters into literature. I have walked alongside them in spirit, felt their battles, and shared their dreams. They came alive in my imagination, in the quiet moments between thought and creation, and then returned to the pages of paper and print.

These stories first found a home in the hearts of readers through the beloved Odia magazine *Kadambini*, which has itself been a part of Odisha's literary history for three years. The encouragement and warm response from its readers inspired me to compile this demanding, research-intensive work into a full-fledged book.

Now, it stands before you.

Each woman here shines with her inner light. Each is remarkable in her own right, noble in her courage, and graceful in her resilience. They are all extraordinary. This book is for those women who walk barefoot on thorny paths, who carry hammers in their hands to shatter society's barriers, and who tear through darkness to carve out new, radiant roads-not just for themselves, but for others to follow.

Let us remember them. Let us learn from them. Let us honour them.

Let us create many more like them.

Iti Samanta

Translators' Note

Translating this book has been a deeply moving experience. Every story held voices that were not just to be translated, but understood and honoured. These women, from many different parts of India's history and culture, spoke through memories, traditions, and emotions that sometimes had no easy equivalent in another language.

This book is not just a series of life stories; it is woven with courage, dreams, and resilience. We stayed true to the spirit of each story, capturing the strength and the struggles that lie behind each woman's journey. Translation here was not just about finding the right words-it was about listening carefully and carrying their voices with care and respect. Through this work, readers will feel the same admiration, sorrow, and inspiration. These women's lives, often forgotten or hidden, deserve to be remembered and celebrated.

Many ideas and words in the original text are deeply tied to Indian culture and history. Some of them have been kept in their original form, with small explanations where needed, so that the richness of these stories is not lost. We want readers to feel as close as possible to the worlds these women lived in-full of meaning, complexity, and strength.

At every step, we tried to stay close to the author Dr. Iti Samanta's voice: thoughtful, compassionate, and clear. It was important to preserve not just the facts, but the emotions-quiet pride, the pain, the hope-that run through these pages. Dr. Iti Samanta, an acclaimed writer, editor, and cultural visionary, has spent decades documenting and amplifying the voices of women across India, particularly from Odisha. She has played a pivotal role in nurturing regional literature and spotlighting grassroots narratives. Her storytelling is grounded in empathy, shaped by both lived experience and a deep scholarly engagement with social issues. This translation is a small tribute to the Indian women whose lives shaped our world, even if their names are not written in history books. Their stories matter, and by sharing them, we keep their spirit alive.

Their courage reminds us that history is not only made by great rulers and famous leaders, but also by everyday women who fought, dreamed, nurtured, and resisted in ways both small and profound. Each act of strength-whether in a household, a village, a courtroom, or a battlefield-added another thread to the fabric of our collective past.

As translators, we are humbled by the chance to carry their stories across languages and borders. We are reminded that translation is not just about changing words, but about carrying emotions, memories, and dreams across time and space. It is a way of saying: you were here; your life mattered; your voice endures.

We hope that as readers walk through these pages, they will not only learn about these extraordinary women but also feel connected to their spirit. May these stories inspire new conversations, new questions, and a deeper understanding of the strength that has always lived-and continues to live-within Indian womanhood.

We are deeply grateful to Prof. Jatindra Kumar Nayak, eminent scholar, litterateur, and mentor, for his constant support, insightful guidance, and generous encouragement throughout the translation of this book. His meticulous editing, thoughtful corrections, and commitment to excellence have greatly enriched the final work. This journey would not have been possible without his patience, expertise, and belief in the importance of bringing these stories to a wider audience. We remain profoundly indebted to him.

Jugal Kishore Mishra
Debamitra Mishra

Acknowledgment

'Maheeyasee Gareeyasee: Bhaaratiya Naree Pratima' book was originally published in Odia during the celebration of Azadi Ka Amrit Mahotsav in the year 2023. The women whose lives and contributions are portrayed in these pages have played significant roles in the history of our nation. They have made sacrifices, shown extraordinary courage, and paved the way for future generations. As I continued writing, so many inspiring characters came to light that the book naturally grew in volume and depth. At the time, I could never have imagined that this work would one day be translated into English and published for a wider audience.

Today, as this English edition comes to life, my heart is filled with gratitude. I sincerely thank the translator, Prof. Jugal Kishore Mishra & Ms. Debamitra Mishra, for the thoughtful rendering of the text, and Prof. Jatindra Kumar Nayak for his meticulous editing. I also extend heartfelt thanks to my Kadambini family for their constant support.

I would like to express my deepest gratitude to my lovable brother Prof. Dr. Achyuta Samanta, who has been a pillar of strength and inspiration in all my literary pursuits. His unwavering support and encouragement have been invaluable to me.

Special mention must go to my only son, Shreejit Abhishek, a scholar who helped me in collecting information about these famous women and encouraged me to go deeper into their characters. Without his support, this would not have been possible!

A special note of appreciation goes to Black Eagle Books and its founder, Mr. Satya Patnaik, whose efforts have made this English edition possible. I am grateful for their dedication and hard work for promotion of Literature.

Contents

Rani Prabhavati Gupta	15
Rani Sugandhadevi	20
Rani Dida	23
Rani Rudrama Devi	26
Khanzada Begum	38
Gulbadan Begum	45
Rani Abbakka Chowta	54
Hamida Banoo Begum	62
Sultana Chand Bibi	69
Noor Jahan	79
Jahanara Begum	92
Rani Ahilyabai Holkar	106
Rani Kittur Chennamma	119
Qudsia Begum	125
Sikander Begum	128
Shajahan Begum	130
Sultan Jahan Begum	132
Rani Jind Kaur	140
Begum Hazrat Mahal	154
Jhalkari Bai	161
Uda Devi	166
Ajijan Bai	169
Manikarnika Tambe a.k.a Rani Lakshmi Bai	171
Savitri Bai Phule	181
Fatima Sheikh	185
Muktabai Salve	188
Tarabai Shinde	198
Pandit Ramabai Saraswati	207

Kadambini Ganguly	218
Bhikaji Rustom Cama	227
Ramabai Ranade	237
Rukhmabai	248
Haimavati Sen	258
Matangini Hazra	272
Sarojini Naidu	277
Muthulakshmi Reddy	283
Amrit Kaur	292
Gulab Kaur	297
Iqbalunnisa Hussain	300
Janaki Ammal	311
Vijaylakshmi Pandit	319
Sucheta Kriplani	328
Begum Aijaz Rasul	338
Bina Das	345
Kamala Sohonie	353
Dakshayani Belayudhan	361
Amrita Shergill	370
Gaidinliu Pamei	380
Ismat Chugtai	388
Chonira Velliappa Muthamma	398
Kanaklata Barua	406
Anna Rajam Malhotra	410
Bibliography of data Reference	415
Bibliography	416
About the author	470

Rani Prabhavati Gupta

History! The more you delve into it, the more information you find. In addition to learning about existing facts, the exploration also yields more information, which makes one want to know more and more. Sometimes it's easy to talk about history, and sometimes it's not. If there is no information, how can we talk? At times, not everyone finds her place in the pages of history; they are not given the attention they deserve. But no matter what the situation is or the problems one has to face; at times, one leaves her mark in such a way that she finds a place in the annals of the past.

Discussions on India's prehistory often overlook women's contributions, reflecting entrenched gender bias. Historians have traditionally marginalized women's roles, mirroring societal attitudes of the time. Nevertheless, women's impact on society-building is undeniable. Emerging facts reveal women in pivotal positions: rulers, advisors, patrons, organizers, and more. Their significance can no longer be ignored.

Although these women have remained historically invisible, their work has given them a unique identity. Available evidence indicates that women definitely leave a mark if they stay on the right path and work hard. No one can erase it. Because the mark of good deeds is there and will remain. Whatever may be the situation and environment, whatever may be the difficulties in their journey, they just need to have the will overcome them. Sometimes life takes a turn where it becomes difficult for a woman to move forward. They can't decide which way is right for them, which way they should move along, or where they should keep their feet steady; such conflicts have come up many times in the lives of women. But they solve the problem very well. The impossible has always been made possible.

Despite historical invisibility, these women's accomplishments have given them a unique identity. Evidence confirms that women who persevere and work diligently, definitely leave a mark if they stay on the right path and work hard. No one can erase it. Because the mark of good deeds is there and will remain. Whatever may be the situation and environment, whatever may be the difficulties in their journey, they just need to have the will overcome them. Sometimes life takes a turn where it becomes difficult for a woman to move forward. They can't decide which way is right for them, which way they should move along, or where they should keep their feet steady; such conflicts have come up many times in the lives of women. But they solve the problem very well. The impossible has always been made possible.

Problems arise over time, and we may wonder why everyone experiences challenges in life. However, women often come to realize that it is not these problems that hold them back. When a woman strays from her goals and fails to give them adequate attention, her problems persist. Conversely, when she sets a clear goal, the path to resolving issues becomes clearer. Women possess the power to tackle all the world's problems and have demonstrated this ability throughout history. Even when society and social structures are shrouded in darkness, women have emerged to illuminate their paths. Regardless of the conflicts society may impose regarding their choices, women face these challenges with courage. Difficult times have led women to make tough decisions, and society has not always embraced those decisions. Despite facing criticism, women continue to forge ahead. They understand that their right actions today will create a positive impact for future generations. Importantly, they know that every problem in the world has a solution.

Here, we discuss three remarkable women whose contributions to society are noteworthy. They have made commendable impacts in their respective fields. Although each of these queens was exceptional in her own right, they were not specifically highlighted in historical records.

A princess named Kuber Nag was sent to the Gupta royal court as part of a royal treaty. Although her arrival occurred at a critical moment, she later established herself as one of the leading queens of the Gupta dynasty. She gave birth to Prabhavati. Prabhavati was active in royal affairs and displayed her mother's proficiency, which ultimately strengthened the Deccan empire, although this is not extensively documented in history.

Prabhavati was fearless, intelligent, and a visionary involved in politics. With her extensive experience, she assisted her father, Chandragupta, in defeating Sakaash of Gujarat in battle. This success brought her fame and made her quite popular among people. Interestingly, she chose not to adopt the Vakatakas' gotra 'Vishnubriddha,' but instead adopted the gotra 'Dharana' from her father's Gupta lineage.

Prabhavati was married to King Rudrasena II of the Vakataka dynasty around 388 CE. After their marriage, King Rudrasena II, who succeeded to the throne of the Vakataka dynasty, was initially a follower of Shaivism but he was influenced by Vaishnavism, and eventually converted to the latter. This shift in belief was certainly a result of Prabhavati's influence on him. She inspired her husband to pursue various cultural, social, and religious improvements. Under his reign, many religious institutions were established during the Gupta period. Prabhavati had two sons, Diwakar Sen and Damodar Sen.

The Vakataka Kingdom was founded around 255 CE, and its most notable ruler was King Prabhasena I, who conducted four Ashvamedha yajnas during his reign. This dynasty played a significant role in the establishment and propagation of Brahmanism in southern India. The Vakataka reign is often regarded as the most prosperous among all the dynasties that ruled in the south, with their rule lasting from the mid-3rd century CE to the 6th century CE. The Vakatakas, who ruled over central and southern India, became well-known through their effective policies. They were primarily Brahmins and belonged to the 'Vishnubriddha' gotra. Maharaja Rudrasena, the third ruler of the Vakataka dynasty, gave A new direction to the dynasty, although he struggled to manage his capital city.

Taking advantage of this situation, Emperor Samudragupta defeated and killed Rudrasena I in the Battle of Kaushambi. The history of the Vakatakas indicates that their successors sank into obscurity for many generations.

Prithvi Sena I was succeeded by his son Rudrasena II, who ruled from 358 to 390 CE. During his reign, the Gupta Empire's influence on the Vakatakas grew, leading to a strong alliance between the two. Influenced by Gupta II, Rudrasena renounced Shaivism and adopted Vaishnavism. Unfortunately, he died young at the age of 30. Following his death, his wife Prabhavati Gupta took on the role of protector of the Vakataka Empire.

After her husband's death in 390 AD, Prabhavati ruled for about 20 years, with her father providing support during her reign. It was quite remarkable for a woman to rule for such an extended period during that time. Prabhavati defended her kingdom until her son became an adult in 405 CE. She shifted the capital from Padmapura to Nandivardhana, which was located at the foot of Ramagiri.

Her father, Chandragupta, had constructed Udayagiri, while Prabhavati built the Ramagiri and Mandhal stupas.

These two edifices were significant because they played an important role in the promotion of Hinduism. During her travels to Nandivardhan, Queen Prabhavati sought to apply a new style of art to high-quality red clay stones. When her son, Diwakar Sen, grew up, he established a new capital for himself at Prabhapuram.

Although there are no reliable historical records, it is believed that Prabhavati died at 70. A monument dedicated to her was erected between Ramagiri and Prabhapura, and it was guarded by a family member from her mother's side, who belonged to the Naga clan. Prabhavati's life and career were fascinating, but her contributions have largely been overlooked by historians. Despite being one of the prominent rulers of her time, historians have not provided many details about her reign.

While Chandragupta II guided her in ruling the Vakataka kingdom, Prabhavati also supported her father in his war against the Shakas, which eventually led to a friendship with the Guptas. She documented the progress of the Uttara Gupta and Vakataka kingdoms on copper plates. Additionally, the coins from her era provide many details about her rule.

□□

Rani Sugandha Devi

Sugandhadevi, born in the ninth century CE, was the first medieval ruler of Kashmir. She was married to Shankaravarman, the Emperor of the Utpala Kingdom, whose reign lasted from 883 to 902 CE. Their marriage proved advantageous, as Sugandhadevi hailed from a noble dynasty, which helped strengthen the empire due to her influential connections.

However, this period of happiness was short-lived. A cloud of sorrow enveloped Sugandhadevi's life when King Shankaravarman was wounded in a battle and could not recover, and passed away. Sugandhadevi was profoundly saddened by her husband's passing, but she found the strength to rise above her grief, driven by a sense her duty and responsibility towards her son, Gopalavarman. She understood that it was her obligation to raise her son with love and respect to ensure the stability of the kingdom and the throne.

Kalhana, a famous poet from 1148 to 1149 AD wrote a poem regarding the history of Kashmir namely Rajatarangini. In this work, he sketches Sugandhadevi colorfully, observing that she was able to summon an army to support her husband in times of war. But historians claim the queen could also have had an affairs with the political representative and minister, Prabhakar. When the affair reached King Shankaravarman's ears, Prabhakar became worried and reportedly hired a sorcerer to arrange for King Shankaravarman to be murdered.

Sugandha's goal of altering the line of succession and crowning a suitable candidate was not particularly beneficial to Gopalavarman. However, she took a commendable step following the death of Shankaravarman by managing the affairs of the kingdom on behalf of her minor son, Gopalavarman. Gradually, Sugandha expanded her power as a ruler and became a favorite among the subjects. She sought to establish herself within the government and gain the support of various political factions in the royal court. Despite her efforts to increase her power and capabilities, these attempts ultimately led to her downfall, and she was overthrown in 914 CE. Her significant role in governance has led historians to refer to her as "Sugandhadevi," meaning the "Goddess of Fragrance."

After the death of Shankaravarman's last descendant, Gopalavarman's brother Samkata ascended the throne, but he mysteriously died ten days afterwards. Sugandha made several attempts, in consultation with Avantivarman, Shankaravarman's father, to ensure that someone within her family occupied the throne, but she was unsuccessful. Kalhana notes, "Though the dynasty of Shankaravarman was on the verge of extinction, Sugandha steadfastly tried to maintain the royal tradition."

Although Sugandha's regency may be seen as unremarkable, her administration was notably effective. Though she ruled Kashmir for a short period, her reign is often referred to as a "Golden Age" in the history of Kashmir. Sugandha founded two cities, Gopalpura and Sugandhapura. Premnath Bajaj says of Queen Sugandha in his book *Daughter of the Vitasta*, "People and subjects loved her very much. The councils believed in her. She was highly respected by the military." However, this talented queen could never enjoy a life of comfort and happiness. At that time, two powerful factions existed in the political landscape of Kashmir, each vying for supremacy. Yet the army held her in high regard.

Sugandha's path was fraught with challenges. She faced opposition from the Tantri group of the army on one side and the security personnel of the royal family, on the other. Amid this power struggle, Sugandhadevi made significant efforts to maintain government control with the support of the group and other loyal councils. In 914 CE, they fought a final battle for the Queen in Srinagar, but it was unsuccessful. Consequently, Queen Sugandha spent her last days as a prisoner in Nispalak Vihar.

The introduction of copper and bronze coins played a crucial role in uncovering the history of Queen Sugandha's empire. Some insights about these coins can be gathered from the debates among avid coin collectors. Additionally, these coins reflect gender disparities prevailing that era. Some argue that Sugandha introduced them to strengthen her dominance in a male-dominated society. Her actions symbolize her role as powerful ruler and her sense of authority.

In her book, *Feminist Theory and the Aesthetics Within*, Anu Aneja discusses the gender disparity prevalent in South India during that time. She states, "Here, I can mention Sugandha's time in the evolution of feminism." Her discussions range from the artifacts of the Indus Valley Civilization to Rekta. Aneja notes, "The struggle between masculinity and femininity accumulated both physically and mentally, leading to many mysterious events."

In modern terms, what we call gender disparity is shaped by the social traditions of the time, revealing different historical truths. The coins issued by Queen Sugandha convey a narrative of power that transcends gender differences between men and women. In *Rajatarangini*, Kalhana describes her as the revered king of the people, comparing her to a full moon on a clear night. He also emphasizes that Sugandha assisting her husband in battle was quite rare in India at the time.

□□

Rani Dida

Queen Dida ruled Kashmir from 958 CE to 1003 CE. She is mentioned in Kalhana's *Rajatarangini*, a 12th-century chronicle of Kashmir written in Sanskrit.

Dida was the daughter of King Sinharaja of Lahore, located in the Pir Panjal region of the North-West Frontier. Her father was very strict with her. Due to a defect in Dida's leg, she earned the nickname 'Lem.' For a long time, her father had no son to inherit the throne, but because of societal norms prevailing at that time in East Kashmir, Dida was unable to claim her father's inheritance.

Dida was married to Kshema Gupta from Kashmir, and the marriage was arranged to merge Lahore with their kingdom. Such marriages were common in feudal societies, often serving political purposes. After her marriage, Dida gradually consolidated her power in the spheres of governance and politics, as evidenced by her and her husband's names appearing on seals issued during that period.

Kshema Gupta died of a fever shortly after returning from a hunt in 958 CE, accompanied by their son, Abhimanyu II, who was still a boy at the time. Following the customs of the empire, Dida initially ruled on behalf of her son. However, she later assumed full control of the throne.

In the struggle for the empire, there were several attempts to overthrow Queen Dida. However, this intelligent queen adeptly outsmarted her opponents each time. Many clans were deeply dissatisfied with Dida's rise to power as regent. The ministers of the royal council felt humiliated under her rule and could not accept the fact that a woman was occupying the throne and managing the kingdom's affairs. Their growing dissatisfaction made cooperation in the administration increasingly unbearable for them. Eventually, these disgruntled feudal lords and council members conspired to overthrow her, but their efforts proved unsuccessful. Dida skillfully thwarted all their plots.

To win over the discontented feudal lords, Dida made every effort to gain their support. Influenced by the political strategy in the puranas (divide and rule), she played on disgruntled factions against one another, which helped her consolidate her power over time. Within about two years, this formerly disgruntled group began to align themselves with her. Dida was as strong as iron and governed with great prudence.

The death of her son Abhimanyu in 972 CE presented a new challenge for her. At that time, her youngest son, Nandigupta, was in critical condition. This situation further enraged the feudal landlords, who could not tolerate Dida's continued success.

Dida skillfully removed Nandigupta and his younger brother, Tribhuvan Gupta from her path, successfully resolving the issue at hand. Later, she established her youngest grandson, Bhimagupta, on the throne.

Dida sought to implement various changes in contemporary society, notably opposing the "purdah" system for women in a male-dominated environment. Above all, she proved to be an effective administrator while enacting these social reforms.

Some suggest that Dida fell in love with a man named Tunga in her middle age. However, this relationship was not accepted by all segments of society, as such unions were uncommon at the time. This love affair challenged prevailing social norms and drew opposition. Nonetheless, Dida became a symbol of feminism and empowerment for women. She was an outspoken and ambitious individual, but also forgiving and far-sighted. Despite her boldness, she skillfully navigated the obstacles in her way.

At the onset of her third grandson's reign, with Tunga's support, Dida consolidated her power and ruled until approximately 980 CE. She appointed Tunga as her Prime Minister, and his support bolstered her governance, enabling her to tackle existing social evils. Their partnership created a compromise that brought order to the regime, allowing Dida to foster a better understanding with her opponents.

It would not be an exaggeration to say that Dida effectively implemented a strong leadership style, using a firm hand to suppress her enemies. Two hundred years later, Razia Sultan faced similar challenges, but it can be argued that Dida was far more adept. She was a realist, sharp, and bold, qualities that her successors lacked. Dida remains recognized as one of the most powerful rulers in the history of Kashmir. Her exceptional talent in establishing peace and initiating changes in the social system through her administrative skills and diplomacy is valued from her time to the present day.

Archaeologist M.A. Stan was greatly impressed by Dida's character. He noted, "Although there are many character flaws to discuss, it must be admitted that as a competent politician, constitutionalist, and diplomat, Dida sat on the throne of Kashmir unchallenged until her last breath." Dida is remembered as one of the most outstanding empresses in Indian history.

Rani Rudrama Devi

Numerous incidents and accidents have been recorded throughout history. They include wars, invasions, conquests, bloodshed, violence, death, and destruction. History focuses on gaining and losing thrones, the expansion and contraction of empires, as well as themes of peace and war. It encapsulates sorrow, remorse, and happiness. By studying our history, we learn about the personalities of powerful, brave, learned, prudent, intelligent, and scholarly kings. We celebrate their skills on the battlefield, showcasing great courage and valor in both expanding the boundaries of their kingdoms and protecting them exercising their royal power. The power of kings is discussed thoroughly, providing a comprehensive understanding of their rule. It is often said that a nation is only as great as its knowledge of history.

History is also written about societies and the events that occur within them, which are extremely important. The term "male-dominated society" has been prevalent for a long time. This phrase highlights the dominance of men in society, which is evident in our historical narratives. There is much discussion about the valor, bravery, erudition, and intelligence of kings; however, considerably less attention is paid to queens and their heroic stories. This disparity is not the outcome of the queens lack intelligence, prudence, erudition, or valor. They are equally capable possessing the ability to rule and defend their people from enemies. Like kings, queens were able to expand the boundaries of their kingdoms, take intelligent evaluation, and demonstrate quality leadership. Unfortunately, they often faced considerable opposition. Just as society accepts the rule of a king, it does not always accept that of a queen. Opportunities for women are limited, leading to less than enthusiastic recognition of their contributions. Yet, despite these challenges, queens have proven their worth as rulers.

Throughout history, there are numerous examples of women who have excelled in leadership roles, at regional and national levels. They are strong figures who have made significant strides through their strengths and abilities. Regardless of whether history acknowledges them or not, these women have made history through their actions. They have set shining examples for us, showing us the way forward and teaching us how to overcome formidable obstacles. They demonstrate that the impossible can become possible.

There are many examples of women's power in India, particularly in the context of its long history. The monarchy has seen periods of rise and fall, and the role of women within this system has been a crucial one. Even in the monarchical structure, women have made their mark, and their sacrifices for the country and society are remembered forever.

One such notable woman is a powerful ruler who led a kingdom in India during the 13th century CE. She belonged to the Kakatiya dynasty. It was rare for a woman to be appointed as the head of a state in India at that time. Despite her exceptional position, she faced the harsh realities of a male-dominated society and had to deal with the backlash of gender discrimination.

Her greatest challenge stemmed from her laying claim to power as a woman. However, she did not allow any obstacles to deter her. Her story teaches us that, despite facing significant resistance, she remained relentlessly steadfast. She proved to be both a formidable warrior and an effective administrator. Ultimately, she gained widespread acceptance and respect for her leadership, which is evident in the legacy of her extensive and enduring rule.

History recognizes her as one of the most famous queens in India. She actively contributed to the nation's development and worked tirelessly to protect the interests of her people. During her reign, her subjects experienced peace despite pressures from neighboring empires. Although she encountered discrimination repeatedly, she viewed it a mere obstacle on her path to progress, and she persevered in her duties.

Her courage in combating social evils transformed societal attitudes, making her a remarkable figure. Through her exemplary actions, she became one of the most famous female in history, paving a new path for future generations to follow and create their own history.

This remarkable figure is the fourth independent ruler of the Kakatiya dynasty, one of the most celebrated rulers of this period. The Kakatiya dynasty lasted from approximately 1150 AD to 1323 AD, with its empire extending over what is now the Telangana region. The Kakatiya dynasty played a pivotal role in shaping the history and civilization of Telangana.

The foundation of the Kakatiya Empire was laid at Hanuman Kunda, a hill located between the Godavari and the Krishna. Warangal, then known as Orugallu, became the capital of the Kakatiya dynasty. Historians generally believe that the Kakatiyas existed as vassal states under the Western Chalukya kings from around the 8th CE, declaring their independence in 1163 CE. King Ganapatideva became the ruler in the late 1190s and succeeded in unifying the Telugu-speaking regions, even conquering parts of coastal Andhra.

However, King Ganapatideva had no sons to inherit the throne, which raised concerns about the line of succession. Some accounts suggest he had one daughter, while others propose he had two: the eldest, Rudrama Devi, and the youngest, Janapama Devi. At that time, the prevalent practice in South India favored male succession, leading to fears that the lack of a male heir could result in the dynasty's downfall and make the kingdom vulnerable to enemies.

In response to these challenges, King Ganapatideva held

discussions with his ministers to devise a solution to the problem. Recognizing the necessity of a successor, he declared his eldest daughter Rudrama Devi by naming her as his "male heir." He had her dressed as a prince and even gave her the name Rudradeva to emphasize her new identity.

Rudrama Devi stands out as a rare example of a woman taking on the role of a male heir within the constraints of her society. King Ganapatideva challenged the prevailing customs and traditions, choosing to name his daughter as his heir despite not having a son. He trained Rudrama Devi in various skills from a young age, instructing her in the art of warfare, royal governance, and making her aware of the importance of connecting with the populace. He empowered her by not only teaching her but also involving her in the affairs of the kingdom, preparing her to be a capable ruler.

Rudrama Devi was likely married to Virabhadra, a member of a minor branch of the Chalukya dynasty in the 1240s. Virabhadra was a prince of Nidadavolu and belonged to the Chalukya clan of the Bengi kingdom, which was conquered by Ganapatideva during the same period. Their marriage was one of political convenience, arranged as part of an alliance with Virabhadra's father. Despite this arrangement, King Ganapatideva did not assign any authority or responsibilities to his son-in-law. He had great confidence in his daughter, whom he had prepared for playing the role of ruler.

King Ganapatideva gradually introduced Rudrama Devi into the governing system. By the 1260s, Rudrama began to understand the workings of the kingdom alongside her father. Ultimately, Ganapatideva named Rudrama Devi as his successor to the Kakatiya throne. Prior to her ascension, she made frequent visits to various places and shrines within her kingdom to familiarize herself with different regions and the people. The father-daughter duo ruled together until Ganapatideva breathed his last.

However, during Rudrama Devi's initial joint rule with her father, their kingdom was thrown into disarray due to the Pandyan invasion led by Jatavarman Sundara Pandyian. The Kakatiyas, along with their allies, suffered a humiliating defeat at the battleground of Sutuku near

Nellore. While the attack was eventually repealed, King Ganapatideva lost extensive territory and prestige as a result. This undermined his control over the feudal kingdoms and left the state vulnerable.

Rudrama Devi's time with her father did not last long; she also lost him in 1267. The same year she lost her husband, Virabhadra. Her marital life was reportedly short-lived and not particularly happy. Virabhadra struggled to accept Rudrama Devi's position as a ruler and her success as an administrator. Jealous of her success, he refused to support her in any administrative duties.

After the deaths of her father and husband, Rudrama Devi was heartbroken but continued to govern the realm effectively. She was officially crowned in 1269, becoming the ruler of the empire. However, her ascension was met with opposition primarily due to her gender. Despite this, she received substantial support, which helped her strengthen her position as an independent ruler.

Unfortunately, Rudrama faced significant resistance, especially from her half-brothers, Harihara Deva and Murari Deva, who refused to recognize her authority and later rebelled against her. Many nobles and relatives felt outraged by the idea of a woman occupying the throne, and led to uprisings against her. Nonetheless, Rudrama Devi remained unperturbed by the rebellions. She confidently sat on the throne dressed in men's clothes, demonstrating her strength and resilience as a leader.

After ascending the throne, Rudrama Devi fought against Harihara Deva, Murari Deva, and other relatives who resisted her rule. Additionally, she faced external threats from the Pandyas and Cholas in the south, but she stoutly defended her kingdom against these incursions. During this tumultuous time, one of her greatest challenges came from the Siuna Yadavas of Devagiri in the west.

Since Rudrama Devi was a woman ruler, the Yadavas of neighboring Devanagari, the Gangas of Kalinga, and the Pandyas of the Tamil kingdom believed she must have been a weak leader. They saw this as an opportunity to conquer the Kakatiya kingdom. Mahadeva, the Yadava ruler of Siuna in Devagiri (present-day Daulatabad in the Aurangabad district of Maharashtra), attacked the fort of Warangal, the capital of the Kakatiya Empire. King Mahadeva hoped to take advantage of the internal instability within the Kakatiya Empire, assuming that because the ruler was a woman, he would easily claim victory. However, Mahadeva underestimated Rudrama's valour and administrative abilities.

Undeterred by his perception, Rudrama Devi did not back down. She courageously confronted the Yadavas and ultimately defeated Mahadeva, driving them away from her territory. Rudrama Devi pursued the Yadava rulers to the Godavari, crossed it, and forced Mahadeva to return to his homeland. Not only that, but she also sought to establish peace, compelling the Yadava king to sign a peace treaty. As part of the agreement, Mahadeva had to pay a substantial sum of money to rid himself of Queen Rudrama and secure peace. Although the treasures from the victory went to her treasury, Rudrama Devi chose to distribute them among her soldiers.

Interestingly, Yadava records presented a different account of the battle's outcome. They claimed that Rudrama Devi was 'spared' by King Mahadeva, who supposedly offered her a chance to win due to her being a woman. This was likely a tactic employed by Mahadeva to protect his image, as it was considered shameful for a man to be defeated by a woman at that time. Such claims were aimed at preserving his honor and prestige in society. Despite this distortion of history, one of Rudrama Devi's most significant victories was indeed over King Mahadeva, after which she adopted the title 'Rai Gaj Keshari,' meaning that she was the supreme ruler.

The opposition to Rudrama Devi was not limited to the Yadavas. In the 1262 CE, the Ganga king of Kalinga, Nrusingha I, captured the Bengi kingdom. It took 15 long years for Rani Rudrama Devi to reclaim this territory, aided by her commanders, Poti Nayak and Proli Nayak.

Rudrama Devi faced both external and internal threats with remarkable courage. Regarding external threats, King Nrusingha I, who had previously been defeated by Ganapati Deva, capitalized on the chaotic situation prevailing in Kakatiya-ruled states to reclaim lost territories in the Godavari tristate area. During the later years of Rudrama Devi's reign, she successfully regained control over these provinces. Her generals, Poti Nayak and Proli Nayak, fought against Bhanudeva, the son and successor of Nrusingha I, along with his allies, including the Odadi Matsya chief, Arjuna Deva. Through these efforts, the Kakatiya power was re-established in coastal Andhra Pradesh.

Rudrama Devi came to power at a young age, initially ruling the kingdom alongside her father as co-regent. After her father, she ruled the kingdom independently and laid a strong foundation for her rule that lasted about four decades. She was recognized as a great warrior, an exceptional monarch, and a skilled administrator in 13th-century India. Under her leadership, the kingdom thrived, leading to her reign being known as the Golden Age of Andhra Pradesh.

Rudrama Devi was one of the longest-serving rulers of the Kakatiya dynasty, despite facing numerous political challenges. She proved an able administrator, implementing numerous projects including the completion of the Warangal Fort, the construction of which had begun. She enhanced the fortifications by raising the height of the walls and adding a moat, transforming the fort into a formidable structure having a grand gateway and entrance. The fort housed beautiful buildings and temples that reflected her dedication to art and architecture.

Her commitment to welfare projects is now widely acknowledged. She got many ponds dug to improve agriculture, significantly increasing production in the state's fields. Rudrama Devi governed from Warangal, the capital of her kingdom, and got a memorial pavilion at the Swayambhu Temple constructed there. She depicted herself as a female warrior, iconically seated on a lion, resembling the fierce goddess Durga, armed with a sword and shield.

In 1994, an inscription found to be carved on a sandalwood slab by a soldier of the Mumadi army indicated that a village pond known as 'Rasamudram' was built during the Kakatiya period.

Rudrama Devi also introduced radical changes in her administrative structure. One of her notable policies was the induction of non-commissioned officers as commanders in the army, which sparked considerable controversy. It is believed she aimed to gain the trust of the common people and win the loyalty of new supporters in the face of opposition within her kingdom. The personal connections Rudrama

Devi sought to establish with her subjects demonstrated her political acumen and ability to wield official power effectively.

The master of the art of warfare had been fundamental to the establishment and success of the Kakatiya dynasty. To continue this tradition, she introduced the Nayankara system in the military, which later became popular during the Vijayanagara rule. In this system, Nayankars or Nayaka officials were granted to groups of villages in exchange for providing troops to the central Kakatiya administration during times of need. This approach not only strengthened the Kakatiya army but also emphasized the creation of loyal officials, diminishing the influence of local nobles who had been growing powerful at her expense.

Her military successes included the capture of key forts like Renadu, Eruva Mullikinadu, and Sati. Overall, her achievements, such as the completion of Warangal Fort, which featured an additional wall and rampart for protection against future sieges, highlight her remarkable leadership skills and vision for the kingdom.

It is said that Queen Rudrama Devi and Virabhadra had three daughters: Mamadama, Ruyama, and Rudrama. However, none of these daughters succeeded Rudrama Devi or ascended the throne. Instead, she appointed her eldest daughter's son, Pratap Rudra, as her successor.

For many years, very few people were aware of the achievements of Rudrama Devi. Although her name later became known, much of the information centered around her portrayal as a man.

The Venetian traveler Marco Polo praised the administrative qualities of Queen Rudrama Devi after visiting her kingdom. He commended her work ethic and impartiality, paying a glowing tribute to her excellent governance and lavishing praise on her as a wise leader. He characterized Rudrama Devi as a woman who constantly strove for justice and equality.

However, Marco Polo misidentified Rudrama Devi as the widow of King Ganapati Deva. He believed she could not be the daughter of Ganapati Deva. This assumption was not entirely unfounded as, during that time, royal heirs were predominantly male. Typically a king's widow would act as his representative until a son succeeded him.

Therefore, Marco Polo's mistake is easily understood. Other historians of the Kakatiya dynasty also referred to Rudrama Devi as the king's queen rather than his daughter.

The historian Cynthia Talbot discovered an inscription that states, "According to historical accounts, a daughter was chosen to succeed her father." In contemporary documents, Rudrama Devi is often depicted as a man. Talbot's research reveals that she is referred to as a maharaja (king) in 52 of the 62 inscriptions (approximately 84%). Her name has been translated as "Rudradeva."

A text compiled during the reign of her successor, Pratap Rudra, in the early fourteenth century states that her father, Ganapati Deva, decided to present Rudrama Devi as a man and called her Rudra. This decision followed an ancient custom that allowed a daughter to be appointed as her father's successor in the absence of a son, despite fierce opposition from the nobles. It is widely believed that Rudrama Devi dressed in men's clothes in public to normalize the situation. However, contemporary historical documents do not reveal how she reacted to these circumstances or how she emotionally coped with concealing her true identity. Nonetheless, the emotional struggles faced by her character are well-depicted in the acclaimed Telugu film "Rani Rudrama Devi" (2015).

Despite popular perceptions, she was often portrayed as a 'man.' Aside from textbooks and pamphlets, other sources indicate that she did not actively try to deceive the public about her identity. Certain scenes from the Kakatiya kingdom suggest that she was depicted as a woman. Notably, she chose to represent herself as a woman on the pillars she erected. Recently discovered relief sculptures in Bolikunda village, located in the Warangal district of Telangana, show that Rudrama Devi died in a fierce battle against a Kshatriya chieftain named Ambadeva. In one of these statues, her power and royal personality are expressed through the gestures of a fierce warrior. Archaeologist Dr. Kannababu's paintings highlight her distinct feminine qualities, featuring an oval face, soft cheeks, wide eyes, a thin nose, and soft lips.

However, despite all her progressive measures

(in the Kakatiya Empire), a small ruler began to revolt against

Rani Rudrama Devi during her reign. A relative of hers aided him in this uprising. Additionally, the Pandyas presented a strong challenge to her rule, and the people of the Kakatiya kingdom also expressed dissatisfaction with her leadership. The Karad state and local councils fiercely opposed being ruled by a female ruler. Gradually, more of her enemies joined the cause, as Rudrama Devi's effective governance, empathy with her people, and ability to confront her enemies boldly made her a threat to them. Under her rule, everyone felt safe, which was intolerable for her opponents. They began to unite against her. However, Rudrama Devi remained calm and collected, displaying great courage and wisdom. Determined to defeat her enemies, she valiantly fought back, achieved victory, and established herself firmly as a queen.

In the south, the kingdom of Nellore fell under Pandya rule and became a vassal state. The Kayastha chief, Jannig Dev, reclaimed vast areas of land from the Nellore kingdom and freed them from Pandyas' control. He and his brother, Tripuradeva (1270-72 CE), continued to govern the Valur kingdom as vassals of Rudrama Devi. However, things changed after their younger brother, Ambadeva, ascended the throne in 1272 CE.

Once Ambadeva became the leader of the Kayasthas in 1273 CE, he began struggling with internal discord. He opposed the dominance of the Kakatiya rulers, who controlled most of southwestern Andhra, now part of Guntur district. Ambadeva, a rebel from the Karad kingdom who sought independence, allied himself with Kakatiya's enemies, including the Pandyas and the Yadavas.

Rudrama Devi could not tolerate Ambadeva's defiance. By that time, her grandson, Pratapa Rudra, had grown strong enough to manage the administration. Pratapa Rudra Dev was a remarkably brave and skilled war strategist. He devised a three-pronged attack against Ambadeva to weaken his support systems and diminish his fighting strength. The first phase involved joint leadership from Rani Rudrama Devi and the commander-in-chief, Mallikarjuna. However, documents from 1283, discovered near Chandupatla in the Nalgonda district, suggest that Ambadeva killed both Rani Rudrama Devi and Mallikarjuna Nayaka during a battle that year. Despite having a strong army, Rudrama Devi's forces faced defeat. Later, her successor, Pratapa

Rudra Deva II, successfully suppressed the Kayastha rebellion, leaving Ambadeva with no opportunity to challenge the Kakatiya Empire further. It is said that Amabadeva died from wounds sustained during the battle in Chandupatla town in Andhra Pradesh.

However, some sources suggest that Rudrama Devi may have died in 1289 during a battle with Ambadeva, while others claim she did not die until 1295. According to legend and available evidence, Rudrama Devi died fighting alongside her soldiers, embodying the spirit of a true warrior. In addition to her conflict with Ambadeva, she faced rebellions from her nobles, including prominent figures like Harihara Deva and Murari Deva.

Queen Rudrama Devi, who made history through her actions and unusual way of life, set an example for others by donning male attire throughout her life. One might wonder about her reasons for choosing to dress as a man for so long. Several explanations could be offered, but ultimately, no one can truly fathom her reasons. However, analyzing her actions reveals that, even if there was a desire to express her femininity, she may have prioritized her role as a ruler above all else. Her dedication and sacrifice were aimed at the administration of the state and the welfare of the people. She fought for development, security, and justice, adopting a masculine image to fulfill her responsibilities. This significant change in societal norms was later emulated by the Vijayanagara Empire.

Historical accounts clearly illustrate that gender discrimination serves as both a barrier and a weapon of oppression.

The 13th century saw the rise of two legendary queens who fell victim to gender antagonism. Iltutmish's daughter, Razia Sultana, ascended the throne of Delhi in 1236. In an era marked by male dominance, queens like Rudrama Devi and Razia Sultan took control of their kingdoms, but they had to fight to retain their power. Tragically, even in the highest positions, attempts were made to suppress these women. Razia's reign lasted less than four years, despite her possessing the admirable qualities required of a ruler, as noted by historian Manhas Siraj. The prevailing social system of the time imposed crippling constraints on her rule.

During a period when the purdah system was a significant aspect of Mughal customs and dress, Razia courageously opposed it. She also adopted traditionally male attire, such as the kaaba and jula, defying societal norms.

In both cases, dress and appearance serve as common denominators. This historical trend of women adopting traditional masculine qualities through their attire was a significant form of protest. For ages, women have concealed their identities as a means to enter the public sphere. From historical figures like Razia Sultan and Rudrama Devi to contemporary women, their relentless efforts to break free from domestic confines have echoed a protest against patriarchal norms.

The extraordinary stories of these remarkable women demonstrate that enthusiasm, courage, perseverance, and determination can empower a woman to excel in any field. Women have historically faced barriers to power; nevertheless, they have made remarkable strides despite these challenges. Often, a woman's accomplishments are overshadowed by those of the male figures in her life, but she continues to strive. Society compelled women in ancient India to prove their worth in a male-dominated environment. Many women have spent their lives adopting masculine principles and behaviours. It is particularly noteworthy that King Ganapati Deva recognized Rudrama Devi's capabilities as a successor, especially considering the gender discrimination prevalent in that era. Had he chosen someone else without considering her, she might have missed the opportunity to display her brilliant leadership quality.

This discussion highlights the ongoing struggle of women to assert their existence, which has endured through the ages. Despite challenges, they remain undeterred. Her journey shows that there is nothing a woman cannot achieve. She is willing to make sacrifices for her family, society, and country. However, waiting or being passive is not an option. A high-class woman like Rani Rudramadevi was compelled by societal expectations to wear men's clothes and rule, yet it is important to note that she could do so precisely because she was a remarkable woman.

◻◻

Khanzada Begum

She was a Taimur Princess! Khanzada Begum was the daughter of Umar Sheikh Mirza II of Fergana and the elder sister of Babur, the founder of the Mughal Empire. She shared a very close relationship with her brother, and fortunately, both enjoyed happiness until the end of their lives.

At that time, the Mirza family ruled a small region in central Asia, but they were able to expand their control over a large area of the Indian subcontinent. Khanzada Begum risked her life for the safety of her family and was the first child of Umar Sheikh Mirza II and his first wife, Qutlugh Nigar Khan, she was born in 1478. She had the strong demeanour of a princess, and her life was marked by sacrifice. Khanzada accompanied her grandmother, Aisan Daulat Begum during the early period of the Mughal Empire. She has been described as the most powerful woman in the Mughal Empire, being a descendant of Genghis Khan on her mother's side and of Taimur on her father's side.

Five years older than Babur, Khanzada endured many sacrifices not only to help establish the Mughal Empire but also to protect and improve her brother's life. Her love for Babur was profound, and she always remained deeply concerned about his well-being. She went to great lengths to ensure his safety, remaining completely devoted to him. It is said that Shaybani Khan was the greatest enemy of their empire.

In order to protect her family, Khanzada surrendered herself to Shaybani Khan, despite his status as the enemy of her empire. She married him and endured immense suffering. When Babur was 17 years old in 1500 CE, he married for the first time, choosing Ayesha Sultan Begum as his wife. Although his love for her was strong, Babur later admitted that his plans failed and his affection faded. During this tumultuous time, Ayesha Sultan became pregnant despite Babur's reluctance and traveled to Samarkand under difficult circumstances. Sadly, their first child, Fakhr Unnisa, died just forty days after birth. Around this period, Babur met his greatest enemy, who drove him out of his birthplace, Samarkand, leaving him in despair.

Babur's hereditary enemy was the Uzbek, who recognized that the Taimur era in Central Asia was coming to an end. He lamented, "Samarkand belonged to our family for about 140 years, then the Uzbeks came and occupied it." Shaybani Khan, the Uzbek chief, besieged Babur and his followers for six months. Babur's uncle and his sons, unfortunately, refused to help him. Determined, Babur decided to rapidly construct a fort in Samarkand and take charge of its security, while his mother and sister remained there.

Conditions continued to deteriorate, and the hope of achieving a respectable victory for Babur was fading. At that time, Babur faced a decision that would irrevocably change the fate of a beloved family member. It was such a shameful arrangement that Babur did not even mention it in his autobiography.

Shaybani Khan sent word to Babur, proposing that if he arranged Shaybani's marriage to his sister, Khanzada Begum, a lasting peace could be established between them.

Reluctantly, Babur accepted Shaybani's proposal. As a result, Khanzada Begum was given to Shaybani as a gift in recognition of

Shaybani Khan's victory in battle. The twenty-three-year-old Khanzada Begum remained in Samarkand as Shaybani's servant. It is evident that Shaybani Khan kept Babur and his companions without food for six months while besieging them. There was no apparent reason to end the conflict; had there been a truce, Babur would not have been forced to leave Samarkand, and Khanzada would not have fallen into Shaybani's hands. As Mirza Haidar notes "Babur gave up Khanzada Begum in exchange for his life and fled." Babur left Samarkand barefoot with two hundred followers, without any weapons, and wearing the slippers of peasants, putting his trust in God.

While writing about Shaybani in his Baburnama, Babur grew restless and failed to address the incident properly, as it was an extremely humiliating experience. With the rise of the Uzbeks, intermarriage between Uzbek warriors and Timurid nobles increased significantly. Babur simply states, "Shaybani started the war of peace, and we made peace." When Babur was leaving with his mother and sister, his sister fell into the hands of Burmwud Khan (Shaybani).

After living with Shaybani, Khanzada gave birth to a son named Khurram, who died shortly after. A few years later, Shaybani divorced Khanzada Begum, accusing her of always remaining loyal to her brother Babur and his family. Following the divorce, she married Sayyad Hadda, a subordinate of Shaybani. Khanzada remained in exile for ten years.

Finally, in 1510, Shah Ismail, a Shia religious leader and the founder of the Safavid dynasty, brought his forces to Iran in a series of conquests and turned his attention to the Sunni Uzbeks. He killed both Shaybani Khan and Sayyad Hadda in the Battle of Merb in 1510. After the war, when Shah Ismail learned that Khanzada was the sister of Emperor Babur Mirza, he sent her back to Babur with some troops at Kunduz, which is located 600 km to the south. At that time, Babur was about twenty-three years old.

Mirza Haidar informed Babur that Khanzada was very happy, and there was no reason to doubt him. Khanzada's relaxed behavior may have contributed to the fact that she holds a unique place in Timurid legacy, unlike other Timurid women who are often associated with stigma. Instead, Khanzada joined Babur's family and was referred to as Padshah. The responsibility of safeguarding Padshah fell not only on Babur but also on his son Humayun and his successors.

Khanzada endured many atrocities. The Mongols were consistently prioritized over her. Reports indicate that Shaybani physically abused Khanzada on several occasions, which she could not endure. Ultimately, he divorced her, and in an additional act of humiliation, he married her off to Sayyad Hadda, a subordinate of Khanzada.

In 1511, Shah Ismail defeated Shaybani at the Battle of Marwa, killing both Shaybani and Sayyad Hadda. After this victory, he sent Khanzada to Babur in Kunduz, after which Babur and Shah Ismail became friends.

Upon returning to her brother Babur, Khanzada remarried Muhammad Mahdi Khwaja. Although she did not have any children of her own, she loved her husband's sister Sultan Begum's daughter as though she were her own. Khanzada aimed to marry her off to Prince Mirza Hindal, the younger brother of Humayun, and successfully accomplished this in 1537.

Khanzada Begum's life revolved around her brother Babur. In the *Baburnama*, Babur expresses his feelings for his sister Khanzada, stating, "You are a heroine, my savior, my goddess, my good-luck charm. I would not be alive without your sacrifices. I would not have survived to conquer Kabul if it weren't for you being in my family. You will be the head of my family; you will be the Padshah Begum because you are our guiding light. We exist because of you."

Khanzada Begum is also mentioned in the *Humayunnama*. Babur bestowed upon her the prestigious title 'Padshah Begum'. After Babur's death, Khanzada became the first female ruler of his empire. She is frequently referenced in the *Baburnama*, with fondness and respect. Her niece, Gulbadan Begum, also mentions her in *Humayunnama*, referring to her as the most beloved woman (Janam). The *Humayunnama* notes that Khanzada Begum often advised her nephews on matters of governance.

When Babur's father died, instability spread across all the states. For this reason, when Babur traveled to Fergana to consolidate his inheritance, he likely found himself alone, as the Timurid princes were seeking territories to govern in various parts of Central Asia at that time.

During this period of uncertainty, Babur quickly consulted his closest advisor and grandmother, Aesan Daulat Begum, to devise a strategic plan. In his autobiography, Babur notes that some women, like his grandmother, excelled in strategy and planning, and many vitally important issues were discussed with her.

On the other hand, Babur frequently described his father as someone who, although capable of ruling, was not gentle. Babur characterized him as short of stature, with a thick beard and a hard face. He also noted that his father was a heavy drinker and had a weakness for majoon, which led to his downfall.

When Babur spoke of his mother, grandmother, and sisters, he did so with affection, love, and respect. He held his grandmother Aesan Daulat Begum in particularly high regard. This admiration is not surprising, considering she was an extraordinary woman in a land known for its strong and courageous women. Previously, Sheikh Jamal-ud-din Khan had held both Aesan Daulat Begum and her husband Yunus Khan captive. Later, Sheikh Jamal gave Aesan Daulat Begum to one of his servants, Khwaja Kalan, as a gift.

The 16th-century historian Mirza Muhammad Haidar Dughlat states that Aesan Daulat did not protest against this treatment; instead, there was jubilation. However, when Khwaja Kalan entered Aesan Daulat's room that evening, her loyal servants locked the door behind him and assassinated him. Aesan Daulat was the mastermind behind this plan. Later that evening, when Sheikh Jamal learned of the murder and sought an explanation from Begum, she responded with unparalleled dignity and pride, saying, "I am the wife of Yunus Khan. Sheikh Jamal gave me to someone else, which is not permitted by Mohammedan law. That is why I killed him; let Sheikh Jamal kill me if he chooses."

However, upon witnessing the courage of this woman, the Sheikh respectfully returned her to her husband.

Aesan Begum was one of the most resolute and courageous women of her time. Following her father's death, she safeguarded her grandson and took a crucial decision to secure their future.

Begum Daulat, along with her daughter and daughter-in-law, Babur's mother Kuklug Nigar Khanam, supported Babur throughout most of his guerrilla wars. He was also accompanied by his eldest sister, Khanzada, who was five years older than him. These were difficult years for them, as they had no fixed place to stay. During this time, Babur made several unsuccessful attempts to besiege Timur and faced exile. Even in these challenging circumstances, his grandmother, mother, and sister remained by his side like shadows.

When Humayun became the Padshah Ghazi of Hindustan, Khanzada, along with some other elderly women from Harman, became a living repository of Babur's memories and Timur's dreams. She was seen as the custodian of a threshold, symbolizing the Mughals' departure from Samarkand in search of solace. No one would have predicted that Khanzada would become the most valued and respected member of Humayun's royal court; this was a reward for her strength to dream.

Khanzada emerged as the most powerful Mughal woman long after Babur's death, earning the title 'Hindustan ki Padshah Begum.' During the two hundred years of Mughal rule, the names of no other 'Padshah Begum' was mentioned. This was no accident; Khanzada truly deserved it, symbolizing the respect accorded to remarkable women who enjoyed significant privileges. Khanzada Begum was childless and had been widowed twice. She assumed her title in recognition of her sacrifices, valor, and the legacy she embodied.

Khanzada died at Vatsal-chak in 1545 while travelling to Kandahar with her nephew Humayun. It is said that she suffered from fever for three days before passing away on the fourth day. She was buried initially in the local graveyard, but three days later, her body was brought to Kabul and interred in the 'Garden of Babur,' next to her beloved brother Babur.

From this account, it becomes clear that the path of life is often filled with challenges, and the struggle to advance is constant. Women, like Khanzada Begum, remain steadfast in their actions. Whenever a duty arises, they courageously fulfill it. Khanzada is one of the most revered figures in our history, exemplifying strong will and unwavering resilience. Her actions reflect a beautiful example of brotherly love; she sacrificed her own happiness to ensure her brother's well-being and happiness, even enduring numerous hardships and humiliations for his sake.

God has created women in various forms, each nurturing and dutiful in her own right. When women fulfil their responsibilities with determination and integrity, not only do they advance, but they also succeed in perform their duties despite any obstacles. In doing so, they shape the course of history.

○□

Gulbadan Begum

Gulbadan Begum was regarded as an educated, intelligent, knowledgeable, virtuous, and pious woman from a noble family in her own time. She possessed immense self-confidence and was an astute observer of royal affairs and various royal treaties. She played a significant role in both society and her family. Gulbadan had a deep appreciation for books, loved to read, and engaged in numerous important activities throughout her life, including extensive charity work. She firmly believed that those who help the poor and the destitute and do charitable deeds with sincerity earn the grace of Allah.

Born into a noble family on February 7, 1523, Gulbadan faced tragedy early in life when her father died when she was just eight years' old. Subsequently, she was raised by her older brother and stepbrother. At the age of 17, she married her distant cousin, Khizr Kwaza Khan, the son of Emman Khwaja Sultan and the grandson of Khan Ahmad Alak, a feudatory of the Chagatai community.

Gulbadan Begum was one of the most celebrated women of her time. She was the daughter of Babur, the founder of the Mughal Empire in India, and her mother was Dildar Begum. The name Gulbadan means "the body of a rose" in Persian. At the time of her birth in 1523, her father Babur had been the ruler of Kabul for 19 years. He also ruled Kunduz and Swat's Badaksthan in Bajapur until 1519, and Kandahar was under his control for one year. For ten of those 19 years, he served as Timur's deputy. Two years after her birth, Babur began his final campaign to cross the Indus and establish his empire in India.

Gulbadan was not Babur's only daughter. He had two sons and three daughters: Gulchhera Begum, Gulbadan Begum, and Gulrang Begum, along with his eldest son, Hindal Mirza. His youngest son, Alwar Mirza, died in infancy. Gulbadan was particularly close to her elder brother, Hindal Mirza, and Humayun was her stepbrother. She spent most of her life in Kabul and traveled to India with her stepmother in 1528. Upon their arrival, her stepmother adopted her as her child at the emperor's request.

Emperor Babur, who came from Central Asia, invaded India after ruling Kabul. He fought the First Battle of Panipat in 1526, where he defeated Ibrahim Lodi and laid the foundation of his empire in India. However, Babur's reign was short-lived, as he passed away four years later, in 1530. His son, Humayun, succeeded him. Before his death, Babur instructed his eldest son to distribute portions of the empire among his other brothers. Humayun, known for his kindness and humility, acted according to his father's wishes.

Humayun's gentle nature renderd him indecisive. In 1540, he was defeated by Sher Shah Suri, the Pathan ruler of Bihar, forcing him to forfeit the empire his father had established. Accompanied by his pregnant wife, Hamida Banu Begum, a concierge, and trusted aides, Humayun first fled to Lahore and then sought refuge in Kabul, where he lived in exile for 15 years in what is now Afghanistan and Persia.

After the loss of Delhi Sultanate in 1540, Gulbadan Begum returned to Kabul with him. Later, Humayun regained strength with the support of other rulers and invaded India in 1555, this time achieving success. He regained control over Delhi and Agra, re-establishing his empire.

Tragically, Humayun died in 1556 under unfortunate circumstances. Two years after his death, his son Akbar requested Gulbadan Begum to join him in India. She arrived at the royal palace in Agra, not just as a passive presence but actively guiding her nephew. Gulbadan Begum managed Akbar's palaces and homes effectively, earning considerable love and respect from him and his mother. Growing up in Kabul, she was influenced by her father Babur, and brother Humayun, and she continuously honed her skills.

Akbar greatly valued his aunt Gulbadan Begum. Her piety, education, humility, and graceful demeanor made her a trusted figure. One of her significant contributions was in the field of writing. While she managed royal affairs, Akbar had complete faith in her writing abilities. During this time, Mughal rulers sought to maintain written records of their empire and administration. The Persian scholar Abul Fazl documented Gulbadan Begum's life writing her biography and recording her artistic contributions, in *Akbarnama*.

Akbar requested his aunt, Gulbadan Begum, to write a biography of his father, Humayun. Unlike biographies of other emperors that were written when they were alive, Humayun's biography was not completed until much later. Akbar asked Gulbadan Begum to document what she recalled about her brother Humayun's life. She was pleased to see him exempting faith in her and the love, reverence, and affection Akbar showed his father. Accepting Akbar's proposal, she began her work with the title "Ahwal Humayun Padshah Jamah Kardom Gulbadan Begum, daughter of Babur Padshah, Ama Akbar Padshah." This biography later came to be known as the *Humayunama*.

Gulbadan Begum is best-known for *Humayun Nama*, a biography of her half-brother Humayun, written at the request of her nephew, Emperor Akbar. In this work, she provides a brief account of Babur and includes special information about Humayun's family life, royal affairs, and rare details about his relationship with his half-brother, Kamran Mirza. Even so, she expresses great sadness and emotion regarding the conflicts between her brothers.

It is noteworthy that Gulbadan, who did not write in the elevated language of the famous writers of her time, chose to use simple language.

Her father, Babur, wrote *Baburnama* in a similar style. Gulbadan followed in his footsteps, revealing everything that transpired during Humayun's time and sharing her thoughts in straightforward language. The accounts of Humayun's reign, life, and struggles provide not only historical facts but also valuable insights into the Mughal family's palaces and other aspects of their lives.

In referring to how she began her work on Akbar's instructions, Gulbadan writes, "There was a manual that said - describe everything you know about Firdaus Makani (Babur) and Janat Ashiyani (Humayun). When Samrat Firdaus Makani left this world, I was only an 8-year-old girl, so I don't remember much. Nevertheless, at the king's command, I will describe all that I know and have heard."

In the first part of the book, Gulbadan Begum describes Humayun's rule following the death of his father, Babur, and his subsequent journeys after being defeated in war. At the time of Babur's death, she was only eight years old, and she offers valuable insights into this period. The book includes stories she heard from Babur's contemporaries and recounts events unfulfilling in the royal court. The next section focuses on events taking place inside the Mughal palace.

One intriguing incident she narrates involves Babur's unusual desire to create a massive gold coin. After establishing his capital in India, he fulfilled this wish. The gold coin was sent to Kabul, where the prominent comedian Asas was commissioned to present it. Blindfolded, Asas had the enormous gold coin hung around his neck. Initially unaware of the value of the heavy object he bore, he complained bitterly until he discovered it was a gold coin. Overjoyed, Asas exclaimed that no one could ever take it from him.

Gulbadan Begum also writes about the death of her father, Babur, particularly during a distressing time when her brother fell ill at the age of 22. Babur was terrified at the prospect of losing his son and spent four days praying to Allah at his bedside, offering to the lord his own life in exchange of that of his ailing son. Miraculously, his son recovered, but sadly, Babur passed away at the age of 47.

After Babur's death, Humayun Shah Hussain Mirza fell in love with his 13-year-old niece, Hamida Banu. However, Hamida initially refused to marry Humayun due to the significant age difference. Eventually, after encouragement from the elder women of the palace, she consented to the marriage. Two years later, in 1542, Hamida Banu gave birth to Akbar, who would become the principal ruler of the Mughal Empire.

In *Humayunama*, Gulbadan Begum humorously narrates many interesting facts about Hamida Banu and Humayun's marriage. She vividly describes the nomadic lifestyle of Mughal women, noting that, from the beginning of the Mughal Empire, even during Shah Jahan's reign, no Mughal woman preferred to stay in one place for an extended period. They enjoyed traveling frequently and would move to different locations at various times. Born into a Mughal family that embraced a nomadic lifestyle, Gulbadan Begum visited Kabul, Agra, and Lahore. She believed that the foundation of the Mughal Empire could not be strengthened if it remained confined to one location. Later, Shah Jahan's daughter, Jahanara Begum, also supported Gulbadan's perspective.

After Humayun ascended the throne, Gulbadan Begum faced increased travel difficulties, prompting her to return to Kabul with one of Humayun's half-brothers. However, this half-brother turned against Humayun and persuaded Gulbadan's husband to support him. Despite Gulbadan Begum's repeated advice to her husband to refrain from taking his side, he refused to listen to her. The consequences were severe: Humayun defeated Gulbadan's husband, who was ultimately expelled. Following this conflict, Gulbadan's husband lost his place in her life, and permission was denied to build his grave near hers.

Humayunama is the only book authored by Gulbadan Begum, the sole female writer of the 16th-century Mughal Empire. There are suspicions that Gulbadan may have originally written it in her mother tongue, Turkish, rather than in Persian; however, the book is known primarily through translation.

In her book, Gulbadan Begum recounts that Humayun died from injuries sustained at the Old Fort of Delhi, but this specific information seems to have been lost over time. The manuscript was completed in 1552, four years before Humayun's death. Kamran Mirza is mentioned at the end of the book. Since it is known that Gulbadan wrote this work at the behest of her nephew, Akbar, it is evident that the writing began long after Humayun's passing. Some believe that the data included is not comprehensive and that Akbar may have instructed his aunt to record memories that would aid Abul Fazl in writing about his own reign. Often, the most influential narratives are crafted by those in power. Historian Angela Wallacourt shows how the book draws attention to feminism and the remarkable contributions of female historians.

Gulbadan Begum's *Humayunama* strikes us as an impressive historical document. It represents the only historical record from 16th-century Mughal-ruled India authored by a female historian. Unfortunately, this important document was lost shortly after its creation, and when it resurfaced later, many pages had been lost, including the last chapter, thus rendering it incomplete. The brief chapters that remain from the original text have prevented it from receiving the recognition it truly deserves.

A copy of this document is preserved in the British Library. The original text was in the possession of Colonel G. W. Hamilton of Britain. His widow sold it to the British Museum in 1868. Its existence became widely known after Annette Beveridge translated it into English in 1900. Beveridge's translation was published as a book in India in 2001. In 2006, Pradesh Chattopadhyay translated *Humayunama* into Bengali.

It can be confidently stated that the historical documents written by Gulbadan have not yet been fully restored. There is little mention of other Mughal writers from that era, particularly during Akbar's reign. Thus, Gulbadan's writings have assumed great significance for historians. Written from a woman's perspective, they provide a wealth of information about the Mughal family and the Mughal palace.

Gulbadan was also a renowned poet, fluent in Persian and Turkish, but none of her poems have survived. Some extracts of her poetry are found in the writings of Bahadur Shah Zafar and Mir Taqi Mir. Unfortunately, many important documents and artistic works of the Mughal Empire were lost in Lucknow and destroyed by the British.

Gulbadan Begum lived for some time in Agra and Sikri, and spent a longer period in Lahore. She resided in Lahore until she travelled to Mecca, accompanied by several noble Muslim women. Gulbadan Begum documented her experiences of the journey to Mecca with Hamidabanu

Begum in her historical accounts. The journey spanned nearly 3,000 miles through rugged mountains and deserts. Despite being born into a noble family, they were ready to face the challenges of life. Akbar arranged all the provisions for her journey, and she was accompanied by servants and guards. She was also given many expensive gifts to use for charity. Her arrival in Mecca created a stir, attracting people from far-away places such as Syria and Asia, all hoping to receive alms.

Gulbadan Begum lived in Mecca for about four years. On her return journey, her ship was wrecked in Aden, preventing her from returning to Agra for several months. She ultimately completed her journey in 1582, after about seven years.

Historian Ruby Lal highlights the significance of texts such as *Akbarnama* and *Ain-i-Akbari* in understanding the methods of governance of the Mughal Empire. These works provide detailed descriptions of the political situation and the governance system of the time. The historical accounts shared by Gulbadan offer crucial insights into her political awareness and acumen.

In her book, Ruby Lal also discusses how male historians have explored themes of feminism and sexism within the palaces. Gulbadan's narratives reveal the dynamics of the harem and rani hanspur, particularly emphasizing age disparities among the women.

There are notable contradictions between Gulbadan's historical accounts of rani hanspur and the historical narratives of the period constructed from a male point of view. It is believed that Gulbadan's writings not only reflect the realities of Akbar's Mughal Empire but also serve as a valuable historical portrait of Mughal-ruled India.

Based on Gulbadan's records, Ruby Lal describes daily life in the Mughal ranihanspur. K.S. Lal (1988) points out certain discrepancies in the data. She provides two examples: "On Sundays and Tuesdays, he would take walks on the other side of the river. During these outings, Azam's (Dildar Begum) sisters and other women would accompany him. Masuma Sultan Begum was often at the forefront of the procession."

Gulbadan Begum adds, "Then Gulrang Begum and Azam Begum would travel, followed by my mother Gulbar Begum and Bega Begum along with other women. They established their office (kar-khana) there and issued various orders. Additionally, they arranged audiences, tents (bargaha), and applicant tents (khaima), where the emperor would come to observe their work and spend time with his begums and sisters. When he stood near Masuma Begum's tent, it instilled in him a sense of respect. We were all part of his family. Whenever he visited any begum or sister's room, all of us would accompany him."

Gulbadan Begum details the daily life of the noble family in her book, providing useful insights into the struggles faced by women from aristocratic backgrounds and the various pressures they had to endure. She highlights how women were influenced by men in managing household affairs and responsibilities. Additionally, she records her experiences during the pilgrimage to Mecca.

Her work, *Ahval-i Humayun Badshah,* also known as *Humayunama,* presents Mughal ranihanspur as a secluded and enchanting haven for all. Young girls were prohibited from attending celebrations because every woman present aimed to attract the ruler's attention and win his affection, feeling empowered by their beauty and social standing. Although there was jealousy among them, these gatherings served as a safe space for women of all ages to enjoy various pleasures of life.

K. S. Lal is not the only historian who has depicted Mughal ranihanspur in a stereotypical light. Other historians like Ruby Lal, John F. Richard, and R. Nath has presented similar portraits, but Gulbadan stands as an exception. Writers such as Susie Tharu and K. Lalita have interpreted Gulbadan's assertiveness, along with the lifestyles and rights of both men and women in aristocratic families, through a modern lens. For instance, Humayun's wife, Hamida, initially hesitated to marry him because she did not want to wed someone older than herself and ultimately resisted the temptation of becoming an empress.

While historians like Abul Fazl and Bayazid Bayat primarily provide accounts of the Mughal Empire, Ruby Lal notes that Gulbadan's writings reveal numerous stories, relationships, and conflicts, portraying both social and political aspects of Babur and Humayun's reigns. Gulbadan's unique perspective presents a comprehensive picture of the empire during the times of Babur, Humayun, and Akbar, derived from her own experiences and memories. Although she vividly recounts daily life in Mughal ranihanspur, she does not delve deeply into her marital life.

Annette S. Beveridge, the translator of the *Humayunama*, notes that Gulbadan Begum spent her childhood in her father's dominions of Kabul and Hindustan. She spent her youth under the guidance of her brother, Humayun, and her adulthood under the mentorship of her nephew, Akbar. Akbar was well aware of Gulbadan's writing skills, which led him to persuade her to compose the *Humayunama*.

Gulbadan Begum also recounts the tragic death of her half-brother, Emperor Humayun, who died after falling from the ramparts of the Old Fort in Delhi. She described the incident as deeply poignant. As Gulbadan wrote the *Humayunama* at Akbar's behest, she, along with Akbar's wife, Salima, played a key role in inspiring Akbar's appreciation for art and culture.

Gulbadan passed away on February 7, 1603, at the age of 80. A few days before her death, she had a slight fever. Rukaiya, the daughter of Hindal, and Hamida Banu Begum were at her bedside, caring for her. Before she closed her eyes, she affectionately addressed Hamida Banu Begum as "jiu" (meaning "you live"). Just before she breathed her last, she opened her eyes and said, "I am going; you live." After saying this, Gulbadan breathed her last.

Akbar carried her body on his shoulders, and she was buried with gifts and decorations. Before her burial be prayed to God for the repose of her soul, following Muslim tradition, as she had no son of her own. It is said that Akbar remembered his beloved aunt until the end of his days.

□□

Rani Abbakka Chowta

The identity of a woman is a complex and expansive concept. If anyone seeks to define it, they may find that days, months, and years will pass without reaching a definitive answer. This uncertainty exists for a reason: a woman cannot be confined to a single identity. It's true—her identity is vast and multifaceted. There is little that she cannot achieve. When her roles and responsibilities extend beyond the horizon, how can she be limited to a specific definition?

This is not a phenomenon exclusive to the present day or contemporary society; it has existed throughout history. Regardless of the circumstances, a woman's instinct to adapt is intrinsic. This adaptability has been her constant companion. No matter the environment or challenges posed to her, she has, time and again, shaped herself to face those situations. That is the pattern of her existence.

It is undeniable that today's women are advancing successfully in every field, but this progress has not come easily. Countless obstacles have historically confronted them. Whether from royal or common backgrounds, women have had to strive to make their mark.

This struggle is exemplified in the life of a royal woman, a queen who faced numerous challenges to secure her place in society and achieve notable accomplishments. Her perseverance not only helped her forge a strong path for herself but also crashed a legacy that inspired many women.

She was the first woman freedom fighter of India and the inaugural Tuluva queen of Ullal (modern-day Mangalore). Crowned in 1525 by her uncle, Tirumala Ray, she ascended the throne as the Queen of Ullal from the Chowta dynasty, which had a matriarchal structure that valued women's roles. While her uncle organized her coronation and arranged her marriage, these events initially brought her joy. Yet, this same system ultimately led to her loss of Ullal and contributed to her tragic end.

During the reign of King Tirumala Raya III of the Chowta dynasty, the capital was Ullal. The Jain kings were originally the feudatories of the Chowtas within the Vijayanagara Empire. In the 12th century, they migrated from Gujarat to Tulunadu, which includes the present-day southern Kannada district of Udupi in Karnataka and the Kasaragod district of Kerala. The Chowtas followed the matrilineal tradition (aliyasantana) of the Digambara Jain community. As matrilineal kings, King Tirumala Raya chose his younger niece Abbaka as his successor, crowning her as the Queen of Ullal.

Rani Abbaka belonged to the Chowta dynasty, which ruled parts of coastal Karnataka (Tulunadu). Their capital was Putig, and at that time, the port city of Ullal served as the auxiliary capital. From a young age, Abbaka received training in various aspects of warfare, including sword fighting, archery, horse riding, military strategy, and diplomacy, guided by her uncle.

When Abbaka was crowned as the first Tuluva Queen of Ullal, the Portuguese began to enter the coastal areas of Ullal. Aware of the risks posed by the Portuguese presence, she took over the reins of the kingdom and resolved to face the threat. Her uncle, Tirumala Raya, arranged a marital alliance between Abbaka Chowta and King Lakshmanapparasa

Bangaraja II of the Bengal royal lineage. This strategic marriage created concern for the Portuguese, who feared that a united Ullal and Banga would be difficult to defeat.

Unfortunately, the marriage between Abbaka and Bangaraja was short-lived. They disagreed on many matters, especially when her husband sought peace with the Portuguese, which Abbaka could not accept. Their marriage ended, and Abbaka returned to Ullal, leaving her husband feeling humiliated. In response, he became vengeful and allied himself with the Portuguese to oppose Rani Abbaka Chowta. As a result, Abbaka faced increased challenges, living with her child while ruling Ullal.

During this period, European colonialism was at its peak, particularly after the Portuguese discovered a new trade route to India with the help of Vasco da Gama. Within 20 years, the Portuguese had established a stronghold on the Indian Ocean due to numerous forts built in India, Indonesia, Sri Lanka, and Macao in China. This dominance led to conflicts with other European traders, transforming the Indian Ocean from a free trade zone into a region subject to trade taxes under Portuguese control.

The Portuguese possessed excellent naval skills and a sizable army, which they used to put down rebellions against their tax regime. Rani Abbaka's small kingdom, located on the western coast of India, attracted the attention of the Portuguese after they captured Goa and established several ports along the Mangalore coast. Ullal, a fertile and prosperous region, was key for the export of spices and textiles. Despite numerous attempts to threaten Queen Abbaka, the Portuguese were unable to collect taxes from her kingdom. Queen Abbaka Chowta firmly refused to accept their unjust demands. Even when attacked by the Portuguese, Abbaka remained undeterred; her ships continued to trade with Arab merchants. She openly defied Portuguese orders by allowing her ships to maintain their trading activities, further intensifying the Portuguese desire to occupy her territory.

The first attempt of the Portuguese to conquer the kingdom of Ullal, failed miserably. They had underestimated the thirty-year-old queen, Abbaka Chowta, believing she would not be able to resist their highly skilled soldiers. However, Abbaka faced the Portuguese onslaught with remarkable skill and won several battles against them.

After capturing Goa, the Portuguese turned their attention to the south, targeting the coastal regions. They first attacked the southern Karnataka coast in 1525 CE, destroying the port of Mangalore. Ullal was a prosperous trading port from which spices were exported to Arab nations and other western countries. As a lucrative trading center, it attracted the competing interests of the Portuguese, Dutch, and British, all vying for control of the region and its trade routes. Nevertheless, the local resistance remained strong enough to prevent their capture of Ullal. The local rulers, setting aside their internal differences, made changes in policies relating to caste and religion, aiming to unite their efforts against the British, Dutch, and Portuguese. Queen Abbaka succeeded in uniting Jains, Hindus, and Muslims, recognizing that cooperation was essential for maintaining independence from foreign invaders.

The arrival of the Dutch, French, and British in India at the beginning of the 17th century altered the dynamics of trade in the Indian Ocean, which had previously functioned as a free trade zone for Indian, Arab, Persian, and African traders. The Portuguese insisted on traders taking paid permits (cartaz). Despite their naval superiority and consistent victories over local rulers, the resistance led by leaders like Queen Abbaka continued to challenge their dominance.

In 1526, the Portuguese captured the port of Mangalore, with their next target being the prosperous port town of Ullal, located between the towering peaks of the Western Ghats and the azure waters of the Arabian Sea.

At that time, Ullal was ruled by Rani Abbakka Chowta, a strong and strategic leader. The Portuguese aimed to gain her respect and influence, although they were primarily focused on profiting from Ullal's successful trade. They attempted to impose taxes on the local populace while seeking the queen's acceptance of their presence.

However, Queen Abbakka firmly rejected their proposals. In 1555, the Portuguese sent Admiral Don Álvaro de Silveira to attack her, but the battle ended in victory for the queen, and the Portuguese were repelled.

Undeterred by their defeat, the Portuguese declared war on

Queen Abbakka once again. In 1556, they assembled a large fleet under Admiral Don Álvaro de Silveira to capture Ullal. Yet, Queen Abbakka stood her ground, bravely leading her forces to another victory over the Portuguese, who were left embarrassed and furious. Their attempts to conquer Ullal were thwarted, and the conflict between the two sides continued.

In 1557, the Portuguese plundered Mangalore, and in 1568, they made another attempt to capture Ullal. In response, the Portuguese Viceroy, António Noronha, dispatched General Joe Picnotto along with a fleet of soldiers. They succeeded in capturing the city and entered the royal palace of Ullal; however, Queen Abbakka evaded arrest by fleeing to a mosque.

That night, she gathered approximately 200 of her soldiers and launched a surprise attack on the Portuguese. In the ensuing battle, General Joe Picnotto was killed, seventeen Portuguese soldiers were captured, and many of the remaining soldiers retreated. The conflict culminated in Abbakka and her supporters killing the Portuguese navy commander, Mascarenhas. As a result, the Portuguese were forced to vacate the fort of Mangalore.

Thus, Queen Abbakka valiantly rebelled against the Portuguese, fighting them and defeating their forces. Once again, the Portuguese were humiliated by a defeat at the hands of Queen Abbakka. The conflict intensified as she formed a diverse coalition made up of people from different castes, religions, and backgrounds, including both men and women in her army and navy. Her forces spanned a variety of groups, from Mogaveeras and Bilva archers to Mapilla warriors. With this army, she fought and won battle after battle, demonstrating remarkable courage and determination.

Subsequent wars were fought in alliance with the Zamorin of Calicut and other Muslim rulers in southern Tulunadu, allowing her to take revenge on the Portuguese. However, the attacks on Abbakka and Ullal continued to increase. In 1568, the Portuguese general Joe Picnotto captured Ullal with his fleet and managed to breach the palace. Faced with this situation, Queen Abbakka fled and took refuge in a mosque. Nevertheless, she refused to give up. Angered by the actions of the foreigners, she was determined to reclaim Ullal. That night, she gathered 200 of her finest men and launched a surprise attack, killing General Joe Picnotto and seventy of his soldiers. This strategic military offensive successfully enabled her to retake the city of Ullal.

With the support of 500 Muslim allies, she also defeated Admiral Mascarenhas and reclaimed the fort of Mangalore, driving the Portuguese from the area. Despite these victories, the Portuguese did not relent in their attacks. Queen Abbakka Chowta was skilled in diplomacy and formed alliances with the Bajipur Sultanate of Ahmednagar and the Zamorin of Calicut.

Maritime trade between the communities of the Arabian Peninsula and the western coast of India had been ongoing since the 7th century, leading to an increase in the trade of spices, textiles, and warhorses. This profitable business attracted the attention of many, including various European powers seeking a sea route to India. Ultimately, the Portuguese became the first European country to discover a sea route to India, with Vasco da Gama reaching Calicut in 1498 after a long journey. Following this, the Portuguese built their first fort at Cochin about five years later. They then established a network of forts across India, Muscat, Mozambique, Sri Lanka, Indonesia, and as far as Macao in China. For the entire 16th century, Portuguese dominance in the region went unchallenged by any other European power.

The Portuguese made numerous attempts to capture Ullal, but Rani Abbakka Chowta withstood every attack for four decades. Renowned for her bravery, she was also known as Abhaya Rani (Brave Queen) and is considered one of India's first female freedom fighters. In Karnataka, she is remembered as the first female warrior and patriot alongside Rani Kittur Chennamma, Keladi Chennamma, Rani Chennabhurai Devi, and Onake Obavva.

As the first Tuluva queen of Ullal, she led the fight against the Portuguese in the late 16th century. During her reign, men from the Beri community served as sailors in her navy. Queen Abbakka personally supervised the construction of the dam at Malali, employing workers from the Beri community for the stonework. Together, they successfully thwarted Portuguese advances. She also received support from the powerful king of Bidnur, Venkatasthanayaka, and remained undeterred by the threats from the Portuguese army.

Despite her repeated victories in battles against the Portuguese, Queen Abbakka was not free from danger. Ultimately, she faced betrayal from her husband. Legend has it that, he sought revenge for his humiliation after they were separated. He conspired with the Portuguese to overthrow Queen Abbakka. With his assistance, they launched another attack on Ullal.

In 1570, Rani Abbakka formed an alliance with the Bijapur Sultan of Ahmednagar and the Zamorin of Calicut, both of whom opposed the Portuguese. The Zamorin's General, Kuti Pokar Markar, fought on behalf of Abbakka and succeeded in destroying the fortifications built by the Portuguese in Mangalore. However, on his way back, he was killed by the Portuguese, marking a significant loss for the Queen.

"Save the motherland. Fight them on land and sea. Fight them in the streets and by the sea. Throw those who are left behind back into the water." These words of Queen Abbakka were repeatedly echoed while showering the Portuguese ships with fire. That night, several ships of the Portuguese battle fleet were set on fire. But the enemy captured her with the help of some chiefs, whom they had bribed. Because of her husband's treachery, Abbakka lost the battle and was imprisoned. She did not give up rebelling against the Portuguese even when she was imprisoned. She rebelled in prison. In the end, Queen Abbakka Chowta breathed her last while battling.

Rani Abbakka Chowta was a warrior queen who sacrificed her life for the freedom and protection of her motherland. Fighting the Portuguese, who were the highest military power of her time, she became a significant obstacle to their ambitions during her reign.

From a very young age, Rani Abbakka Chowta was trained to be an effective ruler. She learned how to wield a sword, fight, strategize militarily, practice archery, and engage in diplomacy, along with other subjects necessary for running a state. She ruled over a kingdom primarily composed of Hindus and Muslims. Although she was a Jain, her administration included both Muslims and Hindus. The diversity of her army transcended racial boundaries, with the Mogaveera Muslim

Kaibarta community serving as a significant asset in her navy during the war against the Portuguese.

Rani Abbakka was also a beloved ruler. Her story has been passed down through generations via folk songs and Yakshagana, a traditional folk drama of coastal Karnataka. The heroic saga of Abbakka Chowta is celebrated in a festival focused on a local dance deity. She is portrayed as a beautiful woman, typically dressed simply, and depicted as a caring queen. It is said that Queen Abbakka was exceptionally skilled in using fire weapons in her battles against the Portuguese. According to some accounts, she had two heroic daughters, who assisted her in the fight against the Portuguese invaders.

Rani Abbakka Chowta is particularly remembered in Ullal, where the 'Veer Rani Abbakka Utsav' is celebrated every year in her honour. During this festival, the Veer Rani Abbakka Prashasti awards are presented to distinguished women. On January 15, 2003, India Post launched a special cover dedicated to Rani Abbakka. There are two brass statues of the queen: one located in Ullal and the other in Bangalore. The Amar Chitra Katha series has published a book titled "Rani Abbakka: The Queen Who Knew No Fear." Her legacy continues through folk songs, stories, and performances.

The 'Tuluvaduku Museum,' built by historian and professor Thukaram Poojary, is located in Bantwal taluk in Karnataka. In her honour, the Indian Navy has named an In-shore Patrol Vessel after her. The Karnataka Academy of History has also proposed renaming Queen's Road in the state capital to Rani Abbakka Devi Road.

Rani Abbakka's life was filled with struggle, yet she never allowed fear to deter her progress. She upheld the dignity of her matriarchal family and defended the honor of women everywhere. History attests to her extraordinary courage, fortitude, and perseverance. She shattered many societal prejudices and bad traditions, becoming a guiding light for generations to come.

□□

Hamida Banoo Begum

When the lives of women are discussed, the focus often falls on their personalities, conduct, work ethic, responsibilities toward family and society, and the recognition they receive for their contributions. However, many aspects of women's lives remain underexplored. Typically, the discussions highlight only those women whose accomplishments are widely acknowledged, many of whom have left their mark in history. Yet, countless other women have made significant contributions to their families and communities; yet their stories go untold.

This has happened even to women living in privilege, such as those in royal palaces. Many authors have highlighted this issue in their writings. For instance, Ira Mukhoty's book, *Daughters of the Sun: Egresses, Queens, and Begums of the Mughal Empire*, sheds light on Mughal women who played essential roles but have not received the recognition they deserve. These women made significant sacrifices for the Mughal Empire—some for the emperor, some for the throne, and others even gave their lives in battle. Unfortunately, little has been said about their contributions.

One remarkable figure in this context is Hamdia Banoo Begum, who was the mother of one of its greatest rulers of the mughal empire. She not only provided an heir to the empire she also worked tirelessly to ensure that her son would be a worthy ruler. Her noble qualities and insights allowed her to guide him effectively, making him a rightful heir to the throne. She possessed the intellect to tackle family issues as well as administrative problems. Additionally, she harbored political aspirations and served as an advisor to the king. Her life exemplifies the intelligence, excellence, and strength of women.

She was born in 1527 into a Persian family. Her father, Sheikh Ali Akbar Jami, was a Shia Muslim who served as an advisor to the Mughal prince Hindal Mirza. A Persian Sufi known as Mian Baba Dost, Sheikh Ali Akbar had a close relationship with Hindal's family, serving as Hindal's spiritual teacher. Hindal Mirza was the youngest son of Babur, the first Mughal emperor, and the younger brother of his successor, Humayun. She was a descendant of Ahmad Jami Zindafil. Her mother, Afroz Begum, was married to Ali Akbar Jami in the Pat region of Sindh.

At the time, she was only fourteen years old. Dildar Begum, the wife of Emperor Babur and the stepmother of Humayun, hosted an extravagant feast, inviting numerous guests. The banquet took place at the residence of Hindal Mirza, who was Babur's youngest son. During this period, Humayun had been defeated by Sher Shah Suri, who aimed to restore Afghan rule in Delhi. As a result of his defeat in the Battle of Kannauj, Humayun was forced to flee from Delhi, losing the kingdom that had been established by his father, Emperor Babur. Together with his half-brother Hindal, Humayun sought refuge with Emperor Shah Hussain during Sindur Thaat's reign. After a long and arduous journey through the desert, Humayun finally reached safety, where he began to regain his composure. His stepmother, eager to lift his spirits, organized the grand feast in his honour.

It was at this banquet, hosted by Dildar Begum, that her life took an unexpected turn. She experienced changes she had never anticipated and had only dreamt of. Most importantly, she received an invitation to the party. The reason for her invitation was that her father was already well acquainted with Hindal Mirza and Dildar Begum due to his advisory role. He frequently visited their home, which is why she was invited to the grand feast where she met Humayun for the first time. Humayun, at 33 years old, was significantly older than the 14-year-old girl he encountered. This meeting took place in 1541 in the city of Shehuan, under the rule of Thatta.

When Humayun met her for the first time, he was mesmerized by her beauty and youthful innocence.

"Who is she? Is she married? Or is her marriage fixed?" Humayun inquired, gazing at her. His stepmother quickly provided him with the information he sought. Upon learning that the young girl was not married, his heart filled with joy, and he immediately expressed his desire to marry her.

However, the proposal was met with refusal. She declined to marry Humayun, regardless of how many offers came her way. Initially, she even refused to meet the emperor. Humayun was aware of her opposition, but he did not accept her decision. He turned to his stepmother, Dildar Begum, and his half-brother, Hindal Mirza, for support. He was determined to marry the young woman, and discussions about the marriage continued.

As the marriage proposal was debated, she strongly opposed it. Hindal, too, voiced his objections to the proposal, raising suspicions about their relationship. At that time, it was believed that she might have feelings for Hindal, although this was merely circumstantial evidence. Gulbadan Begum, Hindal's sister, wrote in *Humayunnama*, "At that time, he was often seen in the room of brother Hindal and in the residence of Mother Dildar Begum."

Hindal Mirza felt insulted by Humayun's marriage proposal. Some sources suggest that Hindal was in love with the young woman, while others believe that this was not the case. Nevertheless, Hindal Mirza declined the offer for different reasons. He was concerned about his family's reputation.

Hindal Mirza told Humayun, "I see the girl as a sister and as my own child. As a king, if you do not provide the appropriate amount of 'meher' (monetary gift), the girl will feel dissatisfied, and I will be dissatisfied as well."

At the time of marriage, a sum of money known as "meher" is given to the bride by the groom or the groom's father. This is a mandatory requirement and serves as a legal obligation. Hindal had reasons to believe that Humayun, having fled his kingdom after being defeated in battle, might not be able to provide the necessary sum of money at the time of marriage. If he could not give the meher to the girl, how could he marry her? Hindal was convinced that Humayun would neither be able to provide the meher nor marry Hamida.

However, Humayun was not ready to give up. He assured Hindal that, despite having lost his kingdom in war, he remained an emperor. Their social status remained unchanged, and he affirmed that he would pay the meher according to his status in order to marry at this time.

Despite the objections of his son, Hindal Mirza, Dildar Begum continued to persuade him to accept the marriage proposal. He was unable to resist Dildar Begum's insistence, and after forty days, he agreed to the marriage.

The wedding took place on the date set by Emperor Humayun. Humayun had a keen interest in astrology, which led him to consult his personal astrologer. On Monday, September 1541 (Jumada al-Awwal 948 AH), Hamida married Humayun at Pat in the Dadu district of Sindh, when she was just 14 years old.

Humayun's first wife, Bega Begum (later known as Haji Begum), had played a significant role in his life. However, marrying Hamida benefited Humayun politically, as it secured support from his opponents during the war.

Two years into their marriage, Hamida traveled through the desert with Humayun, reaching Umerkot on August 22, 1542. The journey was arduous, especially because she was pregnant. At that time, Rana Prasad, the Rajput king, ruled the area. He graciously provided refuge to Humayun, allowing them to reside in a small town. Hamida gave birth to their son on October 15, 1542, just two months after their arrival.

In the following years, Hamida faced numerous challenges while following her husband. Initially, when their son was only 10 or 15 days old, they had to live in a camp. In 1543, they trekked through the desert again, heading towards Sindh with the aim of reaching Kandahar.

Humayun had to leave his location quickly, and travelled to Persia, accompanied by his wife. There, he visited Abdil in Iran, which is a Shia pilgrimage site and also the birthplace of his ancestors, Ahmad-e-Jami and the Safavid dynasty, whose support would prove beneficial later. However, she was unable to bring their newborn son along when they left. In 1544, she gave birth to a daughter at a camp located 93 miles from Sabzabar. Afterward, she returned to Persia with the troops provided to Humayun by the Shah of Iran.

During her return journey, she met her stepmother-in-law, Dildar Begum, and Hindal Mirza in Kandahar. Her travels were dictated by her husband's circumstances, and she did not see her son until November 15, 1545. They were finally reunited that year.

Due to the ongoing situations, their child had been deprived of his mother's love. Hamida had to accompany her husband, and happily, three years later, she was able to reconnect with her son, whom she had left when he was only 10 to 15 days old. Remarkably, the boy recognized her as his mother.

Akbar, who would become the third Mughal emperor of India, was born to Hamida Banu Begum, the virtuous wife of Humayun, the second Mughal emperor. According to Akbar's biography, *Akbarnama*, when Hamida Banu returned three years later to reunite with her abandoned infant son, Akbar recognized her among many other women. In 1548, Hamida Banu Begum traveled to Kabul with her husband, Humayun, and their son, Akbar.

Sher Shah Suri died in 1545, and his successor, Islam Shah, also passed away in 1554. This marked the end of the Suri dynasty. In November 1554, when Humayun left for India, he made a stop in Kabul. Although Emperor Humayun managed to conquer Delhi in 1555, his rule was short-lived, and he died in 1556 after just one year in power. At the time of his death, his son Akbar was only thirteen years old, making him the next in line for the throne.

Hamida Banu Begum arrived from Kabul in 1557 to stay with her son

Akbar. She was highly intelligent and had experience in administration. With her wisdom, Hamida Banu guided Akbar in governing the empire. She was actively involved in politics and supported him in all his endeavors.

Hamida played a key role in the ousting of the influential Mughal minister, Bairam Khan, in 1560. Additionally, she took care of her granddaughter, Shehzad Khanum.

During Akbar's reign, there were several occasions when women from the royal family intervened in court cases to show mercy to wrongdoers. On one such occasion, Hamida Banu and her daughter-in-law, Rukeya Sultan Begum, tried to intercede on behalf of a Sunni Muslim from Lahore, who had killed a Shia Muslim due to religious animosity. However, Akbar ultimately refused to grant him a pardon.

The Mughal Empire is one of the most renowned periods in the history of the Indian subcontinent, with Akbar recognized as its greatest ruler. He is celebrated as a secular emperor who fostered improved relations between Hindus and Muslims, which contributed to a flourishing economy. A significant influence during this period of transformative changes was Hamida Banu Begum, Akbar's mother. She was a wise and gentle woman who played a pivotal role in promoting social change.

Hamida Banu married at a young age to an emperor who had lost his kingdom in battle and faced numerous challenges staying by her husband's side. Despite the difficulties, she remained steadfast, supporting him every step of the way. Even as a young girl, she exhibited patience and resilience, standing by her husband in wartime. She sacrificed much of her youth for the sake of her husband, family, and state, notably fighting beside Humayun in the Battle of Kannauj. Her strength and influence during Akbar's reign mark her as a pioneering figure, and she is often regarded as a feminist queen.

Hamida Banu was highly respected by Akbar. According to the English traveller Thomas Coryat, while she was traveling from Lahore to Agra, Akbar carried her palanquin across a river. When Akbar's son, Prince Salim, rebelled against his father, Hamida Banu was instrumental in persuading her grandson to seek reconciliation with her father.

Eventually, a compromise was reached between Akbar and Salim, although Salim later plotted to assassinate Akbar's favorite minister, Abu Fazl.

Hamida Banu passed away on August 29, 1604, nearly fifty years after Humayun's death and a year before Akbar's. She was laid to rest at Humayun's Tomb. Notably, Akbar shaved his beard and hair only twice in his life: once upon the death of his foster mother, Jiji Anga, and again after the death of his mother, Hamida Banu.

After her death, Hamida Banu was given the title 'Maryam Makani.' She was also known as Hamida Banu Begum, a name bestowed upon her by her son, Akbar, who considered it a symbol of innocence. In the court histories of Akbar and Jahangir, she is referred to as 'Hazrat' (Her Majesty). Her life is documented in the *Humayunama*, written by Gulbadan Begum, Humayun's sister. Both the *Akbarnama* and the *Ain-i-Akbari* were composed during Akbar's reign.

A comprehensive look at Hamida Banu's life reveals that Mughal women were not only exquisitely dressed and adorned but also confident and independent-minded. Hamida Banu Begum was a queen who, whether knowingly or unknowingly, promoted secularism—a rarity in her society. Her secular policies aided her son in consolidating his empire. As a teenager, she supported her husband in various tasks and later helped her son in his endeavors. She was known as a devoted wife and mother.

By examining the social customs and practices of the time, along with Hamida Banu Begum's working style, it is evident how progressive she was. She made her presence felt in every aspect of life. Despite the challenges she faced, she unwaveringly supported her husband in his duties, standing by him in every arena—from family matters and palace affairs to state governance and military campaigns. Her role in advising her son and helping him emerge as a great emperor was significant. Even today, when we look for ideals, we should remember Hamida Banu Begum, who was truly ahead of her time.

□□

Sultana Chand Bibi

Men and women are two integral parts of society, and both are equally important. Throughout history, society has been predominantly male-dominated. The reasons for this are complex and hard to pinpoint. Women often have to fight to achieve recognition and rights, while men have typically taken the lead. Without struggle, it is nearly impossible for a woman to assert their position in a male-dominated environment. However, despite the challenges, women continue to fight for their rights and often succeed in their battles. This struggle not only aids women's progress but also contributes to the advancement of society as a whole, benefiting families and communities.

Women have a long history of fishing for their rights. Sometimes, their struggles have created powerful narratives, and at other times, they have shaped history itself. They fight hard, whether within the family, the community, or even on the battlefield. One notable historical figure exemplifies this challenge: a courageous warrior queen of the Deccan, who faced numerous adversities to strengthen her position in society.

Her story emphasizes the importance of resilience and fighting for one's rights.

Despite various obstacles, she firmly established her leadership during a tumultuous time. A brave warrior, she was born in 1550 as to Hussain Nizam Shah I of Ahmednagar. Her brother, Burhan Nizam Shah II, was the Sultan of Ahmadnagar. She ruled both her father's kingdom of Ahmednagar (now in Maharashtra) and her husband's kingdom of Bijapur simultaneously. In 1595, she famously led her forces against the Mughal army of Akbar, achieving a significant victory that brought pride to Ahmednagar.

The Deccan region, which was her birthplace, has long been characterized by its rich cultural and religious diversity. Today, researchers are uncovering many historical facts about this area. The northern part of the Deccan stretches from the western southern peninsula to the Western Ghats and the Eastern Ghats in the east, and it once served as a cultural and economic hub where people of various faiths, religions, and cultures converged.

Throughout history, the Deccan has been home to several influential figures in India, including Krishna Deva Raya, Malik Ambar, the Adil Shahi dynasty, and Shivaji. These individuals are examples of multi-talented personalities. The region has also produced many poets, musicians, painters, and craftsmen. Artists and artisans from all over the world have come here, and the royal courts of Vijayanagar, Golconda, Bijapur, and Hyderabad have been centers of learning and culture.

During this period, traders from China, Iran, Iraq, Europe, and Africa flocked to this prosperous region for commerce. Persian was the language of the court, while Marathi, Kannada, and Telugu were also recognized. Under the patronage of the Bahmani rulers, southern languages gained recognition in literature as well. Although distinct from Urdu, these languages were prevalent in the north.

The beauty of the Deccan often attracted foreign invaders, and numerous battles were fought between the Marathas and invaders, such as the Qutbshahi dynasty and the Mughals, in their attempts to seize control of the region. This tumultuous history contributed to the diverse cultural, religious, and ethnic fabric of the area. For instance, the architecture of the temples in Vijayanagar reflects Arabic and Turkish influences, while Ibrahim Adil Shahi of the Adil Shahi Empire was deeply influenced by Hinduism and mythology. The emperor identified himself as the son of the deities Saraswati and Ganesha.

An important figure in the history of India from this region is the woman historian Sultana Chandbibi. She was married at a very young age. In 1565, during her father's struggle against Vijayanagar, he formed a political alliance with the Bijapur Empire. According to the treaty, her father, Hussain Nizam Shah I, arranged her marriage to Ali Adil Shah I of Bijapur. Remarkably, even as a teenager, Chandbibi was skilled in navigating complex political affairs. Influenced by her parents, she became a strong and capable leader.

Chandbibi actively participated in discussions with her husband regarding the administration of the state and voiced her opinions on important court decisions. During Bijapur's reign, she assisted her husband in organizing the kingdom's army and worked to improve the state's administration. Despite rumors about her husband's relationships with eunuchs, she maintained her trust in him and did not allow these whispers to damage their bond. The strength of their relationship was widely recognized and respected. Ali Adil Shah even constructed a stepwell at the border of the Bijapur kingdom named after Chandbibi, highlighting the depth of their connection.

Ali Adil Shah's father, Ibrahim Adil Shah I, divided his power among several groups, including Sunnis, the Habs, and the rulers of the Deccan. Sultan Ali Adil Shah of Bijapur led a life of luxury. Although he was a Muslim, he was the adopted son of a Hindu king from Vijayanagar. Notably, in 1565, their armies clashed in the Battle of Sangam. However, during his reign, there was significant multi-dimensional development of the arts. Authentic documents from that time, written by Nukum-al-Uloom of Bijapur, provide valuable information about this period. These detail various methods for preparing halwa and sesame, and contain discussions on mythology.

It is said that Ali Adil Shah II would carry books along with his 80,000 horsemen to various battlefields. Many ships sailed the seas during his reign, and numerous poets and writers celebrated him in their works. He had a particular fondness for food, famously consuming 12 eggs every morning.

Around 1580, Ali met the prominent industrialist Albit, who portrayed his lifestyle. It is said that two eunuchs excercised a significant influence on his life for a long time, and all of this was documented by him.

However, Ali's marriage did not last long. Sultan Adil Shah died in battle, and during this tumultuous period, the kingdom of Bijapur experienced considerable political instability. Ali had no children, so his nephews were considered successors to the throne. Unfortunately, before they reached the age to be enthroned, they became very cruel. In this critical situation, Chandbibi not only strengthened her kingdom but also resisted Mughal invasion.

Her only nephew was the heir to the kingdom and was only nine years old at the time, and thus unable to govern. However, Chandbibi did not remain passive. Instead, her actions following her husband's death were remarkable. After his death, she faced numerous challenges in consolidating her father's and husband's kingdoms. She worked tirelessly to secure the throne against various prospective successors.

After Ali's death in 1580, his nine-year-old nephew, Ibrahim Adil Shah II, was proclaimed ruler. Despite facing significant opposition, Chandbibi managed the administration of the kingdom efficiently as the representative for her young nephew. During this time, she confronted greedy rivals for the throne on three occasions. Initially, her trusted minister, Kamal Khan—a prominent warrior of the Deccan region—attempted to oust her from power. However, with the help of one of her loyal supporters, Haji Quisha Khan, Chandbibi defeated Kamal Khan and imprisoned him in the fort.

The struggle did not end there. Haji Quisha Khan, who had been loyal, eventually turned greedy for power himself. A few years later, he captured Chandbibi and proclaimed himself Sultan. Later on, Ikhlas Khan came to Chandbibi's aid. With his assistance, she was able to capture Haji Quisha Khan, but control of the administration remained with Ikhlas, preventing Chandbibi from regaining her power.

Due to the unstable political situation and the weakness of the state, the rulers of neighboring Ahmednagar and Golconda launched attacks against it. Ikhlas Khan was unable to resist these assaults, leading to power returning to Chandbibi. Meanwhile, in 1580, the political situation in Ahmednagar, her father's kingdom, was dire.

Chandbibi's mother was arrested by her brother, but later, she set fire to her son's bedroom, resulting in his death. Her obsessive craving for power earned her the nickname Diwana, meaning "insane," among her advisors. Another brother of Chandbibi defied her and, with the assistance of the Mughals, became the Sultan of Ahmednagar in 1591. However, his loyalty to Akbar dwindled over time, and he rejected the supremacy of the Mughal Empire, leading to his exile. One Mughal historian commented, "Chandbibi's brother needed to demonstrate significantly more loyalty and gratitude to the Mughal ruler. By failing to do so, he lost his power."

Kishbar Khan served as the second regent for Ibrahim and represented the Bijapur forces in a well-organized battle against the Ahmednagar Sultan at Dharaseo, where he captured many of the enemy's horsemen. After winning the battle, Kishbar Khan ordered the other Bijapur vassals to gather all the captured elephants. This order was met with resentment, as they felt insulted and did not wish to serve him, expressing their displeasure openly. During this period of discontent, Chandbibi joined their cause. Together, they conspired to depose of Kishbar Khan with the assistance of Mustafa Khan, the feudatory of Bankapur.

Kishbar Khan's spies informed him of Mustafa Khan's plans, prompting him to send soldiers to capture Mustafa Khan, who was ultimately killed in the battle. Chandbibi did not remain quiet; she raised her voice against Kishbar Khan. In response, Kishbar Khan imprisoned Chandbibi in Satara Fort and declared himself king.

However, Kishbar Khan's rule was not easily accepted by the other feudatories. He soon faced a united resistance from three major feudal leaders: Ikhlas Khan, Hamid Khan, and Dilawar Khan. In an attempt to assert his authority in Ahmednagar, Kishbar Khan travelled to Golconda, where he was killed by a friend of Mustafa Khan. Following his death,

Chandbibi was released from prison and she held power again, albeit for a brief time.

During this period of political instability in Bijapur, the Nizam Shahi Sultan of Ahmednagar planned an attack with the support of the Qutb Shahi from Golconda. Fortunately, Chandbibi was able to avert this crisis with the assistance of a Shia vassal named Abdul Ul Hassan.

Ikhlas Khan then launched an attack on Dilawar Khan to subjugate Bijapur but was defeated. Consequently, Bijapur remained under Dilawar Khan's control from 1582 to 1591. After the situation in Bijapur stabilized, Chandbibi returned to Ahmednagar.

In 1591, Akbar sent a message to the four sultans of the Deccan, urging them to accept his suzerainty. The sultans agreed to submit to Akbar's authority in order to protect themselves. King Ibrahim Nizam Shah of the Ahmednagar Empire died while fighting Ibrahim Adil Shah II of Bijapur at Shahdurg, located about 40 miles from Ahmednagar. After his death, some of his vassals considered proclaiming his young son, Bahadur Shah, as king was to govern the realm under the guidance of his father's aunt, Chandbibi. However, in 1595, the Deccan minister Mian Manju declared Shah Tohir's 12-year-old son, Ahmad Nizam Shah II, as the heir to the throne. This move was opposed by other nobles of Ahmednagar led by Ikhlas Khan.

A rebel faction among the vassals gained the support of Mian Manju and persuaded Akbar's son, Murad Mirza, who was in Gujarat, to bring his troops to Ahmednagar. When Murad reached Malwa, he was joined by Mughal troops under Abdul Rahim Khan I Khanna, and Raja Ali Khan's forces later joined them at Mandu. Together, these forces marched toward Ahmednagar.

As Murad made his way to Ahmednagar, many feudatories abandoned Ikhlas Khan to support Mian Manju. Mian Manju ultimately defeated Ikhlas Khan but later regretted his involvement with the Mughals. By then, it was too late; he went to Ahmednagar with Ahmad Shah II, requesting Chandbibi to assume the regency.

Ikhlas Khan was also defeated by the Mughals while trying to flee through Paithan. Chandbibi took over the throne and declared Bahadur Shah the king of Ahmednagar.

In 1595, the Mughals launched an assault on Ahmednagar. Chandbibi skillfully commanded the defense and secured the fort. Later, Shah Murad sent an emissary to inform Chandbibi that he and his troops were completely surrounded and under house arrest, requesting the transfer of power. Facing severe famine, Chandbibi reluctantly decided to transfer authority to Murad in 1596.

Chandbibi later persuaded her nephews, Ibrahim Adil Shah II of Bijapur and Muhammad Qutb Shah of Golconda, to join forces against the Mughal army. Ibrahim Adil Shah II dispatched 25,000 soldiers under the command of Sohail Khan, who allied with Ikhlas Khan's troops at Naldurg. Eventually, 6,000 soldiers from Golconda joined them.

During this time, Chandbibi appointed Muhammad Khan as her minister, but he turned out to be a traitor. He made an agreement with Khan-i-Khanna to surrender the entire state to the Mughals. Sohail Khan then returned to Bijapur and launched an attack on the Mughal forces led by Khan-i-Khanna. The Mughal troops led by Khan-i-Khanna and Mirza Shah Rukh retreated to Murad's camp at Shahpur in Berar.

The battle involving Bijapur, Ahmednagar, and Golconda took place between February 8 and 9, 1597, at Sunpet, alongside the banks of the Godavari River. In this battle, the Mughals emerged victorious; however, their forces were weakened and they subsequently retreated to Shahpur. One of the Mughal commanders was killed during the conflict, and there were frequent disagreements among the other commanders. As a result, in 1597, Akbar ordered Khan-i-Khanna to return. Soon after, Murad died, and Akbar then dispatched his sons, Daniel and Khan-i-Khanna, along with fresh troops.

Chandbibi's reign in Ahmednagar was revitalized under the leadership of Minister Nehang Khan. Taking advantage of Khan-i-Khanna's absence and the onset of the rainy season, Nehang Khan successfully recaptured the city of Bid.

In 1599, Akbar sent Daniel, Mirza Yusuf Khan, and Khan-i-Khanna to liberate the governor of Bid. Nehang Khan also planned to travel to Jaipur with the intention of meeting the Mughals via the Kotli road. However, Daniel managed to block this route to Kotli and reached the fort of Ahmednagar, ultimately capturing it.

Chand Bibi once again lost her fort and decided to negotiate a deal with Daniel. However, a feudatory named Hamid Khan exaggerated the situation and spread false rumors that Chand Bibi had formed an alliance with the Mughals. A servant of hers, Jita Khan, an eunuch labeled her a traitor and a betrayer. As a result, Chand Bibi fell victim to the anger of her soldiers and was killed. After her death, the forces led by Daniel and Mirza Yusuf Khan captured the fort of Ahmednagar. In reality, Chand Bibi had escaped to confront the Mughal army, devising a strategy to exhaust them in battle. Unfortunately, her plan failed. Doubting her soldiers' capabilities, she sought to negotiate with the Mughals. However, misleading rumours stating that she was attempting to make peace without fighting circulated. Upon hearing this, her soldiers and vassals stormed the palace intending to overthrow her, ultimately leading to her death.

Chand Bibi followed in her father's footsteps, dedicating her life to uniting all the vassals of the Deccan against the Mughals. In response, Prince Murad sought to consolidate the cities around Ahmednagar and faced the combined forces of the Deccan feudatories. Although Prince Murad won the battle, he was ordered by Akbar to retreat before entering the city. The strong alliance Chand Bibi had formed in the Deccan region was significant enough that Akbar himself had to confront it. This incident showcases Chand Bibi's intelligence and her remarkable skill in the management of political affairs.

The political instability and hostility of the vassals in the Deccan region deeply distressed Chandbibi. She was skeptical about her troops' ability to fight against the Mughals, so she sought to defeat them through diplomatic initiatives. However, when false rumors spread that she intended to make peace with the Mughals without engaging in battle, her own soldiers and vassals stormed her palace with plans to overthrow and kill her.

Chandbibi, who had fought bravely to protect her kingdom from external threats, ultimately met her demise at the hands of someone close to her. Soon after her death, the Deccan region fell under Mughal control. Despite her repeated attempts to dislodge the Mughals from her empire, she ultimately failed. In 1599, while enemies sought to capture Ahmednagar, high-ranking officials within the fort were embroiled in conflicts driven by personal interests. During this turmoil, Chandbibi worked tirelessly to restore peace by addressing both external foes and internal strife, but she was unable to succeed. Tragically, she was killed not by a foreign enemy but by her own people. According to one historian, she was drowned in a pool of blood inside her palace.

Following her death, the Mughals seized Ahmednagar and executed her killers. Although they were her enemies, they referred to her as "Chand Sultana," reflecting a level of respect for her legacy. Without children and having developed animosity toward her father-in-law in Ahmednagar, she saw no future for herself in Bijapur. Chandbibi had married Ali as a political compromise during wartime and spent her life as a warrior for the Deccan Empire.

Chandbibi dedicated her entire life to the unification of the Deccan region, now known as Maharashtra. In Indian history, she stands out as an extraordinary woman. Her life, marked by constant struggle for rights and recognition, ended tragically. Not only skilled in warfare and weaponry, she was also an accomplished painter, with her works included in the Metropolitan Museum of Muslim Art. Fluent in Arabic, Persian, Turkish, Marathi, and Kannada, Chandbibi enjoyed playing the sitar and creating exquisite artworks. Her paintings are celebrated in both Deccan and Mughal styles.

Chandbibi transcended the limitations placed on women of her time, expressing her ideas as a princess and empress. A notable example of her artistry is a painting in which she is depicted riding a white horse, its lower half painted red, perhaps symbolizing the horror and bravery of war. Her sense of nobility is also evident in her sunset paintings.

A woman's life is filled with many significant events, some of which can be quite challenging, even deadly. Nevertheless, she has faced each incident with remarkable courage. No matter how terrifying the situation, she was never afraid to confront it. She approached all challenges with patience, often fighting bravely, sometimes with weapons in her hands. She accepted victory and losses gracefully. Despite setbacks, she did not give up; she rose again and continued to fight.

There is much to learn from this woman's life. Her life exemplified sobriety, patience, perseverance, and self-restraint, as she navigated her circumstances with wisdom. In addition to leading an admirable married life during her husband's lifetime, she supported him in all his endeavors, as he was the ruler of the kingdom. She also proved to be an effective ruler herself.

Today's women have made significant strides, but the struggle for rights continues. Reflecting on the past, we see that the path has often been thorny and filled with challenges. Yet, women have never ceased to fight for their rights.

□□

Noor Jahan

India has been ruled by various rulers throughout its history, with different empires expanding their influence in the region. One of the most significant among these was the great Mughal empire, which governed millions of people and unified the majority of India under a single administration for many years. This period was marked by considerable progress in both political and cultural fields.

It is important to note that women were not excluded from this process, although opportunities for them were often limited. Regardless of the circumstances, a determined woman can carve out a significant place for herself. History shows us that there have been remarkable women who, navigating uncongenial circumstances, became role models for others.

One such woman was born in Kandahar and became a famous historical figure. She was of Persian descent, with her family migrating to India from Tehran in search of a better life. From a young age, she was known for her extraordinary beauty and virtue. She was the daughter of the noble Persian family of Mirza Ghiyasbeg and Asmat Begum, being their fourth child and second daughter.

Before her birth in 1577, her family faced significant hardships in Persia, which compelled them to leave their homeland. At the time, her mother was pregnant with her. Ghiyasbeg had set out with his entire family, hoping to improve their financial situation and provide a comfortable life for his wife and children. He believed that seeking employment in the court of Mughal emperor Akbar—known then as a center for commerce and culture—would be beneficial. However, their journey was fraught with challenges, including an attack by robbers who looted their possessions.

After this unfortunate incident, Ghiyasbeg managed to reach Kandahar with his pregnant wife and two children, Muhammad Sharif and Asaf Khan. It was during this difficult time that Asmat Begum gave birth to a daughter. Despite the dire circumstances, a kind merchant named Malik Masud helped the struggling family, ultimately bringing them to the court of Mughal Emperor Akbar with his assistance.

Ghiyasbeg was appointed to the court, which brought relief to his family from their financial crisis. Amidst these changes, Ghiyasbeg believed that the birth of his daughter brought him such good fortune. This marked a turning point in the family's fortunes; he named her Mehrunnisa, which means "sun among women."

In 1577, Ghiyasbeg was assigned a responsibility of 300 mansabs, which marked the beginning of his career in India. He was later entrusted with the administration of the entire region of Kabul and appointed as diwan. Thanks to his managerial skills and loyalty, Ghiyasbeg quickly rose high in Akbar's court. His outstanding performance earned him the title Itimad-ud-daulah (Pillar of the State). Ghiyasbeg always believed that his daughter's birth was the reason for his success, leading him to ensure that she received higher education. Mehrunnisa completed her education, becoming proficient in Arabic and Persian languages, as well as excelling in painting, literature, music, and dance. Noted poet and writer Vidyadhar Mahajan recognized her as a woman of sharp intellect, wit, and extraordinary courage.

At age 17, Mehrunnisa married Alikuli Istajal, a refugee from

Persia. He had attended the funeral of Khan I-Khana Abdur Rahim, a famous poet and high-ranking counselor in Akbar's court, and later joined the Mughal army, serving both Akbar and Jahangir.

Both Akbar and Jahangir were pleased with Alikuli's work. Impressed by his loyalty, Akbar arranged his marriage to Mehrunnisa. The couple welcomed a daughter, Ladli Begum, born in 1605. Alikuli Istajal earned the title "Sher Afghan," or "Tiger Tosser," for his leadership in a battle at Mewar under Emperor Akbar's eldest son, Salim. He effectively managed a well-organized war against the Rana of Udaipur, and some accounts suggest that he saved Salim from a ferocious tigress, leading to his title.

In 1607, Alikuli was killed in battle against Qutbuddin Khan, the governor of Bengal. There are differing accounts regarding his death; some suggest he was killed by troops sent by Khan in defiance of the governor's orders. After Salim and Akbar's relationship soured, Alikuli also had conflicts with Salim. Following Akbar's death in 1605, Salim ascended the throne as Emperor Jahangir and sent Alikuli to distant Bengal. Some speculate that Jahangir was involved in these decisions, though none of these claims have been substantiated.

After the death of Alikuli Isstajlu, also known as Ser Afrighan, his young widow Meherunnisa and their daughter Ladli were brought to Agra. Salima Sultan, Akbar's wife and Jahangir's stepmother, appointed Meherunnisa to serve her. However, Meherunnisa didn't confine herself to serving Salima Sultan; she also engaged in various tasks that showcased her education, skills, and intelligence, earning her the affection of those around her. During her nearly four-year stay in the harem, she became a favourite among the Mughal women due to her exceptional embroidery and sewing skills.

Despite dressing very simply, she created vibrant and colorful garments for the women of the harem using purple tissue and silk cloth. The diverse styles of clothing she designed have remained popular ever since. She introduced several fashionable elements, including Dudami (Floral Muslin), Pesawaj (front-open kurta), Panchotliha (a new style of dress), Badla (embroidery work on metal), Kinari (lace), and Faras-i-Chandini (embroidered cloth draping down to the floor), all of which were highly admired at the time. Additionally, she was innovative with jewelry and gold crafts.

During Akbar's reign, a Meena Bazar was established, held at the beginning of every new year, where noble ladies of the harem showcased their handicrafts and talents.

Meherunnisa attended a Meena Bazar in 1611 to exhibit her artistry, where she first caught the attention of Emperor Jahangir. At that time, she was shopping with her patron queen Rukaiya, and the occasion coincided with the New Year celebration of Navroz. Jahangir fell in love with Meherunnisa at first sight and made a marriage proposal to her. They were married on 25 May 1611 (Wednesday, 12th Rabi-Val-Awal, 1020 AH / 25 May 1611). Meherunnisa thus became the Queen of the Mughal empire, known as Noor Jahan.

At the time of her marriage, Noor Jahan was 34 years old and this was her second marriage. Some historians suggest that Prince Salim, who later became Jahangir, was in love with Meherunnisa their first encounter. His deep affection for her led to her being married off to the Persian nobleman Alikuli, supposedly to keep her away from Salim, who was heir to the throne.

There are various intriguing theories surrounding Meherunnisa's love life and relationships. Some even claim that Salim was so deeply in love with Meherunnisa that he got Alikuli killed. However, later historical researchers, such as Satish Chandra, a scholar of medieval history, dispute this claim. Alikuli died in 1607, and four years later, in 1611, Meherunnisa married Jahangir.

Emperor Jehangir deeply loved his last wife, Meherunnisa, who was renowned for her beauty and loyalty. After their marriage in 1611, he affectionately named her "Nurmahal," which means "Light of the Palace." Five years later, in 1616, he bestowed upon her the title "Noor Jahan," meaning "Light of the World."

Jehangir placed immense trust in Noor Jahan. His extraordinary love and unwavering faith in her enabled her to play an influential role in the administration of the kingdom. Although she did not come from a noble family like other queens, Noor Jahan made the most of her education and demonstrated remarkable intelligence. She trusted her husband's governing abilities, and during a time when only senior women of the royal family held the power to advise the emperor, Noor Jahan, despite her youth, gained considerable influence at the Mughal court. Jahangir's excessive use of opium and narcotics allowed her to exert her influence over governance on several occasions. For many years, she effectively ruled from behind the throne, often sitting beside him at the window, observing the public, issuing various orders, and managing the administration of numerous jagirs. She even exercised the power to issue edicts, a privilege typically reserved for men of the aristocracy.

Noor Jahan is often regarded as the first woman in a Muslim-controlled region to have enjoyed such authority and recognition, and she certainly deserved it. According to Indian historian Ruby Lal, it is important to note that "Mughal blood did not flow in her veins." She did not belong to the same lineage as powerful figures like Queen Elizabeth I of England or Queen Christina of Sweden. Noor Jahan's influence in the Mughal court was unparalleled and similar to that of elderly women who advised the emperor. Although she was not from a noble background—her mother was an educated and accomplished woman who invented rose water and perfume from heated rose petals—Noor Jahan achieved a level of fame unmatched by others. The circulation of coins bearing her image, alongside the king's, is evidence of her authority.

Noor Jahan also commanded an army and was a skilled archer. She not only oversaw military operations but also led troops when necessary. When Jahangir was imprisoned by a disgruntled employee, Noor Jahan took action and attempted to rescue her husband with the soldiers under her command. Analysis of the available information about Noor Jahan reveals her skills and political acumen, further demonstrating her pivotal role she played in history.

It is said that Noor Jahan was the only woman who gave a new direction to the Mughal empire. During a visit to the court of Emperor Jahangir, the British visitor Thomas Row expressed his frustration with Noor Jahan's interference in his application for a trade permit. However, he was impressed by her intelligence, discernment, and straightforward manner of expressing her views. He notes, "At every nook and cranny of the meeting place, Noor Jahan proved that women cannot be treated as mere objects. They are capable of making important decisions and are not incompetent in business or innovation." This demonstrates how the young Prince Salim was likely influenced by Noor Jahan's personality.

According to some historians, Noor Jahan and Jahangir had two children, but the true identity of the mothers of many of Jahangir's children is unclear due to a lack of proper documents. For instance, while some sources describe Noor Jahan as the mother of Shah Jahan, it was actually Jahangir's wife, a Rajput by the name of Jagat Gosaini, who was his mother.

Women of the Mughal family typically received education in literature, philosophy, religion, music, and painting from experienced tutors. Noor Jahan was no exception; she was clever and sharp-minded. She wrote many poems in Persian under the pen name 'Makhfi' and other pseudonyms, and she also published poems in the names of Salima Sultan Begum of the Mughal court and Aurangzeb's daughter, Zebunnisa Begum. Additionally, Mughal women were taught the art of war, weaponry, swordsmanship, and more, and Noor Jahan excelled in these areas. She frequently accompanied Jahangir on tiger hunts.

In his memoir, *Tuzuk-e-Jahangir*, Jahangir recounts an incident from 1619: "The poachers informed me that a tiger was troubling the area near Mathura. I ordered them to bring elephants and encircle the area. We remained there almost all night. I decided not to kill any animal myself, so I asked Noor Jahan to fire my gun. The elephants became restless at the smell of the tiger, which made it challenging to watch. Mirza Rustam, who was supposed to take the shot after me, also failed, missing three or four times from the back of an elephant. Noor Jahan, however, killed the tiger with her first shot."

In another incident, Jahangir noted that Noor Jahan fired six bullets and killed four tigers, and on another occasion, she killed two tigers with just four shots. For her remarkable achievements, he rewarded her with precious diamond jewelry and presented her with a thousand asarfi (Mughal rupees).

Noor Jahan had a deep passion for art, which was one of the reasons why Emperor Jahangir was so captivated by her. Her mother,

Asmat Begum, was known for inventing perfume and rose water, but it was Noor Jahan's remarkable efforts in popularizing these products that truly stood out. She also devoted herself to caring for many orphaned children, particularly young girls, and arranged marriages for those without family. It is believed that Noor Jahan helped marry off around 500 girls who had no one to support them.

Additionally, Noor Jahan had a keen interest in architecture. She got numerous palaces, mosques, and gardens constructed. One of her notable achievements is a grand pillar built in memory of her father, Ghiyasbeg, located in Agra, which exemplifies the Indo-Persian style of architecture. It is also said that she inspired the construction of the Taj Mahal and built a stone mosque in Srinagar.

However, there are accounts suggesting that Noor Jahan's excessive involvement in governance contributed to political instability during Jahangir's reign. Their third son, Prince Khurram, later known as Shah Jahan, was particularly rebellious against Jahangir. Some historians speculate that Noor Jahan was an ambitious woman who took control of the empire, leveraging Jahangir's infatuation and his struggle with drug addiction. Nonetheless, historians like Satish Chandra have challenged this perspective, arguing that such views are influenced by the male dominance prevalent in Indian society at that time. Jahangir himself remarked about Noor Jahan, saying, "Before I married her, I did not understand the true meaning of marriage. She gradually reduced my drug use and guided me away from unhealthy habits and wrong paths."

It is evident from various accounts that when Jahangir fell ill, Noor Jahan took charge of his health and managed the affairs of the government with his permission. She carried out her responsibilities diligently, effectively ongoing affairs of the state. Noor Jahan exercised all powers of the emperor, except for the religious duties associated with the khutar (prayer to the emperor). She issued government orders and placed her name on the imperial seal. Coins were minted in her name between 1623 and 1627.

Moreover, Noor Jahan continued the tradition started by Emperor Akbar, where the emperor would show himself to the public from a window after daily prayers. Alongside Emperor Jahangir, she would also appear at the window to give darshan to the people.

Not only did Noor Jahan rise to prominence, but her father and brother also achieved high positions during Emperor Jahangir's reign due to their skills. Jahangir himself stated, "Because of loyalty, diligence, and experience towards the ruler, I deemed it appropriate to elevate Itimad-ud-daulah to the post of Wazir of the empire." These events illustrate Noor Jahan's mastery of royal affairs. Jahangir's affection and deep respect for Noor Jahan are evident in his words. This highlights the honorable place of women in Jahangir's life.

According to Professor Nurul Hasan, Itimad-ud-daulah and his family prospered after around 1616, when Noor Jahan became less involved in politics. She re-emerged into the spotlight following Jahangir's illness in 1622. When Jahangir's son, Shah Jahan, began to openly oppose her, his father was no longer there to guide her. At this time, some ambitious feudal lords sought to exploit the situation, but they underestimated Noor Jahan's influence and power.

Noor Jahan frequently travelled the country with the emperor, allowing her to enact many laws during these excursions. She also participated in hunting trips with Jahangir, where she hunted numerous tigers. In many respects, she was seen as equal to the king and was recognized as a legislator. However, this did not make her powerless. In 1622, Shah Jahan rebelled against Noor Jahan after she chose his younger brother, Shahryar, as a suitable match for her daughter Ladli. This rebellion demonstrated that Shah Jahan was wary of Noor Jahan's strength.

Despite this tension, there was also an understanding between Shah Jahan and Noor Jahan. In 1622, as criticism began to arise suggesting that Noor Jahan was sowing discord between father and son, Mahabat Khan, who would later capture Jahangir in 1626, travelled with them to Kashmir. During this journey, he remarked to Jahangir, "Being a man, he will face many unfortunate situations due to being led by a woman." This incident further illustrates the complexities of Noor Jahan's position and the perceptions of her power at that time.

In 1626, Noor Jahan's courage and intelligence shone through when she undertook a daring mission to save the life of Emperor Jahangir. She crossed the river on the back of an elephant, instructing her brother Asaf Khan and other counselors to rescue the ailing emperor. With her sharp intellect and foresight, she managed to save Jahangir's life. This incident led to the introduction of the term 'Fitna,' which has importance in Islamic history. Originally used during the Shia-Sunni conflict, the term referred to Aisha, the beloved wife of the Prophet Muhammad, during her conflict with Ali, the leader of the Shias. Over time, 'Fitna' evolved to describe women's abilities and sexuality. Since 1626, it has been specifically associated with the chaos resulting from Noor Jahan's power. Critics of the Shah Jahanama later cited her influence as a source of turmoil, as the text emphasized male supremacy while critiquing Noor Jahan's relationship with the emperor.

When Jahangir fell ill in 1626, Noor Jahan appointed her brother, Asaf Khan, as prime minister. However, Mahabat Khan, a chief counselor and Mughal vassal, was not satisfied with this arrangement. Concerned about potential dangers, Mahabat Khan ordered Noor Jahan to deliver the surviving elephants to the emperor and sent some sepoys to assist her. Meanwhile, he, along with his loyal Rajput soldiers, captured the emperor while he was crossing the Jhelum River on his way to Kabul. Mu'tamad Khan, the author of *Iqbal Naam-e-Jahangir*, was present and documented the incident.

Upon reaching her brother's house after crossing the river, Noor Jahan was furious. She gathered everyone together and addressed them angrily, stating, "All this happened due to your negligence and managerial lapses. This could never have been imagined. None of you seem aware of what has transpired. The way the emperor has been imprisoned shows your disloyalty. You have proven yourselves unfaithful to him, both before God and the Emperor. You should all be ashamed. Correct your mistakes as soon as possible, and do your utmost to rectify this error and succeed."

Empress Noor Jahan was determined not to let this setback defeat her. She declared war to free Jahangir from captivity and made frantic efforts to liberate him from Mahabat Khan's grasp. The enemy forces launched a heavy attack, but she continued her campaign with bravery and resolve, facing the fierce onslaught without hesitation. Even when her elephant was wounded in deep water, she kept fighting back at the enemy. Despite her relentless efforts to free Emperor Jahangir, she unfortunately could not succeed in her mission.

Surprisingly, the queen did not give up. She returned to Lahore, seeking another way to free Jahangir, but was unsuccessful. She feared for both their lives after being separated from the emperor. Concerned for their safety, she joined Jahangir in Kabul at his request. At that time, Mahabat Khan had seized all powers, yet Noor Jahan continued to make every effort to secure Jahangir's freedom.

According to Mu'tamad Khan, Noor Jahan was actively engaged in both public and private resistance against Mahabat Khan. To secure the support of the nobles, she promised financial incentives to many of them, and won their loyalty. She looked for weaknesses in Mahabat Khan's position and ultimately succeeded. Within six months, Noor Jahan took advantage of Mahabat Khan's vulnerabilities, winning over most nobles and counselors to her side. Feeling insecure, Mahabat Khan left the court, allowing Noor Jahan to outsmart him through her intelligence, prudence, and foresight. However, her success was short-lived; Jahangir died in Lahore in 1627. After Shah Jahan ascended to the throne, Noor Jahan withdrew from the court, and Mahabat Khan aligned himself with Shah Jahan, remaining by his side for the duration of his rule.

According to Dutch traveler Pelat, edifices built under Noor Jahan's supervision display exceptional artistic skills. "In every corner of her empire, she built rest areas for travelers and merchants, as well as magnificent gardens and palaces unlike anything seen before," Pelat noted. In 1620, Noor Jahan constructed a grand *Sarai Ghar* in the Jalandhar district, located 15 miles southeast of Sultanpur; at that time, it was the largest city in the region. Sujauddin described *Sarai Noormahal* as comparable to a grand palace in its magnificence.

After Itmadullah's death in 1622, Noor Jahan invested considerable time and resources in building a monumental tomb for him, which took six years (1622-1628) to complete. This impressive structure is situated in Itmadullah's own garden by the Yamuna in Agra and is approximately 69 feet square, featuring four facing pillars. The central dome encompasses the graves of Itmadullah and his wife Asmat Begum, Noor Jahan's mother. Their exquisite royal lifestyle is beautifully depicted on the walls of this chamber. According to historian Vincent Smith, the intricate carvings found on the monument exemplify ancient Indian architecture perfectly.

Noor Jahan also constructed her own memorial in Lahore and the Patar Mosque in Srinagar. Historians assert that she made notable contributions to various forms of fine arts and painting, often expressing her artistry under the name 'Khafi Khan'. According to Alison Banks, "Noor Jahan pioneered many innovations in trade, commerce, and industry. She possessed a remarkable taste for beauty and created many new garments and fabrics, such as Panchtulia Badla (silver embroidered cloth) and Kinari (silver lace)."

Noor Jahan was among the first women in Indian history to marry a half-Hindu Rajput and a Sunni Muslim. She stands out as the only woman to rule the entire Mughal Empire. Whether hunting, issuing edicts, constructing palaces, or aiding impoverished women, she set a remarkable example that distinguished her from other women in her time. She truly lived up to her name by attempting to rescue the ruler from the grips of his enemies with the support of her elite army.

Noor Jahan was the last and twentieth wife of Mughal emperor Jahangir, although some sources claim she was his 18th and final wife. In 1611, she married Jahangir as his second wife. There are differing accounts regarding her age; some say she was 34, while others state that she was 42 at the time of their marriage. Regardless of her age, Noor Jahan made history by showcasing her talents and intelligence in a remarkable way, serving as a mentor and guide to others. She was Jahangir's favourite wife; her skills and acumen earned her deep appreciation from her husband and made her his confidante. Jahangir had great confidence in her, which allowed Noor Jahan considerable freedom in various matters. She utilized this freedom responsibly, proving that women could achieve the extraordinary when given the opportunity.

Notably, Noor Jahan, who had married a commoner under Mughal rule, lost her husband at the age of 35 and became a widow. She caught

Jahangir's attention during her period of mourning. Within a few years, Meherunnisa, later known as Noor Jahan, had established herself as one of the most powerful women in the Mughal Empire. She played a crucial role in issuing coins in her name, enforcing various laws, negotiating with foreign merchants, and discussing pressing issues. Jahangir's love for Noor Jahan, often depicted in films, stemmed from her extensive knowledge, fierce bravery, and politically astute management, which significantly influenced his reign. For instance, in 1619, while travelling to the foothills of the Himalayas, Noor Jahan hunted a man-eating tiger near Mathura.

When a baby girl is born, questions often arise regarding her future: What should she do? What can she achieve for herself, her parents, society, and her country? These questions persist even in today's world, despite the advancements women have made. Yet, time and again, women prove such doubts wrong—Noor Jahan is a prime example. Her parents could not have anticipated that their daughter would rise to such prominence.

Jahangir fell deeply in love with Meherunnisa, seeking to marry her, but it took years for her to agree. While some historians suggest that Meherunnisa had a romantic connection with Salim during her marriage to Sher Afghan, there is no concrete evidence to support this. Rather, reliable sources suggest that Salim was infatuated with Meherunnisa from their first meeting while he was in Afghanistan, despite Emperor Akbar's opposition to their union. Ultimately, after Sher Afghan's death, Noor Jahan's power and influence increased significantly upon marrying Jahangir. As a capable, strong, and highly educated woman, she earned her husband's trust and became a notable figure in the Mughal court.

At the peak of her influence, Noor Jahan was one of the most powerful women during Jahangir's reign. Historians assert that she was more decisive and progressive than her husband, managing the Mughal throne for 15 years, whether directly or indirectly. She enjoyed special honours and exercised powers unprecedented for any Muslim ruler before or after her, being the only one in whose name coins were minted.

Later, Jahangir's son, Shah Jahan, became the new ruler of the Mughal Empire. Noor Jahan spent the rest of her life in a grand palace in Lahore with her daughter, Ladli. Shah Jahan provided her with Rs 2 lakh. During this time, she completed the construction of the monument dedicated to her father, the Itmad-ud-Daulah Memorial, in Agra, which she had begun in 1622.

Noor Jahan passed away in Lahore in 1645 at the age of 72. The memorial she built for herself in Sadar Bagh in Lahore was where she was ultimately buried. This monument is located just a short distance from the tomb of her husband, Emperor Jahangir. "No one will light a lamp or place a rose on this monument, nor will a butterfly fly here or a bird chirp here," reads her memorial.

Since time immemorial, a woman is like a river. If she flows like a stream, she benefits society; if she is stable, she also contributes to its welfare. Just as the banks of a flowing river cannot be blocked, the path of a woman's journey cannot be obstructed. She continues to pursue her dreams regardless of the obstacles in her way. She becomes the creator of a new era. Given the chance, a woman can make history. No matter how many storms she faces, she can carve out a path for herself by confronting every challenge. Many more will follow her example in the future!

□□

Jahanara Begum

History! These letters hold great significance. When we speak of the past, we refer to history. Through history, we learn about the present and the past of our homeland. It reveals the lives of our ancestors, their whereabouts, deeds, and achievements. Understanding history allows us to better comprehend today and helps us to take steps toward the future.

To discuss history, we utilize various mediums, such as books, newspapers, letters, gossip, poems, essays, and even the experiences of people and animals. One such medium, *Kadambini*, the first monthly family magazine of Odisha, has highlighted figures from history in its numerous issues.

Women have undeniably played a vital role in history. Indeed, it is true that women have shaped history in significant ways.

Among these remarkable women is a figure who stands out for her exemplary contributions in work, duties, and responsibilities, garnering attention in her own time as well as in the present. This woman is a famous princess—a princess of princesses.

She was an outstanding princess and empress of the Mughal Empire from 1631 to 1681. Born in 1614 in Ajmer, she was the eldest daughter of the fifth Mughal emperor, Shah Jahan, and his beloved wife, Mumtaz Mahal. As a member of one of the most powerful empires in the world, she lived amidst the rituals and customs of the Mughal royal family, enjoying many luxuries. Her life was filled with joy and happiness. She adorned herself in expensive clothing and dined from gold utensils. She was also the eldest sister of Prince Dara Shukoh and Mughal Emperor Aurangzeb, earning her the title of Begum Sahiba, or the Princess of Princes.

Referred to as "Jani" by her close relatives, she was the beloved daughter of Mughal emperor Shah Jahan and held many important responsibilities as the most powerful woman in the Mughal Empire. Jani was the eldest sister of Shah Jahan's four sons: Dara Shikoh, Aurangzeb, Shuja, and Murad, as well as two daughters, Jahanara and Roshanara Begum.

Mughal emperor Jahangir died on October 28, 1627. Seizing the opportunity, Khurram and his family took possession of the palace in Fatehpur Sikri, Rajasthan. In the western part of the Deccan region, Nazim Sahi's family sought refuge within the kingdom's precincts to escape rebels, traitors, and assassins, engaging in various agricultural activities and animal husbandry. Traditionally, the eldest son would become king after their father's death. However, in the Mughal Empire, it was not guaranteed that only the eldest son would inherit the throne. After the father's death, whoever among the sons was stronger and could defeat the others in battle would be accepted as the ruler, especially by the king's cabinet.

In this context, following Jahangir's death, Khurram orchestrated a dramatic scheme to claim the throne. According to the story, after his father's death, Khurram took a goat's blood in a trunk, pretended to vomit it, and feigned a death-like condition to instill fear in everyone's minds. He later declared himself dead. Believing Khurram's act to be genuine, his brothers and rivals were convinced that he was truly dead, which removed obstacles for them in their quest for the throne.

For many days, Jahanara was deeply saddened by the news of the death of her beloved father. However, Khurram eventually arrived in Rajasthan with his attendants, discarded his disguise, and ascended the throne of the Mughal Empire. He eliminated Shahryar and other claimants to the crown, bringing Noor Jahan under his protection. Noor Jahan was a strong and fierce woman. Khurram then took the title of Shah Jahan, also known as the Emperor of the World, and Arzumand became 'Mumtaz Mahal,' which means 'the best beauty of the palace.' During this time, Jahanara enjoyed many luxuries in the Mughal palace.

Since childhood, Jahanara had been energetic and full of life. She spent her days drawing, writing poetry, and discussing various architectural projects with her father. Living in the palace, she was surrounded by women, from maids to stepmothers, and had no intention of engaging romantically with anyone. She shared a close bond with her brother, Dara, and they often talked about art. In contrast, she harbored strong feelings against Roshanara and Aurangzeb, unable to accept their cunning behavior and lack of respect for their parents. They treated the younger palace employees harshly, and Shah Jahan's Hindu and Christian wives also faced disrespect from them. This created an atmosphere within the palace that often resulted in Jahanara getting scolded.

The children in the palace received instruction from many learned individuals, including Sati-un-Nisha, or Sati, who was a close aide of Mumtaz. Their education included teachings from the Quran. Unfortunately, instead of becoming educated and wise, this upbringing led Aurangzeb to become narrow-minded and fanatical.

As a young girl, Jahanara traveled with her father to numerous kingdoms and palaces. They visited the snow-covered Dal Lake in Srinagar, Kashmir, and the incomparable Red Fort, which her father, Emperor Shah Jahan, had built. The Nine Days Bazaar, which had nearly closed during Jahangir's reign, was revived under Shah Jahan, with Jahanara actively participating in the activities. By 14, she was regarded as a powerful figure in her father's court, known as Begum Sahiba, or the Princess of Princes, in honor of her lineage.

Shah Jahan created many magnificent works of art during his reign, including the Taj Mahal, the Red Fort, and the remarkable Peacock Throne. This grand throne was square in shape and featured four pillars adorned with precious stones such as diamonds, blue vaidurya (cat's eye), and rubies. During his reign, Shah Jahan fought several wars, conquering parts of the Deccan region and regaining control of Kandahar.

Shah Jahan built his first palace in Fatehpur Sikri, remodelling all the rooms in his residence. Among them, the room of his beloved daughter, Jahanara, was particularly beautifully decorated and is still visible today. Although the beauty of the palace has faded over time, it still reflects the craftsmanship and aesthetics of that era. The walls of Jahanara's room were embellished with floral motifs and precious stones, including rubies, diamonds, sapphires, pearls, and emeralds. The space included a water body for her bath, and the floor was adorned with precious ornaments. To highlight Jahanara's special status and nobility, her room and bath were decorated with lights and precious stones, creating an exquisitely beautiful environment.

Jahanara completed her primary education under the tutelage of Sati-al-Nisha Khanum, the sister of Talib Amuli, a renowned poet in Jahangir's court. Sati-al-Nisha possessed great erudition and deep knowledge of the Koran, Persian literature, aristocratic customs, palace management, and medicine. She also served as a key aide and colleague to Mumtaz Mahal.

Many women of the palace were interested in household work, reading, writing poetry, and painting. They often engaged in activities such as playing polo and chess, as well as going out hunting. They carried books on various religions and on Persian, Turkish, and Indian literatures to the grand library founded by Akbar. Jahanara, in particular, excelled in these areas and, at a young age, became a prominent sculptor.

In 1631, the family faced a significant storm when Empress Mumtaz died on June 17 while giving birth to her 14th child. At the time of her mother's death, Jahanara was just 17 years old, but the newborn baby survived. Following her mother's passing, Jahanara assumed responsibility for the infant and took on additional duties. She stepped into her mother's role, caring for her younger siblings and making efforts to help alleviate her father's depression.

Jahanara managed various responsibilities, including overseeing the palace, preparing food and clothing, arranging travel, and ensuring that her siblings received proper education. She wielded considerable power within the empire and the palace, becoming the most influential figure after her father, Shah Jahan. As his most beloved daughter, Jahanara played a key role in making important administrative decisions.

It is said that when Aurangzeb, one of her brothers, opposed her, Jahanara removed him from his royal honors, although he was later restored to his position based on her decision. Shah Jahan had three other queens in addition to his beloved Mumtaz, but none could fill her role after her death. Only Jahanara was recognized as her mother's successor, becoming the first woman, or Padshah Begum, of the Mughal Empire. She earned this recognition due to her dedication, influence, and intelligence.

After the title of Begum Sahib or Empress was bestowed on her, Jahanara frequently spent her evenings playing chess with her father, Shah Jahan. They discussed royal affairs, the management of the royal family, and the construction of various monuments. Shah Jahan often consulted Jahanara before making important decisions or signing documents.

Shah Jahan's deep love for Jahanara was evident through the many titles he granted her, including Shahibat Al Zamani (Lady of the Age), Padshah Begum (Lady Emperor), and Begum Sahib (Princess of Princes). Jahanara held considerable power within Shah Jahan's empire and even had her own mansion outside Agra Fort.

Shah Jahan was very protective of her; if a young man entered Jahanara's room, he would face severe consequences. The French traveller François Bernier, in his account of the Mughal Empire, noted that "Shah Jahan had unwavering faith in his beloved daughter. She closely monitored his security, and no food was served to him without her direct supervision."

Jahanara was especially close to her brother Dara Shukoh, who was one of Shah Jahan's favourite sons. She deeply loved and supported him as a potential successor to their father.

Moinuddin Chishti was a saviour of the poor and a hermit who found God at the age of 15. He was a scholar and philosopher of Islam who wrote extensively on the behavior and practices of Sufis. Moinuddin traveled to many countries, studying in Samarkand and Bukhara. He also visited Medina in the Middle East before coming to India. It is said that Muhammad blessed him in a dream, which inspired him to come to India. After staying in Lahore for a few days, he arrived in Ajmer during the reign of Muhammad Ghori. As a result, Ajmer became an iconic religious center and a significant pilgrimage site.

The Chishti sect is considered the founder of Sufism in India. Many of Moinuddin's disciples later became Sufis, awakening spiritual consciousness in India, especially in the Mughal Empire. He served as a bridge between Muslims and non-Muslims, his main goal being to love and serve all people. Moinuddin stated, "Religion is such a service to humanity that it is as compassionate and flexible as a river, as affectionate as the sun, and as hospitable as the earth. Those who serve the downtrodden can reach God. Fulfilling the needs of the distressed, alleviating their suffering, helping the helpless, and above all, feeding the hungry is true sacrifice, duty, and service. This is the best work of renunciation and Dharma."

Sufism represents religious beliefs and practices within Islam which lead Muslims to seek to understand God through the acquisition of knowledge, truth, and love. There are many divine paths through which individuals experience God and are filled with His love. Sufi saints, often referred to as faqirs, sought to point the spiritual path to Muslims. Sufi literature was written in various languages, including Persian, Turkish, Urdu, Sindhi, and Punjabi. The goal of Sufi saints was to spread the message of the Prophet Muhammad throughout the world through poetry, delivering various verses of the Quran to the people in a simple and fluent manner.

Jahanara was deeply influenced by Moinuddin and Sufism. Together with her brother Dara Shukoh, she became a disciple of

Mula Shah Badakhshi. Jahanara wrote *Munis-al-Arwah*, a biography of Moinuddin Chishti, the founder of the Chishti religious tradition in India. She also authored *Risalah-i-Sahabiyah*, which details the life of Mula Shah. The biography of Moinuddin Chishti was well received and reflected her profound literary knowledge. In this work, she expressed her admiration for Khwaja Moinuddin and her immersion in Sufi thought.

Jahanara articulated Moinuddin's philosophy of life, stating, "A lover's heart is like a fireplace of love. Anyone who comes in contact with it burns with it. There is no greater fire in the world than love." She also likened the human experience to a waterfall that makes sounds while flowing, which disappears when it joins the river. She emphasized that a person continues seeking until they find God, at which point they forget their own self and gradually shed materialism. Jahanara promoted Sufism so effectively that Mulla Sahib intended to make her his successor in 1641, but this was not feasible due to existing rules. During a visit to Ajmer, Shah Jahan gifted his beloved daughter precious jewels and the jagirdari of Surat.

On February 6, 1628, Jahanara's coronation took place. On this occasion, Shah Jahan presented his wife, Mumtaz Mahal, with 100,000 Asarfi (Persian gold coins), 600,000 coins, and one million Swars coins. He also gifted Jahanara 100,000 Asarfi, 400,000 coins, and 600,000 gold coins. After the death of Mumtaz Mahal, Jahanara received half of her annual salary, while her siblings received the other half. As part of her inheritance, Jahanara gained ownership of several gardens, including Bagh-e-Jahanara, Bagh-e-Noor, and Bagh-e-Safa, as well as villages such as Achol, Farzahara, Bachhol, Doraf, and the Panipat Parganas.

Jahangir's mother owned a ship that facilitated trade between Surat and the Indian Ocean. Following in her footsteps, Noor Jahan engaged in trading textiles and gemstones. She owned numerous ships and conducted trade with both the English and the Dutch. According to the traveller Niccolò Manucci, "the Dutch merchants were impressed by the personality of the empress, who had a sharp intellect, strong leadership, and an open personality."

Jahanara also established a factory that brought valuable goods from Surat. Her remarkable courage, combined with Sufi guidance, inspired her to undertake many initiatives. Jahanara made significant contributions to the construction of the city of Delhi, playing a crucial role in the development of a large rectangular garden known as *Begum ka Bagh* and a canal in Shahjahanabad, which was later named Chandni Chowk.

Jahanara not only accumulated wealth for herself but also found great fulfillment in helping others. She was renowned for her kindness and generosity; on significant occasions, she would assist the poor and needy and provide financial aid to pilgrims travelling to Mecca. She also supported the fields of painting, education, and literature, facilitating the publication of many books on Islamic mythology. Notably, on October 29, 1643, when her ship *Sahib* embarked on its maiden voyage to Medina, Jahanara ordered it to carry 50 koni (where one koni equals 4 manas, or 151 pounds) worth of coins, rice, and marrow for the destitute in Madina. This charitable act became an annual tradition at her encouragement. As the First Lady of the Muslim Empire, Jahanara was responsible, generous to people of all faiths, and compassionate towards the poor.

Jahanara's generosity extended beyond financial contributions. She supported various causes, including education and art, and played a significant role in both areas. She was instrumental in publishing numerous books on Islamic mysticism and engaged in discussions about the popular work on Mughal India, *Commentaries on Rumi's Mathnawi*, which focuses on mysticism. Ira Mukhoty reveals that Jahanara was generous to subordinate kings and made donations to several service organizations.

As a passionate promoter of art and culture, Jahanara contributed significantly to the translation of classical literature and explored many literary topics. Two of her notable Sufi works include *Sahabiyyah* (1661), a biography of her teacher Mulla Shah, and *Mu-nis-al-arwa*, based on the play *Anis-al-arwa* by Moinuddin Chishti, which serves as a biography of Moinuddin Chishti himself. Jahanara gathered information from various sources, including her brother Dara Shukoh's own book on Sufism, *Safinat al-awliya*, to craft these works. Each of these publications stands as a testament to her remarkable talent.

Jahanara is said to have been more erudite than her father, Shah Jahan. Interestingly, they once had a disagreement regarding the origin of the great saint, Khwaja Moinuddin Muhammad Chishti. There was some research on this topic. Jahanara claimed that he was the son of a Prophet and that he belonged to the Sayyid lineage. Shah Jahan was skeptical at first, but later, after reading the *Akbarnama*—the biography of Akbar written by Abu Al-Fazl—he came to agree with her. Both Shah Jahan and Jahanara often engaged in discussions about scriptures and religion.

Like other noblewomen of the royal family, Jahanara spent her days in her fort outside Agra. She received special recognition for her interest in literature and the arts, and she owned a large collection of valuable books in her library. Not only did she lead a noble life herself, but she also cared deeply about the well-being and prosperity of her subjects and the poor.

Contributions to the Art:

When discussing Indian art and architecture during the Mughal period, the names of Shah Jahan, Akbar, and Jahangir automatically come to mind. The forts, monuments, mosques, and gardens built by them adorn North India and can also be seen in present-day Pakistan. However, in these discussions, we often overlook the contributions of women. These women played a vital role in establishing what is now the capital city of Delhi.

Humayun's first wife, Bega Begum (also known as Haji Begum), built the Zeenat-ul-Nisha monument in honor of her husband. Other Mughal princesses, such as Fatehpuri Begum and Begum Sambhru, constructed notable monuments including the Fatehpuri Masjid and Zeenat-ul-Masjid (now known as Begum Samur's Palace). Jahanara was deeply influenced by her surroundings, her father's interest in the arts, and the unique feats of Indian architecture at that time, such as the Taj Mahal in Agra, the Red Fort, Jama Masjid in Delhi, Shalimar Gardens in Lahore, Lahore Fort, and the Jahangir monument. She interacted with many prominent artists, craftsmen, and architects which further inspired her artistic pursuits. Her artistry was expressed through various paintings and poems, and Shah Jahan often held discussions with her on these.

According to Sir Thomas Ophillus in 1843, Jahanara Begum was the real architect of or guiding force behind present-day Chandni Chowk. She built the Jami Masjid in the old city of Agra in 1648, which remains one of the major monuments of the city. Jahanara constructed this mosque with the intention of promoting education, using her own funds to support this cause.

Jahanara played a pivotal role in the construction of the capital Shahjahanabad. She oversaw the building of five out of the 18 palaces in Shahjahanabad, with the completion of these structures occurring around 1650. Hubert Charles Fanshawe described a large garden located to the east of Chandni Chowk in Delhi in his writings.

Envisioning a bustling market at Chandni Chowk, Jahanara established shops offering various precious jewels, fine crafts, and handicrafts found in Delhi. Notably, the North Brook Clock Tower and the ornate entrance to the Queen's Garden were part of this development. The entrance later became associated with Jahanara Begum's caravan inn, named *Shah Begum*. This Caravan Sarai is one of the most ornate buildings in Delhi, showcasing exquisite and attractive architecture in its rooms and front portico. Today, a beautiful town hall and a large clock house have been built in the middle of the square pond where the inn once stood.

Stephen Breck, in his book *Shahjahanabad: One of the Wealthiest Cities of the Mughal Empire*, notes that the Chandni Chowk area was hexagonally shaped, with a large pool at its center. Jahanara constructed a gateway on the northern side. In the middle of this area, there was a garden and a bathhouse. The name *Chandni Chowk* means Moonlight Square, as the moonlight reflected in the pond water at midnight illuminated the entire area. The market, stretching from Lahore Gate to Fatehpur Masjid, was also part of Chandni Chowk. A canal flowed through this market, helping to keep the trees on both sides of the road evergreen. Jahanara also built a tavern to the north of the central pool and a hot bath to the south. A mid-18th-century writer, Chaturman Roy, described this area in his book *Chahar Gulshan*. The canal ran from Shahadullah Khan Chowk through Paharganj to Ajmeri Gate, contributing to the greenery of Delhi.

All the streets of Delhi are interconnected, and the wells have always been filled with water. The French traveller François Bernier, who visited Delhi in the 17th century, noted that the beauty of the tavern located in Chandni Chowk rivaled that of Bagh Sahibabad. He praised its remarkable architecture, second only to that of the Jama Masjid in the city. According to Blake's descriptions, wealthy merchants from Persia and Uzbekistan often sought refuge in this area.

Currently, the historic buildings of Chandni Chowk are becoming increasingly difficult to see, as new shops, large poles, and noise have taken over the area. This market, which was established in 1650, did not initially gain much fame. However, Jahanara's efforts remarkably enhanced its reputation and widened its reach. The market extended from the Lahori Gate of Shahjahanabad to the Fatehpuri Masjid, which was built by Shah Jahan's wife, Fatehpuri Begum. It was about 120 feet wide and spanned more than one kilometer, comprising around 1,560 shops that sold a variety of goods, including gemstones, luxury items crafted from precious materials, and glassware from China.

The Urdu Bazaar area was home to clerks and artists of the Mughal court, with the Ashrafi and Johari bazaars serving as their economic centers. The coffee house in the market became a gathering place for high-ranking military personnel and senior officers, where they discussed daily news and engaged in various games. Jahanara aimed to make this market not only a commercial hub but also a venue for cultural integration.

One of Jahanara's most ambitious projects was the *Sahibabad Garden*, which spread over approximately 50 acres and was designed for the royal family. The Paradise Canal flowed through the garden, irrigating many trees and ensuring that they bore abundant fruits. Each corner of the garden featured a large pillar, and a hot bath was installed in the center, which was connected to Jahanara's palace. The garden was accessible only to women and children.

Jahanara also constructed a grand tavern for Persian and Uzbek merchants, located where the town hall now stands. This tavern, named Begumabad or Begum Ka Bagh, was built on an area of fifty acres, featuring a large wall, a pond, bathrooms, and a courtyard, complete with artificial fountains. Many festivals were celebrated in this beautiful setting, the most notable being the *Pankhon Ka Mela*. This fair was meant exclusively for women and lasted for seven days. It showcased a vast collection of exquisite handicrafts, including kurta, dhoti, colorful bangles, jewelry, toys, delicious food, beautiful utensils, home appliances, paintings, clay art, and more. Various cultural programs, such as singing and dancing, were also organized, allowing everyone to enjoy the seven-day event.

There is a fascinating story about Begum Ka Bagh. Only women and children were allowed to enter the garden. A Persian poet from Shah Jahan's court was eager to see this market, attracted by the beauty of the princess, Chandni Chowk, and the vastness of the market itself. One day, the poet entered the garden in disguise, wearing a burqa. When he arrived, he saw the royal women playing pranks on each other. He was so captivated by Jahanara's beauty and personality that he immediately began writing a poem on the spot.

However, Jahanara noticed him as he sat writing. She approached him and asked what he was doing. The poet introduced himself and explained he was a poet. Upon learning of his identity and intentions, Jahanara commanded that he be punished.

In response, the poet pleaded, "I request you to listen to this poem I am writing before you punish me." Jahanara, moved, allowed him to recite his poem.

As the poet recited, his words enchanted Jahanara and the other women present. They were all amazed by his talent. Eventually, those in attendance requested that the poet not be punished. Jahanara finally relented. Instead of punishment, she handed him a bag of gold coins, saying, "Do not linger here any longer. Leave at once and never return."

In 1857, during the reign of Queen Victoria, the name of the garden was changed to Queen's Garden. After undergoing many transformations, Begum Samru's palace was renamed Bhagirath Palace, which has now become one of the largest electronic markets in Delhi. The vast garden area is no longer visible; only a small section remains, and is now known as Gandhi Park.

Throughout this time, Jahanara continued to trade with the English and the Dutch, maintaining her family's traditions.

Jahanara played a key role in the Mughal Empire for around thirty years, caring for her father as a privileged daughter for the remainder of her life. During Shah Jahan's illness, his sons—Dara, Aurangzeb, Suja, and Murad—fought among themselves to seize their father's throne. Ultimately, Aurangzeb emerged victorious. After defeating his three brothers, he declared himself king while Shah Jahan was still alive and confined the latter to an underground chamber in the Agra Palace. Following Shah Jahan's death in 1666, Jahanara supported her brother Dara in the conflict. She later entered the Agra Fort to stay with her father. Even then, Jahanara did not neglect her responsibilities, taking care of Shah Jahan until his passing.

While in captivity, Shah Jahan often looked to the river in search of a reflection of the Taj Mahal, his most renowned masterpiece. The construction of the Taj Mahal began in 1631 and continued until 1648. Jahanara played a crucial role in planning its architectural style. A monument dedicated to Mumtaz was built there, and later, one for Shah Jahan was also constructed. It is said that Shah Jahan intended to build another marble structure akin to the Taj Mahal opposite it.

Shah Jahan died on October 22, 1666, at the age of 74. Jahanara was present during her father's final moments.

Devastated by his death, Jahanara returned to the palace, only to find that the conservative and inflexible Aurangzeb had usurped the throne. As a narrow-minded ruler, Aurangzeb oppressed the non-Muslim women of the royal family, stripping them of many privileges. Consequently, Jahanara's power and authority were diminished. However, she was later reinstated to the title of Padshah Begum at Aurangzeb's request. Jahanara opposed Aurangzeb's ideals and practices by wearing salwar kameez and supporting Hindu and Christian women.

Much about Jahanara's life remains a mystery. In her later years, while living in her father's hometown of Delhi, she dedicated herself to creating various works of art and architecture. Jahanara expressed the love of her parents in many of her poems and paintings. During this time, her sister Roshanara remained close to Aurangzeb and felt a strong jealousy toward Jahanara. Aurangzeb had five wives, and Jahanara took on the responsibility of caring for his six sons and daughters. She never married and chose to remain a spinster from the time of her father's reign until Aurangzeb's era.

Jahanara died in 1681 at the age of 67. She contributed immensely to her father's empire through her efficiency, perseverance, and leadership skills. Her influence can be seen in many artifacts, architectural works, and monuments of the Mughal Empire.

True to her modest outlook, Jahanara chose the Nizamuddin Dargah as her final resting place even before her death. Unlike her parents, who were buried in lavishly decorated graves, her monument was built under an open sky with bare marble columns. According to her dictum written in Persian, "My grave should not be covered with any precious thing except grass, because this green grass is the most beloved sheet of the poor."

The more one learns about this remarkable woman, the more fascinating she appears. Everyone knows about the two great epics of our country, India—the *Ramayana* and the *Mahabharata*. I have often discussed their characters, especially the female figures, and explored their virtues, thoughts, behavior, and resilience. However, it is important to note that these characters are imaginary, whereas Jahanara was a real person. Her personality mirrors the progressive women of modern society. She excelled in education, commerce, politics, art, literature, culture, religion, philosophy, and home management, as well as in service and charity.

Jahanara faced her own battles, yet she was a courageous woman, who managed everything with her knowledge and skill. The feminism we discuss today can be seen as embodied in her qualities. She shared her joys with the world, placing humanity above religion. Jahanara worked towards understanding the true essence of religious philosophy and its application in serving humanity. She was a model of sacrifice, resilience, and fortitude. Even the powerful Aurangzeb respected her. It is hard to believe that a woman could wield such influence in the Mughal era. Jahanara was well-versed in art, literature, music, and philosophy. Indian women have a long history of exemplary achievements, and they will continue to shine brightly.

□□

Rani Ahilyabai Holkar

It was nighttime in the rural environment of Chaundi village, located in Jamkhed, Ahmednagar district, in present-day Maharashtra. The evening was spent at a Shiva temple at one end of the village, where the sound of a bell resonated alongside a soft-voiced Shiva stotra.

Mahlar Rao Holkar, a feudatory of the Maratha Peshwa Bajirao and the chief of the Malwa region, was passing through the village while returning from a visit. Suddenly, a soft voice whispered in his ear, capturing his attention. He stopped his horse, fascinated by the sound, tied it to a tree, and walked towards the temple.

Inside, an eight-year-old girl was singing hymns to Lord Shiva as the worship took place. The feudatory remained silent, completely absorbed in the moment.

As the prayer concluded and the girl stopped singing, Mahlar Rao Holkar looked on in amazement. The priest approached him.

"Who is that girl? Whose voice is that?" he asked the priest.

"Who are you?" the priest asked, somewhat taken aback.

Understanding the unspoken questions on the priest's face, Mahlar Rao reassured him. "I see you have doubts about me. I'm new to this town and travelling. This is my first visit here, so it's natural for you to be curious. I am Mahlar Rao Holkar, the chief of the Malwa region. I stopped here to rest, but the melodious voice of this girl has captivated me, and I want to know who this little girl is."

The priest was delighted to learn of his identity. "She is the daughter of the chief of our Chaundi village. Allow me to introduce you to him."

He introduced Mahlar Rao to Mankoji Scindia, the chief of Chaundi village, who hailed from a well-to-do family in Beed district. Mahlar Rao was pleased to meet Mankoji and welcomed him warmly into the village. Mankoji invited him to stay that night in the village. Although Mahlar Rao initially hesitated to accept the invitation, but the cordiality of Mankoji overcame his hesitation for him. However, he had another motive for accepting the invitation: a strong desire to meet the girl whose voice had enchanted him.

"I would like to meet your daughter," he requested Mankoji. "She has a truly melodious voice."

Mankoji replied, "Please understand, my daughter is currently praying and distributing prasad to the beggars over there. After she finishes her chores, she will return home after completing her night's work." He pointed to the girl, who was still engaged in her tasks.

Mahlar Rao looked at the little girl with loving eyes, fascinated by her simplicity. His heart brimmed with joy as he closely observed her conduct, behavior, and conversation with everyone around her. He had heard stories of her benevolence—how she was saddened by the suffering of others, how she shared their happiness, how she fed the hungry, and offered wholehearted assistance to those in need. The more he learned about her, the happier he became.

He began to wonder why he felt so happy when someone talked about her. It was then he realized he was searching for a girl just like her; only such a girl would be fit to take care of his son—the future ruler and the heir to his throne. That night, during his visit to the house of Mankoji Scindia, he decided to propose that this little girl become the bride of his only son. Not only did he make the decision in his heart, he also shared his thoughts openly with Mankoji. Happiness filled every corner of Mankoji Scindia's home, and he felt exceptionally fortunate.

"It is a matter of great fortune that my only daughter will become the daughter-in-law of the Holkar family. I am overjoyed to receive such a proposal for my daughter," Mankoji Scindia exclaimed. The wishes of Peshwa Holkar of Malwa were fulfilled, bringing him immense happiness. Hello thought that such a daughter-in-law would render the foundation of his kingdom firmer.

The girl was married at the tender age of eight, becoming the daughter-in-law of Mahlar Rao Holkar, the Peshwa of Malwa. Her husband was Khanderao Holkar. At that time, women were not allowed to attend school, but her father took the initiative to teach her to read and write, skills that would prove invaluable later in her life. Even after her marriage, she remained committed to her studies, fueled by a passion for reading. Her father-in-law, Mahlar Rao, recognized her interests and nurtured her education. He taught her politics and administration, while her mother-in-law guided her in household chores and royal traditions.

She adored her husband, Khanderao, who was initially indifferent to governance. However, she instilled in him a sense of purpose and transformed him into a passionate warrior for their state. Together, they worked alongside her father-in-law. Whenever Mahlar Rao traveled outside the state for official duties, he entrusted her with the responsibility of governance, fully confident in her abilities. She did not betray that trust; she managed the state exceptionally well.

Tragically, her husband, father-in-law, and only son passed away, leaving her to take charge of the administration during a critical time. Despite facing numerous challenges, she navigated her responsibilities with remarkable skill, establishing good governance and carving out her own identity. This remarkable woman earned immense respect in the country for her contributions, ideals, and unique governance style. She was not only a warrior and skilled ruler but also a senior politician, effective leader, social reformer, and visionary. Most importantly, during her lifetime, the people revered her, affectionately calling her Devi Mata, Lokmata, and Rajmata.

Queen Ahilyabai Holkar is one of the most renowned women in Indian history. She was born on May 31, 1725, in Jamkhed, Ahmednagar, Maharashtra, and belonged to the Sardar family of the Maratha Empire. Her life was filled with challenges, and her story serves as a significant example in history.

Tragically, her husband died during the siege of Kunger in 1754. Khanderao Holkar, leading an army under the command of his father, Mahlar Rao, fought against Jaat Maharaj Suraj Mal of Bharatpur State to capture the fort of Kuhmer, supporting the Mughal commander Imad Ul Mukh. During the battle, Khanderao was mortally wounded by a Jaat soldier while riding an open palanquin.

Though Khanderao had other queens, he shared a deep bond with Ahilyabai, and they loved each other deeply. Following his death, Ahilyabai was devastated and believed she could not live without him. At the age of 21, she faced the harsh reality of widowhood. Initially, she considered following the practice of sati, like Khanderao's other wives. However, her subjects pleaded with her not to go through with it, and many tried to persuade her to reconsider her decision.

Her father-in-law, Mahlar Rao Holkar, made a heartfelt appeal, saying, "The son I had hoped would support me in old age has left me alone. Will you also abandon an old man like me in this hopeless situation? If you choose to follow your husband, let me die first." This emotional plea moved Ahilyabai, and she ultimately decided against becoming a sati.

Recognizing her potential, Mahlar Rao trained Ahilyabai in the arts of warfare and administration and placed her on the throne. He believed that his daughter-in-law was more capable than his son and would govern Malwa effectively. Thus, he arranged for her to assume control of the administration whenever he was away on military campaigns. Even during his absences, he would communicate with her through letters, discussing various matters of state.

Mahlar Rao Holkar died in 1766, twelve years after the death of his son Khanderao. Following this, Malerao Holkar—Mahlar Rao's grandson and the only son of Ahilyabai and Khanderao—ascended the throne of Indore in 1766 under Ahilyabai's guardianship. However, Malerao was mentally ill and died on April 5, 1767, just a few months after becoming king. After her son's death, Ahilyabai ascended the throne of Indore. Even after the death of her father-in-law, she continued to govern his kingdom with the approval of the Maratha ruler, the Peshwa.

Ahilyabai established her kingdom in Maheshwar, located on the banks of the Narmada River, south of Indore, and ruled from 1765 to 1795. She worked tirelessly to protect her country from enemies and actively led military campaigns. Remarkably, she could shoot four arrows simultaneously while riding an elephant. Ahilyabai appointed Tukojirao Holkar, a loyal supporter of Malhar Rao, as the commander-in-chief of her army.

During her reign, she built many forts and roads, and promoted agriculture and trade. To gain the support of Brahmins, she constructed numerous ghats, temples, and pathshalas at sacred sites such as Kashi, Gaya, Somnath, and Dwarka. As a devoted reformer and patron of Hinduism, she established several Hindu temples and dharamshalas across India. One of her significant achievements was the reconstruction of the Kashi Vishwanath Temple in Varanasi in 1780. This important Hindu site had been destroyed by the Mughal ruler Aurangzeb in 1696 and converted into a mosque, later returning to a Shiva temple through Ahilyabai's efforts.

Influenced by Ahilyabai's leadership, the Scottish poet Joanna Baillie praised her system of governance in her poem written in 1849. She wrote:

During her 30 years of peaceful reign, the kingdom was blessed and flourishing.

Everyone blessed her.

The children and the elderly all lived happily.

The children listened to lullabies on their mothers' laps,

As if this great ruler reigned with the blessings of Prajapati Brahma.

Her heart was full of love and compassion.

Ahilya truly justified her name.

Her father-in-law Mahlar Rao's letter to her in 1765, which expressed faith in her abilities and ordered her to head the military forces in the artillery campaign at Gwalior, demonstrates her father-in-law's trust in her. In the letter Malhar Rao said, "Cross the Chambal valley and go to Gwalior. You can stay there for four days. You must make correct arrangements for the cannons you have and as much ammunition as feasible. A substantial portion of the cannon must be held in Gwalior, and for a month you must plan how to fire it in a controlled manner." This letter clearly demonstrates that Ahilyabai was not only a superb warrior, but also an exceptional leader and administrator. Coming from an ordinary family like hers in India, such an important decision of women's governance really shocks everyone.

After Abdali's arrival in India in 1765, Mahlar Rao fought the forces of Abdali and Rohilla at Delhi. At the same time, on the instructions of Mahlar Rao, Ahilyabai captured the Gohada fort near Gwalior and captured many guns and ammunition.

After Mahlar's death, Ahilyabai requested the Peshwa to take over the governance of Malwa. However, several angry residents opposed her request. Despite the opposition, Ahilyabai received strong support from Holkar's army. She represented the army herself, riding her favorite elephant and carrying an arrow-shaped pole along with four bows on her shoulders.

On December 11, 1767, the Peshwa granted her request. Subedar Tukojirao Holkar, Mahlar Rao's adopted son, was given command of the army, and Ahilyabai journeyed to Malwa. Despite objections from the Brahmins, she ascended the throne and made it a point to interact with the common people daily. She provided immediate assistance to anyone in need. Throughout her reign, she remained vigilant about the British rulers' thoughts and plans.

Ahilyabai was aware of the menace of British rule, even though the Peshwa remained unaware of it. In a letter to the Peshwa in 1772, she wrote, "A wild animal like a tiger can be killed through force or skill, but defeating a bear is much more difficult. If struck directly in the face, the bear will die; otherwise, if its powerful claws catch its prey, it will tear it apart. The English are similar in nature. Therefore, overcoming them is a challenging task."

Within 30 years of her reign, Indore transformed from a small town into a thriving city. Ahilyabai built numerous forts, roads, and Hindu temples throughout Malwa. She generously donated to various festivals, and many temples, ghats, wells, and other structures across the region which serve as reminders of her benevolent nature. Access to water was difficult at that time, so she constructed many dwellings for this purpose. Additionally, she established a ghat in Varanasi.

Ahilyabai's significant contributions to the prosperity of Indore are well documented, but her influence extended beyond this region. She established her capital near Maheshwar on the banks of the Narmada. She generously donated funds for the daily worship associated with various Hindu festivals and temples.

Her philanthropic efforts benefited many pilgrimage sites in southern and northern India. She built temples in many sacred locations, including Kashi, Gaya, Somnath, Ayodhya, Mathura, Haridwar, Kanchu, Avanti, Dwarika, Badrinarayan, Rameshwar, and Jagannath Puri. Beyond merely building temples, she appointed Sanskrit scholars to oversee temple activities, ensuring that all information about the temples was meticulously recorded.

It is said that Ahilyabai constructed many temples from Badrinath to Puri, restoring old temples and creating new ones. Furthermore, she encouraged merchants, farmers, and small traders, by refraining from collecting any revenue from their profits.

It is no exaggeration to say that her capital city is a vibrant confluence of music and culture. Her court was always open to erudite scholars, including the Marathi poet Moropant, Sahir Anantapahandi, and the Sanskrit scholar Khushali Ram. Painters, craftsmen, and weavers were rewarded for their hard work. Ahilyabai also established a textile mill in her hometown and extended patronage to poets, weavers, and artists such as Moropant and Sahir Anantapahandi. She started the trend of Maheshwari sarees, and even today, Maheshwar is renowned for its quality cotton and silk fabrics. After the textile mill was established by Ahilyabai, the weavers were encouraged to find ways to earn a living. She was always present in court, resolving various issues and assisting those who sought her help. Historians note that she provided ample opportunities for everyone within her palace to develop their skills and talents.

According to Anne Besant, "During Ahilyabai's reign, large trees were planted along the sides of long and wide roads to provide shade to pedestrians. Wells were dug in the middle of the roads to supply drinking water, and taverns were established in many places. The poor, homeless, and orphans were assisted according to their needs. The nomadic and warlike Bhils, who came from the upper reaches of the hills, made their living by farming in the lowlands. Both Hindus and Muslims wished the queen a long and prosperous life."

Ahilyabai did not distinguish between the king and the people. She was very effective at dispensing justice. It is said that when robbers entered her kingdom, causing serious trouble to the public, she called a meeting of all the Rajput chieftains of her state. At the meeting, she announced that she would marry her daughter to the brave man who could capture the robbers. A courageous young man from an ordinary family succeeded in capturing the robbers and married her daughter, Muktabai.

There are many examples of her kindness. Once, when one of her ministers refused to adopt a helpless child because she was not dressed properly, Ahilyabai went out of her way to defend the custom of adoption. She provided the child with clothes and issued a certificate of adoption. Importantly, whenever she received a gift, she would present it to someone nearby.

Ahilyabai could prevent the infiltration of Bhil and Gond castes into her kingdom, but she allowed them to earn a livelihood by farming in the foothills. She also permitted a small amount to be collected from the goods they produced.

The work accomplished by this remarkable woman during her lifetime as an able ruler is truly impressive. At one point, Mahlar Rao informed Ahilyabai in a letter of his intention to build an ordnance factory in Gwalior. This project required a large number of staff, observers, and artillerymen, and it needed to be completed in a very short timeframe.

Ahilyabai had a unique talent for selecting skilled workers for any task. As a result, Mahlar Rao entrusted her with this responsibility, and she successfully completed the project.

After the death of Mahlar Rao, Ahilyabai's son, Malerao, became the subedar. However, he was not mentally stable and accidentally killed a weaver. Ahilyabai appointed an impartial committee to investigate the incident objectively. After the investigation confirmed the weaver's innocence, Malerao was punished. It is said that this guilt further deteriorated his mental state, leading eventually to his death.

Malerao's death posed a great threat to Ahilyabai's kingdom. Her manager Gangabatya persuaded Raghoba Dada, the Peshwa of Pune, to invade Maheshwar and capture Ahilyabai's capital, because he thought that, since there was no male ruler at that time, the throne could be easily gained by defeating Ahilyabai. But Ahilyabai greatly strengthened her intelligence department. There were many loyal people in her army and intelligence department. So, when Ahilyabai received the news that Raghobadada was about to set out for Maheshwar, she initially formed a large army consisting only of women. Later, Ahilyabai wrote a letter to him and informed him, "I hear you are coming to attack my kingdom. All right, come on, attack. Conquer my kingdom as well. I'm waiting for you. You know I'll fight with you and it will not affect me as much as it will affect you. The outcome of this battle will hurt your reputation. You think we are weak, so come and see what we can do. If you win this battle, you win over the weak. If you lose this battle, people will say you lost to the weak. Tell me which one you like and which one you can accept. "

When Raghobadada arrived in Ujjain, Ahilyabai traveled there to meet him. Accompanied by her entire army, she was supported by the common people of her kingdom. Raghobadada was compelled to retreat, and Ahilyabai's reign continued without interruption.

Ahilyabai was one of the few rulers and intellectuals in India who recognized the British conspiracy. To strengthen her military, she appointed a French minister to train her army.

Ahilyabai passed away in 1795 at the age of 70. After her death,

Tukojirao Holkar assumed the position of army chief. However, in 1797, he abdicated the throne in favor of his son, Kashirao Holkar.

The 18th century was a period of healthy progress in the history of Malwa. Peshwa Malhar Rao, the founder of the Holkar Empire, played a significant role as a well-wisher in guiding Ahilyabai's life, contributing to her emergence as a great ruler. Under her leadership, Malwa not only became a progressive kingdom but also enriched the cultural, spiritual, and social life of India.

Ahilyabai built the Trimbakeshwar Shiva Temple in 1780 and also established the Nagar Bhairav Temple in Miri, the Mahadev Temple in Uttar Pradesh, Nimsar Dharamshala, the Shri Ram Mandir in Panchvati, Ramghat, Dharamshala, nine temples at Banpur, seven temples at Mansi Devi Peeth, and Dharamshala Kund in Bharatpur. These constructions are clear evidence of Ahilyabai's service and dedication.

To honour her outstanding contributions, the Government of India issued a stamp in her name in 1996. Additionally, an Indore-based organization annually awards the Ahilyabai Samman to individuals for their significant contributions to the social sector. The first recipient of this award was Nanaji Deshmukh, who was honored by the Prime Minister of India. Furthermore, Indore Airport has been renamed Devi Ahilyabai Airport, and Indore University has been renamed Devi Ahilyabai University in her honor.

Jawaharlal Nehru, India's first Prime Minister, mentioned in his book *The Discovery of India*' (1946) that the thirty years of Ahilyabai's rule in Indore were marked by great prosperity. Her governance and rule of law ensured happiness for the people of her kingdom. Ahilyabai was an accomplished ruler who was respected throughout her life and continues to hold a revered place in the hearts of people due to her remarkable contributions to the nation.

In 1820, British officer Sir John Malcolm wrote about her in his book *Memoirs of Middle India*, stating, "Ahilyabai had extraordinary powers. Marathas like Nana Fadnavis also respected her. She was considered an incarnation of divinity in her birthplace, Malwa, and beyond. She emerged from a difficult situation with exceptional skill. Her calm, steady, and serious nature remains an example for all."

According to Anne Besant, during Ahilyabai's reign, her kingdom reached its peak of prosperity. She provided everyone the opportunity to work according to their abilities and did her best to help the poor and needy. She made provisions for farmers, merchants, travelers, and others. During her rule, Hindus and Muslims coexisted peacefully and shared a desire for the queen's long life. However, the greatest tragedy of her life was the death of her son-in-law, Jaswant Rao, and her daughter, who followed the practice of sati.

Historian Jadunath Sarkar supports the argument that Ahilyabai's support was instrumental in Mahadji Shinde consolidating his position in the politics of North India at that time, as evidenced by various letters and historical sources.

Arvind Javlekar notes that Ahilyabai was influenced by the ideas of Plato and Bhattacharya. She also embodied the qualities of great figures like Shri Ram, Shri Krishna, Janak, and Yudhishthir, evident in her governance, delivery of justice, social service, and ability to handle various situations. History finds in her, after a long time, a ruler who truly possessed these admirable qualities. Without a doubt, she was an ideal leader.

In his book, *Ahilyabai Holkar*, Khadapkar describes this Maratha ruler as a shining example of idealism, morality, and intelligence. While Akbar is unique among male rulers, Ahilyabai stands out as a singular figure among female rulers.

The phrase "less is more" aptly describes the greatness of this remarkable woman who made history through her efficiency and good governance. She was a devout believer in God and dedicated herself and all her work to Shivshankar. During her rule, she issued her verdicts while holding the statue of Shivshankar in her lap. She made every effort to provide good governance to her people, treating them as her own children. As a result, there were very few problems during her reign. Another notable aspect of her life was her commitment to simplicity. To enhance the efficiency of her administration, she divided her kingdom into tehsils.

She held women in great respect and understood challenges they faced. She believed that women are strong and should not show weakness. She never allowed women to greet her in a submissive manner, often encouraging them not to consider themselves weak, as they are always strong. Women's respect and dignity were her top priorities. She was deeply concerned about women's education and equal rights, taking action wherever necessary. She established schools for women's education and introduced new rules for widowed women. During that time, wives were not entitled to inherit their husband's property, but she set guidelines to ensure that widows could receive compensation after their husbands' deaths.

During Ahilyabai's reign, her kingdom resembled Ramrajya—a model of good governance that attracted people from different states who wanted to live under her rule. According to her system, the minister was the first point of contact for anyone with a problem. If justice was not served by the minister or if he failed to provide satisfactory results, Ahilyabai would personally address the issue. To ensure proper justice for women, she would meet with them privately to listen to their grievances. She understood that women might find it difficult to express their feelings or problems in the presence of men.

She always used to say one thing: first, I am the mother of my people; then, a woman; and finally, a queen. Not only did she express this belief, but she also applied it in her own life. She was loved by all for her simplicity. She protected the culture of her state and established a new standard of good governance. "I live to serve others, and I will serve others as long as I live." That was her guiding principle.

What I have been discussing is not a very old story; it dates back to the 18th century. She was a noble exemplar of womanhood at that time. But her impact did not stop there; her legacy has endured through the ages. We often read about her in the pages of history, drawing inspiration from her example and sharing it with others. We frequently celebrate great warriors and skilled rulers, such as Rani Lakshmibai, the Queen of Jhansi, of whom we have been very proud. However, if we examine history closely, we find greatness in ruler Ahilyabai that is unparalleled. Perhaps we don't talk about her as much, but her achievements predate those of Rani Lakshmibai. Just as leaders like Rani Lakshmibai transformed the nature of governance in India, Ahilyabai set a new course for Indian governance even earlier.

She exemplified unparalleled courage and determination. Ahilyabai demonstrated that a woman can achieve the impossible if she possesses perseverance, righteous intentions, and strength. Evil forces are ultimately compelled to surrender to the truth, resilience, and perseverance of women. Women have accomplished this before and continue to do so today. When a woman is strong and approaches challenges with positive thinking, she can raise herself, her family, and society to a higher level. This paves the way for the next generation. We are indeed fortunate that the presence of such remarkable women in our country has enriched it immensely.

Rani Kittur Chennamma

Dharwad in Karnataka is famous for being the place of origin of the world-renowned Dharwad Peda. A key historical figure associated with this region is Kittur Chennamma, born on October 23, 1778, in a small village called Kakati in the Belagavi district of Karnataka.

Chennamma grew up as the beloved daughter of Dhulopa Desai, the king of a small kingdom, making her a cherished star in her father's eyes. Born into the Lingayat community, she displayed extraordinary courage from a young age. Her beauty and radiant smile were also notable, contributing to her popularity in her village. During her childhood, she learned to ride horses, practiced swordsmanship, engaged in martial arts, and mastered archery—skills she acquired rapidly due to her keen interest in learning.

As Chennamma approached marriageable age, her father was eager to arrange a match for her. He had a great proposal in mind and did not want to delay her wedding. At the age of 15, Chennamma married Malasarja Desai, the king of Kittur, with great pomp and celebration.

The entire village rejoiced, honored to be connected to the daughter of a noble lineage. After the wedding, when Chennamma visited her village, the locals expressed their admiration, saying, "Our Chennamma is very fortunate," as she had married into a respected family. Her sweet nature, humility, and her beauty continued to endear her to the villagers.

At that time, Kittur was a small princely state located in Mysore, positioned between the Maratha and the Kingdom of Mysore. The Kittur dynasty was established in 1585, and it was fortunate to be a small yet prosperous state, attracting envy from the surrounding kingdoms. Many merchants traveled from afar to trade in gold and silver, contributing to Kittur's wealth. Chennamma was living a happy life; she not only enjoyed a fulfilling married life but also assisted her husband in governing the state. King Malasarja had great affection for Chennamma and was influenced by her actions.

During his reign, the importance of art and culture flourished. Chennamma gave birth to a son, marking a joyous time in her life. However, this happiness was short-lived as King Malasarja Desai passed away unexpectedly in 1816. Following his death, Chennamma and her only son were plunged into a life filled with despair. Despite her grief, the queen did not resign herself to fate; she took upon herself the responsibility of ruling the state in her husband's absence. Her foremost concern was to protect Kittur from British colonization. Chennamma tirelessly dedicated herself to raising her son and maintaining the state's independence, though sadness lingered in her heart. Her devastation was compounded by the loss of her only son in 1824. She faced intense pressure as she was aware that the British were closely monitoring Kittur since the king's death. She feared that their awareness of the king's passing could lead to Kittur's subjugation.

Burying her profound sorrow, Chennamma prioritized the freedom and security of her people. To distract herself from her grief, she immersed herself in the administration of the state. Rudrama, the first queen of Raja Malasarja Desai, had two sons: Shivlingappa and Veerarudra Sarala. Chennamma loved Rudramma's sons as if they were her own. In the same year that her only son died, Chennamma adopted Rudramma's son Shivalingappa, appointing him to govern the state. Shivalingappa was installed as the successor to the king's throne, bringing new hope for the kingdom. Chennamma ruled alongside Shivalingappa, and slowly the administration began to function effectively.

Although Chennamma felt reassured, her struggles were far from over. The East India Company resented her decision to make Shivalingappa the successor since they harbored ambitions for Kittur's wealth. Chennamma was aware of their true motives; the British could invade and conquer Kittur at any moment, leaving her fearful of losing everything. She was not only apprehensive but also acutely aware of the British's dismissive attitudes.

Chennamma's fears became real when the British ordered Shivalingappa to be ousted from the throne, using the pretext of the Doctrine of Lapse, introduced by Lord Dalhousie, the then Governor-General. This policy aimed to conquer independent Indian states. The British rejected Shivalingappa's adoption, claiming he was not a legitimate heir since the British government had not been informed of the adoption. Consequently, they began a policy of abolishing revenue in an attempt to banish Shivalingappa. According to this law, if a ruler had no biological children, they could not adopt an heir, leading to British annexation of the kingdom upon the ruler's death. This policy was formally enacted by the British government under Lord Dalhousie, resulting in the state of Kittur being handed over to St. John Thackeray, the collector of Dharwad.

At this time, Chaplin was the commissioner. Since both the new rulers and the local population were unfamiliar with the territory, the British sought to impose control over it. However, Queen Chennamma resisted the British order to remove Shivalingappa, sending a request to Lieutenant Governor Mountstuart Elphinstone of the Bombay Presidency. Unfortunately, Lord Elphinstone rejected her request, advising her to surrender her kingdom to East India Company. Once again, Queen Chennamma defied the British order, leading to the outbreak of war.

Initially, the British attempted to seize Kittur's treasures and jewels. They then launched an attack on Kittur, aiming to plunder its immense wealth, estimated to be worth around Rs 15 lakh. By the time the news of the British assault reached Queen Chennamma, they had surrounded the entire fort. The people of Kittur were terrified, but the queen remained undaunted. She reassured her subjects with courage and patience, declaring, "No one can take over this state until the last drop of blood is left in my body. No one can take our region away from us."

Queen Chennamma did not sit idly by; she rallied the people of Kittur to resist the British invasion. The first battle between Queen Chennamma and the British took place on October 21, 1824. The British forces, consisting of 20,797 men and 437 guns, suffered a crushing defeat at the hands of Chennamma and her army. The British collector and political agent, St. John Thackray, was killed during the battle, which resulted in heavy losses for the British troops. Amatur Balagi, the commander of Rani Chennamma, played a crucial role in inflicting heavy casualties on the British. Additionally, two British officers, Sir Walter Elliot and Stevenson, were taken as hostages during this conflict.

In an effort to prevent further destruction and warfare, Queen Chennamma negotiated with the British Commissioner Chaplin and the Governor of Bombay, under whose jurisdiction Kittur fell. Her proposal involved the British ending the war and allowing her adopted son, Sivalingappa, to rule Kittur in exchange for the release of the hostages. Commissioner Chaplin signed the treaty on behalf of the East India Company, which included a promise that the British would not attack Kittur again and that there would be no further war. Trusting this agreement, Queen Chennamma freed the British hostages.

However, the British promise turned out to be a deception. Despite having a smaller army, Queen Chennamma successfully fought valiantly against the British in the first battle, leading to their humiliation as they suffered defeat at the hands of a female ruler from a small Indian state. Angered and insulted, Chaplin betrayed Queen Chennamma and attacked Kittur once more, this time with larger forces from Mysore and Sholapur.

Undeterred, Chennamma bravely engaged the British with the support of her representative Sangolli Rayanna and follower Guru Siddappa. The second battle commenced, during which Sir Thomas

Munro, the nephew of Sub-Collector Munro of Sholapur, was killed. For twelve days, Chennamma and her army fought fiercely to defend their fort. Unfortunately, they were ultimately betrayed by two of their own soldiers, Malasa Shetty and Venkat Rao, who sabotaged their gunpowder by mixing it with mud and cow dung.

In the end, despite her resilience, Kittur Chennamma and her forces were defeated by the British army. After enduring so many struggles, the British arrested her and imprisoned her in the Bailhongal Fort. Her most trusted representative, Sangolli Rayanna, continued to wage guerrilla warfare against the British in her absence until 1829, aiming to place Shivlingappa, Chennamma's adopted son, on the throne of Kittur. However, that plan was thwarted as the British captured him and sentenced him to death, since Sivalingappa showed no interest in ruling and failed to recognize his friends and enemies. In seeking help from the British to avenge his father's death, he too was deceived, resulting in his arrest.

After being captured by the British, Queen Chennamma spent the last five years of her life at Bailhongal Fort, where she dedicated herself to reading various holy texts. She died in the fort on February 21, 1829.

Queen Chennamma's burial site is still located in Bailhongal and is maintained by government agencies. This site is cleaned and honored during the 'Kittur Utsav' and 'Kannada Rajotsava' celebrations.

Kittur Queen Chennamma is remembered for her unparalleled valour. She was one of the first Indian rulers to lead an armed rebellion against East India Company, preceding Rani Lakshmibai. Chennamma once achieved a remarkable victory over the powerful British Empire, setting an inspiring example for all. Born in 1778, years before the 1857 revolt led by Rani Lakshmibai, she stands as one of the first women freedom fighters who valiantly fought British rule. Though her rebellion ultimately ended with her imprisonment, she became a symbol of resistance in Karnataka and throughout India. Despite not winning the second conflict against the British, her courageous fight inspired future freedom fighters.

Chennamma's resistance against British forces has been celebrated through various plays and folk songs, including Lavani. The 'Kittur

Utsav,' held every year from October 22 to 24 in Karnataka, honours her first victory against British forces. This festival is celebrated with great fervour.

A historical film has also been made about Kittur Chennamma, and a popular Indian train connecting Bangalore and Kolhapur is named the 'Rani Chennamma Express.' On September 11, 2007, a statue of the queen was unveiled in the Indian Parliament House in New Delhi by Smt. Pratibha Singh Patil, the first woman President of India. The statue was crafted by Vijay Gaur of the Kingur Rani Chennamma Memorial Committee. Additionally, two other statues of Rani Chennamma have been installed in Bangalore and Kittur.

Chennamma was a great warrior who sacrificed her life to protect her country. Her unwavering spirit and determination inspired Sangolli Rayanna, another prominent freedom fighter from Karnataka, to continue the fight against the British. Unfortunately, the conflict did not last long for him either, as he was captured and eventually hanged. Rani Chennamma's adopted son, Shivalingappa, was also arrested. Despite her capture and death, her legacy of resistance against the British remains an enduring source of inspiration for the people of Kittur and the nation.

□□

Qudsia Begum

India has a rich and ancient history. Discussion in this subject often focuses on well-known events and influential people. The people include men and women. Both have played key roles throughout history. However, although women have historically contributed immensely to the country's development and progress, yet they are often overlooked or mentioned only in passing.

In this context, we aim to highlight some remarkable women from history who made contributions to society. Despite the limited recognition their achievements have received, their efforts have guided society towards positive change. Their profound impact on the reconstruction and renewal of the country cannot be ignored.

Women continue to be a source of inspiration, and it is important that we remember their legacies. The light they have shown in the world guides us even today.

In the traditional Indian monarchical system, sons were deemed to be the rightful heirs to the throne, inheriting it through paternal descent. Nevertheless, women have played vital roles in shaping the course of history. Notably, four Muslim women ruled established kingdoms, demonstrating their capabilities not only in governance but also in state management. These women were the four Begums of the princely state of Bhopal during British rule: Qudsia Begum, Sikandar Begum, Shahjahan Begum, and Sultan Jahan Begum.

These four Begums set a remarkable example for society by breaking away from the purdah system and resisting customs prevailing in their time. During their reigns, they prioritized education and social reform, valiantly working to maintain the independence of their state against neighboring powers. Their initiatives to provide education to girls and revitalize religious institutions were noteworthy. Their activities demonstrate the courage they displayed and the valuable contributions they made to society during that era. While historians have often overlooked these brave women, their influence on political transformation of the country cannot be overlooked. The matrilineal tradition they initiated began in 1819 and lasted for 107 years, concluding in 1926.

The modern city of Bhopal was founded in the early 18th century by Dost Mohammad Khan, a member of the Orakzai Pathan community from Afghanistan. It quickly grew to become the second-largest city in India, after Hyderabad, and was a key center in India's struggle for independence in 1858.

The rule of the Begums in Bhopal began in 1819 after the death of Nawab Mohammad Khan. At the time, his daughter, Sikandar, was just fifteen months old, making her ineligible to take the throne. However, her mother, Qudsia, took charge of the state despite being illiterate. Breaking free from the purdah system, she appeared in court and addressed the assembly, declaring, "Our dynasty is dedicated to the state of Bhopal. I am responsible on behalf of my daughter until she is of age."

The British authorities supported Qudsia's rule until her daughter became eligible. Qudsia boldly argued that if Queen Victoria could rule Britain, then so could she. It was a remarkable moment in Bhopal's history when Qudsia Begum stepped out of the purdah and voiced her opinions publicly, all before she turned 20.

This marked the beginning of Qudsia Begum's reign and the establishment of female Nawabs in South Asia. Muslim women were granted political rights, with Qudsia being the first female Nawab. She dedicated herself to the welfare of her people, ensuring that she would eat only after all her subjects had been fed. To consolidate her authority, Qudsia worked to reshape perceptions of women in leadership within the Muslim community. She became the first to draft a legal document with the help of Qazis and Muftis that recognized women's political rights. Qudsia proclaimed, "Women should not be denied political rights in Islam."

Qudsia Begum ruled from 1819 until 1837, and after her reign, she was succeeded by her daughter, Sikandar Begum.

Sikandar Begum

Begum Qudsia of Bhopal, overcoming various objections, declared her daughter Sikandar as her successor. This decision reflected Qudsia's progressive mindset, transcending the religious and political norms of contemporary society. Sikandar Begum was intelligent and skilled in weaponry. After her husband's death in 1844, she effectively assumed her responsibilities as a ruler and became a reliable ally of the British authorities. Although the British were initially reluctant to grant power to women, they later approved of the Begums' actions.

Sikandar Begum's deeds impressed the British to the extent that they officially recognized her as the ruler of her kingdom. By 1861, she was acknowledged as one of the most powerful women in the British dominions, second only to Queen Victoria. Like other Begums of Bhopal, she took pride in her Afghan heritage. Sikandar strongly opposed the practice of purdah and actively participated in various women's programs in her state. To counter a male-dominated society, she excelled in both academics and military endeavours.

She engaged in various social and sports activities, including horse riding, hunting, and polo. Sikandar Begum also trained in archery, sword fighting, and painting.

While overseeing her army, administration, and finances, Sikandar focused on improving the management of her administration. She made it a point to visit villages within her jurisdiction to understand the needs and issues of her people, as well as to supervise various development initiatives. Sikandar Begum implemented revolutionary changes in agriculture and took groundbreaking steps to provide technical education of girls. She established the Victoria School for Girls, where a range of skills, from handicrafts to various academic subjects, were taught.

During her reign, Sikandar Begum laid a solid foundation for women rulers and established several schools to promote women's education. She introduced a quality education system in these schools, naming one Victoria School. Gauri Srivastava's dissertation, *The Role of the Begums of Bhopal in Girls' Education*, describes the changing attendance figures in schools during her time. Education was scarce for girls from ordinary families, so Sikandar made efforts to educate not only her staff and their children but also children from ordinary households by establishing Urdu and Hindi medium schools in the state. She hired a tutor to teach her daughter Shahjahan English and algebra regularly. Sikandar Begum continued to rule until 1868.

◻◻

Shahjahan Begum

Sikandar Begum was succeeded by her daughter, Shah Jahan Begum, and later by her granddaughter, Sultan Jahan Begum. Seventeen days after Sikandar Begum's death, Shah Jahan Begum came to the throne at the age of 30, when her daughter, Sultan Jahan Begum, was only 10 years old. While she was alive, Sikandar Begum had arranged for both her daughter and granddaughter to inherit the throne and had made a deal with the British government to secure this transition.

Shah Jahan Begum proved to be a strong ruler, much like her mother. During her reign, she undertook significant reforms in the tax system. Although she had many talents, Shah Jahan Begum was not interested in warfare; instead, she had a profound interest in literature and the arts. Under her rule, Bhopal saw a flourishing of both. She actively encouraged women's participation in poetry and published her own writings. Her contributions to housing, education, health, and technology have been well-documented in history. Notably, Shah Jahan Begum also wrote a book addressing the status of women in Islam.

Among her most significant achievements was the establishment of the Lady Lanzdon Hospital, specifically designed for women from the purdah tradition. Prior to this, there were no medical facilities available for women adhering to purdah in Bhopal. Understanding the challenges faced by women in her noble family and in society, she took multiple steps to improve their circumstances. She also built several mosques and commendably performed her responsibilities as a ruler in line with the customs of her time. Her progressive attitude towards women's education was particularly noteworthy. Sikandar Begum reigned from 1868 to 1901.

Sultan Jahan Begum

Sultan Jahan, the fourth Begum of Bhopal, cared deeply for her subjects and prioritized their welfare during her reign from 1901 to 1926. Ruling her kingdom for 25 years, she promoted the development of her people, focusing on education and women's health. In addition, she worked to implement various social and governance reforms at the grassroots level, which is recognized as a fundamental goal for any progressive nation today. Due to her dedication, the people of her state reverently referred to her as 'Sarkar Amma.'

In 1925, Sultan Jahan engaged in a significant battle for her younger son, Hamidullah Khan, the 13th and last Nawab of Bhopal, during a time of considerable change. She championed initiatives related to women's education, self-reliance, and health. Her contributions to women's education and emancipation were particularly noteworthy. She laid a strong foundation for education in Bhopal by advocating against the social evils, prejudices, and stereotypes that had persisted for almost a century. She observed that Hindu girls were unwilling to attend schools designated for Muslim girls, which led her to establish the Birjisiya Higher Secondary School, named after her daughter, exclusively for Hindu girls.

Like her mother and grandmother, Begum Sultan Jahan was also a social reformer. She founded several. She placed special emphasis on women's education, establishing numerous technical institutions and working to increase the number of skilled teachers. Notably, she served as the founder and chancellor of Aligarh Muslim University from 1920 until her death, making her the only woman to hold the position in the university's history.

Another significant milestone of her reign was the establishment of modern municipalities in her state in 1903. She introduced free and compulsory primary education in 1918 and established the Legislative Council in 1922. Following in the footsteps of her predecessors, she undertook various development projects, reforming the army, police, judiciary, prisons, and treasury. Throughout her rule, she undertook several development initiatives, including water supply systems, healthcare provisions, vaccination campaigns, cleanliness efforts, and women's health programmes.

In 1912, Sultan Jahan Begum published her autobiography, *My Life Story*, in three parts. In it, she described the reign and style of her great-grandmother, Qudsia Begum; her grandmother, Sikandar Begum; and her mother, Shah Jahan Begum. The autobiography also furnishes an interesting account of the noble family's history, as well as the diplomatic situation of the time. It includes various maps, charts, official proclamations, letters, and government orders bearing the stamp of British rule, along with many images of Bhopal, to narrate its history.

Sultan Jahan greatly admired her mother's generosity, stating, "My mother's rule was a better regime in all aspects." She emphasized the far-sightedness and sharp-wittedness of the rulers of that era. Shah Jahan Begum was not only a visionary and respected leader but also a kind, humble, gentle, and just ruler. She was faithful in both her words and deeds.

Through this statement, Sultan Jahan indirectly highlighted the status of the male-dominated society of her time, the conditions of the government machinery, and her mother's strength as a Muslim woman. Acknowledging her mother's organizational skills and leadership, she noted that Shah Jahan had revamped the treasury and allocated funds for the salaries of soldiers, police departments, and other critical needs. Additionally, she invested in the construction of dams, the dredging of lakes, and efforts to protect the people from epidemics like the plague. Shah Jahan sought to improve the economic conditions of her subjects by strengthening the agricultural system in the state.

Sultan Jahan also wrote extensively, publishing many books in Urdu. In *Gohar-e-Iqbal*, she chronicled significant events and provided details about the political, social, and economic situation in Bhopal during the first seven years of her rule. The English translation of *Gauhar-e-Iqbal* is *An Account of My Life*. The second part of this work, titled *Akhtar-e-Iqbal*, was written by her mentor, C.H. Paynng. In 1918, she authored *Ift-ul-Muslimat*, which discusses the practices of the veil and hijab in Europe, Asia, and Egypt.

One of her notable achievements was the construction of the Taj-ul-Masjid, one of the largest mosques in India, located in Bhopal. Sultan Jahan was also a regular contributor to the Muhammadan Anglo-Oriental College in Aligarh, which later became Aligarh Muslim University. Furthermore, she oversaw the development of a railway line from Hoshangabad to Bhopal.

Following in the footsteps of her mother and grandmother, she undertook notable initiatives in the fields of women's empowerment and education. In her writings, she discusses the oppressive rule of various male leaders and the delirious impact of British colonialism. During this time, Sultan Jahan provided considerable freedom to women who were vocal in advocating for social change.

In her autobiography, she reflects on the challenges she faced while managing her life after the deaths of her mother, daughter, and husband. "I will devote all my energies and capabilities to fulfilling the major responsibilities entrusted to me," she stated. She believed that hard work is the best remedy for a troubled mind. "I must confront all the political and social challenges of my time alone. Perhaps this is God's will, and He is my only helper and guide." This sense of loneliness fueled Sultan Jahan's determination to fight against adversity and persist in the face of numerous obstacles. During her time, most women were confined to the domestic roles as daughters-in-law, mothers, sisters, and daughters. Sultan Jahan's ability to manage the empire on her own after enduring such painful losses, while also being a champion of social change, demonstrates her extraordinary capability and determination.

One of the most crucial initiatives of her government was promoting women's education. "I had a strong interest in working in the field of women's education and was particularly motivated to pursue this direction. It was essential to eliminate the discrimination between men and women in education within a male-dominated society. I was not against women's education; rather, I worked to ensure that girls in Bhopal received educational opportunities similar to those of boys. While there was some progress in Bhopal's social conditions, education for girls was largely confined to the *Quran* and Urdu. In many cases, girls relied on their fathers or brothers for literacy, making it a significant challenge to promote a more progressive approach to education."

Sultan Jahan was one of the first Muslim women to advocate against educational discrimination based on gender. She was deeply committed to the idea that girls and women should have equal access to learning, extending beyond the confines of Quranic and Urdu instruction.

She took concrete actions to establish numerous educational institutions within the state, recognizing that women's education is vital for social development and the well-being of families. "We often forget that women make up half of society. Therefore, we cannot think of social progress without considering the education and development of this segment."

Sultan Jahan took the initiative to establish a school for girls. Before launching the school, she consulted wise members of society and her advisors. While some supported her idea, many opposed it, largely due to the prevailing system of Purdah in society. As a conscious citizen and social worker, Sultan Jahan took thoughtful steps to ensure that girls could receive an education despite these challenges. She arranged for girls to study in designated areas where parents felt comfortable sending their daughters. This initiative was successful, and girls began attending school with their parents' permission. Through her dedicated efforts, Sultan Jahan strove to improving society while maintaining social harmony, despite the opposition she faced.

In addition to founding schools for girls, Sultan Jahan aimed to make them self-reliant through education. She emphasized that education should extend beyond traditional classroom learning. In her autobiography, she noted that girls were taught various skills, including translation of the Quran, Urdu, algebra, geography, housework, and economics.

Sultan Jahan believed that a girl's education should not be confined to theoretical knowledge; it should empower them to excel in practical fields, enabling them to become self-sufficient. She recognized that, although Muslim women were educated, many still struggled to attain independence, and she worked diligently to change that.

Sultan Jahan was particularly concerned about the rehabilitation of poor widows and widowed women in her kingdom. To achieve this end, she established a school specifically for these women, teaching them sewing, handicrafts, and various vocational courses. During her reign, Bhopal emerged as a center for education in the country. Furthermore, Sultan Jahan implemented financial assistance programmes and government incentives to ensure the safety and support of women. She was always focused on creating a healthy social environment by eliminating gender discrimination.

Sultan Jahan's vision included funding the construction of a mosque in Iraq, financing the Muslim University in Aligarh, and establishing a school for girls in Delhi in the early 1920s. Such actions were quite groundbreaking for a ruler in her time, reflecting her commitment to advancing women's education.

Sultan Jahan Begum adopted important measures to improve the health of women and children in her state. She founded the Prince of Wales Hospital for men and the Lady Lansdowne Hospital for women. Additionally, she established the Lady Hardinge Infant Home for children. To ensure quality training for midwives, she arranged daily education programmes and directed them to work under the guidance and supervision of female doctors at the Lady Lansdowne Hospital. In her autobiography, she emphasized, "No state can solve the problems of female foeticide and improve women's health without quality training for midwives."

Sultan Jahan Begum received numerous awards and honors, which she attributed to her exceptional administrative skills. The British government recognized her contributions through various accolades, and she also served as the president of the All India Muslim Women's Association.

During her 25 years in office, Nawab Sultan Jahan implemented many progressive initiatives across various fields, leading to paradigm shifts that transformed the health and social status of adolescent girls and women.

The Begums' Contribution to Architecture

The Begums of Bhopal had a deep passion for art, which gave a new identity to Bhopal's architecture. She got famous mosques such as Jama Masjid, Moti Masjid, and Taj-ul-Masjid constructed in various important areas of the city. These structures enhanced the beauty of Shahar-e-Khas, Khirtiwala Maidan, and Shahjahanabad, promoting religious harmony between Hindus and Muslims. The mosques built by the Begums reflect their piety, commitment to social harmony, and cultural vibrancy.

Qudsia Begum's Jami Masjid, built in 1833 in Shahr-i-Khas, is renowned for its unique architecture. It is constructed on high pillars, with access to the lower part via stairs. The mosque features artistically designed rooms and balconies, along with three entrances.

Sikandar Begum's Moti Masjid: Moti Masjid was constructed in 1847 to the southwest of the Jami Masjid. Its design was influenced by the Jama Masjid in Delhi, incorporating elements such as construction style, materials, and the use of red and white marble. The masjid occupies a large area in the city.

Shah Jahan Begum's Taj-ul-Masjid: Named after Shah Jahan Begum, Taj-ul-Masjid was built in Shahjahanabad, Bhopal. The newly constructed city of Shahjahanabad was surrounded by high-rise buildings, schools, and libraries catering to the city's elite. There were three significant ponds in the area: Munshi Hussain Talab, Nurmahal Talab, and Modia Talab. Influenced by the Begum's commitment to Islam, several other mosques were also established in the vicinity. The construction of Taj-ul-Masjid was completed in 1901 under the supervision of Sultan Jahan Begum, following the death of its main architect.

These mosques, built by the Begums, feature a triangular style with complex, subtle, and multi-sensory architecture.

Many changes have taken place over time. In some contexts, women wore the burqa, while in others, they chose to abandon it. The Begums acknowledged the profound influence of their mothers and grandmothers in their lives. Despite the pressures of radical modernity, they remained grounded in their religious and cultural values. They actively encouraged research on Islam, emphasized respect for the Quran, and championed the principle of equality between men and women enshrined in their faith. Sarojini Naidu notes how Mahatma Gandhi, upon visiting Bhopal in 1920, was struck by their simple lifestyle and modest attire.

Historically, women have played limited roles in Islamic politics. Although there is no clear record of which Begum of Bhopal first adopted the title of 'Nawab Begums,' their governance style demonstrated that they were as competent and accomplished as their male counterparts. Their diaries, written in accordance with Islamic tradition, give insight into their political, cultural, and traditional practices. The Begums of Bhopal established a distinctive trend in Indian governance by combating gender discrimination. Their efforts to enhance women's health and education reflect their genuine commitment to the principles of Islam. It can be said that these Begums have transcended religious boundaries and served as a source of inspiration for women everywhere.

Above all, it is obvious that women have consistently contributed to the improvement of society. They have fought for their rights and faced various obstacles, yet they charted their own paths. The most crucial aspect is women's empowerment. They recognized that education is the fundamental key to women's progress. Only through education can women gain knowledge, express their views on various issues, and, most importantly, achieve independence. Notably, four Begums governed the Hindu-majority state of Bhopal for over 100 years. Their lifestyle and approach demonstrate the importance of empowering their daughters for future success.

Efforts were made from the very beginning to involve women in governance independently. They have been educating girls about these issues for a long time. At that time, they did not adhere to any single religion. They respected their own beliefs as well as those of others and worked towards fostering this respect.

They understood the true meaning of religion and conveyed to others that its essence lies in the equality between men and women. They respected men, collaborated with them, and grasped the essence of modernity. They moved beyond tradition to embrace modern values, recognizing that true modernity transcends the superficial. They comprehended the fundamental principle of the joint religious tradition of 'Ganga-Yamuni tehzeeb' and made their subjects aware of its significance. They endeavored to communicate the essence of this tradition—a blending of the cultural and religious values central to both Hinduism and Islam. They proclaimed, "We are proud to be Hindus, and we are proud to be Muslims."

The Begums of Bhopal championed the cause of women's empowerment. As rulers, these women were powerful and influential. Above all, they set a shining example by transcending barriers related to education, health, tradition, culture, religion, and caste.

□□

Rani Jind Kaur

We all remember a fairy tale at some point in our lives. Since childhood, we have been hearing these stories. A fairy tale is something that we not only hear but also pass down to our children, and they will share it with their children as well. It could have been my mother or my father telling the tale! This is a story that has been told for generations. We've all heard them!

Unlike many other stories that we may forget over time, the characters of fairy tales often linger in our minds, especially the angelic figure within them. These tales leave a deep impression on us. We understand the core message: no matter how stuck someone may feel in a problem, once the angel arrives, all challenges can be overcome. This reflects a profound truth—that no matter how difficult a situation may seem, there is always a solution. The fairy, often depicted with a magic wand, embodies the ability to resolve everything.

For ages, we have seen that fairy as a woman. One thing is clear: women hold the potential to solve any problem. They strive to find solutions, regardless of the struggles or suffering they may face. Their efforts often inspire change and provide new direction for society.

Similarly, we can see the challenges that arise regarding a woman's character and her life story, which is rich and impactful.

She was born in 1817 into a Jat family near Chachar in present-day Gujranwala, Pakistan. Her father, Manna Singh Aulakh, was the caretaker for the noble families' dogs. He performed his duties well and managed to support his family effectively. She was the youngest of three children, with two brothers and one sister. Her brother was named Johar Singh Aulakh, and her elder sister was married to Sardar Jwala Singh Padhania, the chief of the Lahore district. The children were raised in a healthy and nurturing environment.

Manna Singh Aulakh had a dream to marry off his youngest daughter to a noble family. While looking after the dogs of one such family, he frequently met Maharaja Ranjit Singh of Punjab. Manna Singh wished to introduce his daughter to the Maharaja and hoped to secure a marriage for her. He believed his daughter was extremely beautiful, brave, and intelligent, and with a marriage into a noble family, she would be able to take care of herself.

Whenever he had the opportunity to meet Maharaja Ranjit Singh, Manna Singh would share details about his daughter's looks, qualities, courage, and intelligence. Ranjit Singh was greatly influenced by Manna Singh's descriptions of his daughter.

After many requests from Manna Singh, Maharaja Ranjit Singh finally agreed to marry Manna Singh Aulakh's youngest daughter. He sent a marriage proposal along with his bow and sword, symbolizing his intent. Manna Singh was elated that his youngest daughter was to marry Maharaja Ranjit Singh, and the marriage took place in 1835.

Maharaja Ranjit Singh was born on November 13, 1780, in Gujranwala, present-day Pakistan. His father, Maha Singh, was the head of the Shukarchakia Misl in Sullia, and Ranjit Singh became the leader of the Shukarchakia Misal in 1792. His mother was Raj Kaur.

A formidable warrior, Ranjit Singh could not tolerate the looting of India by the Afghans and took the initiative to attack Afghanistan. He successfully captured Peshawar and continued expanding his empire, reaching as far as Jammu and Kashmir and Anandpur. Ranjit Singh assembled a large army known as the Sikh Khalsa and established the Sikh Empire, becoming its first ruler. His contributions to Punjab are remembered, as his name is inscribed in golden letters in history.

Ranjit Singh was a powerful king known for his leadership and compassion. He implemented significant developments in education and art in his state. Notably, he is said to have never executed anyone during his reign and made Punjab a strong and prosperous region. He achieved complete victory over Afghanistan and captured the Khyber Pass, effectively safeguarding India from external threats.

Ranjit Singh treated all religions with equality and, despite enduring illness since childhood, he had a notable radiance about him. He was a benevolent and capable ruler who captured Lahore and later Amritsar. On April 12, 1801, he was crowned in Lahore as an independent ruler of India and declared himself Maharaja. He captured Amritsar in 1805, establishing Lahore as his political capital and Amritsar as his religious capital. By the age of 20, he became the king of the entire Punjab region.

At that time, although the East India Company and the British occupied many areas of India, they were unable to conquer Punjab or Ranjit Singh. This was due to Ranjit Singh's strong and skilled army. He recognized the need for modern tactics to effectively combat the British forces. To enhance his army's capabilities, he brought in foreign instructors and even invited an army general from abroad to teach new strategies. Additionally, he provided language training for his soldiers.

The British were concerned about the expansion of Ranjit Singh's kingdom and found it difficult to defeat him. Rather than engaging in direct conflict, they sought to negotiate. However, negotiating with Ranjit Singh was not easy; he was known to be shrewd in his dealings. Initially, he was hesitant to agree to a treaty, but when faced with British threats of attack, he reconsidered and agreed to a deal under the given circumstances. This led to the signing of the Treaty of Amritsar in 1809 between Charles T. Metcalfe and Maharaja Ranjit Singh. According to this treaty, the Sutlej River was established as the western boundary of Ranjit Singh's territory, with British troops stationed in Ludhiana.

All lands east of the Sutlej were under British control; however, Ranjit Singh continued to expand his empire beyond the river. He captured Peshawar for the Sikh kingdom in 1834 and brought the entire region of Kashmir under his reign by 1821.

Maharaja Ranjit Singh's rule was referred to as the Khalsa Sarkar. During his reign, Sikhs, Hindus, and Muslims were treated equally. He was known as an able, courageous, and magnanimous ruler, respected not only in India but throughout the world. Ranjit Singh possessed many precious jewels and had expressed a desire to donate the Kohinoor diamond to Lord Jagannath, the presiding deity of Odisha, but unfortunately, he passed away before he could fulfill this wish.

Jind Kaur was the youngest queen to marry such a great ruler. Before marrying her, Maharaja Ranjit Singh had four other queens: Datar Kaur, Gulab Kaur, Raj Ban Soo, and Gul Bahar Begum. The sons of these queens included Kharak Singh, Sher Singh, Ishwar Singh, Kashmira Singh, Tara Singh, Multana Singh, and Pashaura Singh. Among all Ranjit Singh's queens, Rani Jind Kaur was noted for her beauty and had a radiant glow.

Rani Jind Kaur came from humble beginnings, as the daughter of a dog keeper, before becoming the queen of the Sikh Empire. Despite being raised in a healthy family environment, transitioning to the lavish lifestyle of the royal family was no small feat for her. The circumstances of her marriage made it difficult for her to maintain her position as the queen throughout her life. Her story is akin to a fairy tale. Though she was born into a modest family, she was fearless and desired to connect with the common people. She had no aspirations for a high status; her life was uniquely her own. Although married to the king, she remained closely linked to the people. She held a deep love for Punjab and its inhabitants, as well as for Maharaja Ranjit Singh. Her goal was to earn a place in the hearts of the people, and she hoped for the genuine love of Maharaja Ranjit Singh, which she ultimately received. The love of Ranjit Singh became her strength. This talented and resilient woman constantly sought to express her independent thoughts without fear.

Rani Jind Kaur was the youngest wife of Maharaja Ranjit Singh, the first ruler of the Sikh Empire, and she gave birth to a son named

Duleep Singh, who would become the last ruler of the Sikh Empire. Jind Kaur played a significant role during this transitional period; however, her marriage to Maharaja Ranjit Singh lasted only four years. In 1838, she gave birth to her only son, Duleep Singh, on September 6, much to the king's delight. He considered Duleep Singh his successor.

Unfortunately, Jind Kaur's life as the queen of such an influential ruler was not filled with happiness. The Sikh Empire, which had been established in 1799 and dominated for 50 years, collapsed following the British East India Company's acquisition in 1849. Maharaja Ranjit Singh passed away in 1839, just a year after Duleep Singh's birth, and this death drastically changed Jind Kaur's life.

Following Ranjit Singh's demise, the political landscape became chaotic, with numerous factions vying for power, including those loyal to the Maharaja and those aligned with the British government. In the absence of a courageous ruler, the administration became paralyzed, creating an atmosphere of anarchy.

After Maharaja Ranjit Singh's death, Rani Jind Kaur and her son Duleep Singh sought refuge with their relative, Raja Dayan Singh of Jammu, where Gulab Singh, Jind Kaur's brother, held rule. Despite the upheaval, Jind Kaur remained resilient. She refused to succumb to despair and gathered a small group of loyalists from the Lahore court to help her manage governance, deliver justice, and address the people's grievances.

On September 16, 1843, after negotiations with the three successors of Ranjit Singh, Maharaja Sher Singh and his council declared five-year-old Duleep Singh as the successor. Duleep Singh was crowned the king of Punjab; however, since he was still a minor, Jind Kaur served as his caretaker and acted on his behalf, which granted her the right to rule.

Initially, Hira Singh, a counselor, was indifferent to Duleep Singh and Jind Kaur, prompting her to raise strong objections. She insisted that the royal court and council must recognize Duleep Singh as king, asserting that without this acknowledgment, the title would appear meaningless. Support for Jind Kaur and Duleep Singh grew among the counselors and the army. Gradually, Jind Kaur consolidated real power in her hands. As an administrator, she reorganized the Supreme Council of Khalsa and maintained harmony between the common people and the armed forces.

Gradually, Rani Jind Kaur proved herself to be a capable ruler, and her people were happy under her leadership. However, her challenges were far from over. Duleep Singh faced many difficulties in securing the throne. His half-brother, Pashaura Singh Karpoor, attempted to dethrone him, while the feudal kings pressured for the return of their zamindari rights and demanded the taxes imposed by Hira Singh. The army soldiers also sought a salary increase, and the overall costs of running the government had risen significantly. Hira Singh's uncle, Gulab Singh Dogra, the Raja of Jammu, had taken a large portion of the treasury from Lahore, leading to further financial strain. Additionally, disputes among the Sikh vassals over state rights were common, and some even secretly negotiated with the British, allowing British soldiers to cross the border.

Despite these obstacles, Jind Kaur was determined to resolve these issues. With the help of Raja Lal Singh, the head of the jagir, and the chief of army staff, she managed to address various problems. To strengthen her position, she arranged for her son, Duleep Singh, to marry the daughter of Chatar Singh Atariwala, an influential representative of the Sikh community and a governor from Hazara. She approved salary increases for the soldiers and brought Gulab Singh back from Lahore to enhance the treasury. Furthermore, she appointed Johar Singh as Wazir, replacing her nephew Hira Singh. Gulab Singh returned with a fine of Rs 68 lakh and a commitment to negotiate better terms in the future.

In January 1845, Pashaura Singh arrived in Lahore and was greeted with honor by Jind Kaur. However, she ordered him to return with the promise of military protection for the empire. He refused to comply, instead attacking the fort and declaring himself ruler of Punjab. A large army led by Chatar Singh defeated him, forcing his retreat. Anticipating further threats from the young king, Johar Singh planned a stealth attack. Unfortunately, he was brutally stabbed to death in front of Maharani Jind Kaur for his efforts.

Maharani Jind Kaur ruled the Sikh Empire from 1843 to 1846. During her reign, she effectively balanced the needs of the common people and the armed forces, implementing a specific payment plan for her troops with the help of Chatar Singh Atariwala. She was a powerful and influential woman who opposed several societal evils, including the Sati and purdah systems. Additionally, she reconstituted the Supreme Khalsa Council and bolstered the economy by promoting trade and commerce in her state. At that time, Jind Kaur was recognized as one of the most powerful women in North India.

In 1845, British Governor-General Sir Henry Hardinge declared the First and Second Anglo-Sikh Wars. Jind Kaur sent her army to the banks of the Sutlej River in an effort to resist the British forces, but the Sikhs suffered defeat. Lal Singh and Raja Tej Singh faced failures in the Anglo-Sikh battles, including defeats at Firoz Shah and Soborn. According to the treaty signed in Lahore in 1846, Duleep Singh remained the Maharaja, and Jind Kaur was appointed as his guardian. Although Duleep Singh ascended to the throne, Sir Henry Lawrence held the real power in government. In December of that year, Jind Kaur was stripped of all her powers and was granted an annual salary of Rs 1.5 lakh.

Rani Jind Kaur did not accept her situation easily. She made efforts to regain control, which posed a significant challenge for the British. Consequently, they viewed her as one of their main obstacles in British-ruled India, even dubbing her the "Messalina of Punjab." Alarmed by her actions and influence, the British captured her and separated her from her nine-year-old son, Maharaja Duleep Singh, who was sent to England.

After the war, the British allied with their supporters, including Tej Singh and Lal Singh. In August 1847, when the British refused to recognize Duleep Singh as the king of Sialkot, Henry Lawrence, a British ruler, imprisoned Queen Jind Kaur in the Summon Tower of Lahore Fort. Ten days later, she was transferred to Sheikhpura, and her salary was drastically reduced to Rs 48,000.

The most tragic event for Rani Jind Kaur was the separation from her son. Duleep, only nine years old, was sent to England, where he was placed in the company of Queen Victoria and her friends. There, he was converted to Christianity and raised to live like an Englishman. Meanwhile, Maharani Jind Kaur was forcibly removed from the assembly in Lahore, dragged by her hair, and imprisoned in Sheikhpura Fort and later in Chunar Fort in Uttar Pradesh.

Despite these hardships, Rani Jind Kaur refused to give up. Even after her arrest, she attempted to escape. Disguised as a common maid, she managed to slip out of the fort. Although she did not publicly demand her son Duleep Singh's return to the throne, she tried to bring him back to Sikhism. Unfortunately, it was too late; the British had already influenced Duleep Singh, who had begun to embrace life as an English gentleman and wished to remain in London.

However, Jind Kaur continued to think of her son and worked to bring him back to India. She wrote a letter to Lawrence expressing her concerns: "He doesn't have any siblings, an uncle, a father, or any other relatives. So under whose care is he?" Sadly, all her efforts were in vain, and she did not see her son again for 13 years. During this time, the new British ruler, Frederick Currie, declared her a renegade and expelled her from Punjab. She was imprisoned at Chunar Fort, 45 kilometers from Varanasi, and all her jewelry was confiscated. The brutal treatment she received from the British deeply affected the Sikh community, and even Dost Mohammad Khan, the Muslim ruler of neighboring Afghanistan, condemned the attack.

A year later, Jind Kaur escaped from Chunar Fort in disguise. She traveled about 800 miles through the forest, eventually reaching Nepal in search of refuge and safety. She arrived in Kathmandu in April 1849.

Before escaping from the fort, Jind Kaur threw money on the floor of her prison cell and left a letter for the soldiers there. The letter read: "You locked me up in a prison cell, but know this: whether you confine me in a cell or a dungeon, I possess the magical power to break free from all your bonds. With that power, I have freed myself from your locks. I told you politely not to be so hard on me. Do not think of my actions as an escape from prison; I have liberated myself without anyone's help, and I don't even consider this liberating. Never think of me as a thief."

The mid-1900s brought significant changes to the political landscape of India under British rule. Bhimsen Thapa, the then Prime Minister of British-ruled Nepal, and Maharaja Ranjit Singh entered into a secret alliance against the British. However, Ranjit Singh's death in

1839 had a profound impact on the Sikh Empire. The young Duleep Singh ascended to the throne with Jind Kaur serving as his caretaker. Under her leadership, the Sikhs declared war on the British in 1845. A letter was sent from Lahore to Kathmandu seeking assistance; however, by that time, Kathmandu had also been divided, and King Rajendra Bikram Shah did not respond to the plea for help.

After Rani Jind Kaur escaped from prison and reached Kathmandu, she initially found refuge in the home of Amar Bikram Shah, the son of General Chautariya Poshkar Shah. Amar Bikram Shah served as the Prime Minister of Nepal from 1838 to 1839. While at Amar Bikram Shah's residence, Jind Kaur received all the royal privileges but chose to introduce herself as an Indian maid whenever she ventured outside.

Rani Jind Kaur stayed at Amar Bikram Shah's house for a few months until she revealed her true identity to the Prime Minister of Nepal, Jung Bahadur Rana, and requested his assistance. Upon learning of her situation, Jung Bahadur Rana provided protection to Jind Kaur and accorded her all royal honors. A palace known as Charburja Durbar was constructed for her at Thapa Thali Durbar, and the Government of Nepal arranged for an annual financial allowance to support her. Despite these provisions, the British remained wary of Rani Jind Kaur, fearing she might unite the Sikhs again. Consequently, the British authorities in Kathmandu kept a close watch on her during her 11 years of residence in Nepal.

Duleep Singh married Bamba Muller, the daughter of Ludwig and Sophia Muller, on June 7, 1864, in London. They had four sons and three daughters, one of whom died in infancy. After the death of his first wife, Duleep Singh married Auda Wetherill, daughter of Charles and Sarah Wetherill, and they had two daughters. Unfortunately, only Duleep Singh's daughter, Sophia Alexandra, survived; all his other children died while he was still alive.

In November 1856, Duleep Singh sent a message to his mother, Jind Kaur. This message was delivered by Jung Bahadur Rana on his behalf to the Governor-General of India. In the message, Duleep Singh requested that his mother be allowed to live with him in England for the rest of her life. However, the British government dismissed his request, considering it a hoax. A few days later, Duleep Singh sent Pundit Nehemila Gore to Kathmandu to inquire about his mother's well-being, but this attempt also failed as Pundit was not given the opportunity to meet the Queen.

Unwilling to give up, Duleep Singh decided to approach his mother himself. He hatched a plan to hunt tigers in Bengal. In 1860, Duleep Singh wrote to the British ruler in Kathmandu and sent a copy to Sir John Login, mentioning the deteriorating condition of his mother as reported by the Nepalese authorities: "The queen has become weak and feeble. Her vision has weakened."

The British were relieved to hear about Rani Jind Kaur from the Nepalese authorities, believing there were no further threats from her. Finally, on January 16, 1861, Rani Jind Kaur was allowed to meet her son at the Spanish Hotel in Calcutta. At that time, many Sikh rulers were returning to Punjab via Calcutta after the Chinese war, creating a festive atmosphere. Thousands of armed Sikh warriors surrounded the hotel in celebration. Under pressure, Governor-General Lord Canning requested Duleep Singh to take his mother to England as soon as possible.

On their way to England, Duleep Singh wrote a letter to Sir John Login, who was his guardian, requesting him to find a house for his mother in the Lancaster Gate area. Upon Jind Kaur's arrival in England, Sir John Login's wife visited her, bringing their three children. She was greatly impressed by Jind Kaur's beauty, courage, strength, and endurance. Sadly, by the time of the meeting, Rani Jind Kaur had fallen ill, and her eyesight had deteriorated, diminishing her once-great beauty. However, her confidence remained unshaken, which surprised Sir John Login's wife. There was no doubt that the extraordinary fortitude and beauty of this woman in the twilight of her life had earned her the nickname "Messalina of the Punjab."

The jewels taken from Rani Jind Kaur were kept in the treasury of Banaras, and Duleep Singh proceeded with an agreement to return them.

After visiting Sir John Login's wife, Rani Jind Kaur received some gifts. With the help of her attendants, she adorned herself with some of these ornaments. Wearing beautiful necklaces and beaded jewelry enhanced the queen's beauty. The jewellery was later auctioned on October 8, 2009, for Rs 55.2 lakh.

Duleep Singh went to stay with his mother, Rani Jind Kaur, at Mulgrave Castle in Yorkshire for a few days. Arrangements were made for Rani Jind Kaur to stay separately from him, but she refused to leave her son. In the last two years of her life, she continually reminded Duleep Singh of his responsibilities. A petition addressed to Queen Victoria, found in the British Library, states that the seeds of the Sikh Empire sown 20 years earlier needed to be replanted. Rani Jind Kaur described the injustices faced by her family. Under her guidance, Duleep Singh rekindled efforts to reunite the Sikhs and revive the vast Sikh Empire established by his father, including its capital. Through her influence, Duleep Singh rediscovered the history, prestige, and traditions of his clan, eventually converting back to Sikhism.

Rani Jind Kaur lived with her son until the end of her life. She passed away in her sleep on August 1, 1863, at the age of 46, in Abingdon, Kensington, London. At that time, cremation was not practiced in Great Britain, which only became common after 1885. Duleep Singh was not permitted to take his mother's body back to Punjab. Instead, Jind Kaur's body was temporarily interred in the Dissenter's Chapel at Kensal Green Cemetery. In the spring of 1864, Duleep Singh gained permission to transfer his mother's body to Bombay, India, where her last rites were performed at Kensal Green Cemetery and subsequently in Nasik, Bombay. Her ashes were eventually brought back by her granddaughter Princess Bamba and Duleep Singh, and placed near the tomb of her husband, Maharaja Ranjit Singh, in Lahore.

Duleep Singh built a memorial for his mother near Panchavati on the banks of the Godavari River. Jind Kaur expressed a desire to be laid to rest in Lahore, but the British government refused this request. Later, Princess Bamba Sutherland moved Jind Kaur's tomb to the vicinity of Ranjit Singh's tomb in Lahore. In 1997, the marble over her tomb at the Dissenter's Chapel in Kensal Green was removed and re-erected in her memory in 2009. Jind Kaur, known as "Rani Jindan," was celebrated for her beauty, courage, and strength. Her remarkable history, marked by courage, perseverance, intelligence, and hard work, has left a lasting impression on many. It is important to discuss and learn from the lives of women like her. Jind Kaur was very popular among the people of British India, which is why she was referred to as 'The Messalina of the Punjab.'

She was deposed by the British Council in December 1846, following the defeat of the Sikhs in the First Anglo-Sikh War. To diminish her influence on the masses and reduce their affection for her, the British imprisoned her and sentenced her to exile. After 13 years, she was finally granted permission to visit her son, who had been taken to England, but even then, she faced restrictions that prevented her from fully expressing a mother's love for her child.

Despite these challenges, she constantly endeavored to uphold the governance and maintain the empire that her husband had left behind. She faced hostility from external forces with courage and intelligence, fiercely fighting to protect her husband's vast empire from British control and striving to place her son on the throne. She succeeded to some extent, but sadly could not keep her son, for whom the king had fought so hard to preserve freedom. This is a poignant story of a mother enduring great sorrow, yet she never gave up the fight. There is no doubt that the Maharani wanted her son, Duleep Singh, to ascend to the throne.

The death of her brother, Johar Singh, deeply impacted the Queen. Many historians attribute the fall of the Khalsa army, at least in part, to the Maharani. Dr. Ganda Singh, who was Lord Alenbro's personal correspondent during the Anglo-Sikh War, noted in a letter dated November 20, 1943, that "the mother of Maharaja Duleep Singh stands by her words, and she is the only one still present in Lahore."

However, as Henry Montgomery Lawrence, Lahore's Home Minister, observed, "Two days before the end of the war, she employed all her tactics. She even led the Sikh Sardars to potential victory in battle, but this was thoroughly suppressed by Frédéric Curie. She altered the course of the 1845-46 war by assigning a non-Punjabi general named Tej Singh important strategies, which ultimately led to the defeat of the Lahore army."

She was an exceptionally brave and courageous woman who changed some of the strict societal rules for women of her time. The

Bhils even joined the army under her influence. She was unrelenting in her criticism of the British. Even after her imprisonment at Chunar Fort, she remained undeterred and sought to escape. Chitra Banerjee Divakaruni, in her book "Sheshrani" about Jind Kaur, highlighted how Maharani Jindan's perseverance and willpower deeply influenced her. Although blinded by her son's infatuation and temporarily out of power, she stood firm in the face of danger and navigated her challenges with intelligence and resilience.

She had made some mistakes in her life. For example, when the Khalsa army brutally killed her brother Johar in front of her, she remained unmoved. This led to the Anglo-Sikh War in Punjab. This decision may have been a mistake, but it showed her loyalty to her family. As a mother, she sought power for her son, Duleep Singh, wanting him to be a king like Maharaja Ranjit Singh. She believed that the British must not be underestimated, understanding that Maharaja Ranjit Singh was powerful and that the British feared subjugating him. She thought her son Duleep Singh could wield similar power, which would ensure the maintenance of freedom.

Lord Dalhousie, the Governor-General of India, remarked about Jind Kaur, "Her Majesty had the power to mobilize all the forces for any objective." Governor-General Lord Ellenborough noted in a letter to Arthur Wellesley in 1843 that "the mother of boy Duleep Singh was unwavering in her mission."

In her book 'The Maharaja's Box,' Christie Campbell writes, "Maharani Jind Kaur was one of the most powerful women in 19th-century Indian Sikh history."

Since the British viewed Jind Kaur as a primary obstacle and enemy, they spread disinformation about her. Most of Maharani Jind Kaur's life was dedicated to expelling the British from India. Only after her capture were the British able to enter Kashmir through the Khyber Pass. Following the death of her husband, Maharaja Ranjit Singh, in 1839, she rebelled against the British to protect her minor son, Duleep Singh, from losing power. During her reign, she fought two fierce battles against the British, but these efforts ultimately led to the downfall of Punjab. Although her lack of age, guidance in administration, and diplomatic experience affected her effectiveness, she remained a formidable ruler. British historian Peter Canse described her as a strong leader who tirelessly strove to make Punjab a well-governed empire.

Nikke Gunider Kaur Singh, a professor at Maniyar Kolbe College, stated, "Maharani Jind Kaur set an example in her society by abolishing the practices of Sati and Purdah. She played a unique role in consulting the Chief Minister and guiding the prominent military leaders. By resisting British authority, she became their main opponent. The British feared that her influence over Duleep Singh might galvanize the Sikhs against them, potentially allowing them to reconquer Punjab. Therefore, they conspired to separate the 9-year-old Duleep Singh from his mother.

Regardless of the challenges, Jind Kaur remained a shrewd, courageous, and strong woman who resisted British power throughout her life. Most significantly, the British feared her—and they only ceased to do so when she fell ill. It is no small feat to intimidate such a powerful and intelligent empire. Despite not coming from a royal background and spending only a few years with her husband, Rani Jind Kaur achieved remarkable feats. Her maturity and ability to leave a lasting impact, even without extensive experience, are nothing short of extraordinary. Her strength, perseverance, truthfulness, courage, patience, intelligence, independent thinking, and determination embody a kind of magical power. With this power, she dared to confront immense challenges, proving that she could make the impossible possible.

◻◻

Begum Hazrat Mahal

From time immemorial, women have traveled the world. If we were ever to estimate the end of this journey, it would never reach a definitive starting or ending point. However, one thing is certain: the journey of women is always moving forward. Their feet never turn back. Women are rising at every level of society. Regardless of the work they do or the struggles they face, they never back down and never succumb to fear. They confront all challenges with courage and perseverance. Our women are brave; they embody patience, endurance, fortitude, resilience, and organizational strength. Formal education may vary, but they acquire these qualities through experience and fight the battles of life, emerging victorious. Whether it is a struggle for themselves, their families, their communities, or their nation, they are ready to confront every challenge. This has been true for ages.

The struggle for freedom is significant, and it's essential to acknowledge how many people were involved—women included. They have surmounted the obstacles before them. With weapons in hand, they fought valiantly and found success. Women have ensured that conflicts are not solely a male domain.

The courageous women of India sacrificed their lives during the first rebellion against the British in 1857. They are remembered as skilled warriors. Many women emerged as key figures when discussing the revolt of 1857. Importantly, this participation was not limited to upper-class or educated women; historians note that many brave individuals from the Dalit community also fought on the frontlines, mounted on elephants, and provided financial, social, and psychological support to the rebels. They often acted secretly as vital conduits for the exchange of information. Unfortunately, history has paid little attention to their contributions because they were a small number of women from specific segments of society. Their sacrifices remain largely untold, and no one has adequately narrated their stories or freely acknowledged the roles of women in a predominantly male society. Yet, these events and sacrifices are imprinted in our memories. Humanity, the best creation of God, does not forget. Over time, many narratives may fade, but these women have not been lost from the hearts of the people. Their stories persist, and we continue to rewrite them. In the same way, the tales of valor from other overlooked heroes are now part of this conversation. We draw inspiration from the stories of their bravery.

Begum Hazrat Mahal is a hero of our country, India—a brave warrior who believed firmly in winning battles. She was not only full of valor, courage, and strategic skill but also possessed tremendous talent. Unfortunately, her contributions receive little recognition in Indian history.

Throughout history, many brave individuals have been celebrated, but numerous others remain overlooked, including Begum Hazrat Mahal. The heroic stories of various historical figures are extensively documented, while the story of this remarkable woman seems to be forgotten. She fervently opposed the British Empire and the British East India Company, valiantly fighting for the freedom of her state during the First War of Independence in 1857. With her combat skills, courage, and organizational abilities, she dealt significant blows to the British forces, making them recognize her power.

Begum Hazrat Mahal, whose real name was Muhammadi Khanum, was born in a small village in the Faizabad district of Awadh, in present-day India. During her time, Nawab Wajid Ali Shah provided education and vocational training to some economically disadvantaged women. This education transformed their attitudes and behaviors, enabling them to live in the royal palace. However, many of these women were ultimately sent back to the harem, where they entertained the Nawabs and were often treated as temporary wives. Hazrat Mahal's life was no different.

It is said that she grew up without a mother, as her family was struggling financially. She was taken in by her maternal aunt, but her aunt did not keep her for long and eventually sold her into a noble harem in Awadh. Hazrat Mahal was known for her striking beauty and talent in dancing, which attracted the attention of Nawab Wajid Ali Shah, the last ruler of Awadh. He quickly selected her from among the other women and honored her with the title of "Mehek Pari." She transitioned from being a housekeeper to becoming a favorite in the Nawab's court.

Gradually, she grew closer to the Nawab and became his second wife, receiving the name Iftikhar-un-Nisa. Later, she gave birth to a son, Prince Brijris Qadr, after which she was granted the title of Begum Hazrat Mahal. However, she was eventually abandoned by the Nawab, much like his other consorts.

The Mughal Empire began to decline after the death of Emperor Aurangzeb on March 3, 1707, which led to the emergence of stronger regional states. The kingdom of Awadh was declared independent in 1722. Nawab Safdarjung (Abdul Masur Khan) was succeeded by his son Shujauddaula, who ruled from 1758 to 1778. In 1773, the Treaty of Banaras was signed between Shujauddaula and Warren Hastings. He was followed by his son Asaf Udaulah, who ruled from 1775 to 1797. Asaf Udaulah moved the capital of Awadh from Faizabad to Lucknow, which remained the capital until the end of the dynasty. The last ruler was Wajid Ali. The territory of Awadh stretched from Kannauj in modern Uttar Pradesh to the east, with its first capital in Faizabad, later becoming Lucknow.

In 1856, the East India Company took control of Awadh under

the Doctrine of Lapse, which had been promulgated by Lord Dalhousie. The region was known for its large-scale production of cotton and sugarcane. Officials of the East India Company identified several errors in the treasury's collection process, and Nawab Wajid Ali Shah was accused of corruption and mismanagement. That same year, Nawab Wajid Ali Shah was overthrown and exiled to Matyabruz in Calcutta (now Kolkata), along with some of his family members. The British then took possession of the land. Meanwhile, Begum Hazrat Mahal remained in Lucknow, overseeing the area along with her 12-year-old son.

However, Begum Hazrat Mahal did not accept British subjugation after the Nawab's exile. She consistently sought to free her country from British rule, employing various means to do so.

On May 10, 1857, the army declared a rebellion against the British East India Company from Meerut. They were soon joined by the forces of Mughal ruler Bahadur Shah II, who was proclaimed Shahenshah-e-Hind. The protests quickly turned violent, as the rebellion saw participation from kings, zamindars, feudal lords, tribals, and common people alike. Begum Hazrat Mahal emerged from her courtyard to join the men and declared war against the East India Company, continuing to resist British authority for an extended period.

She was supported by notable figures such as Sarfad Dola, Maharaj Balkrishna, Raja Jailal, Mamukhan, Rani Beni Madhobasko of Biswara, Raja Digvijay Singh of Mohana, Maulvi Ahmad Ullasah of Faizabad, Raja Man Singh, and Raja Jailal Singh. Zamindars and merchants also backed her in the 1857 uprising.

Prince Brijris Qadr was ceremoniously anointed at Quasi Bagh, Baradari. Following the victory at the Battle of Chinhat on June 5, 1857, she, with the backing of the Mughal forces, installed her 12-year-old son as the ruler of Awadh. British troops were compelled to withdraw from Lucknow. Since the prince was still a minor, Hazrat Mahal acted as his guardian for nearly ten months. She earned acclaim for her organizational skills, issuing notices and declarations in her capacity as the guardian of her son.

William Howard Russell's "My Indian Mutiny Diary" highlights that Begum Hazrat Mahal was a shrewd and powerful woman who made all the important decisions for her son. She garnered unwavering loyalty from her supporters and fought bravely against British forces. Hazrat Mahal exemplified the qualities of a fighter and displayed the skills of an ideal legislator. She was never defeated and upheld her self-respect throughout her life. During her tenure, she accomplished significant work and stood firm against the gender inequality prevalent in society at the time.

Begum Hazrat Mahal was vocal in her beliefs and had no religious biases; she respected all religions equally. She rejected the authority of the East India Company, and under her leadership, Lucknow emerged as a stronghold of resistance against the British during the First Indian War of Liberation in 1857. In response to Queen Victoria's proclamation regarding the provinces of India under the East India Company, she issued a counter-declaration. Her effective governance and popularity resonated with the people of her state. She succeeded in uniting the population of Awadh and assembling a formidable anti-British army.

Compared to Nawab Wajid Ali, Begum Hazrat Mahal was known as a strong and capable ruler. She possessed exceptional skills in politics, warfare, and administration. Despite coming from humble beginnings—her parents were caretakers and she spent her early life in a brothel—she prioritized her self-esteem and dignity in every aspect of her life. Historical records indicate that during her time in the brothels, she strongly objected to any inappropriate behavior directed toward her. She was determined to create her own identity and did not adhere blindly to all social norms. From an early age, she advocated against injustice and inspired others to do the same, standing firmly for her dignity as a woman and her identity.

Her struggle to establish her own identity later helped her mobilize the masses against the British. However, the freedom of Awadh was not her only goal.

She wanted India to be free from British rule and had a solid strategy for achieving that goal. Constantly striving to preserve her kingdom's independence, she dedicated herself to her state and its people, setting aside her personal struggles. A fierce warrior, she not only fought in battles but also stood alongside her soldiers to boost their morale. She encouraged them in various ways and taught them new tactics of warfare. She viewed all religions with equal respect. Most notably, she formed a women's army and rallied her troops from the back of an elephant to resist the British soldiers.

Begum Hazrat Mahal maintained a strong relationship with Nana Saheb, a childhood friend of Rani Lakshmibai, working together on several occasions. When the British attempted to assert their authority over Lucknow using their war booty, she rejected the pension offered by the East India Company and left the city. Subsequently, she allied with the Maulvis of Faizabad and continued her fight against the British until 1859. One significant event of this period was the Shahjahanpur attack, where Sir Henry Lawrence, the Chief Commissioner of Awadh, was defeated at the battle of Chinhat.

Her struggle continued until the end of her life as she did everything she could to save her country. When Nawab Wajid Ali Shah was exiled to Calcutta in 1856, Hazrat Mahal felt a tremendous sense of empowerment, which she skillfully utilized. However, she was ultimately defeated by the British and sought refuge in Nepal, where she spent most of her life. The Prime Minister of Nepal accepted her as a refugee. She passed away in 1879, and her body was buried near the Jama Masjid in Kathmandu. Unfortunately, her grave is now in a dilapidated state.

The conditions of her resting place can be observed in the area managed by the Jama Masjid Committee. The sacrifices she made and the challenges she faced are reflected in the inscription on her tomb: "Today my house, my market is being looted. Hazrat Mahal, only you can understand the pain of the poor and give them shelter. Hazrat Mahal."

Thus ends the story of a woman who has served as an inspiration for generations. She was a tenacious individual who never surrendered, confronting all adversities and forging her own path. Reflecting on her journey, it raises the question of how long she lived happily without any struggle. While she may not have derived inspiration from anyone, her character, behavior, ideals, perseverance, integrity, and actions made her an inspiration for many. Regrettably, Begum Hazrat Mahal did not receive the same recognition as other Indian women fighters of her era. Often overlooked due to her lineage, religion, traditions, and social status, she emerged from the lower strata of society to defend the Nawab and challenge the vast British Empire, yet she is not celebrated as a dignified queen. Her contributions have been largely ignored in history.

The capital city of Awadh, including Lucknow, played an active role in the first war of independence against British rule under the strong leadership of Begum Hazrat Mahal. Her courage and sacrifice for freedom have immortalized her in history. In 1962, Begum Hazrat Mahal Park was established in Hazratganj, Lucknow, in her honor. On May 10, 1984, the Government of India issued a postage stamp to commemorate Begum Hazrat Mahal.

Jhalkari Bai

The historical narrative of Dalits has remained largely untold for a long time. The sacrifices made by Dalits have not been adequately highlighted in the writings of historians, resulting in many remarkable figures being overlooked. However, several Dalit women have made significant contributions to India's history and cultural life, showcasing their sacrifices for the country and their homeland.

One notable Dalit woman is Jhalkari Bai, who played a crucial role in the organized struggle led by Rani Lakshmibai of Jhansi in 1857. Born into a Dalit family, Jhalkari became a skilled warrior and a devoted follower of Lakshmibai.

Jhalkari was born on November 22, 1830, to Sadovar Singh and Yamuna Devi in Bhojla village near Jhansi. As a member of the Kori tribe, she was raised by her father after her mother's death. He was determined to empower her, often defying societal norms. Although formal education was not accessible to her at that time, she developed into an astute warrior from a young age, skilled in handling weapons and riding.

Jhalkari's reputation for bravery emerged early in her life. To support her family, she tended to animals and collected firewood from the forest. In one notable incident, she killed a leopard that attacked her cattle while she was gathering wood. On another occasion, she bravely drove away robbers who were harassing a local businessman. Her courage and fighting skills caught the attention of Puram, a renowned wrestler, archer, horseman, and firefighter from the Kori tribe of Namapur near Jhansi. Puram sought permission from his mother to marry Jhalkari, and her father agreed to the proposal. The couple married in 1843.

The Revolt of 1857 had a profound impact on both Jhalkari Bai and the Dalit community. This uprising marked the first strong and organized resistance against British rule in India. However, the sacrifices of Dalits, who contributed immensely to this rebellion, have not been adequately recognized in our historical accounts. Jhalkari's story highlights the prevailing caste system in society. Her extraordinary bravery during the struggle of 1857 serves as a testament to the valiant efforts of Dalit women, who fought alongside their male counterparts in the rebellion and demonstrated the strength of their community.

Many historians note that Jhalkari Bai, who belonged to the Kori sect, assisted her husband in his weaving craft and occasionally visited the palace with him. From a young age, the brave Jhalkari Bai learned wrestling and horseback riding from her husband after their marriage. Her husband, Puram, was renowned for his bravery in the army of Rani Lakshmibai.

During the Gowri Puja in her village, Jhalkari Bai, along with other women from the village, went to welcome Rani Lakshmibai. Rani Lakshmibai was surprised to see Jhalkari, as she bore a striking resemblance to the queen. Hearing stories of Jhalkari's bravery elated Rani Lakshmibai, and Jhalkari subsequently joined her women's army, known as 'Durga Dal.' There, she learned to shoot guns and operate cannons. Already skilled in the art of warfare, Jhalkari became even more proficient and was appointed commander of the Durga army. She not only led the women's wing of the Jhansi Regiment but also shared a close personal relationship with Rani Lakshmibai, assisting her in various ways.

The revolt of 1857 primarily aimed to protect the royal thrones of the nobles, while the Dalits sought true independence. Due to Lord Delhousie's policy on state ownership, the British prevented the adoption of the childless Lakshmibai, hoping that her childlessness would allow them to usurp her kingdom. In response, Lakshmibai took up arms against the British.

On March 23, 1858, General Hurose attacked Jhansi with a large army. Rani Lakshmibai led her troops from within the fort. Despite the strategies of the British and some local opposition leaders failing, one of the queen's soldiers betrayed her by opening the fort gates for the British. As the fall of the fort became inevitable, some loyal companions advised the queen to flee. She had no choice but to leave the fort on horseback with a faithful companion. This was made possible by Jhalkari, who used her resemblance to Rani Lakshmibai to keep the British distracted. They mistakenly believed they had captured the queen of Jhansi.

While the British surrounded the Jhansi fort, Jhalkari Bai fiercely fought them off. She even requested to meet General Hurose, leading the British Army to believe that the queen was about to surrender. However, this was a tactical move; her goal was to keep the British occupied while Rani Lakshmibai escaped safely from the fort, allowing her to gather more strength and reinforcements for the upcoming battle. Through her immense courage, sharp intellect, and strong willpower, Jhalkari Bai successfully misled the British army, enabling Lakshmibai to escape safely and regroup for future confrontations.

Jhalkari Bai was solely in charge of the Bhandari Gate and the Uno Gate. Her husband, Puram, was martyred in battle. When the news of her husband's death reached her, she was overwhelmed with grief but did not stop fighting. Taking on the fierce spirit of a tigress, she killed many British soldiers.

General Hurose mistakenly believed Jhalkari to be Rani Lakshmibai and asked her, "What should we do with you?"

"Hang me until death," she immediately replied.

The general was impressed by her bravery and response, stating, "If only one percent of Indian women were like her, the British would soon have to leave India."

Some accounts suggest she was shot multiple times during the battle, leading to her death, while others claim that the British released her upon discovering her true identity, allowing her to live until 1890. Jhalkari Bai was a prominent member of the 'Durga Dal,' the women's militia of Jhansi.

While her husband served as a soldier in the Jhansi army, Jhalkari Bai herself was skilled in archery and martial arts. Due to the many similarities between her face and that of Lakshmibai, she often helped devise strategies for the soldiers of Jhansi. This resemblance also allowed Lakshmibai to escape safely from the fort of Jhansi without the British noticing. After her arrest, the British learned of Jhalkari's true identity and eventually released her, allowing her to live until 1890.

Many other women, such as Sundari Bai, Mundari Bai, and Moti Bai, also sacrificed for their queen and motherland as part of the Durga Dal in Jhansi. Jhalkari Bai played a significant role in the story of Rani Lakshmibai, helping her cross the forest into Nepal with the ruler of Pratapgarh to survive.

For many years, Jhalkari's story has been intertwined with the memories of Bundelkhand. Even today, her tale can be heard in numerous folk songs from the region. Jhalkari's indomitable courage and valor foster a sense of cultural unity among the Dalit community in North India. On April 5, 1857, Jhalkari Bai fought fiercely against British soldiers while disguised as the Rani of Jhansi. That day remains unforgettable for the people of Bundelkhand, who keep her memory alive in many poems, capturing the intensity of the battle.

According to reports, Jhalkari's story was initially shared orally before being documented by historians. The oppressive caste system of that time played a significant role in why her story was published in detail; however, the saga of her sacrifice cannot be overlooked. Jhalkari's unparalleled bravery highlights the contributions of Dalits in Indian history. Later literature, textbooks, and historians have illuminated the social status and communal discrimination faced by Dalit women at that time. It often appears that because Jhalkari was not a queen, the British neglected to mention her in their records.

Many poets and writers have created poems and stories inspired by the story of Jhalkari Bai. Additionally, there are numerous children's books, novels, and plays dedicated to her legacy. Several publications and institutions bear her name.

Among the literary works inspired by her, titles such as "Veerangana," "Jhalkari Bai Kavya," "Jhansi Ki Sherni," "Veerangana Jhalkari Bai Ka Jeevan Charitra," "Veerangana Jhalkari Bai Mahakavya," and "Nrityanatika" are notable folk plays. Furthermore, a magazine called "Jhalkari Bai Sandesh" was published in her honor.

"Splendid! You have fought valiantly, possessing the strength to confront the British. Your valor has become legendary among heroes.

Your story is extraordinary. Alongside the Queen of Jhansi, you led Jhansi to victory, standing resolutely against the British at the Datia Gate. You fought fiercely like the goddess Kali, decimating the enemy. The British artilleryman who dared to meet your gaze met his demise. We continue to hear tales of your bravery."

Additionally, many folk songs and dramas created by Dalit communities have been inspired by Jhalkari's life story. Her narrative celebrates the self-respect of the Dalit community.

Jhalkari Bai was a true braveheart, not born into royalty nor did she occupy a throne, and she possessed neither a palace nor wealth. Yet, she fought fearlessly against the British until the very end. Her sacrifices are a testament to her courage.

Uda Devi

A statue of a beautiful young woman made of stone stands in the central square of Sikandra Bagh in Lucknow. With a rifle resting on her shoulder, she appears to be walking forward in a line. This striking statue represents Uda Devi Pasi, a heroine of the 1857 revolt.

In November 1857, a fierce battle occurred at Sikandra Bagh in Lucknow. Thousands of Indian soldiers lost their lives in this conflict, which aimed to liberate Europeans held by the British under the leadership of Commander Corlani Campbell. By 1857, North India was a prosperous region, and residents of Delhi, Jhansi, and Kanpur began protesting against the exploitation and oppression of the British East India Company. Along the shores of the Gomati River, some British soldiers found themselves surrounded by rebels. As they faced a shortage of food and ammunition, their morale gradually weakened. In September, British forces attempted to rescue them but were repelled by a rebel encirclement. In November, under General Corlani Campbell's command, some British soldiers were released. For the second time,

Campbell's 93rd Regiment advanced south of the Gomati River and reached Sikandra Bagh Palace.

Intense fighting broke out between the rebels and the British, resulting in the deaths of about 2,000 rebel soldiers.

During the assault on Sikandra Bagh, a British officer observed that many of his soldiers were being struck by bullets. He moved closer to investigate and discovered someone firing at British troops from a nearby peepal tree. He ordered his men to set fire around the tree. After some time, the body of one of the militants fell to the ground. Later, the British learned that the rebel was a Dalit woman named Uda Devi Pasi, who had disguised herself as a man to fight against the British soldiers.

Uda Devi was born in a small village in Awadh, Uttar Pradesh. She approached Begum Hazrat Mahal and proposed initiating a war in response to the widespread anger and opposition of Indians against British rule. In support, Begum Hazrat Mahal sent an army of women to assist Uda Devi. Together with her Dalit sisters, Uda Devi fought valiantly in the struggle against the British during the uprising of 1857.

Uda Devi has become a powerful source of inspiration for Dalit women in modern times. Every year on November 16th, people from her community gather at her memorial to honor her unparalleled contributions to the Indian freedom struggle. Women come from various parts of the country, including West Bengal, Bihar, and Madhya Pradesh. Born into the Pasi caste, traditionally associated with rearing pigs and producing local liquor, Uda Devi was martyred for the sake of her country's freedom. Therefore, women from the Dalit community come together in her memory, chanting slogans like "Uda Devi Amar Rahe" and "Uda Devi Zindabad."

Although the story of Uda Devi's sacrifice dates back many years, her bravery and courage continue to resonate with Dalit women today. Unfortunately, the history of the Pasi people is being lost globally, with little evidence of their existence recognized by either British or contemporary society.

The sacrifices of the Pasi and other Dalit castes, often at the hands of the upper castes, have not been adequately highlighted. As one poet noted, "Some call them Africans, some call them untouchables, some call them helpless, while others call them brave."

Additionally, many women from Africa worked as guards in the harem of the Nawab of Awadh and actively participated in the revolt of 1857 in Lucknow. This demonstrates that women from the Dalit community, as well as upper-class women, played significant roles in the Indian freedom struggle; however, not all of their contributions are equally recognized in our history books.

In his work "The Great Mutiny," Forbes-Miguel described Uda Devi as "armed with a pistol on her shoulder and a bullet in her abdomen, fiercely attacking British soldiers from the edge of the trees." Before her capture, she had already killed several British soldiers. Similarly, 22-year-old Mahaviri Devi from Mundabahar village in Muzaffarnagar district had also taken down multiple British soldiers during the 1857 uprising. Unfortunately, these brave women fighters were ultimately captured and killed by the British.

□□

Ajijan Bai

Ajijan Bai of Kanpur served in Nana Saheb's army and fought against the British. She had no personal animosity toward anyone; her sole motivation was the independence of the country. Her legacy lives on in the hearts of the people of Kanpur. Like Rani Laxmibai, she rode into battle on horseback, dressed in men's clothing and wielding a pistol. After Nana Saheb's victory, she proudly marched at the front of the army's victory procession, holding the flag of Kanpur.

In her book "Making the Margin Visible," Lata Singh notes that Ajijan was well-liked among the sepoys of Kanpur and was particularly loyal to a sepoy named Shamsuddin. Meetings were held at his house where soldiers secretly discussed their plans. Ajijan even formed a women's group that bravely assisted the rebels, delivering weapons and providing various forms of support. During the Kanpur Rebellion, she worked closely with the rebels and was instrumental in helping them.

The other rebels mentioned in Rudyard Kipling's book "On the City Wall" were also active in the anti-British movement of 1857. Almost all buildings in the city served as meeting places for the rebels, leading the British to seal many of them off. Muzaffarnagar in Uttar Pradesh was one such location. Women like Asha Devi, Bhaktabari, Habiba, Bhagwati Devi Tyagi, Indra Kaur, Jamila Khan, Mankor, Rahimi, Rajkor, Shobhadevi, and Umra played significant roles in the fight for freedom. Tragically, many of these courageous women were executed at a young age or burned alive. Similarly, Rani Avantibai of Raigarh and Rani Draupadi of Dhar opposed the Law of Lapse, yet their contributions are often overlooked in history. There are few accounts of women from minority groups who fought valiantly. Nevertheless, the stories of these brave women will always be remembered.

□□

Manikarnika Tambe a.k.a Rani Lakshmibai

Many people have fought for the country's independence, and many have sacrificed their lives in this struggle. They include kings, ministers, generals, military personnel, members of the royal family, and ordinary citizens. It is important to recognize that the fight for freedom was not limited to kings and men; women also played a significant role in this. Just as kings fought bravely and gave their lives for the cause, queens also participated in the freedom struggle and made sacrifices. Over time, history has recorded their contributions. Here is the story of one such queen whose legacy has been remembered for generations.

She was born on November 19, 1828, into a Marathi Karhade Brahmin family in Varanasi. Her father, Moropant Tambe, and her mother, Bhagirathi Bai, were originally from Maharashtra. Her mother was her dear companion. Although her father initially desired a son to carry on the family name, he was blessed with a daughter. He did not feel disappointed. "This is my daughter, and she is my son, too," he declared, deciding to raise her as if she were a son. They named their daughter Manikarnika Tambe, but the family affectionately called her 'Mano.' The Peshwa referred to her as 'Chhabili,' meaning 'joyous,' reflecting how much everyone adored her.

Unfortunately, her mother passed away when Manikarnika was just four years old, leaving a void in her life. However, her father continued to shower her with love and attention. After her mother's death, he ensured that Manikarnika received the care and affection of both her parents.

From a young age, Manikarnika was active and eager to learn. Her father provided her with the same opportunities he would have given a son. He even taught her the art of warfare, wanting her to stand out. Indeed, she grew to be self-reliant and confident, differentiating herself from her peers. People often remarked on how unique Manikarnika was!

She quickly developed skills in shooting, horse riding, martial arts, and archery. She also regularly practiced yoga. Manikarnika cultivated strong relationships with those older than her. Her best friend, Nana Sahib, was ten years her senior, and Tantia Tope was also a cherished friend. Together, Manikarnika, Nana Sahib, and Tantia Tope formed a close-knit friendship as they grew up.

As a child, Manikarnika was independent and free-spirited. She was a strong independent thinker and an outspoken opponent of the many social restrictions placed on women in contemporary society. She had a natural affinity for horses, and both cycling and horseback riding were her passions. Often, she would ride alone or travel from the palace to the temple accompanied by attendants on palanquins. Her beloved horses, Sarangi, Pavan, and Badal, were very dear to her.

There is an anecdote about how Manikarnika once saw Nana Saheb sitting atop an elephant. Desiring to do the same, she expressed her wish, but Nana Saheb refused. Undeterred, she asserted that she would one day ride an elephant, and eventually, she fulfilled that dream.

In May 1842, at the age of 13 or 14, Manikarnika married Maharaja Gangadhar Rao Newalkar, a middle-aged king of Jhansi. Following

Maharashtrian tradition, she changed her name upon marriage and became Lakshmibai Newalkar, later known simply as Lakshmibai. From the very beginning, Lakshmibai focused on governance alongside her husband.

In 1851, Lakshmibai gave birth to a son named Damodar Rao. Gangadhar Rao was overjoyed by the arrival of his son; however, tragedy struck when Damodar Rao passed away just four months after birth. The Maharaja was heartbroken and struggled to cope with the loss.

In response to this crisis, Maharaja Gangadhar Rao adopted Anand Rao, the son of a relative, as his heir. At that time, the British authorities maintained that a king without biological heirs could not rule. Consequently, the East India Company would take control of the state and offer the king a pension of Rs 60,000 per year. Maharaja Gangadhar Rao appealed to the British government for adopting a son. Following the Maharaja's request, the adoption ceremony took place in the presence of British officials. In his application, Gangadhar Rao assured that all necessary facilities and respect would be granted to the adopted child, and that his wife, Rani Lakshmibai, would continue to manage Jhansi for the rest of her life.

Even after adopting a son, King Gangadhar Rao struggled to come to terms with the loss of his biological son. In November 1853, Maharaja Gangadhar Rao Newalkar of Jhansi died just a day after adopting a son. Rani Lakshmibai, though deeply saddened, remained resolute. She fulfilled her royal duties with heroic fortitude.

Rani Lakshmibai was known for her rigorous morning routine, which included weightlifting, boxing, and horse racing, all before breakfast. Dressed in simple clothing, this clever and intelligent woman governed Jhansi with great efficiency. At that time, the Governor General of India was Lord Dalhousie.

Following Gangadhar Rao's death, his adopted son, Damodar Rao (whose real name was Anand Rao), was not recognized by the East India Company. Despite Gangadhar Rao having completed all necessary paperwork for the adoption, the British rejected it. Lord Dalhousie, the Governor-General of the British East India Company, enforced the

Doctrine of Lapse to invalidate Damodar Rao's claim to the princely state, subsequently placing Jhansi under British control.

Upon learning this, Rani Lakshmibai voiced her strong opposition, declaring, "I will not give it to anyone." In 1854, the British ordered her to vacate the fort of Jhansi and offered her an annual allowance of Rs 60,000 instead. They insisted that she abandon the fort and leave Jhansi.

Until that point, Rani Lakshmibai had been hesitant to rebel against the British, but in June 1857, the 12th Bengal Infantry captured the fort of Jhansi, looting both treasure and many valuable books.

Four days after the massacre, Indian soldiers under British command took a substantial amount of money from the queen and ordered her to renounce the royal palace. The Queen communicated this to Major Eriksen, the Commissioner of the Saugor Division, in a letter. On July 2, Eriksen requested the Queen to maintain control of the situation until the British Superintendent arrived.

The rebellion organized by Sadashiva Rao, the nephew of Maharaja Gangadhar Rao, was suppressed by the Rani's soldiers. Additionally, a dispute erupted between the troops of Company Adhunsu Oorja and Datia of Jhansi regarding the division of Jhansi into two parts. Lakshmibai appealed to the British Governor-General to intervene and resolve the conflict. However, the Governor-General blamed the Queen for the massacre and did not respond to her request. Nevertheless, Rani Lakshmibai did not remain passive.

She positioned cannons on the walls of the Jhansi fort, alerted her army, and, with the assistance of various feudatories, quelled the rebellion. Until then, she had been trying to keep Jhansi under her control on behalf of the British.

As a prominent warrior of the Sepoy Mutiny of 1857, she set an example by opposing British rule. Rani Lakshmibai became a source of inspiration for Indian freedom fighters.

The Indian freedom struggle began in Meerut on May 10, 1857. When news of the rebellion reached Jhansi, Rani Lakshmibai sent a letter to British officer Captain Alexander Skane, requesting for protection. Skane agreed to offer her support, and at that time, peace prevailed in the city. In the summer of 1857, Rani Lakshmibai gathered all the women of Jhansi and celebrated a turmeric and kumkum festival with great enthusiasm. She tried to assure the people of her state that there was no threat to them or Jhansi from the British.

From August 1857 to January 1858, peace prevailed in Jhansi under the rule of Rani Lakshmibai. The British announced that they would send troops to Jhansi solely to maintain peace and control groups opposing British rule. However, in March, when the British army arrived in Jhansi, they discovered that the fort was well-equipped with weapons, and the surrounding area could be devastated by cannon fire.

Some historians report that Hagros, the commander of the British army, ordered the soldiers of Jhansi to surrender. In response, Rani Lakshmibai declared, "We are fighting for freedom. According to Lord Krishna, if we seek success, we can strive for the sweet fruits of victory. If we die on the battlefield, we will surely gain glory and attain salvation." There is no record of any intent to surrender.

On March 23, 1858, when Sir George besieged Jhansi, Rani Lakshmibai fought valiantly alongside her soldiers to protect the fort from the British forces.

Heavy shelling began in the vicinity of Jhansi on March 24. A message was sent to Tantia Tope for assistance. He arrived with 20,000 soldiers, but they were unable to defeat the British. During the battle with Tantia Tope's army, on April 2, the British resorted to diplomacy and launched a fierce, multi-directional attack on the fort. Despite resistance from Rani Lakshmibai's forces, the British troops entered the palace and exterminated soldiers in the streets. Tragically, even women and children were not spared. Thomas Lowe described this incident as a deeply tragic event.

After this, the queen decided to leave the fort and planned to return once the situation improved in the city. At this time, she chose to align herself with either Tantia Tope or Rao Saheb, the nephew of Nana Saheb.

According to legend, the queen, with Damodar Rao on her back, jumped off the fort on her horse, Badal. Although both she and her son survived, the horse perished. Under the cover of night, the queen escaped from the fort alongside her loyal soldiers. They managed to reach Kalpi in the company of generals Khudabaksh, Basahrat Ali, Ghulam Ghaus Khan, Dost Khan, Lalabhau Bhakti, Moti Bai, Sunder Mundar, Kashibai, Diwan Raghunath Singh, and Diwan Jawahar Singh. Together, they captured Kalpi along with Tantia Tope and other rebels.

However, on May 22, the British attacked and fought against Rani Lakshmibai's army, successfully recapturing Kalpi.

Rani Lakshmibai, along with Tantia Tope, Bandar Nawab, and Rao Saheb, escaped once again and joined other Indian soldiers at Gwalior. They aligned with the defeated Maharaja Scindia of Agra at Morar. Without facing any resistance, they captured Gwalior and took control of Gwalior Fort. The rebels in Gwalior nominated Rao Saheb as their Subedar. However, Rani Lakshmibai struggled to persuade the other rebels to unite with Gwalior and launch an attack on the British. General Rose took command of Morar on June 16.

On June 17, at Court Ki Sarai near Phool Bagh in Gwalior, soldiers of the 8th Royal Irish King's Hussars, led by Captain Hege, engaged the large Indian army of the Queen, who was attempting to escape. Approximately 5,000 Indian soldiers were killed in the conflict, and many were attacked and killed by gunfire. According to eyewitness accounts, Rani Lakshmibai, dressed as a common soldier, fought a Hussar on foot and was gravely wounded. After being injured, she rested on the street, where she encountered another soldier and bravely attacked him with a pistol, only to be killed by a carbine shot. Some reports suggest Rani Lakshmibai was dressed as a horsewoman when she was wounded.

To ensure her body would not fall into British hands, she instructed her loyal soldiers to cremate her secretly after her death. Following her demise on June 18, 1858, her last rites were performed in the presence of local people. The British suppressed the rebellion by November 1858. Three days after her death, Gwalior was captured by the British forces.

Rani Lakshmibai was known for her beauty, intelligence, and bravery, standing out as one of the most courageous leaders of the Indian rebellion. After her death, she was cremated in a grand ceremony on a large boulder at the base of a tamarind tree in Gwalior. Her bones and ashes are said to have been preserved, and an impressive memorial has been erected in her honour at Phool Bagh in Gwalior. Colonel Malction, in Part III of his *History of Indian Mutiny* published in London 20 years after her death in 1878, noted that while she was considered guilty in the eyes of the British, she remains a hero in the memory of her countrymen, celebrated as a rebel who lived and died for India. Her sacrifice will never be forgotten.

The young prince of Jhansi, Damodar Rao, joined his mother's army during the Battle of Gwalior. After escaping the battle, he led a group of 60 soldiers, along with 60 camels and 22 horses, toward Rao Saheb's camp at Bithoor. However, the people of Bundelkhand refused him shelter out of fear of the British, presenting many obstacles in his journey. Eventually, he escaped into the woods, and after two years, only 12 of his men survived. Another group of about 24 soldiers was killed in Jhalrapatan town but later regrouped with some refugees from Jhansi. Forced to surrender to the British, Damodar Rao was granted a pension of ten thousand rupees, administered by Munshi Dharmanarayan, for the rest of his life. Y.N. Kelkar refers to these incidents in his book *Ithihasachaya Sahali*, although much about the prince's life remains unknown. He is believed to have died in 1860.

Throughout India, there are images of Lakshmibai riding a horse and fighting valiantly with her prince on her back. In her memory, several institutions have been established, including the Lakshmibai National University of Physical Education in Gwalior, the Lakshmibai National College of Physical Education in Thiruvananthapuram, and the Maharani Lakshmibai Medical College in Jhansi. The Rani Lakshmibai Central Agricultural University was founded in 2013, and the Rani Jhansi Marine National Park in the Andaman and Nicobar Islands is named in her honor. Additionally, the women's wing of the Indian Army is known as the Rani Jhansi Regiment, and her palace has recently been transformed into a museum, housing a collection of archaeological and historical artifacts from the 9th to the 12th century CE. In 1957, two postage stamps were issued to commemorate the centenary of the Revolt of 1857.

The Indian Coast Guard's ICGS has also been named in her honour.

Numerous literary works have been written about the life and struggles of this queen of Jhansi, including novels, poems, and films that highlight her dedication to the Indian freedom struggle. Many patriotic songs have been written about her, and one of the most famous Hindi poems by Subhadra Kumari Chauhan, which recounts her life story, has gained unprecedented popularity. Some of these poems celebrating the legendary life of Jhansi Rani are included in the curriculum of schools across India.

A prime example of this is the legacy of Rani Lakshmibai, the Queen of Jhansi, who is honoured in numerous works of literature and media.

> *We have heard this story from the people of Bundela.*
> *She fought bravely like a man; she was the queen of Jhansi.*
> *You were born in this land;*
> *you took up arms to protect it,*
> *igniting the flame of rebellion in everyone's mind.*
> *Oh dear! You bravely fought the British and finally rested here.*

According to B.R. Tambe's Marathi ballad, "In a field near Gwalior, this braveheart attained valor from the warrior Karuka."

Many novels have also been written about her life. These include Brindlal Verma's *Jhansi Rani*, Jayshree Mishra's *Rani* (2007, English), Janmast's *Night Runners* (1951, English), Christopher Nicholl's *Manu and Queen of Glory* (published in two parts), and Michelle Moran's *Rebel Queen*. Emilio Salgari's work, *Just After a Throne* (1907), describes Rani Lakshmibai's assistance to a rebel camp in Assam. George MacDonald Fraser's *Flashman in the Great Game* depicts a meeting between the Queen and Flashman, while French writer Michel de Gris imagines a love affair between Rani Lakshmibai and English lawyer Puckett in *La Femme Sacrée* (1988).

Philip Meadows' *Sita* (1872) explores the relationship between O'Toole and the Queen, while Gillen, a British military officer, portrays the Queen's resoluteness in his novel *The Queen* (1887).

Numerous movies and television shows have been made about her as well. The story of the 1857 uprising was adapted in the serial

Bharat Ek Khoj, produced and directed by Shyam Benegal, which was aired on Doordarshan in 1988, featuring Ratna Pathak Shah as Rani Lakshmibai. In another Doordarshan segment, *Jhansiki Rani,* Varsha Usgaonkar portrayed the Queen. In 2001, a historical drama titled *1857 Kranti* was aired on DD National with Barkha Madan playing the role of Lakshmibai. Varsha Usgaonkar also played Lakshmibai in Ketan Mehta's 2005 film *Mangal Pandey.* In 2012, Rajesh Mitral made a Hindi film, *Jhansi Ki Rani Lakshmibai,* with Vandana Sen Kashish in the lead role. Kangana Ranaut took the role of Lakshmibai in the 2019 Hindi film *Manikarnika: The Queen of Jhansi.* Anushka Shetty portrayed Lakshmi Bai in the Telugu film *Sera Narasimha Reddy* (2019), and Devika Bhise played the role in the British film *The Warrior Queen of Jhansi* (2019). In the 1985 Tamil film *Jhansi Rani,* directed by Karnan, M. Pandharibai played the lead. The 2009 Zee TV serial *Jhansi Ki Rani* features Ulka Gupta as the young Lakshmibai and Kratika Sengar as the adult character. Anushka Sen starred as Lakshmi Bai in the Hindi serial *Khoob Ladi Mardaani Jhansi Ki Rani,* which aired on Colors TV in 2019. Additionally, the story of Lakshmibai was made into the Hindi film *Jhansi Ki Rani* (1953), directed by Sohrab Modi, which also has an English version titled *The Tiger and the Flame.*

Who would have thought that a girl, raised with abundant love since childhood, would face such challenges in life? Despite growing up without a father, she blossomed into a star. Surrounded by the love and support of her family, she grew stronger with each passing year. This strength became a cornerstone in her journey through life.

She faced numerous challenges head-on, including the death of her husband, ruling a kingdom as a single parent, shaping her son into a good man, and ensuring that he received his rightful place. She bore each of these burdens to the best of her ability, remaining fiercely dedicated until the very end. Despite the harshness of British rule, she never yielded to injustice. She protested in various ways against the British and addressed the wrongs. Though she had no inclination to engage in war under normal circumstances, she chose to fight with courage when necessary, striving to protect her kingdom from British domination. Her desire for freedom remained unwavering.

Tragically, she lost her life at the end of the conflict. Such a brave and courageous woman deserves our respect. Though that era has passed and times have changed, her legacy continues to endure. The story of her courage transcends generations. Every pursuit she undertook was dedicated to society, her country, and her people. She consistently prioritized the interests of her state and her subjects above her own. Her actions serve as a powerful example.

Moreover, it is important to recognize that the impact a woman leaves through her selfless service and hard work is timeless. A woman's contributions extend beyond her family or household; they encompass the broader society.

☐☐

Savitri Bai Phule

To live harmoniously in society and to enjoy a healthy and fulfilling life, individuals engage in a variety of activities. These activities are so intricately woven into daily routines that without them, a person becomes stagnant, finding it difficult to progress. This connection is crucial since human advancement relies on these activities. It is widely understood that essentials such as water, air, food, clothing, and shelter are fundamental to daily living. As a person's life evolves, the need for education is also felt. Education is the pathway to progress; it is an illuminating force in life. Without education, life resembles darkness. Education symbolizes growth and civilization. The more educated a person, the more cultivated and enlightened their environment will be.

However, acquiring invaluable gems of knowledge is not a straightforward process. Understanding its importance and integrating it into one's life presents considerable challenges. Despite the collective acknowledgment of education's significance, access to it is not uniform. Historically, only a privileged few had the opportunity for receiving education, while many faced overwhelming obstacles. Gender disparities further complicate this situation. Nevertheless, we must remember that education is a guiding light that can never be extinguished, even if the journey to find that light is an arduous one.

Women play a pivotal role in the advancement of society and education. Recognizing the critical nature of women's roles in societal progress is essential; raising awareness about women's education is vital. Born on January 3, 1831, one exceptional woman exemplified this struggle. Like many daughters of her time, she had no formal education until her marriage. Afterwards, she began her learning journey in her husband's home, where he made it his mission to educate her. He collaborated with American missionaries to establish a school for girls in Ahmednagar, facing considerable hardships along the way. His family opposed this initiative, especially her father-in-law, leading them to leave their home. Despite these challenges, she remained dedicated to learning, completing her primary education with her husband's support.

After receiving her primary education, she expressed a desire for further learning. At her husband's request, her friends Sakharam Yashwant Paranjpe and Keshav Shivram Bhavalkar helped her continue her education. This newfound knowledge excited her, but her thoughts often turned to the countless other women who deserved the same opportunity to shine. She recognized that educating women is crucial for a nation's progress. Both men and women must be educated to ensure societal advancement, and it is through their cooperation that true progress can be made. With this conviction, she resolved to work tirelessly for the betterment of society and the advancement of women, undergoing additional training with the help of two more teachers.

Savitribai Phule received her initial training at the Cynthia School in Ahmednagar, which was run by American missionaries, and continued her education at Normal School in Pune. After completing her teacher training, she began teaching in Mahawada, Pune. Her work was supported by her husband's mentor, Saguna Bai, who ardently advocated women's rights.

In 1848, Savitribai and her husband established their own school in Bhide Wada, Pune, which had the distinction of being the first girls' school in India. Bhide Wada was also the birthplace of Tatyasaheb Bhide, who warmly appreciated their efforts. The curriculum of their school emphasized both traditional and western teaching methods, incorporating subjects such as mathematics, science, and social studies. By the end of 1851, they had started three girls' schools in Pune, in which approximately 150 girls enrolled. The teaching methods in these schools were far superior to those added at government schools, resulting in the girls recording better academic performance than boys in those institutions.

Savitribai Phule is renowned for pioneering women's education in India amidst numerous challenges. In partnership with her husband, Jyotirao Phule, she undertook various initiatives to promote education for women and advocate for their rights. Consequently, she became the first female teacher in India, often regarded as a mother figure for the women's rights movements in the country. Savitribai Phule was a prominent social activist, significantly contributing to the eradication of superstitions, untouchability, and other forms of social injustice. She was also a public welfare advocate and a writer in Marathi.

Despite her groundbreaking contributions, Savitribai and her husband faced considerable opposition due to the conservative attitudes of society prevalent at the time. Rao Bahadur Kandukuri Veerasalingam Pandul noted that Savitribai often carried an extra saree while going to school because she faced verbal harassment and sometimes physical assaults such as having dirt thrown at her. She encountered strong resistance due to the caste and communal discrimination then pervasive in society, with many communities opposing formal education for years. The efforts of Savitribai and Jyotirao were often condemned, and they were labelled as sinful. Nevertheless, Savitribai persisted in her activism and dedication to education.

Savitri Bai and Jyotirao lived in Jyotirao's ancestral home until 1849. However, their work faced strong opposition from members of the upper castes and various communities, which led Jyotirao's father to evict them from the family home that year. Despite this setback, they remained defiantly resilient. After being thrown out, Jyotirao took Savitribai to the home of his friend Usman Shaikh.

On September 15, 1853, the journal of Christian missionaries, *Dnyanodaya*, published Jyotirao's statement regarding the work of both Savitribai and himself. He emphasized, "A mother plays an important role in the growth and development of a child. Therefore, those who aspire for the growth, happiness, and true progress of the country must focus on educating women. It is essential to pay attention to their lifestyle and their rights. I supported this idea and worked to educate women, but the prevailing caste system in society, including opposition from my own father, posed significant challenges. People were unwilling to fund schools, and many refused to send their children to school. However, Lahuji Ragh Raut Mang Ranba Mahar taught the importance of education to the members of their community."

Together with her husband, Savitribai educated many children across caste and community lines and established about 18 schools. They also founded an institution called the 'Child-Killing Prohibition Home' to protect rape victims, pregnant women, and children. The University of Poona was later renamed Savitribai Phule Poona University in her honor. The Maharashtra government has introduced several awards in her name, and there is a serial on Doordarshan that depicts her life. The history of India has duly recognized her contributions, and she has received significant praise and recognition from the public.

□□

Fatima Sheikh

While Savitribai Phule was determined to advocate for women's rights by prioritizing women's education and overcoming obstacles, she found a great ally in Fatima Sheikh, whom she considered a beloved friend. During that time, only upper-caste men had the right to education, but Savitribai and her husband refused to accept this inequality. They began their mission to educate the women of their caste and started teaching children at home. Though it wasn't easy and the path was fraught with challenges, Savitribai remained steadfast in her decision. The couple eventually had to leave their home to pursue this work, but they did not lose heart.

Fatima Sheikh and her brother Usman provided shelter to Savitribai and her husband in Pune's Gupte area. When their own community rejected them for rendering social service, Fatima and Usman not only offered them a place to stay, they also shared their dreams. Fatima assisted Savitribai in opening the first girls' school and tribal library in her home. This girls' school later expanded to their residence.

Despite the uncongenial social climate of the time, both Fatima and Usman courageously faced opposition. Fatima taught girls at the school founded by Phule in Bhide Wada and went from door to door to raise awareness about the importance of sending daughters to school. With Fatima's support, Savitribai's educational initiative for girls achieved significant success.

Fatima Sheikh's contributions as an educator and social organizer were as important as those of Savitribai. She encountered numerous challenges but remained committed to the cause of promoting girls' education and fighting against casteism. Although Savitribai and Fatima worked in different environments, they supported each other wholeheartedly.

Fatima's work focused on education, which is allowed for girls in Islam. However, she not only aimed to educate girls in her community but also reached out to girls from other communities, implementing modern educational methods in her pedagogical practices. It is believed that she was the first Muslim teacher in India. Researchers indicate that Usman, influenced by the Phule couple, encouraged Fatima to pursue higher education and spread modern education within their community. Together with Savitribai, she participated in teacher training programmes and began teaching others.

Although Savitribai was not deeply versed in the cultural and literary history of India, she actively worked to eradicate casteism, gender discrimination, and untouchability while promoting girls' education. Alongside her husband Jyotirao Phule, she was instrumental in combating social evils and bringing about a significant shift in women's rights within Hindu families.

In the 21st century, we can observe the impact on traditional Hindu families in Maharashtra, particularly through the contributions of Savitribai Phule and Fatima Sheikh. Both played pivotal roles in initiating social change, with Fatima Sheikh significantly aiding the realization of their shared vision.

Despite facing opposition rooted in caste norms, Fatima and Savitribai established girls' schools and participated in teacher training programs to promote quality education. Their efforts emphasized the importance of women's rights in India. Through her collaboration with social worker Saguna Bai, Fatima opened another school, which further accelerated their social service work. Together, she and Savitribai taught in all five schools that had been established until about 1856. However, in late 1856, Savitribai fell ill and returned to her mother's home.

When Fatima began attending the school founded by Savitribai and Jyotirao Phule, she encountered significant resistance from the upper classes of society. They would throw stones and cow dung at her, believing that women from lower classes had no right to education. Nevertheless, Fatima persisted in her mission, undeterred by such protests.

The friendship between Fatima and Savitribai went beyond mere companionship; it was built on mutual trust, a shared desire to effect change, and a deep commitment to their mission. Savitribai frequently expressed her deep appreciation for Fatima's dedication in her letters to Rao, highlighting the strong bond that united them. Their close friendship had a significant impact on their work, ultimately laying the foundation for women's education in India, a legacy that is still felt today.

Every educated Indian woman today should express profound gratitude to Savitribai Phule and Fatima Sheikh for their invaluable contributions. Efforts have been made to honour them and raise awareness of their work; textbook published in Maharashtra by the government includes Fatima Sheikh's contributions alongside those of Savitribai. This recognition was included in the draft curriculum by the Maharashtra State Bureau of Textbook Production and Curriculum Research in 2014.

☐☐

Muktabai Salve

In the past, our social system made it unimaginable for women to step out of their homes to pursue education. If a woman had dreams of receiving education, those dreams often remained unspoken, and are concealed in her mind and heart. While this was not true for everyone, it was the case for many. For a small number of women who had the opportunity to learn, they had to overcome formidable challenges. Fortunately, despite the severity of the situation, women did not give up hope or resign themselves to silence in the corners of their homes. The desire for education and empowerment often broke through these barriers, transforming dreams into reality.

Within women's movements, there were individuals from various social classes, including the rich, the poor, and the impoverished. While it was somewhat easier for upper-class women to access education, Dalit women faced considerable obstacles in stepping outside their homes to pursue learning and assert their presence in society.

The challenges were immense, yet women managed to break free and learn to fight for their rights. Dalit feminists argue that, within the broader social system, women's experiences and access to education are heavily constricted. They highlight the "social divide" that manifests itself in numerous areas of life. This divide necessitates discussions on caste and gender discrimination as critical issues in the articulation of Dalit women's rights.

Jyotiba Phule, a renowned social reformer, thinker, and writer, championed women's rights and education. He was married to Savitribai Phule, India's first female teacher. His works often reveal the male-centered family dynamics prevalent in Hindu society, illustrating how these norms deprived women of their rights and hindered their awakening in India. In 1916, Dr. Bhimrao Ambedkar published an article titled "Caste System in India," wherein he addressed consanguineous marriage practices used to control women's lives and sexuality. Practices such as Sati, the prohibition against women of certain castes covering their upper bodies, and child marriage exemplify the systemic oppression women faced. Ambedkar's writings concerning discrimination against Dalit women and the denial of women's rights contributed significantly to reform in Indian society.

In the late 1990s, a notable shift occurred. At that time, the ideas of Dalit feminists began to diverge from those of upper-caste feminists. To fully understand this divergence, we must cite to an instance from the class of Jyotiba Phule, where a student from the Mang caste spoke out in 1855 about the struggles faced by the *Mahar and Mang* castes.

"Our women bear children without even a roof over their heads; they endure the harshness of summer and winter," he wrote, illustrating the stark contrast between the experiences of upper-caste women and those of Dalit women. Only those who have lived through such hardships can truly understand this difference.

This distinction between the perspectives of upper-caste feminists and those of Dalit feminists regarding women's awakening is significant. As we explore this further, the rural story of *Nangeli* from the Izhava caste reveals the severe caste oppression faced by these women, who were compelled to expose their upper bodies to show respect to the upper castes. There is little surviving evidence of these struggles, as much of it has been erased from history. The caste regulations imposed by the Nairs in the Travancore kingdom in 1800, along with Ambedkar's writings on Dalit history, strongly highlight these injustices.

The names of Bhimrao Ambedkar and Jyotiba Phule are often discussed as the leading figures in the Dalit movement within Indian society. They highlighted the discriminatory social conditions prevalent at the time and encouraged others to explore different perspectives. However, many other prominent social reformers contributed significantly to this movement. Among them was a student of Jyotiba Phule, who courageously raised her voice against the caste system. As a prominent social reformer, she played a pioneering role in challenging and removing harmful practices from society.

The anti-caste movement was a long and arduous struggle. Her contributions were so significant that she has frequently been associated with Ambedkar and Phule in the context of *Dalit History*. She is recognized as the first Dalit woman writer in India, driven by her passion for social justice. This passion often filled her with anger, which she could not contain.

She strongly opposed the caste system and articulated her dissent through her writings. In her work, she challenged the so-called upper castes, questioning why the Shudras were treated so poorly.

The issue of 'Education for All' is not a new one; it has been a point of ongoing discussion. While debates about this topic had traditionally been superficial, there is now a more profound dialogue surrounding it. Today, education plays a crucial role in shaping political, cultural, and social transformation within the country.

Education is often described as the "third eye" of human life. Without it, everything remains in darkness.

In his Marathi play *The Third Gem*, Jyotiba Phule illustrated how education was provided to the upper classes, helping to foster religious and social harmony. However, Phule did not stop there; he recognized education as essential for social improvement and urged everyone to embrace it as their 'third eye.' Only through education could society correct its flaws. Sharmila Rege, in her work *Phule-Ambedkar Feminist*

Survey, stated, "Education is the channel through which knowledge and power can be combined."

Savitribai Phule and her husband Jyotirao Govindrao Phule understood the significance of education profoundly. They consistently sought ways to help others grasp this vital concept, which led them to establish a school. A girl who studied at their institution came to recognize the importance of education and made strides in social reform. Before Jyotiba and Savitribai Phule founded the Vetal Peth girls' school in Pune in 1852, many girls, including her, lacked educational opportunities. The school was notable for providing education to girls of all castes and creeds.

She began her education at this school, assisting Savitribai in establishing the first girls' school in Pune in 1848, which opened on January 8. Enrolled as a student at just 14, she quickly grasped the importance of education and became aware of women's low status in society, which deeply troubled her. In her writings, she articulated the plight of Dalit women during that era. She was acutely aware of her surroundings, including the thoughts, feelings, and actions of others. Her words were clear and impactful, as she vehemently opposed the caste system of 19th-century Indian society. She questioned, "Have the upper classes, who wrap themselves in sacred garments, ever felt even a moment's bitterness or sadness when we, labeled as untouchables and lower castes, are subjected to neglect and exploitation?"

Moreover, she remarked, "O wise scholars, by your selfish knowledge, you close your ears with false compassion; listen to what I am saying."

Her writings and speeches demonstrate the depth of her understanding of the importance of education. Every piece of her work reflects her role as a catalyst for social change during her time. She advocated a transformative view on education: "Education should not be confined to the classroom but should permeate society." This assertion illustrates her belief that education goes beyond mere literacy; it empowers individuals to challenge injustices within society. Unfortunately, discussions about racial, religious, and gender discrimination are often avoided in schools, leading to a reluctance to confront societal issues openly. It is crucial that students are made aware of and supported in addressing these realities rather than being shielded from them. Sadly, racial, religious, and gender discrimination remains not only a frequent occurrence outside the classroom but a routine experience for many students.

Despite the numerous obstacles and prejudices of her time, she fearlessly challenged societal norms and fought for change.

According to the caste system, she belonged to the Mong caste, which was considered the lowest caste in society at that time. She was the first Dalit woman to raise her voice against the caste and gender discrimination prevalent in India during the 19th century. In 1855, at the age of 14, she wrote "Mang Maharasya Dukkha Bhisra," an article that addressed the plight of Mahars and Mangjati women. This article was published in the journal "Dnyanodaya." History bears eloquent testimony to the oppression faced by Dalits at the hands of the upper castes in Indian society. The article strongly condemned the atrocities committed against Dalits and has since been translated into several languages. It is recognized as the first work of Dalit literature.

She declared, "Abandon that religion! In a religion where only one class receives all the privileges, others are marginalized and neglected in society." Through her writings, she protested against the caste system in a clear and assertive manner. This excerpt from her essay is arguably the first powerfully articulated protest by a Dalit woman. The history of Dalits has often been overlooked by upper castes, who have ignored their narratives. The awakening of women is closely linked to the caste system, which is why the writings of this remarkable woman are acknowledged as pioneering contributions that highlight the struggle for the freedom of Dalit women.

Analytical thinking can often give rise to rational thought. She was one of the first Dalit women to vocalize her opposition to the caste system during the 19th century. While fighting against caste discrimination and gender inequality, she, along with the Phule couple, also worked tirelessly for asserting the rights of Shudras and untouchables.

One of these women was someone who could not remain silent even while learning. Instead, she initiated a powerful struggle, embracing the ideals and education she had received. She wrote a book that made a significant impact on society, marking a transformative era.

"The Brahmins consider us very abominable, they even consider us inferior to cows and bulls. They did not hesitate to consider us as inferior to donkeys during the reign of Bajirao Peshwa. If you beat a sick donkey, its owner will definitely protest, but who is raising his voice against the regular atrocities on our mahars and mangas? During the reign of Bajirao, if a person belonging to the Mang or Mahar caste passed through the gymnasium with his head held high, his head was cut off and a game of batball was played. Their swords were used as bats and our heads as balls. Where is the question of freedom and education when we have to go to their doorstep and get punished? "- In a powerful expression of her experiences, she shed light on the historical treatment of her community by higher castes. Citing past injustices, she reflected on how individuals belonging to the Mang and Mahar castes faced severe discrimination, even to the point of being dehumanized. Drawing upon her inheritance as the granddaughter of a noted revolutionary, she emphasized her commitment to social change and equity.

Her narrative included stark observations about the struggles faced by Dalits, particularly the hardships endured by women, including a lack of basic medical care during childbirth. She gave an impassioned call for reflection on societal norms, questioning why rules were enforced selectively and highlighting the need for inclusivity and respect for all.

Through her discourse, she challenged the status quo maintained by certain upper castes and underscored the importance of addressing the fundamental needs of every individual, such as those for education and basic rights. Her words resonated with a vision for a more equitable society, urging a collective acknowledgment of past wrongs and a commitment to future justice.

She firmly believed that education was the key to overcoming obstacles and transforming the lives of the downtrodden. Through education, she thought, society could eliminate various prejudices, the caste system, and superstitions. Most importantly, she felt a significant change in herself after receiving just three years of education. However, she faced considerable criticism for this from orthodox Brahmins who deeply adhered to casteism.

She used to say, "There is an unknown fear in the minds of both those on the higher rungs and those on the lower rungs of society. They attribute their circumstances to luck, believing that we are destined to suffer. If a woman is born into a low caste, she is expected to live like a slave for the rest of her life."

Despite this, she never viewed herself as inferior to number of upper classes. She understood that education would empower her to reject this mindset. Without education, people rarely question or challenge societal norms, but those who are educated are more likely to raise objections. She didn't just talk about it; she actively demonstrated this belief.

At that time, it was significant for a Dalit girl to come forward and voice her opposition to the caste system, gender discrimination, and religious inequality. Her writings emerged in the 19th century, a period dominated by caste and a male-centric society that affected all strata of life.

Her actions were a welcome development and had a profound impact on Dalit women.

She could feel the pain of women from the lower strata of society who struggled to find a place in the traditional lifestyle of the village. "They are treated as outsiders in Hindu society." Women from these lower strata face far greater challenges compared to those from higher social classes. In her essay, she emphasized the oppression of Dalit women and the dominance of men within society. "The situation in India varies significantly from one region to another, creating different circumstances based on caste, gender, and religion."

"O Mahars and Mongas - you are poor, you are weak, only the medicine of education can cure you, give you relief. "This was another theme to her essay. This article of hers was published in the journal *Gyanodaya* in 1855. Incidentally that year was the first year of the publication of Jyotiba Phule's writings. Part of this article was published in 1868 under the title 'The Third Gem' in N.V. Joshi's book *Description of Pune City*. The text was later translated into English and published by Susie Tharu and K. Lalitha from 600 BCE to 1991. This is the only article we are currently discussing. It is difficult to find more information about the author and her work. However, by examining this single piece, we have access to the history of approximately 100 years prior to 1950. Researchers S.G. Mali and Hari Narke state, "Many non-Brahmin and Dalit women writers and social reformers are being systematically erased from the pages of history." Currently, her works are only referenced in the context of Jyotiba Phule and Savitri Phule, while her name is absent from historical accounts.

'Muktabai Salve' is a remarkable woman who recognized the importance of education at that time. She broke through societal barriers, pursued her education, and illuminated the path of learning.

Inspired by the ideals of Jyotiba Phule and Savitribai Phule, she became the first Dalit woman writer in our country. Born into a Maharashtrian family, she quickly recognized how the hierarchical structures in society permeate to its very core. Through her writing, she gave shape to her experiences and thoughts. Her main argument was that Brahmins were consolidating all societal power in their hands, depriving others of education and basic rights.

In her article, she expressed, "These people hate us, strangle us by calling us poor Mongs and Mahars, remove us from our own land, and build high-rise buildings there. They do not hesitate to treat us in the most despicable manner, throwing us under the foundations of their buildings while constructing on top of us. This has been happening to us for generations." In the same article, published in 1855, she further stated, "Abandon such a religion in which all facilities are available to only one class, while others are literally disappearing from this earth. How can we take pride in such a religion?" She also described how the upper castes deceive the lower castes under the guise of political interests and for the sake of votes.

She understood and firmly believed that education is more than just literacy. It should serve as a medium and a means to raise awareness against the superstitions, prejudices, and injustices present in society. Education should foster self-awareness among all individuals, regardless of caste, creed, class, or gender. This is a topic that requires thorough discussion. By achieving this, education can not only balance society but also regulate it.

Though this is the only work of Mukta discovered so far, it clearly reflects her lifestyle and ideals. Her article demonstrates that her thoughts stem from a place of consciousness.

She deviated from the traditional path and advocated for the acceptance of innovation, highlighting the importance of education in a person's life. Even today, her work inspires many and instills hope in their minds. She firmly believed that education is the only means to rescue those exploited by social institutions. It is the tool that strengthens self-confidence, enabling individuals to question various issues and raise their voices against injustice. Although they are the majority in society, they often remain silent and fail to ask questions. Education is the key through which they can change this prevailing mindset. By acquiring knowledge, they can improve their mental and social conditions and attain independence.

In modern India, the voice of Muktabai Salve, through her speeches and writings, is recognized as that of the first Dalit woman to advocate for social change. She spoke out against the social injustices perpetuated by the upper classes long before notable figures like Tarabai Shinde and Pandita Ramabai. Today, many Dalit women writers are emerging and raising their voices against social discrimination, yet their works often remain unheard. Caste and gender discrimination continue to persist in Indian society. Dalit literature and Dalit feminism were significantly influenced by Muktabai Salve, who highlighted the oppression faced by Dalit women in her writings.

However, many questions remain about this pioneering Dalit woman writer and her impactful contributions. What happened to Muktabai Salve? Did she continue writing, and if so, where did her work go? If not, what were the reasons behind her absence from the literary scene? Unfortunately, answers to these questions are elusive. To this day, she is primarily remembered for just one article, which is quite disheartening. Nevertheless, that singular piece has conveyed a powerful message for social and epochal change.

While we may not know much about her later activities, we do understand a great deal about her character. She reminds us of other women from earlier generations who fought for social change. Muktabai Salve emphasized that education is the beacon of light in life, illuminating the way from darkness to brightness. She held a strong belief that education opens pathways to a better life. There has been research and a call for change inspired by her work. Observing the current landscape, it is evident that despite numerous challenges, the struggle she initiated for women's education has made significant strides.

Today, women are more aware of their rights and can discern right from wrong. They have found their own voices. When women strive for positive change, adhere to the right principles, and take strong stances, transformation is inevitable. However, such a journey requires immense perseverance. Muktabai Salve exemplified courage, and her struggle continues to inspire ongoing change.

□□

Tarabai Shinde

International Women's Day is celebrated every year on 8th March. This day is not just an occasion for celebration but also one which should be with love, reverence, affection, and, above all, faith. The origins of International Women's Day deserve thoughtful consideration. The day was first celebrated in 1975, and in 1977, the United Nations General Assembly designated 8th March as International Women's Day. The purpose of this holiday is to promote world peace and women's rights. Importantly, this day is not solely dedicated to women. It carries a deeper intention: to uplift women in every field of society, making their journey easier and helping them overcome obstacles. Women should strive for progress in all spheres, including political, cultural, economic, social, and educational domains. They must be resolute in their pursuits, as they possess the same rights as men, and there should be no discrimination.

The aim is for women to progress and prosper in a sustainable manner. The fundamental truth is that women are powerful and invincible. They are the true agents of social change and can contribute meaningfully to progress at every level of society.

Every year, various events are organized to celebrate Women's Day. The theme for Women's Day in 2022 was "Gender Equality Today for a Sustainable Tomorrow," encompassing the idea of 'Breaking the Bias'. This emphasizes that, if there is gender equality today, tomorrow will be secure. Discussions and debates about gender equality in society have been going on for a long time. The feminist movement and its debates have existed for years, often initiated by women advocating for their rights and safety, including issues related to working from home.

These discussions have been prominent in our society for some time but are currently more visible, particularly in urban areas. The recent global movements, such as the Me Too movement, have highlighted the fact that the discourse surrounding feminism will continue, despite opposition.

In reflecting on this, one might say: "Dear God, you are most powerful and completely unbiased. But if you created both men and women, why do men receive all the happiness while women endure pain? Your will may have been fulfilled, but for centuries, women have been suffering."

Whoever has asked God with sorrow why happiness is bestowed upon men while women endure all the pain—this thought is often expressed by women themselves. In our discussion on gender equality, we must remember a remarkable pioneer who played a vital role in this movement. She was born in 1850 in Budhana, Maharashtra, into a poor Marathi family and was raised in a challenging environment. As a child, she did not receive any formal education. Her father, Hari Shinde, was a dutiful employee working as a clerk in the revenue department, and he also published a book titled *Hints to the Educated Natives* in 1871. With no schools available for girls in the area, he took it upon himself to educate his only daughter at home. She showed a keen interest in learning and studied Sanskrit, English, and Marathi under his guidance. Her extensive knowledge of both classical and modern literature set her apart from other women of her time.

Although she married at a very young age, she did not adhere strictly to traditional customs. In a significant departure from patriarchal norms, her husband moved into her home after their marriage. Even after getting married, she faced tough decisions influenced by societal expectations. At that time, a married woman without children had to cope with severe social stigma and harassment. To address this, she made the courageous choice to remain childless, aiming to emphasize that the life of a woman without children is just as valuable as anyone else's. This was not an easy decision, especially given the social pressures of the time. However, she stood firm, fully aware of the position and difficulties faced by women in society.

Witnessing the injustices directed at childless women deeply troubled her, and she would not tolerate the disrespect shown to them. Rather than accepting the status quo, she resolved to enact change. As an active member of Jyotirao Phule and Savitribai Phule's "Satyashodhak Samaj," she worked tirelessly to combat gender and caste discrimination. Alongside these social activists, she dedicated herself to improving the plight of women and promoting equality within society.

She worked tirelessly to fight for justice for women across all fields, aiming to eliminate gender inequality and secure equal rights for them. In an era when women were denied education, she resolutely rejected these limitations. Many women were forced into marriages and then subjected to widowhood against their will. They troubled her deeply. The treatment meted out to widows was especially painful to witness. Additionally, sexual violence within marriage was another significant issue affecting women at that time. Society was highly conservative, with most members upholding restrictive norms about how women should behave and be treated. Remarkably, few women expressed dissatisfaction with the constraints placed upon them. However, Tarabai stood firmly against the oppression of women, distinguishing herself from others in society with her courage and resolve.

Tarabai Shinde was one such woman who forged a unique path for herself by confronting societal norms and circumstances to effect change. She was a feminist activist who challenged patriarchy and casteism in Indian society during the 19th century. She engaged with women from diverse backgrounds, wanting to understand their experiences. Working with upper-caste widows, she became aware of the oppression they faced from their own families, including instances of unwanted pregnancies, which deeply distressed her. She could not tolerate the denial of education to low-caste girls and the restrictions placed on high-caste widows, who were forced to remarry or were ostracized. Appalled by society's treatment of women, she sought ways to support and rehabilitate them, striving to provide shelter for those who had been excluded. As a member of the Satyashodhak Samaj, she worked to offer refuge to women marginalized by society. Alongside promoting gender equality, she also connected with Phule to understand the detrimental effects of the caste system. This fusion of ideas laid the groundwork for challenging oppressive social norms.

Tarabai was a member of Satyashodhak Samaj, working alongside Jyotirao and Savitribai Phule. The Phule couple established a school for Dalit girls in 1848 and later, in 1854, created a shelter home for upper-caste widows who were denied the right to remarry and were marginalized by mainstream society. Tarabai joined their efforts after some time, gaining valuable insights from her experiences while working with them. Both Savitribai Phule and Tarabai shared similar views on caste and gender discriminations in Indian society.

Rosalind O'Hanlon, a professor of Indian history, has researched the ideas of Jyotirao Phule, highlighting his belief that the Brahmin community oppressed lower castes. In contrast, Tarabai Sathe argued that women faced oppression primarily because of male dominance in society. O'Hanlon's work delves into Phule's life and activism.

Tarabai not only sought to change the status of women in society but consistently worked towards this goal. She organized various literary programmes and used her writings to guide societal change. Her most famous book, *A Comparison Between Women and Men*, offers a strong critique of the caste system and the patriarchal views inherent in Hindu belief-systems. According to Sushi Tharu and K. Lalitha, this work represents perhaps the first thorough feminist argument emerging after the Bhakti poetry movement. Originally published in Marathi in 1882, Tarabai's book posed a provocative question: "Don't men have the same faults that women have?" This question resonated with many women who had felt they were voiceless.

In *A Comparison Between Women and Men*, Tarabai addressed the inequitable treatment of women and criticized the religious traditions that perpetuated their oppression. This was her first published book and presented a powerful critique of upper-caste patriarchy. Notably, it is considered one of the first modern feminist texts in India, as it sharply interrogated Hindu religious texts that contributed to the subjugation of women—an idea that remains contentious even today.

In 1881, *The Pune Vaibhav*, an orthodox newspaper known for its conservative and anti-reform stance, published an article about a controversial criminal case involving a Brahmin widow named Vijayalakshmi from Surat. The article was part of a series titled "New Loose Ethics," which disparaged her. Depicted in a negative light, Vijayalakshmi faced a public backlash after aborting an illegitimate child to avoid humiliation and ostracism. She was initially sentenced to death for this act, although her punishment was later commuted to life imprisonment.

The incident sparked outrage in Tarabai, prompting her to respond with her book *Stri Purush Tulana* (A Comparison of Women with Men). In this 52-page work, Tarabai systematically refuted the derogatory writings, emphasizing the different standards applied to men and women and asserting that women deserve equal rights. Despite the significance of her arguments, her work faced criticism as sexist by some.

The book was published by Shri Shivaji Press, with an initial print run of 500 copies priced at 9 annas each. However, contemporary society and the press did not welcome Tarabai's work, which resulted in her book not being printed for a second time despite receiving much praise. Although Jyotirao Phule commended her effort, the negative reception from the press hindered its reprinting.

In 1885, Phule addressed Tarabai, stating, "Chiranjeevini (dear daughter), you have done a great job." He encouraged his co-workers to read her book. The book was also reviewed and praised in the second issue of *Satsar*, a journal founded by Jyotirao Phule and associated with Satyashodhak Samaj.

Following the discussion in the magazine, Tarabai's book gained renewed attention. Phule noted, "Tarabai had to face a lot of criticism for her book *A Comparison Between Women and Men* because newspapers were published by those whom she had criticised." After this point, however, there was little further discussion about the book.

Tarabai's work was particularly significant, as many intellectuals at the time focused on visible atrocities committed against Hindu widows. In contrast, she explored different and more nuanced issues, boldly challenging patriarchal ideas by asserting that women are equal to men on all levels.

In her book, she urged readers to consider the notion that "Man is not an indestructible being who is free from all mistakes, but he is as flawed as the women he criticizes." She consistently highlighted and countered the faults attributed to women. Tarabai also pointed out the hypocrisy of men who championed widow remarriage while imposing restrictive codes of conduct on women.

She criticized the patriarchal norms prevalent in Hinduism at the time, arguing that these norms adversely affected women. This criticism laid the groundwork for feminist thought in India.

Regarding adultery, Tarabai emphasized a woman's right to choose and condemned men for their inability to keep women satisfied. She challenged the patriarchal structure of marriage, which she believed is a system designed to subjugate women.

Tarabai wrote, "In this world, women are suffering from hard work, hunger, and thirst. Yet, all they seek is a kind word from you. Though you may go out and earn money, is a woman sitting idle, or is she managing the household? You claim she is obedient, which shows you want women to remain ignorant. Women toil until their bodies are worn out. Their hands may remain intact, and their blood may not be shed, but do not forget that a woman's eyes are always on your face. Acknowledging her efforts with a smile is all she desires. This small recognition encourages her to work harder, bear burdens, learn, and take on diverse tasks." It's important to note that this was the perspective offered in the nineteenth century.

Maharashtra has a long history of women making their mark in the social sector. During the Bhakti movement, women poets challenged Brahminical patriarchy. Women from upper-caste Brahmin families received education, while in the 19th century, many began advocating for greater privacy within the home. Some became teachers, others pursued careers in medicine, and some started magazines to discuss women's emancipation.

Although learning was less difficult for Maratha girls, Tarabai Shinde's bold statements posed a greater challenge, as she questioned the superiority of men. By the 19th century, many male and female volunteers were advocating for the abolition of practices such as sari. They campaigned for widow remarriage, girls' education. These efforts were diligent, but they primarily focused on women's upliftment. In contrast, Tarabai Shinde's challenge was completely different and radical; she called for equality between men and women. Before her, no one had made such a direct appeal against the patriarchal social order and cultural traditions that underpin male chauvinism. Historian Ramachandra Guha highlights this in his book, *Makers of Modern India*.

Tarabai accused society on behalf of women, arguing that, while women may be at fault, their crimes were not more serious than those committed by men. She asserted that the focus should be on dismantling the norms of marriage based on income and behavior that are imposed on women. She stressed the need for the abolition of child marriage and caste discriminations. Her arguments remain relevant in today's world.

The backlash she faced from local publishers for her book, *A Comparison Between Women and Men*, was both outrageous and humiliating. According to some historians, her work was so widely condemned that it led her to stop writing altogether. Following the publication of her book, it was subjected to harsh criticism in local newspapers. This widespread disapproval likely silenced her, as she did not publish any more books afterward. The only person to mention her writings was Jyotirao Phule, who noted that she had been criticized by those whom she had offended with her intelligence.

Tarabai raised her voice against the stereotyping of both men and women and addressed the unfair treatment faced by different castes in India. Her work encouraged citizens to question societal standards for women.

It is important to understand why Tarabai was referred to as the "sand of time." She created an alternative model by building on existing standards. Her writings represent the first comprehensive argument following the values embodied in the poetry of Bhaktivada.

In the 19th century, women in the Indian subcontinent faced forced marriages and were denied access to education. They were subjected to sexual violence both within and outside the family and were often kept in confinement. Tarabai opposed these injustices in her public life and fought against the prevailing norms concerning how women should be treated. In a world enveloped in darkness, she shined as a beacon of courage, daring to speak out against an oppressive system. She was a pioneer of revolution at a time when many were more focused on religion than on the pressing social issues of the day.

Tarabai was one of the few women willing to voice her concerns. While many intellectuals and activists highlighted the visible oppression of women, Tarabai focused on a different yet equally important issue: improving women's futures in society. She expanded the conversation to address the ethical evolution of patriarchal society as a whole. She often stated, "Women are oppressed everywhere," a sentiment that has become a foundational aspect of feminism in India.

Simone de Beauvoir's *The Second Sex* is considered a seminal text in modern feminism. However, Tarabai Shinde's work, *A Comparison Between Women and Men*, was published in India nearly a century before *The Second Sex*. This addressed feminist themes and established Tarabai as India's first feminist literary critic. Long before de Beauvoir's work became a cornerstone of feminist discourse, Tarabai Shinde had already offered a trenchant critique of patriarchal systems and orthodoxy. Through her impactful writings and activism, she challenged male-centric societal norms. Tarabai's literary contributions and social efforts reveal hers was a unique intervention.

To understand Tarabai Shinde's immense contribution to feminist discourse in India, it is essential to consider her the context of her contemporary social environment. Tarabai often stated that remembering the history of feminism in India and striving to connect with its rich legacy would lead to a radical feminist path. She was a persistent thinker who could foresee the implications of societal traditions and adeptly used irony and silences to keep her arguments relevant.

Through her work, Tarabai created a model for women that contrasted sharply with earlier concepts. She was one of the pioneering activists who refused to remain passive in the face of problems. Instead of merely taking only a few steps forward, she sought to analyze the issues within the broader moral fabric of a patriarchal society. Tarabai strongly rejected the notion of male superiority based on gender, asserting that women had their own unique challenges to address. At that time, she believed that women's issues were not less important than those affecting men. This stance was central to her philosophy, which ultimately made Tarabai a revolutionary figure in the Indian feminist movement.

It's insufficient to merely discuss her revolutionary ideas and work; the effort she invested in them to bring about success is commendable. Women have come a long way, evolving alongside a changing environment and society. They are continually making history through their struggle. Yet, a woman's present and past remain subjects of concern and discussion, particularly as gender equality continues to enter the dialogue. Fortunately, women have forged their own paths. Many times, they have come to understand this clearly for themselves. They are actively shaping their futures, having broken down barriers.

Living in the present, they shape a beautiful future while striving to make their dreams a reality. Their efforts have often been successful, rooted in their strong will and attitude. Women have the power to create and to endure. The strength of a resilient woman is beyond words. It raises her above the level of ordinary humanity and endows her with qualities of the divine.

□□

Pandita Ramabai Saraswati

Sometimes, one struggles against the caste system, while at other times one fights the limitations placed on education. This fight represents a determination to break free from darkness. However, these struggles serve a greater purpose—not just for the benefit of others, but for the empowerment of women in society as a whole. With a strong desire for change, these women face numerous difficulties, in the hope that the next generation will not have to endure the same hardships.

What was once a challenge for them, often seeming insuperable, fuels their determination to make a better future accessible to others. They are committed to working towards societal betterment and improving the lives of generations that follow. This requires immense effort and perseverance.

To lead for others through a difficult path filled with obstacles, one must take brave steps forward. We must confront societal norms and values. Our women are bravely engaging in this battle against oppressive and unjust societal customs, fighting for their rights, their dignity, and their right to education. Time is precious, and they are determined to secure a better future for themselves and those who will come after them.

Sometimes, the environment can offer some individuals ample opportunities for personal gain. They may be born into families which face no hardships, they are not victims of caste discrimination, and receiving an education presents no problem for them. To them, life might seem relatively easy. Yet, despite these advantages, they still face challenges. They must confront society's unanswered questions. Nevertheless, they refuse to be constrained by societal norms. They create new paths for themselves.

She was one of those rare individuals.

For her, caste discriminations and illiteracy were not obstacles, yet she still challenges.

Born on April 23, 1858, in a Marathi-speaking Brahmin family, her father, Anant Shastri Dogre, was a Sanskrit scholar who made his living by reading Puranas in a temple. Thankfully, as a scholar, he wished to teach Sanskrit to his wife. He also taught Sanskrit himself, treating men and women equally in matters of education. Sadly, this led to his being ostracised by society; the other Brahmins in his village condemned him for teaching Sanskrit to a woman. The attitude of his fellow Brahmins was unbearable for him, forcing him to leave his home and village. He eventually built a house in the woods.

Living in isolation for a short time, Anant Shastri Dogre welcomed a daughter, the youngest of his three children. Her birth brought significant changes to his family. They no longer remained in their forest home, and when she was very young, they began to move from forest to forest, village to village, and city to city.

The extraordinary dedication of the Dogre family, particularly the daughter, united them in their shared beliefs. She travelled extensively across the country with her family, visiting various religious sites along the way. Anant Shastri Dogre, her father, had a profound influence on her, as he believed that education should not be imparted only to men. He actively worked to promote this idea.

Anant Shastri organized campaigns advocating for girls' education and taught his younger daughter Sanskrit at home. This education instilled a strong sense of enthusiasm in her. She excelled in her studies, mastering both her mother tongue, Marathi, and Sanskrit. Whenever her father delivered religious discourses, she accompanied her family to listen to him. This experience further enriched her knowledge, and she began to give sermons at various religious locations, earning some money for the family.

Inspired by her father's work, she joined him in promoting the idea that education for girls should not be neglected and that young girls should not be married off prematurely. By the time she turned sixteen, she had gained significant recognition as a woman dedicated to these causes.

Between 1876 and 1878, she and her brother Srinivas travelled throughout the country, aiming to make Sanskrit texts accessible to the common people. Her remarkable proficiency in Sanskrit led to an invitation to Calcutta, where she took on the challenge of advocating for social change. She encouraged women in Calcutta and across the Bengal Presidency to seek education and empowerment. Her efforts were notably successful, making her a respected teacher by the age of 20. Together with her brother, she worked tirelessly for the education and upliftment of women nationwide.

Later, she became a professor at the University of Calcutta. In 1878, Calcutta University awarded her the titles of Pandit and Saraswati in recognition of her extensive knowledge and proficiency in Sanskrit. She pursued higher education in the United States after studying in the United Kingdom. Following her studies, she delivered speeches at convocations in Japan and Australia.

She played an important role in the Bharatiya Narimukti Andolan, advocating for women's rights and empowerment.

She learned as much as she could from the teachings, morals, and ideals of the missionaries, their friends, and their superiors to apply this knowledge in her work. She recognized that the impact of caste on Hindu society was profound, feeling that the caste system was responsible for physical abuse and also hindered the democratic development of the country by instilling in people a sense of inferiority complex.

Her remarkable contributions to education had a great influence on her contemporaries. However, her association with the Christian community displeased some prominent figures in Western India. She believed that their anger stemmed from the fact that most of her students were from the upper classes, suggesting that if her students had come from underprivileged backgrounds, there would have been no issues.

She married a Bengali lawyer, Bipinbehari Medhbi, on November 13, 1880. It is important to note that she did not marry a Brahmin; her husband, Bipin Bihari Medhbi, belonged to the Bengali Kshatriya community, marking their union as an interfaith marriage. This marriage was not widely accepted in society, and the couple faced a lot resistance, but she remained undeterred.

She lived a happy life with her husband and wanted to demonstrate that marriage should not be restricted by caste. Her beliefs were a testament to Indian culture. Bipin Bihari Medhbi supported her in all her endeavours and served as an inspiration to her. Notably, she was one of the few women in India at that time who engaged in social reform with her husband's encouragement, although she did not always seek his advice while taking her decisions; she often made strong independent choices.

Her efforts met with success, and although she was born into a Brahmin family, she was educated, capable of differentiating right from wrong, and able to make her own decisions. She approached every task with determination, not just for herself but for the greater good of society. Despite facing opposition and backlash from others, her resolve remained unwavering. She did not hesitate to take a stand. She founded the Arya Mahila Samaj, a women's organization dedicated to women's education.

Influenced by Hindu social reforms and the Brahmo Samaj, she dedicated her efforts to the education of women, their rights, and the abolition of child marriage. Her actions are a testament to her commitment to social reform. She believed that meaningful change in society could only come from the transformation of individuals.

Later, she became involved in various development programs. Initially, she struggled to accept the Hindu way of life due to family influences and her understanding of Hindu ideology. However, she eventually participated in various initiatives led by missionaries. In 1882, the Government of India appointed the Hunter Education Commission to revitalize education in the country. She made several proposals aimed at improving the education system.

She suggested that teachers should receive special training for their roles and advocated for the employment of more women in the educational sector. Additionally, she emphasized the need for more women in health care, as female practitioners are essential for certain types of ailments. Her recommendations included appointing female school inspectors and teacher trainers.

Her words reached Queen Victoria. Before the Hunter Commission, she stated, "In 99% of cases, educated men in this country are opposed to women's education and progress. If they see a woman's mistake as a mustard seed in any field, it does not take long for them to exaggerate it into a mountain, and they do not hesitate to destroy her character."

Her speech was no mere speech; it exercised a significant impact. The Women's Medical Movement was initiated by Lord Dufferin. She advocated for the improvement of women's education and health by collaborating with Christian organizations in Maharashtra, including the Anglican Nuns and the Centenary Virgin Committee.

This remarkable woman, who made history through her work, is Ramabai. She was a prominent activist for women's rights, security, education, the freedom movement, and social service in India. Ramabai was the first woman in India to be awarded the title of 'Pandit' for her advanced studies in Sanskrit. After receiving this title, she became known as Pandit Ramabai. Upon joining the University of Calcutta as a lecturer, she was granted the title of 'Saraswati' and subsequently became known as Saraswati Ramabai Dogre.

In addition to her social reform efforts, she authored numerous books throughout her career. Her first book, "Morals for Women," was published in 1882. In 1883, she traveled to England to join the Community of St. Mary the Virgin (CSMV) but was not selected for training there. During her stay in Britain, she converted to Christianity, a decision that was met with criticism from others. Despite the backlash, she remained steadfast in her choice.

On her conversion, she stated, "Due to the orthodox thinking of Hinduism, I changed my religion because of the prejudices towards women." In her autobiography, she reflected, "Women have been looked down upon in various scriptures, puranas, and modern poetry. They are often regarded as inferior and are believed to be unable to attain salvation like men." She strongly believed that this is not an acceptable way to treat women.

In England, she came into close contact with her Anglican mentor, Sister Geraldine. From the beginning, she was a vegetarian and she did not engage in any illegal activities. After converting to Christianity, she changed her name to Mary. Following her conversion, church officials asked her to make various changes in her conduct, including wearing a cross and studying Latin mythology instead of Sanskrit. However, she chose to ignore their directives, continued to wear Indian clothing, and remained a vegetarian.

In 1886, at the invitation of Dr. Rachel Bodley, Dean of the Pennsylvania Woman's Medical College, she travelled from Britain to the United States to observe the graduate education of her relative, Anandabai Joshi, the first female Indian doctor. She was inspired by the lifestyle of the American women and showed new horizons to the girls of modern India. During her stay, Pandit Ramabai translated several textbooks and delivered lectures across the United States and Canada. She also dedicated her book, *High Caste Hindu Women*, in English to her close friend Dr. Joshi. The book reveals the dark realities of the lives of upper-class Hindu women, addressing issues such as child marriage, early widowhood, and the oppression of women under British rule in India. Through her speeches, she raised about 60,000 rupees with the help of her associates, which she used to establish a school for widowed Hindu girls. According to her, this was one of the worst periods in the lives of Hindu women, as the Brahmin community did not allow widow remarriage. Widows often shaved their heads to remain inconspicuous, dressed in plain clothes, and covered their heads, while being deprived of many food items. They frequently faced physical and sexual abuse, and girls suffered from child marriage at a very young age. This situation significantly impacted women, prompting the formation of the American Ramabai

Association in the United States to raise funds to assist Ramabai in achieving her goals.

She generated funds by selling her books and speaking at various events.

After returning to India in 1890, she established an institution called Sharda Sadan for widows in Pune, receiving support from the prominent Hindu reformer M. G. Ranade. She founded the organization with the aim of empowering women. At Sharda Sadan, girls were taught subjects such as history and geography. It became the first institution in India where Brahmin women were given the opportunity to study in a hostel setting. It was also the first place where they received instruction according to a formal school curriculum along with vocational education, enabling them to become economically self-sufficient. Additionally, their social status improved perceptibly. The curriculum included practical skills such as gardening, carpentry, and sewing. As the institution grew, it could accommodate up to 700 girls, many of whom went on to become teachers, nurses, and managed cattle stations and printing presses. This legacy continues to resonate today.

She was one of only ten women elected to Congress in 1889. In 1890, she founded the Mukti Mission in the village of Kedgaon, located about 40 miles east of Pune. This mission later became known as the Pandita Ramabai Mukti Mission.

At that time, Ramabai was a well-known figure. She traveled to the United States to fulfill various assignments related to her efforts in India. The primary purpose of her visit was to explore ways to help young widows in India become self-reliant. An article about her was published in *The New York Times* and the *Philadelphia Bulletin*, arousing the curiosity of Americans about her work. A Christian convert with a clear English accent, a fair complexion, and the title of "Pandit," Ramabai presented herself as an Indian woman.

Ramabai believed, "There is joy in complete freedom. That is the invisible wealth." Through her writings, she highlighted the conflict between Native Americans and the migrants from Africa who settled in America.

In her narratives, Ramabai shared numerous experiences, joys, sorrows, incidents, and challenges from her life. One of the American coordinators was surprised to see her walking barefoot in their home. She also recounted how, on a small ship, when she hosted a banquet with fellow Indians, the Europeans did not attend. In her travelogue, which detailed her stay in the United States from March 1886 to November 1888, Ramabai offered more than just geographical observations. It reflected her unique style and perspective.

At the age of 28, after losing her parents, brother, and husband, Ramabai described the beauty of America, its blue skies, mountains, and waterfalls, in eloquent language. She chose not to dwell on the cultural differences she noticed. Despite criticism regarding her views on U.S. policies, she handled the situation adeptly.

On one occasion, she stayed with an American family in Gilbert Valley, where she was accompanied by a student named George from Cornell University. The mother of the family proudly mentioned that her daughter would soon join George at Cornell. Ramabai noted, "Her mother felt proud when she told me about it. I will be very happy on the day when parents in our country want their daughters to strive for success in life. When the misconception of gender differences is eradicated from their minds, and the idea that men are superior to women disappears."

At 28, Ramabai carried the weight of her loneliness and loss. Additionally, her writings revealed a keen interest in economics. She not only closely observed American life but also contemplated how the American economic model could be applied in India. She envisioned a new direction for India by fostering public opinion in America against British colonial rule. Her thoughts were centered on how American economic development could be implemented in India, and she succeeded in this endeavor.

Expressing her frustration with the monarchy, she stated, "What else can we do? Instead of exporting copper, we sold our gold. We have shut down our handlooms and imported clothes from abroad. We have brought in expensive glass bottles and glasses filled with wine, replacing our own resources. Now, those glasses are shattered, and the glass shards are scattered at our feet. Drugs are ruining our lives and are gradually taking over our country. What a great tragedy!"

At the same time, she had much to say about American society. She praised its positive aspects while also highlighting its flaws. Her writings addressed significant issues such as drug abuse, racism, gender discrimination, and social prejudices within American society. Although she received support from various non-American individuals and organizations, she firmly rejected any unethical practices associated with them. She could not accept such actions. Additionally, she was critical of the vices, errors, and prejudices present in Indian society, demonstrating her deep love for her country.

In 1887, she met Frances Willard during a speech at an event in the United States, where Willard sought support for her ongoing work in India. Willard invited Ramabai to speak at a conference of the Woman's Christian Temperance Union (WCTU). Ramabai returned to India in June 1888 as a representative of the WCTU. Mary Greenleaf Clement Leavitt was the first president of the WCTU. In 1893, Ramabai began collaborating with the WCTU of India, receiving encouragement from many social reformers who were impressed by her dedication to and love for her homeland.

Although Ramabai did not actively promote conversion to Christianity, she did not hide her own Christian faith. When some of her students converted, however, Hindu reform organizations in Pune withdrew their support for her. In 1889, a movement for women's awakening emerged in Pune, prompting the government to impose restrictions on the activities of prominent leaders, particularly those associated with Sharda Sadan. In response, Ramabai moved her school to Kedgaon, near Pune, and named it Mukti Mission. There, she acquired about 100 acres of land and established the Mukti Mission, providing women and young girls a place to study.

At Mukti Mission, widows were also given the opportunity to learn various skills such as carpentry, printing, and more. Ramabai created avenues for many women to access an education that was previously difficult for them to attain. She arranged for lessons in subjects like botany, zoology, physical education, environmental education, painting, woodworking, sewing, weaving, farming, and gardening.

In 1896, during another major women's liberation struggle, Ramabai traveled to various villages in a bullock cart, rescuing many Dalit girls, widows, orphaned children, and helpless women, bringing them to the Mukti Mission in Maharashtra. By 1900, approximately 1,500 women had joined the Mukti Mission.

Ramabai was proficient in her mother tongue, Marathi, as well as Hebrew and Greek. She utilized her education in multiple ways. As an educated woman, she translated the Bible into Marathi, her native language. The 'Pandita Ramabai Mukti Mission' continues to empower women by providing education, vocational training, and support for many widows, orphans, and the blind.

In the 19th century, Ramabai travelled throughout India, contributing significantly to the women's liberation movement and establishing the first women's shelter in the country. At a time when learning Sanskrit was predominantly reserved for Brahmin men, Ramabai defied societal norms and pursued her studies in Sanskrit as a woman. She also married into a different caste, making her an exception within the rigid social structure of her time. She embraced Christianity without fear of intense social backlash, boldly challenging the rules of orthodox society. As a widow, she chose to remain in the public eye rather than retreat into obscurity, making her own decisions and advocating for women's empowerment and education.

However, as a woman in that era, achieving her goals was fraught with challenges. Her straightforward approach to social change drew harsh criticism. Conservative elements within society condemned her actions, accusing her of promoting conversions to Christianity. A notable newspaper even reported that she was engaging in religious conversions in league with foreigners.

Despite facing significant backlash for her reformist views and advocacy for Christianity, Ramabai remained undeterred. She maintained a strong relationship with Jyotiba Phule and his wife, Savitribai Phule. Biographers and historians have highlighted her relentless efforts to bring women into the mainstream of society. Numerous researchers and writers from both the East and the West have published articles about Ramabai, with scholars like Meera Kosambi and Uma Chakraborty contributing to the discourse. More research on Pandita Ramabai is being conducted, and her ideas and emancipation movement continue to inspire many women and girls today. Ramabai holds a unique place among the leaders of the women's liberation movement in Maharashtra.

Ramabai was dedicated to educating her only daughter, Manorama. After bringing her daughter into the world, Ramabai soon lost her husband, leaving her to navigate life alone. Manorama completed her graduation from Bombay University and then pursued higher education in the United States. Upon returning to India, she was appointed the principal of Sardar Sadan in Mumbai. With support from Pandita Ramabai, she established a school in Gulbarga (now in Karnataka) in 1912 and later became the principal of that school. During this time, Manorama was living with nuns in England, but Ramabai consistently encouraged her through her letters. In one such letter, she shared the inspiring story of Harriet Tubman, an abolitionist and anti-slavery activist, emphasizing the importance of helping oppressed women in India.

Manorama was a great support to her mother, assisting her with school and mission work. However, her dedication to these responsibilities took a toll on her health, leading to her untimely death at the age of forty. The loss of her daughter deeply impacted Ramabai, who could not continue her work after Manorama's passing. Just a few days later, on April 5, 1922, Ramabai passed away at the age of 63. Both women lived extraordinary lives dedicated to service and education.

Looking at Ramabai's life's journey and her approach to her work, it is evident that women often faced closed doors. These doors were not easily opened, and when they were, life was full of challenges. Achieving success requires a strong mind, determination, and patience. Pandita Ramabai confronted numerous difficulties, overcame many obstacles, and opened countless doors for women, making access to education, identity, free thinking, and change much more achievable for future generations.

Kadambini Ganguly

There was a time when a woman's place in society was the home. Her movements were confined within the four walls of her house, and her world revolved around her family, as she performed the usual household chores. However, some women became exceptions to this norm. Despite facing numerous obstacles, they broke through the barriers and stepped out of their homes, firmly establishing themselves in the world.

These women had a strong desire to forge their own paths. They sought opportunities that aligned with their interests and opened new avenues for themselves, paving the way for future generations. Their determination and desire to create new paths made history for those who followed.

When a woman pursues her goals, she not only carves a new path for herself but also offers future generations a new direction, contributing to the process of societal change. This process is filled with possibilities, hopes, and assurances, creating a legacy that has been passed down through generations. Women are destined for greatness, and their contributions continue to be celebrated.

During the late 19th and early 20th centuries, the province of Bengal witnessed a Renaissance. This period brought about significant changes in the religious, social, and educational fields. Amidst this cultural transformation, a girl was born in Bengal during a challenging time. Despite the difficulties faced by girls in obtaining an education, she persevered and overcame obstacles to establish her identity in society. She received higher education and distinguished herself, becoming an inspiring example for other women.

Kadambini Bose was deeply inspired by her father, Brajkishore Bose. An active member of the Brahmo Samaj, she played a significant role in the reorganization of Hindu society. She co-founded the Bhagalpur Mahila Samiti, India's first women's rights organization, and served as the principal of Bhagalpur School.

When she became the headmaster of her school, she recognized the vital role education plays in everyone's life and was determined that her daughter would not be deprived of this opportunity. Understanding the societal challenges women faced regarding education, she passionately advocated for her daughter's right to learn. In a period when Indian women were largely denied access to education, and often struggled to even dream of attending school, Kadambini's mother was a beacon of strength and encouragement.

Kadambini Bose was born on July 18, 1861, in Bhagalpur, Bengal (in present-day Bangladesh). She completed her schooling in Dhaka and Calcutta (now Kolkata). Pursuing higher education was a difficult task for women at that time. Kadambini firmly believed that as long as women were prohibited from receiving higher education, she would fight against this injustice. She received unwavering support from Dwarkanath Ganguly, a teacher at Bethune School and a prominent member of the Brahmo Samaj.

Ultimately, the University of Calcutta recognized Kadambini's determination, and she successfully passed the entrance examination in 1878, securing a place at Bethune College. In 1882, Kadambini graduated from the University of Calcutta with a degree in arts, becoming one of the first female graduates in India, alongside Chandramukhi Basu from Dehradun. Their achievements marked a historic milestone in women's education in India and the entire British Empire.

Both Kadambini Ganguly and Chandramukhi Basu graduated from Bethune College as the first female graduates in both the country and the province under British rule. They were among the first two female doctors in India and the British Empire. In 1884, Chandramukhi Basu became the first woman to earn an MA from the University of Calcutta in British India. These two women set the shining example of how modern women in post-independent India can assert their freedom and rights in society.

In the late 19th century, Kadambini Ganguly gained recognition as a professional physician and was the first female doctor to practice medicine in a foreign country. She actively raised her voice against societal evils such as the practice of sati and child marriage, inspiring other women to advocate for their education and rights.

In 1932, a 21-year-old widow protested at the University of Calcutta against the Governor of Bengal, Stanley Jackson. Bethune College served as a significant institution where many women, including Kadambini, learned to view undivided Bengal as their motherland and fought against the British Empire.

Kamala Das Gupta, Kalpana Dutta, and Pritilata Waddedar played pivotal roles in the Indian freedom struggle. They spearheaded movements in the pre-independence era aimed at promoting education, literacy, and the rights of women, alongside figures like Saraladevi Choudhury, Kadambini Ganguly, and Chandramukhi Basu.

Bethune College was India's first private girls' educational institution, established with government support. Despite initial resistance from conservative neighbours and friends, who discouraged families from sending their daughters to school, the institution grew. Initially, there were only seven students, but over time, some girls who had dropped out returned, and enrollment rose to 34.

John Elliot Drinkwater Bethune arrived in India in 1848 as a legal adviser to the Governor-General's Council. Inspired by his noble initiatives, local philanthropic Indians became involved in social work.

For instance, just 15 days after Bethune's institution was established, Raja Radhakanta Deo set up a school for girls in his palatial compound. Following this, Bethune purchased a plot of land from the Bengal government and established another girls' school at Cornwallis Square in 1849. This initiative was carried out with the support of Dakshinaranjan Mukherjee as an extension of the Calcutta Women's School.

In 1850, Bethune appointed Ishwar Chandra Vidyasagar as the secretary of the Hindu Women's School, which was a timely decision. According to Vidyasagar's biographer, Shambhu Chandra Vidyaratna, many Hindu families, influenced by Vidyasagar, began sending their daughters to study at Bethune School. Efforts were also initiated through the 'Calcutta Female School' to promote the education of girls across Asia. The transformative impact of Bethune College is evident in the lives of women like Kadambini Ganguly.

After completing her graduation, Kadambini planned to pursue further studies at Medical College. In 1875, while women were allowed to study at Madras Medical College, Calcutta Medical College did not permit women to enroll there. In response, Kadambini and Dwarakanath initiated a strong protest against this policy. Meanwhile, June 12, 1883, became a memorable day for Kadambini as she married Dwarkanath Ganguly just before being admitted to Calcutta Medical College. After her marriage, she became Kadambini Ganguly. Dwarkanath, a 39-year-old teacher at Banga Mahila Vidyalaya and a prominent member of Brahmo Samaj, was previously married and had lived alone for many years after his wife's death. He was 17 years older than Kadambini and had six children from his first marriage. Kadambini took on the role of mother to Dwarkanath's daughters and later gave birth to two more children with him.

Dwarkanath fully supported Kadambini in both her education and career. They faced resistance from the members of the upper class and many elders in Brahmo Samaj, but despite this, they led a happy married life.

After their marriage, both Kadambini and Dwarkanath focused on facilitating women's access to medical education. Kadambini strongly challenged the rule that barred women from studying at Calcutta

Medical College. Their efforts to change this policy were ultimately successful. As a result, in 1884, Kadambini became the first female student of Calcutta Medical College. Notably, she was selected to study in the department of medicine with her monthly stipend increased by Rs 20.

Following her graduation, Kadambini briefly worked at the Lady Dufferin Woman's Hospital, earning a salary of Rs 200 per month before moving to London in 1892. However, she faced a hostile environment in the male-dominated society of the time. Many of her classmates and hospital colleagues found it difficult to accept a woman's economic independence. Nonetheless, her achievements marked a significant milestone in the history of women's education in the country, as the presence of a female doctor was not easily accepted in contemporary society.

Even a professor at Calcutta Medical College did not allow Kadambini to pass in a particular subject. As a result, instead of receiving an MB degree, Kadambini graduated as a Graduate of the Medical College of Bengal (GMCB) in 1886. She faced disdain from other British women doctors because she lacked an MB degree. Despite this, Kadambini continued her private practice, but she was often regarded as a mere midwife.

This is evident from one particular incident.

Once, Kadambini, along with one of her associates, went to treat a wealthy patient at their home. They were served food on the verandah, and after the meal, they were instructed to clean the utensils they had used and the area where they had sat.

In the same year, Kadambini was appointed to Lady Dufferin Woman's Hospital. However, due to her lack of an MB degree, she could not gain the support of her colleagues there. This made her feel sad, and she thought about how she could improve her situation. After much thought, she decided that to earn the respect of her peers, she needed to enhance her educational qualifications. She promptly made the decision to pursue a diploma course in three disciplines of medical sciences at Scottish College in Edinburgh. Having already completed her BA degree from Calcutta University and her GMCB degree from

CMC College, she was able to finish her diploma in a very short time. Kadambini arrived in London on March 23, 1893, and completed her training in Dublin, Glasgow, and Edinburgh. She was the only woman among 14 students and became the first Indian woman to achieve this distinction. She also trained in pediatrics and gynecology, earning the Licentiate of the Royal College of Physicians, Edinburgh (LRCP), the Licentiate of the Royal College of Surgeons, Glasgow (LRCS), and the Licentiate of the Faculty of Physicians and Surgeons, Dublin (LFPS).

In 1886, she became the first female doctor in British India. That same year, Anandibai Joshi graduated from medical school in faraway Philadelphia. In 1885, the Dufferin Fund (later renamed the National Association for Supplying Female Medical Aid) was established for the benefit of Indian women. Kadambini applied for a position there and was appointed as a doctor at Lady Dufferin College, earning a salary of Rs 300 per month, which would be equivalent to Rs 4,50,000 today. She was the first woman to practice medicine in South Asia.

Upon her return to India, Kadambini Ganguly resumed her private medical practice and was appointed as a senior physician. She holds the distinction of being the first female doctor in South Asia who had been taught Western medicine. During her brief stay abroad, Kadambini's intelligence, prudence, and self-confidence were greatly enhanced.

It is important to acknowledge that Kadambini lived in a social environment where it was very challenging for women to break free from traditional roles. Overcoming these obstacles and firmly establishing herself in society was particularly difficult for a girl of her time. As a successful doctor, a devoted wife, and a caring mother of eight children, Kadambini successfully managed to fulfill all her roles. However, conservative men in orthodox Hindu society did not refrain from criticizing her lifestyle.

Due to her professional commitments, she often needed to visit patients at night, which draw negative comments from various segments of society. In 1891, a local conservative newspaper called *Bangabasi* described her as a misguided woman and even went so far as to portray her as a "prostitute." In response, her husband stood up against the editor and sought legal recourse.

Dwarakanath, along with other members of the Brahmo Committee, who were advocating for women's emancipation, strongly condemned the disparaging remarks published in an article in the *Indian Messenger* column by Brahmo Prakashan Sanstha. The article criticized the notion that women's self-reliance conflicted with their moral and social responsibilities. As a result, Mahesh Chandra Pal, the editor of *Bangabasi*, was sentenced to six months in prison and fined Rs 100.

During 1895-96, she treated and successfully cured the Rajmata of Nepal, which led to requests for her services from many noble families. In one notable incident, a girl complained of pain in her lower abdomen, and while other doctors diagnosed it as a tumour, Kadambini found that the girl was pregnant and safely delivered the baby.

In 1888, Florence Nightingale wrote a letter to a friend praising Kadambini. She noted, "Kadambini had excelled from the very beginning in the field of medicine and surgery." The young woman, who wished to become a doctor after her marriage, rejoined her education just 13 days after giving birth to her second child. Nightingale also recommended Kadambini for a position in the women's wing of Lady Dufferin Hospital.

American historian David Kopf published a book in 1979 titled *The Brahmo Samaj and the Shaping of the Modern Indian Mind*, in which he described Kadambini as a shining example for women in contemporary society. He noted that her relationship with her husband, Ganguly, was unique and based on mutual understanding and love, contrasting with the experiences of women within the Brahmin, Christian, and Bengali societies of the time. With her determination and perseverance, Kadambini rose above the typical status of a Brahmo Samaj woman and became a representative for the women of Bengal.

In her book *How India Wrought for Freedom*, Annie Besant mentions that Kadambini was the only woman invited to thank the President at a National Congress meeting. This illustrates how the Indian freedom struggle contributed to the empowerment and dignity of women.

While continuing her medical practice, Kadambini treated many noblewomen, including members of the royal family of Nepal. Grateful for her treatment, the Nepalese Rajmata presented Kadambini with valuable gifts, including a special breed of pony. This small horse quickly became a favorite among Kadambini's two children and her step-grandchildren. The clinic adjacent to Kadambini's reading room became a wonderland for them, they were specially intrigued by the human skeleton.

Despite being a busy woman, Kadambini was very devoted to her children and grandchildren. Against fierce societal opposition, she came to be dearly loved by many for choosing a profession that was beneficial to women and focused on safeguarding their health. Kadambini would travel by a horse-cart to visit her patients.

Kadambini Ganguly was dedicated to ensuring that no child or mother died during challenging times. She played a significant role in various spheres of the Indian freedom struggle and was the first woman member of the Indian National Congress. During the partition of Bengal, she organized several programs, including a women's conference in Calcutta in 1908. Kadambini championed for the rights of women working in the coal mines of eastern India and served as the president of the Transvaal Indian Association until her death in 1923.

Despite facing challenges regarding her decision to continue her education after marriage, Kadambini remained steadfast. She balanced her responsibilities as a mother of eight children while remaining fully committed to her personal goals. Along with Swami Dwarkanath, she fought for the rights of women working in tea gardens in Assam. In 1922, alongside poet Kamini Roy, she served on the Increase Commission appointed by the government to examine the status of women workers in the coal mines of Bihar and Odisha. Kadambini was not only an dedicated activist but also a talented artist, skilled in fine handicrafts and sewing.

There is often debate over who should be recognized as India's first woman doctor—Kadambini Ganguly or Anandibai Gopal Joshi. Anandibai obtained her MB degree from the Women's Medical College in Pennsylvania in 1886, while Kadambini earned her medical degree in India. Anandibai passed away in 1887, one year after returning to India due to complications from tuberculosis. Thus, it is clear that while Kadambini was the first woman to practice medicine in India, Anandibai

Joshi was the first woman to obtain a medical degree abroad. Another contemporary of Kadambini was Anne Janathan, who graduated from Madras Medical College, making her the first woman graduate in the science stream. Like Kadambini, she traveled to Scotland to pursue a diploma in three disciplines, but sadly, she also succumbed to tuberculosis just two years after returning to India.

Kadambini Ganguly, a remarkable woman who dedicated her life to serving her fellow countrymen and engaging in various social welfare activities, passed away on October 3, 1923. Despite suffering from high blood pressure, she never allowed her illness to hinder her work. At the age of 63, she fell ill after undergoing a complicated surgery and sadly died that evening.

Her life teaches us many valuable lessons. As a successful medical doctor, she balanced her role as an ideal wife and a responsible mother of eight children while leaving an indelible mark in numerous other fields. She was not only a freedom fighter and a doctor but also a social worker who championed women's rights. However, aside from this information about Kadambini, there is a surprising lack of recognition for such a legendary figure in history. Even photographs of her are not easily available. It is crucial to preserve the memory of this influential personality by uncovering any information that can be retrieved from the past.

Women continue to strive for societal change and are unafraid to fight for achieving success. However, they also understand that bringing about change in society is only possible when women themselves evolve. When women are given bigger roles, the progress of families and society as a whole will follow, since families and communities revolve around them. Education plays a vital role in women's development. An educated woman deserves respect, which is a victory in itself. In societies that respect women and celebrate their achievements, the trees of transformation are sure to flourish.

Bhikaji Rustom Cama

The country was in turmoil at that time, under British rule. A nationwide struggle to eliminate slavery was unfolding not just in India, but around the world. Indians living abroad were equally concerned about the situation in their homeland, showing little regard for the countries in which they resided. Many freedom fighters had also settled overseas, united in their desire to end slavery in India.

As oppression from the British government intensified, Indians both at home and abroad grew increasingly rebellious. Amidst this growing unrest, one woman emerged as a prominent figure in the fight for India's freedom. She played a crucial role, diligently holding meetings at various locations and delivering powerful speeches about independence. Her speeches were incredibly inspiring, stirring emotions and igniting a sense of urgency among her listeners.

However, her impact came at a cost. While many Indians were deeply moved by her words, she also became a target of British anger. Fearing her growing influence on the ongoing struggle for freedom, the

British authorities banished her from the country. She was forced to leave for London, intending to spend the rest of her life there.

Despite her exile, she remained undeterred and continued her mission. She began her career in London, where the opportunities were vast. Her commitment to her country had been established in her childhood. She developed an intense hatred for the British and colonialism early on. From a young age, she delivered speeches against colonialism on various platforms, despite disapproval of her teachers and concern from her parents.

Despite their worries about her behavior and views, she remained steadfast in her beliefs. Her mind was consumed with thoughts of rebellion and anger towards the British, and she refused to change.

This led to a discussion among the parents, resulting in a decision about her marriage. They organized a wedding for their daughter and found a suitable groom from a wealthy family in Mumbai. On August 3, 1885, at the age of 24, she was married to Rustom Kama, the son of K.R. Kama. Rustom was a well-known lawyer in British India.

They married young. Her husband came from a rich and noble family. His wife later became a prominent lawyer. However, her married life was not happy. It wasn't a matter of wealth, but of mentality and differing life goals. Their attitudes and ideologies clashed with each other significantly. While she had a strong desire to serve her country, her husband showed no interest in nationalism. She was vehemently opposed to British rule, while he supported it, believing it brought progress to India. He thought the British were working for the betterment of India and its people, but she believed they were exploiting Indians for their own gain.

This fundamental disagreement led to frequent quarrels between them. She was focused on improving India's economic conditions and argued that the spinning wheel (charkha) needed to be preserved. Their conflicting views on British rule created tension in their marriage. She was dedicated to social work and various service activities, while her husband remained an ardent supporter of British rule.

Despite his opposition, she got increasingly involved in the freedom struggle, which had a profound impact on her life. She was firm in her beliefs and could not reconcile them with her husband's views. As he opposed her more, she found herself drawn further into the fight for freedom and devoted most of her time to charity and social work. Her dissatisfaction with her married life grew intense.

A session of the Indian National Congress was held in Bombay under the chairmanship of Umesh Chandra Banerjee. The sessions were led by Sri Aurobindo from Bengal and Bal Gangadhar Tilak from Maharashtra. Anti-British sentiments spread throughout the world, and the movement for independence became more active. Many individuals played significant roles in the freedom struggle.

In 1896, bubonic plague broke out in Bombay. A woman like her felt compelled to act and could not remain idle during this crisis. She quickly organized a group of volunteers to serve the plague patients and joined the volunteer team at the Grand Medical College. The impact of the outbreak was devastating, and many people in the city succumbed to the disease. Unfortunately, she contracted the infection while attending to the patients. After receiving medical care, she managed to recover from plague, but her health continued to deteriorate. Despite having survived, she was physically weakened and required further treatment. Her family and friends advised her to seek better medical care in London, leading them to insist that she make the journey.

In 1902, she arrived in Britain.

There, she came into direct contact with Indian freedom fighters living in Europe. Through nationalist leader Shyamji Krishna Varma, she met Dadabhai Naoroji, the founder of the Indian National Congress and the first Indian member of the British Parliament. She became her personal secretary. It was under her leadership that the freedom movement began gaining momentum in Britain. In 1908, she met Bipin Chandra Pal and engaged with many students and European intellectuals who supported India's independence. She collected funds from various Indian revolutionaries, including Shyamji Krishna Varma, Veer Rana, Sardar Singh Rana, Mukund Desai, and Veer Savarkar, as well as from revolutionaries from other countries, to finance the cause of independence. Her efforts proved instrumental in advancing the freedom struggle.

London became a center of political activity, where she openly opposed British rule. With the help of notable social reformers Shyamji Krishna Varma and Lala Hardayal, she founded the Indian Home Rule Society. Her active participation in the country's freedom struggle greatly influenced various initiatives implemented in India.

Every one of her speeches focused on the revolution. She often stated, "The idea that a woman should stay away from revolutions and wars in our society must be opposed. It is essential for its own uniqueness. There was a time when I didn't believe in that idea. Three years ago, I couldn't stand hearing the word 'violence.' It made me feel terrible. But I no longer feel that way. There's a reason for this change. I developed this perspective due to the failures of liberal thinking. If the enemy resorts to violence, then what options do we have left?" This demonstrates her deep commitment to equality between men and women. She also reflected on how women should be treated, which fuelled her activism. "Women have an important role to play in nation-building."

After meeting various personalities in the United Kingdom, she realized that the power of one's opinion can bring about significant changes in society. She sought to make the people of India aware of this confidence, believing it could help ensure justice for the Indian protesters. In the 20th century, she campaigned for women's voting rights in the United Kingdom under the banner of "Protecting Women's Rights." When this news reached India, the British banned her from returning.

She also exchanged letters with Lenin and was fluent in many languages. She published articles on the Indian freedom struggle in magazines such as *Madan's Talwar* and *Vande Mataram*. She translated Veer Savarkar's book into French. Shyamji Krishna Verma, a prominent nationalist leader among Indians in London, delivered impassioned speeches about the Indian freedom struggle at Hyde Park. In 1904, she came into contact with Shyamji Krishna Verma and later returned to India. However, in 1905, when she expressed her desire to return, the British imposed a significant condition: she could return only if she agreed to stay away from activities related to the Indian freedom struggle.

The British ultimately rejected her proposal. She made the decision to remain in a foreign country for the rest of her life, dedicating herself to India's freedom struggle while refusing to serve the British. In February 1905, Dadabhai Nairoji and Singh Revabhai Rana, among others, raised funds for the Indian Home Rule Society. That same year, S.R. Rana and Munchershah, alongside political activists like Burjorji Godrej, established the Paris Indian Society as an offshoot of the Home Rule Movement. This organization later became one of the leading institutions of the Indian freedom struggle outside India. She and other prominent members of the freedom movement created *Vande Mataram* and *Madan's Talwar* in the Netherlands and Switzerland, publishing articles on the Indian freedom struggle in various weekly magazines. These publications were secretly brought to India by the French colony of Pondicherry. After the British banned her writings in India, she supported the Indian freedom fighters by raising funds for their struggle.

Her anger grew day by day, just as the anger of the British was escalating. Ultimately, the British government decided to eliminate her, and this news reached her.

To save her life, she crossed the English Channel to France before the British government could act against her. Her efforts didn't stop there; her house in Paris became a refuge for Indian freedom fighters. It evolved into one of the most important offices for these activists outside India. Political discussions took place, and she even had weapons stored in her home, carefully managing their delivery. Sometimes they were disguised as toys, other times as gifts. Despite the British government's vigilance, she skillfully delivered weapons to Indian revolutionaries.

In August 1907, the largest conference of socialists was held in Germany, attracting a significant number of participants. On the final day of the conference, she joined it as one of the leading agitators and took part in the most prominent meeting. While addressing the gathering, she informed everyone about the arbitrary rule in the colonies. "This flag is the symbol of India's independence," she declared, raising the cloth she held to represent equality, freedom, and human rights for every individual. "Its foundation has been laid, and the blood of young men has been spilled. I call upon everyone present to rise and salute this flag, which symbolizes our independence."

The hall erupted with cheers and applause as she unveiled the flag of Indian independence. Designed by her and Shyamji Krishna Verma, this flag is a predecessor to the current national flag. It featured eight blossoming lotuses in green at the top, representing the eight provinces of pre-independence India, and 'Vande Mataram' written in orange Hindi letters at the center. The bottom of the flag was red, adorned with a crescent on the right and another on the left. The rising sun signified the unity of Hindus and Muslims.

Addressing the gathering, she stated, "I am here. I appeal to all freedom-loving people to join hands for the freedom of the entire world."

This was her unique challenge—a powerful speech against British repression. At the time of the conference, the freedom movement in India was not particularly vigorous. However, her words resonated with everyone and inspired the youth of India to fight for independence. Moved by her speech, the delegates stood up and paid their respects to the Indian flag. Her speech was published in its entirety by a German socialist newspaper, marking a memorable event. She was the first woman to raise the Indian flag in a foreign land, and most importantly, she had sewn the flag with her own hands. Today, the flag is preserved for public viewing at the Maratha and Kesari libraries in Pune.

At that time, the British government and society viewed Bhikaji Rustom Cama as a formidable revolutionary leader. They were afraid of her, and as a result, her every action and program were closely monitored. She was subjected to constant surveillance, which led her to stop visiting India and reside in Paris for 30 years. Finally, in 1936, after falling seriously ill, the British government permitted her to return to her homeland.

Bhikaji Cama (24 September 1861 - 13 August 1936) was a keen figure in the Indian freedom struggle. Born in Bombay (now Mumbai) to a prominent Parsi Zoroastrian family, her parents, Sorabji Framji Patel and Jaijibai Sorabji Patel, were well-known in the community. Her father was a lawyer and businessman, actively involved in Parsi affairs. Like many Parsi girls of her time, Bhikaji received her education at the Alexandra Garges English Institution, founded by Judge Manakji

Karsetji and women's education reformers. From an early age, she was responsible and disciplined, proficient in multiple languages.

Political discussions were constantly held in her household, which greatly influenced her. As a result, Bhikaji Cama took part in the freedom struggle from an early age, discussing various national issues. The failure of her marriage and the devastating bubonic plague pushed her further into political activism. She began her journey as a social activist in London and eventually became known as the mother of the Indian freedom struggle. Sadly, she spent much of her life away from her homeland. As a social worker, she dedicated significant time to public service, particularly in assisting the victims of the plague epidemic that struck Bombay.

Bhikaji Cama tirelessly worked to highlight issues such as poverty, illiteracy, and the need for inquiry among Indians. She sought to bring global attention to the oppression faced by Indians under colonial rule and the harsh punishment meted out to freedom-fighters by the British.

Cama was also a strong advocate for women's rights and gender equality. When two Parsi women confronted the issue of women's voting rights, she encouraged them to prioritize Indian independence, asserting that, once India was free, women would not only gain the right to vote but would also secure all their rights. Additionally, she fought for equal rights for women in British-ruled India. The British government eventually prohibited her from staying in France. Although Lenin, the socialist leader of the Soviet Union, invited her to stay in Russia, Bhikaji Cama declined and chose to travel across America as an agitator. She was an ardent supporter of women's education, firmly believing that the success of the Indian national movement depended on women's participation. However, her views were often contested by some nationalist leaders who believed that an educated woman could not fulfill her primary responsibilities as a wife and mother.

Cama expressed her view, stating, "We need educators and trainers. More than focusing on the weaknesses of women, we should emphasize their strengths and potential, as these are key factors in our progress. Education is our birthright. Women are the mothers of this country; a child receives their first education from their mother. The hand that manages numerous difficult household tasks also has the power to rule the world without any hindrance. According to Sarojini Naidu, 'Women all over the world are bound together by the sacred virtues of motherhood.' Similarly, Surendranath Banerjee, in one of his speeches, urged women to set aside any internalized discrimination by embracing the sanctity of motherhood and called for unity.

In 1910, at a national convention in Cairo, Egypt, Bhikaji Cama said, "Who are the other half of the Egyptian people? I see only half the men of this country here. Where are the mothers? Where are the sisters? Never forget that the hand that can hold a child in its arms can also shape a man."

She consistently spoke the truth, even when it was unpopular. Her inherent motherly love always resonated within her. Cama was profoundly disturbed by the arrest of Lala Lajpat Rai by the British, and her emotional outburst left everyone shocked.

"All men and women of India must rise against this arbitrary rule. Take a pledge that you will no longer tolerate such captivity and will not put your lives in danger. Brave Rajputs, Sikhs, Pathans, Marathas, Bengalis, Parsis, Jains, Hindus—why do you forget your rich culture and heritage? What compels you to accept such slavery? Break free from these chains and create your own system of governance based on equality. Brothers and sisters, continue to fight for human rights and let the foreigners know that we too have much to teach them. As William Wordsworth, the grandson of the famed poet, said, the English are 'white-robed evils.' I believe that if I can escape, I can free Lala Lajpat Rai. Unity is our strength. Let us come together. If we all follow in the footsteps of Lala Lajpat Rai, we will form a single voice. Then the British government will have to construct immense jails and forts to contain us. Our population is around fifty million; if we strive to emulate Lala Lajpat Rai, it won't be long before we achieve unity. Let's advance towards our goal together. His suffering is intertwined with our lives." Cama believed that those working for freedom worldwide should be united in purpose.

In 1909, Scotland Yard issued a warrant for the arrest of several leading figures in Great Britain, including Madanlal Dhingra, for the murder of William Hutt Curzon Wyllie, the British representative to

India. The British government requested the French government to extradite Bhikaji Cama, but the French government refused, leading the British to seal Cama's house. Despite this opposition, the British government could not halt Bhikaji Cama's nationalist efforts. During World War I, the friendship between Britain and France resulted in the French government placing her under police surveillance, but this did not deter her. She returned to her home in Paris, where she lived until 1935. That year, she suffered a heart attack that left her with severe paralysis. Despite her condition, she appealed to the British government through Sir Cowasji Jehangir for permission to return to her homeland. In a letter dated June 24, 1935, she expressed her desire to return to India. Given her age, the British government had no valid reason for denying her request. After spending most of her life away from her motherland, she finally returned to India in November 1935, accompanied by Jehangir. Sadly, she passed away nine months later, at the age of 74, in the Paris General Hospital on August 13, 1936. Our country lost a remarkable leader before the dawn of independence.

Bhikaji Cama spent the last nine months of her life in her birthplace, where she had fought so passionately for freedom. No matter how much we discuss this great woman in our history, our discussion will always be inadequate. Bhikaji Cama was a learned woman with a strong personality and a broad perspective on many subjects. As a woman, she traveled extensively to achieve her goals and faced significant opposition. She played a crucial role in advancing the national struggle, standing shoulder to shoulder with her male counterparts in the fight for India's freedom. Most notably, she dedicated her entire life to the Indian national movement, significantly contributing to its international recognition. With her strong leadership, organizational skills, and unique presentation style, she helped transform the Indian freedom struggle into a mass movement. She emphasized the vital role that women play in nation-building.

Cama asserted that true freedom cannot exist without equality between men and women. She played a pivotal role in the early phases of the Indian freedom struggle and consistently worked to strengthen the position of women in society. A dedicated patriot, she strived to place the Indian freedom movement on the international stage.

Despite her immense sacrifices and dedication, Bhikaji Cama's story remains largely unknown to the public. While we often read about the contributions of figures like Raja Rammohun Roy in social reforms and Bal Gangadhar Tilak's leadership in the national struggle, Cama's efforts have received far less attention. It is crucial that we remember and honour the contributions of all those who fought for national freedom, especially women like Bhikaji Cama. We must never forget the countless women who played a crucial role in the fight for our country's freedom.

Eleven years following her death, our country gained independence. During the freedom struggle, women supported men as mothers, sisters, and wives, and among them was a remarkable figure. She chose a path of struggle, leaving behind the wealth of her father's household as well as the comfort and prosperity of her husband's home. She donated all her belongings to an organization dedicated to orphaned girls in need, which became the Framji Nusserwanali Patel Educational Institution in Mazgaon, South Bombay.

Regardless of the difficulties and obstacles she faced, she remained steadfast in her commitment and worked tirelessly to realise her goals. Ultimately, she sacrificed herself for the country.

She demonstrated that when a woman is determined, she can overcome any challenge, no matter how great. Nothing can deter her. This remarkable woman is known as the "Mother of the Revolution." She is also referred to as Madame Cama, and her name has been honoured by naming several cities and towns across India after her. A prominent area in South Delhi, where multinational companies such as Jindal, SAIL, and GAIL have their offices, is named after Bhikaji Cama.

In 1962, on the occasion of the 13th Republic Day, the Indian Postal Department issued a postage stamp in her memory. In 1997, the Indian Coast Guard named one of its defense ships after her. Indulal Yagnik secretly brought the national flag back to India. Looking at the life journey of Bhikaji Cama, it becomes clear that nothing is impossible for a woman, regardless of the circumstances or the environment.

Ramabai Ranade

With the mindset of "I can, it can be done by me," she not only worked tirelessly but also overcame numerous obstacles in her path. Her determination led her to success. Her primary aim in life was to bring about change in society, and she accomplished this. However, it wasn't just any change; it was the most significant change. She emerged as one of the most influential figures of the 19th century, becoming the first female volunteer who successfully fought for women's rights.

"Anyone, regardless of their caste, can bring about a significant change in society," she stated. She felt strongly that education was essential for all women and consistently advocated for the education of women from all social classes. While most organizations of that time typically admitted women from only middle-class families, she opened her own organization to accept women from poor and laboring backgrounds. As a result, a large number of women joined her organization, increasing female participation significantly.

She understood the societal position of women and the challenges they faced. She aimed to raise awareness among them in a way that allowed them to advance not in opposition to society, but alongside it. She effectively communicated the traditional roles of women and the concept of motherhood, framing them as important facets of societal reform. All her efforts eventually paid off.

During that time, the primary role assigned to women was to manage the household and care for members of their families, including their husbands and children. It was widely believed that women who ventured outside home to work would create difficulties for their families. Many women who aspired to work felt that their household responsibilities would hinder their ambitions. However, Ramabai sought to convey that being at home and caring for the family should not be viewed as a limitation.

As one of India's first female volunteers, she overcame the challenges facing her. Although she was completely illiterate, she married a prominent educationist 21 years her senior at the age of 11. Nevertheless, she went on to lead an exemplary life by educating herself and advocating for women's upliftment. As a strong-willed woman, she was both forward-thinking and rational in many ways. Through her reforms, she brought about significant changes in Marathi society. She inspired many women to enter the public sphere and voice their concerns. She initiated a new movement through education to transform the attitudes and roles of both men and women in society, skillfully balancing the development of the Marathi family and society, which ultimately altered their social and cultural landscape.

She played a crucial role in the empowerment of women in Maharashtra. She often said that love and service to others are qualities of motherhood. Every woman should embody these qualities for the betterment of society. She actively participated in various social welfare activities and political movements. She regularly visited patients, students, and jail inmates, engaging with them and providing essential items. She fought for workers' rights in Kenya and Fiji and advocated for making primary education compulsory for girls. Additionally, she was part of the delegation led by Sarojini Naidu to support the Indian women's suffrage movement in 1917, which helped organize the women's suffrage movement in Maharashtra in 1921-22.

Moreover, she held strong views on motherhood and consistently championed women's rights. She understood the status of women in society well and aimed to drive gradual yet effective change. She successfully propagated her feminist ideas while respecting traditional notions of womanhood and motherhood. She rejected the Marxist perspective that motherhood and the care of husbands and children hinder women's development, asserting instead that motherhood is a service. In doing so, she skillfully balanced modern and traditional ideologies within Marathi society.

Born on January 25, 1862 into a Kurlekar family in a small village in the Sangli district of Maharashtra, her childhood name was Yamuna Kurlekar. At that time, her father did not send her to school because facilities for providing education to girls were not available then. She was married to Mahadev Govind Ranade in 1873 when she was only 11 years old and became known as Ramabai Ranade.

Although Mahadev Govind Ranade was a judge by profession, he was also a prominent educationist and was often referred to as the Prince of Bombay University. He graduated with first-class honors from Elphinstone College in Bombay in 1862 and studied law for four years, earning his law degree in 1866. He settled in Pune as a sub-judge in 1871, where he became known as Justice Ranade. Govind Ranade was an accomplished oriental translator and social reformer who engaged deeply in social service activities. He was an influential member of the Prarthana Samaj, a movement founded by Asaram Pandurang in Bombay on March 31, 1867, aimed at promoting social and religious reform.

Ranade was actively involved in fighting against social evils, superstitions, and practices like child marriage, sati, the caste system, untouchability, and dishonesty. He believed that society is a living institution that requires change in all aspects. By the age of 30, he had gained considerable popularity in Maharashtra due to his strong personality, educational attainments, knowledge, and relentless efforts to improve society, inspiring many people in the process.

Mahadev Govind Ranade was a remarkable individual, known for his learning and progressive ideas. In contrast, his wife, Ramabai, was completely illiterate. However, she was deeply impressed and inspired by her husband's personality and work. Ramabai loved everything her husband did and wanted to contribute to his endeavours. Recognizing the barriers posed by her lack of education, she was determined to change her situation.

With a strong desire to learn, Ramabai took the initiative to educate herself. She aspired to gain knowledge not only to assist her husband but also to understand his actions and to support him fully. During that time, women were generally not allowed to attend school, but Govind Ranade encouraged her to pursue her education.

Fortunately, Ranade actively supported her studies. He began teaching Ramabai Marathi, covering subjects such as history, geography, and mathematics. She later ventured into learning English, mastering both reading and writing. Education became a mission for Ramabai, and she dedicated herself to her studies, working tirelessly day and night. Her husband inspired her to read the daily newspaper and engage in discussions on contemporary issues, suggestions that Ramabai wholeheartedly embraced. She became an ardent admirer of Govind Ranade, absorbing his teachings and cherishing to his guidance. Over time, she became her husband's trusted friend and secretary.

In 1882, after losing her husband, the renowned social reformer Pandita Ramabai arrived in Pune and received support from the Ranade couple. When the topic of Pandita Ramabai's education arose, Govind Ranade arranged for a Christian missionary woman to come to their home, enabling both Ramabai Ranade and Pandita Ramabai to learn English together.

When Ramabai Ranade spoke at a public meeting as the chief guest during an event at Nashik High School, she delivered a speech that her husband, Justice Ranade, had written for her. Together with her husband, she became involved in the Prayer Society of Bombay and also established the Arya Mahila Samaj in the city. By 1878, she had fully committed herself to social service. Starting in 1880, Ramabai actively participated in the Prayer Society, where she encountered liberal ideas and social systems. Through her involvement in various programs organized by the Prarthana Samaj, she learned the significance of education and the skills necessary for public speaking. In this way, she adopted and propagated the liberal ideas of her husband, influencing the social structure of her time.

These ideas were shared among women through various social programs. Women often gathered for rituals such as Haldikunku, the practice of applying turmeric and vermilion, as well as kirtan. While these gatherings typically revolved around prevailing customs and traditions, Ramabai transformed them into social events. From 1893 to 1901, she gained popularity for her dedication to social service. The Hindu Ladies Social and Literary Club was established to educate women in languages, general knowledge, sewing, and handicrafts. Swami Govind Ranade played a significant role in supporting and inspiring her social endeavours, which further fuelled Ramabai's interest in social work.

However, Ramabai's happiness was short-lived. Her husband, Govind Ranade, who had been a mentor, well-wisher, and friend to her, passed away in 1901 when she was only 38 years old. Devastated by his death, she left Mumbai and returned to her home in Pune's Phule Market, where she lived alone for a year. During this period, she isolated herself, not leaving the house or attending meetings. However, she eventually re-emerged as a social reformer and found a way to overcome her loneliness and to continue her work.

In 1904, Ramabai presided over the first Indian Women's Conference held in Bombay at the request of Ramkrishna Gopal Bhandarkar and Shri Vazhekar. During this time, she developed her speaking style, becoming a skilled orator. Starting as a speaker at Nashik High School, she went on to attend numerous meetings, where she delivered speeches in both Marathi and English. Over time, Ramabai gained popularity among women due to her leadership skills and eloquence. She founded the Hindu Literary and Social Ladies Club, where women were also taught the art of public speaking. Her efforts were aimed at improving society, and she actively participated in the Arya Mahila Samaj in Bombay.

In 1908, Persian social reformers B.M. Malvari and Dayaram Gidumal approached Ramabai with a proposal to establish a home for women that would impart training in nursing. The house, suggested by Ramachai, became known as the House of Service. Ramabai tirelessly worked to combat child marriage, and as a result of her efforts, the service center was established in Bombay, providing shelter to many women in distress, particularly widows. Ramabai's involvement in this initiative is a remarkable example of her dedication to social reform.

An interesting incident unfolded during the annual festival of Sevasadan. which included a prize distribution ceremony. One of the awardees was a woman who had arrived dressed in a traditional widow's saris, with her veil neatly secured at her waist. As soon as she stepped onto the stage, the entire hall erupted in whistles. Ramabai was deeply hurt by this disrespectful behavior towards women, and she chose not to remain silent. When it was her turn to give a brief Thank You speech, she could hardly control her emotions.

"You are college students, but how can you call yourselves educated?" she began. "Those who do not sympathize with their sisters, who endure cruel fates and social pressures, deserve to be ridiculed. How can we call this education? Some of you may have a widow in your own home—be it a mother, a sister, or a relative. If you had that in mind, you would not have behaved so poorly towards this woman today."

Ramabai's sharp and poignant words had a profound impact, instantly silencing the hall. Everyone listened, captivated and awestruck by her commanding presence.

Ramabai began her service at her ancestral home in Pune, which eventually developed into an institution offering various facilities, including hostels, training schools, business centers, and sales outlets. As Sevasadan gained popularity, so did Ramabai's reputation. Her contributions to the welfare of middle-class women were immense. Initially starting with a school for women, Sevasadan expanded its services under Ramabai's leadership. She provided vocational education for women and girls, enabling them to become self-reliant. Particularly, she focused on offering training to poor women and widows.

At a time when many institutions admitted only middle-class women, Ramabai opened her doors to women from poorer backgrounds, providing them with the opportunity for education and training. As a result of her efforts, a sizable number of women joined the school; by 1920, the institution that had just six members in 1909 had over 1,000 members. Furthermore, there were eight additional branches across Maharashtra where women received education.

Pune Sevasadan was registered as a society in 1915. Over time, this society expanded its scope and initiated various new projects. It established a training college and three hostels for women, one of which was designated for medical students and another for trained nurses.

After the death of her husband, Ramabai devoted herself entirely to the welfare of women in India. Her commitment to the social awakening of women, addressing grievances, and establishing services for oppressed women distinguished her from others. Although she had been publicly active since 1878, she fully committed herself to the cause of women's emancipation after her husband's death in 1901.

In 1913, Ramabai traveled to Kathiyavad in Gujarat to assist victims of untimely deaths of relatives. She regularly visited women inmates in the Central Jail and shared sweets with students at local schools. She also made it a point to visit patients in hospitals, where she distributed fruits, flowers, and books.

Ramabai presided over the first Women's Conference held in Bombay in 1921-22, where she spoke to the Governor on behalf of Indian women. She advocated for Indian workers in Fiji and Kenya and fought for women's rights. Although many admired her work, she often described herself as living in the shadow of her husband.

She utilized her experience from working in Prarthana Samaj to improve women's conditions in the service sector. Ramabai consistently emphasized the importance of women's education in various meetings organized for women. Additionally, she provided them training in public speaking. These meetings served as platforms for social interaction among women. Ramabai also organized writing competitions and seminars within her institution, enabling her to share her progressive ideas with a broader audience and educate them.

Ramabai has made significant contributions to literature, particularly through her autobiography, *Amchya Ayushyatil Kuchh Aathvani*, which was published in Marathi in 1910. She was the first woman to write an autobiography in Marathi. In her autobiography, she details how her husband, Govind Ranade, inspired her in various ways and encouraged her to educate herself. She provides a comprehensive account of her experiences, work, and thoughts on her married life as a social reformer. This work has also been translated into English by Catherine Van Akin Gate, titled *Himself: The Autobiography of the Hindu Lady*. Additionally, she had a passion for reading English literature.

In her book, *The Emergence of Feminism in India, 1850-1920*, Padma Anagol states, "Ramabai spread liberal ideas by organizing educational activities such as lectures and essay competitions."

Ramabai played a crucial role in supporting various women's empowerment groups by designing and managing their services. Her liberal ideas significantly contributed to women's empowerment, as she recognized the importance of civil society, community, and entrepreneurship in the development of women. For this reason, Ramabai dedicated her life to financially empowering women and inspiring them to lead lives filled with personal dignity.

Ramabai was an important liberal figure in the history of India, whose efforts greatly improved the status of Indian women. What makes her even more inspiring is that during her time, there were few role models for women to emulate. She was among the few women in India who fought for the education and political rights of girls. Often referring to herself as the shadow of her husband, she drew inspiration from his ideology, which motivated her to engage in social service. It is clear that Ramabai's work fundamentally challenged the patriarchal and oppressive society that existed at the time.

Growing up in an environment where educating women was ridiculed as a waste of resources, Ramabai faced numerous adversities. Nevertheless, she worked tirelessly to not only prove her worth as a woman but also to awaken the potential in many others. She serves as a source of inspiration for women everywhere.

Ramabai was not someone who sought to dominate others in society; rather, she was one of the leading social reformers of pre-independence India. At a time when it was extremely difficult for women to step into the public sphere, and they played little role in social work or decision-making, her life was nothing short of revolutionary.

One of Ramabai's most admirable qualities was her commitment to living by her own advice. Her most important contribution was the establishment of Sevasadan. Initially, this initiative was proposed by Dayaram Gidumal and B.M. Malvari, with the goal of training women as nurses. Ramabai joined the Bombay branch of Seva Sadan and later founded the Pune Seva Sadan. By the time of her death, more than a thousand women were being trained by this organization, marking an important achievement in that era. At the time, women were not given much importance, and many traditionalists opposed Ramabai's efforts. Despite such challenges, the organization expanded under her leadership.

Sevasadan included a women's training college, three women's hostels, and various other departments that not only provided education but also offered vocational training. Women who were widowed or marginalized found refuge in the service quarters in Bombay. Importantly, there was no discrimination based on caste, creed, or financial status. Women from all backgrounds were treated equally, thanks to Ramabai's dedicated efforts. Under her guidance, Sevasadan successfully progressed, overcoming obstacles and prevailing against traditional norms.

Later, eight branches of the service were established in Maharashtra. This service provided women with training in crafting pachchis, pickles, and other household products, alongside nursing and health-related training to help them achieve financial independence. Ramabai played a significant role in changing prevalent perceptions about working women. She successfully blended various forms of femininity with simplicity and a liberal ideology. She encouraged women to embrace their roles as wives and mothers while also pursuing economic independence, training, and modern ideals.

Over time, Ramabai's efforts became focused on two primary areas: girls' education and women's suffrage. Her work in these domains significantly contributed to liberalizing Indian society and challenging patriarchal structures. Ramabai emphasized the importance of girls' education and established the Poona Native Girls' High School in Pune, which is now known as Huzurpaga. This institution is recognized as the oldest girls' school in the country.

In 1921-1922, Ramabai was a key figure in organizing the women's suffrage movement in Bombay, advocating for political and social empowerment. This was a defining moment in the Indian freedom movement. At the end of 1917, the Women's Indian Association was founded in Madras, led by Sarojini Naidu, to demand the inclusion of women's suffrage in the new suffrage bill. The Colonial government remained silent on this issue. Ramabai, along with other women leaders, sent a telegram of support to Foreign Minister Edwin Montagu, marking her as one of the earliest advocates for equal political rights for women in India.

Under Ramabai's leadership, a cooperative society for women was established, where women received training in producing household items like pickles, toys, and baskets. Although they established nursing and medical associations, training was extended beyond nurses to include doctors, health visitors, and midwives in various capacities. Additionally, health care programs, including first aid, hygiene, private nursing, sanitation, and public health, were organized to further empower women in the community.

Ramabai, along with other activists, worked to eradicate the stereotype of women in the nursing profession. Women were often discouraged from pursuing nursing as a career because it involved physical contact with male patients. Ramabai believed that a woman could serve men as a brother, father, or son. Her efforts were successful, leading many disadvantaged women to undergo nursing training.

Additionally, a health awareness campaign was launched in the House, where people received information, clothing, and medicines.

Ramabai also dedicated remarkable efforts to ending child marriage. Throughout her life, she continued to work for the church, focusing primarily on women's empowerment. It can be said that Ramabai's most significant legacy is her commitment to empowering women, which has strongly inspired future generations to take action and move forward.

This remarkable woman passed away in 1924. Even in her final days, she travelled to Alandi to serve women pilgrims visiting the Sant Gyaneshwar temple, alongside the volunteers active during the

Ashadha and Kartik fairs. Through her efforts, the foundation for a new approach to social service for women was laid.

Two of her most significant contributions were the organization of the movement for compulsory primary education for girls and the establishment of the women's suffrage movement in the Bombay Presidency. Her unique stance in the last moments of her life was a glowing tribute Mahatma Gandhi paid to her. After her passing, Gandhiji said in his condolence message, "Ramabai Ranade's death is a great national loss. She embodied what a Hindu widow could be. She was her husband's best friend and confidante."

Ramabai played a key role in advancing the modern women's movement in India and beyond. Seva Sadan is India's largest women's organization, with thousands of women still associated with it today. Ramabai Ranade was a pioneer of this movement. The 'Seva Sadan' she founded became a highly successful Indian women's organization. In Mumbai, the shelter home for the service volunteers continues to operate on Pandita Ramabai Road, and a girls' school on Gamdevi Road is also named in her honour.

On her birth centenary, August 14, 1962, Australia Post issued a postage stamp featuring Ramabai in recognition of her great contributions to Indian society. In March 2012, a television serial titled *Unch Maja Joka*, depicting Ramabai's life and activities, was aired on Zee Marathi.

The film was a major success in Maharashtra, and her autobiography is now regarded as a classic in Marathi literature. Even today, Ramabai Ranade continues to inspire many.

Regardless of the time or social circumstances, when a woman is determined and confident of her goals, she will persevere. Despite the challenges and struggles she may face, she continues on her journey, serving as a beacon of change. Her efforts provide new directions for women, families, and society as a whole, making her an inspiring and exemplary figure for all.

□□

Rukhmabai

In her address to the nation on the occasion of the 74th Independence Day, Prime Minister Narendra Modi made an important statement regarding the age of marriage for girls. The Hon'ble Prime Minister said, "We have constituted a committee to reconsider the age of marriage for girls. The government will make a decision after the committee submits its report."

The minimum age for marriage has been a contentious issue, facing opposition from various social and religious communities. After overcoming many obstacles, we have finally reached this stage, where the minimum age for marriage is established as 21 for boys and 18 for girls. While this minimum age differs from the age of majority, it highlights gender disparity. According to the Indian Majority Act of 1875, an individual is considered a minor until they reach the age of 18, but this differs in the context of marriage.

On June 2, 2020, an investigation team was formed under the Ministry of Women and Child Development. The main task of this research team is to investigate the age of motherhood, the maternal mortality rate, and women's nutritional growth. The team will explore the relationship between the age of marriage and gestational age, as well as the health, healthcare, and nutrition of both mother and child from conception to childbirth and beyond. They will also examine child mortality rates, maternal mortality rates, total mortality rates, and the sex ratio at birth, along with the potential to raise the minimum age of marriage for girls from 18 to 21 years, as recently proposed.

Different religious communities have their own rules regarding marriage; however, the existing laws have been effective in preventing child marriage and protecting the rights of adolescent girls. According to Section 5 of the Hindu Marriage Act of 1955, the minimum age of marriage is 21 years for boys and 18 years for girls. Even if minors marry of their own free will, such marriages cannot be legally recognized.

The Marriage Act of 1954 and the Child Marriage Restraint Act of 2006 establish the minimum legal age for marriage as 21 for boys and 18 for girls. Furthermore, if a minor girl engages in sexual intercourse with the consent of a minor boy, it is still considered rape, as she is not mature enough to provide informed consent at a young age.

In 1860, the Indian Penal Code set a specific age of consent for girls, initially limiting it to the age of 10 years. Sexual intercourse with girls below that age was made a criminal offense. In 1927, it was defined as rape, and marriage with girls under 12 years of age was banned. At that time, many Indian leaders believed that these laws reflected British interference in India's cultural and social life. Consequently, leaders of the Indian National Movement opposed such practices. The tradition of establishing a minimum age for marriage in India began in the 1880s. Under the Child Marriage Restraint Act of 1929, the legal age for marriage was set at 16 for girls and 18 for boys. This law, commonly known as the Sharda Rule, was introduced by Harvilas Sharda, a prominent member of the Arya Samaj and a former judge.

To address gender discrimination, there have been numerous arguments supporting the increase of the legal marriage age for girls. Early pregnancies are contributing to rising infant mortality rates, and the health of young mothers deteriorates significantly. Although sexual relations with a minor are deemed criminal under the law, child marriage remains prevalent in our country. In 2014, the case of National Legal Services Authority of India vs. Union of India was brought before the Supreme Court, addressing the status of transgender individuals and affirming that every human being should have equal rights under the law.

In 2019, in the case of Joseph Shine vs. Union of India, Supreme Court declared it a crime to treat women differently based on gender discrimination. The wedding in question was scheduled for July 2, 2020. According to the United Nations Population Fund (UNFPA), despite child marriage being banned in almost every country worldwide, approximately 33,000 child marriages still occur daily in various corners of the globe. It is estimated that around 650 million girls continue to live in child marriages, and by 2030, an additional 150 million girls are projected to be married off. As of 2018, India accounted for nearly 50% of all child marriages in South Asia, and about 18.46% of these marriages occurred in families living below the poverty line. According to UNICEF, about 1.5 million girls under the age of 18 are married in India every year, making the country rank third in the world in terms of child marriage. Recently, around 16% of girls aged 15-19 years have been married.

Whenever there is a discussion about the age of marriage for daughters or the issue of child marriage, one remarkable woman from our country often comes to mind. This woman's historic contribution to the fight against child marriage is significant. It was not easy for her to take such a bold step; she faced numerous obstacles along the way. Given the social norms of that time, considering such a change was unfathomable, but she had the courage to stand firm. She encountered social ostracism but never lost her composure or determination. When a woman aims to bring about social change, she becomes empowered. Once her mind is made up, fear and apprehension fade away. We must recognize that no problem, evil, or harmful tradition can be eradicated from society without the intervention of women.

This brings us to one of the extraordinary Indian women in question, a doctor who was one of the most prominent female physicians in Indian society in her time. She took legal action between 1884 and 1888 to address the challenges posed by her own child marriage in British-ruled India. The tension her case generated between traditional customs and legal reforms, as well as between orthodox thinking and social change, was felt both in India and England. This led to the enactment of the Age of Consent Act in 1891, which emphasized the importance of a girl's consent. This remarkable achievement, which seemed impossible in the social context of that era, was made possible through the relentless struggle of this brave woman.

Rukhmabai was born on November 22, 1864, into a poor family. Her father, Janardan Pandurang, and her mother, Jayantibai, faced many hardships. Tragically, her mother passed away when Rukhmabai was just 17, and her father had died when she was only 2 years old. Six years after her husband's death, Jayantibai remarried a man named Sakharam Arjun, a well-known doctor in Bombay at the time. This was a widow's remarriage, which was accepted in the Varela community. Sakharam Arjun was not just a skilled doctor; he was also a social worker who passionately advocated for social reforms and aimed to eradicate societal evils. After her mother remarried, Rukhmabai remained under the care of her stepfather.

At the age of 11, Rukhmabai was married to Dadaji Bhikaji, who was 19 at the time and a cousin of her stepfather. However, she did not go to live with her husband. In a departure from societal norms, her stepfather, Sakharam Arjun, decided to keep Rukhmabai in his own home. Consequently, her husband, Dadaji Bhikaji, moved in with her family and lived as a domestic help. Rukhmabai's family took full responsibility for his upbringing and education, believing that since he married their daughter and became a son-in-law, it was their duty to help him grow into a good human being. They thought that if Bhikaji received an education, he could develop independent thinking and contribute positively to society, which would ultimately make Rukhmabai happy and empower them both.

Unfortunately, despite their efforts, things didn't go as planned. Bhikaji turned out to be indifferent and opposed to the advancement of women. Rukhmabai began to menstruate about six months after their wedding and later became pregnant. A traditional feast was held to celebrate this, but her father was deeply troubled. As a doctor, he understood that pregnancy at such a young age could harm both mother and child, and he opposed this early pregnancy on both medical and social grounds.

Bhikaji, now 20, did not share her father's concern. He resented the arrangement made by Sakharam to have him study at home, as he had little interest in education beyond the sixth grade. Despite Sakharam's support and encouragement, Bhikaji struggled to concentrate on his studies. During this time, Bhikaji's mother passed away. His uncle wanted to take him away, but Sakharam intervened, believing that if Bhikaji left his home, he would fall further behind in his education.

Despite Sakharam's opposition, Bhikaji's uncle, Narayan Dhurmaji, took him away to his home, which created an environment that led Bhikaji astray. Narayan insisted on taking Rukhmabai with him and demanded a share of her property. Rukhmabai strongly opposed this decision, defending her right to choose, and received unwavering support from her stepfather. Sakharam, understanding that a woman cannot be forced into marriage against her will, bolstered Rukhmabai's morale during the lengthy legal battle that ensued, lasting for three long years.

In that year, Rukhmabai continued her studies at home by reading books from the French Church Mission Library. Her father, Sakharam, was a social reformer who connected with Vishnushastri Pandit, a notable organizer and reformer. This exposure brought him into contact with many highly educated men and women from Europe, which had a significant impact on Rukhmabai. She had the opportunity to meet several distinguished individuals and regularly attended gatherings of the Prarthana Samaj and Arya Mahila Samaj with her mother.

However, Rukhmabai's husband did not remain passive about the situation. In March 1884, Bhikaji sent a legal notice to Sakharam Arjun through his lawyers, Chak and Waqar. The notice contained allegations that Sakharam, who was Rukhmabai's stepfather, was keeping her away from her husband. In response, Sakharam Arjun defended Rukhmabai through his lawyers, Payne-Gilbert and Sammanni.

In 1885, the court began hearing the case titled "Restitution of Conjugal Rights," officially named "Bhikaji vs. Rukhmabai." The case was presided over by Justice Robert Hill Pinhey. He concluded that, according to English law, an adult cannot be forced to live with someone against their will. Justice Pinhey noted the difference between English law and Indian Hindu law, stating, "Rukhmabai was married at a tender age, so she cannot be forced to go to her husband."

Justice Pinhey retired shortly after this hearing, but this was not the end of the case.

The trial began in 1886, with hearings attended by JD Inverarity Jr. and Kashinath Trimbak Telang. The incident caused a significant uproar within the Indian community. Many believed it undermined the moral and cultural integrity of Hindus. There was extensive criticism, especially of Pinhey's decision, featured in the Anglo-Marathi weekly (1833-1889), overseen by Vishwanath Narayan Mandlik, a supporter of Bhikaji.

A weekly newspaper called *The Maratha*, published in Pune by Bal Gangadhar Tilak, featured criticisms of Justice Pinhey. Tilak stated, "Pinhey should not have made such a decision without understanding Hindu culture." During this time, the *Times of India* published articles that critiqued public opinion regarding this incident, revealing that these writings were authored by Rukhmabai herself.

The public reacted with deep resentment to regarding the conflict between 'Hindu Law and English Law.' The case was heard on March 18, 1886, by Chief Justice Sir Charles Sargent and Justice L.H. Bailey. Ultimately, the law favored Rukhmabai's husband, ordering Rukhmabai to live with him. The court further mandated that, if Rukhmabai defied this order, she would face six months in jail.

On March 4, 1887, Justice Faran ruled based on the Hindu Marriage Act, affirming that Rukhmabai must stay with her husband or serve six months in jail.

Despite hearing the verdict, Rukhmabai did not break down or accept the court's decision. Instead, she responded with determination, stating, "In such a situation, I would prefer to be jailed."

The incident sparked considerable controversy. Bal Gangadhar Tilak remarked in his publication, *Kesari*, that "Rukhmabai's fight is a consequence of English education and jeopardizes Hindu culture." In contrast, Max Muller asserted, "Legal action is not the solution to Rukhmabai's problems; her education has empowered her to make decisions about her own life."

After a lengthy trial, Rukhmabai presented her case to Queen Victoria. She wrote to the Queen:

"Queen! It is widely acknowledged that, by the grace of God, we live under the fearless shelter of our beloved Queen Victoria. She is recognized around the world for her fair and transparent rule. If such a government cannot liberate oppressed Hindu women like us, then who can?

On the 50th anniversary of your reign, residents from every village and city under your rule are joyfully praying for your well-being. We all pray to God to bless you with peace and prosperity. In the light of the conditions in our society, may I ask if the Mother Queen could spare some time? I have faith that you will heed the appeal of young Indian girls like myself.

The age requirements set for girls and boys in the Hindu Marriage Act, along with the voices raised against it, should prompt a reconsideration of this marriage law when the issue reaches the courts. In just a few sentences, you can grasp the unspeakable pain that girls experience in our Indian society due to child marriage. If you permit it, minor changes can be made to the Hindu marriage rules. This would be the greatest gift to Hindu women on the occasion of your 50 years of reign. God can make it happen in an instant; otherwise, all your efforts could be in vain.

Your Majesty, I humbly ask for your forgiveness for taking up so much of your precious time.

With all good wishes,

Your faithfully,

Rukhmabai."

This appeal was published in the Daily Telegraph on July 15, 1887, and presented to the Government of India. The event was attended by Queen Victoria, who intervened in the matter. She later overturned the court order, declaring the marriage null and void, despite no evidence or documentation being presented to her.

In 1888, a compromise document was presented to Bhikaji, who rejected Rukhmabai's demand for Rs 2,000. In 1889, Bhikaji remarried, while Rukhmabai continued her medical studies and became increasingly active in the women's rights movement. This activism gained traction both in India and the UK. Prominent figures like Beheramji Maibari (1853-1912), Bal Gangadhar Tilak, and various writers and social organizations discussed women's rights in British women's magazines.

As a result, Rukhmabai's case garnered significant public attention, leading to an increase in the age of consent for marriage in British India, raised from 10 to 12 years.

During this time, Dr. Edith Peche was working at Cama Hospital and became interested in Rukhmabai's actions. He admired her and supported her on various levels, both mentally and financially. Dr. Peche not only encouraged Rukhmabai to pursue higher education but also provided her with financial assistance for it. Other supporters included Shivajirao Holkar, who donated money to help "raise awareness against prevailing traditional practices." With the help of social activists like Eva McLaren, Walter McLaren, Adelaide Manning, and others, the Rukhmabai Defence Committee was formed. The committee's primary objective was to raise funds for Rukhmabai's higher education, which they successfully achieved. The money raised enabled Rukhmabai to pursue her studies. Following her divorce from Bhikaji in 1888, she travelled to England to study medicine.

In 1894, Rukhmabai completed her medical education at the London School of Medicine for Women and also studied at the Royal Free Hospital. In December 1886, Dr. Anandi Gopal Joshi and Kadambini Ganguly became the first female doctors in India. However, only Kadambini Ganguly was able to devote herself fully to medical service. After her, Rukhmabai became the second woman doctor to serve the community.

After finishing her education in 1895, Rukhmabai returned to India and was appointed Chief Medical Officer at the Woman's Hospital in Surat. In 1918, she was offered the position of Chief Executive Officer of the premier women's hospital in Rajkot, but she chose not to accept the offer.

She refused to accept such a position, preferring instead to work with women at Rajkot hospital. She continued her work in Surat until her retirement in 1929, during which time she founded the Red Cross in Rajkot. After retiring, she settled in Bombay and dedicated around 35 years of her life to serving in Surat, Rajkot, and Bombay. Following the death of Bhikaji in 1904, Rukhmabai adopted the traditional Hindu custom of wearing white clothing. After her retirement, she published a small booklet titled *Parda*, which discussed the contributions of widows to the Indian social system and the opposition they faced.

At a time when Indian women lacked the right to speak openly, Rukhmabai became a beacon of hope and possibility. She endured harassment from her husband, who did not believe in women's education or progress. Despite these challenges, Rukhmabai lived with her mother and stepfather to pursue higher education and establish herself as a respected doctor. After returning from London, she encountered numerous social obstacles but remained determined. She took on the role of chief medical officer and actively campaigned against child marriage.

Rukhmabai's case became a turning point in the struggle for the abolition of child marriage and the battle women's suffrage in India. It captured attention in the British media regarding child marriage and the call for equal rights for women. Pandita Ramabai, a prominent educator and social worker advocating for women's rights, remarked, "When a highly educated woman physically and mentally refuses to accept the subjugation of a man, the British government resorts to law and imprisons that woman."

In a letter to *The Times of India*, on June 20, 1885, Rukhmabai stated, "This rotten tradition of child marriage has destroyed all the happiness of my life. It has significantly impacted my education and development. Unfortunately, I was viewed differently by others, even my younger sisters regarded me with suspicion."

Despite facing numerous protests, Rukhmabai remained unmarried and established herself as a self-respecting woman doctor in

India. Defying social opposition with immense resilience, she devoted her life to advocating for the rights and dignity of women.

Rukhmabai passed away on September 25, 1955. Though she is no longer with us, her courage, determination, and perseverance continue to inspire women to raise their voices against injustice. There is much to learn from her life. Rukhmabai's biography serves as a call to all Indian women to prioritize education and self-sufficiency over submitting to oppressive men.

Haimavati Sen

Woman!

This simple five-letter word carries immense significance. The Creator has beautifully designed this epitome of beauty. A woman is endowed with the incredible ability to create—she becomes a creator in her own right. A man is born of a woman and is shaped by her.

Yet, it is deeply saddening that women often struggle to establish their identities within families and societies that frequently overlook their existence. A woman fights for her place not only in her family but also in society and, most importantly, to be treated with dignity and respect by the men around her. Despite facing overwhelming challenges, women have persevered, confronted obstacles, and affirmed their existence. Unfortunately, this journey has come at a cost. To gain something valuable, one often has to endure loss, and women have to make numerous sacrifices.

Nevertheless, women continue to move forward, overcoming

immense hurdles. They have emerged victorious, serving as inspiring examples for future generations.

Writing an autobiography is a unique way to share one's life with others. Historically, women faced many restrictions when they wanted to write their autobiographies. During times when they struggled for their very existence, who would grant them the authority to express their lives in writing? Opportunities were scarce. According to historians, Indian women began writing their autobiographies toward the end of the 19th century, influenced mainly by Western literature and culture.

Despite these limitations, women wrote their stories in their own ways. As family and social structures changed, alongside the impacts of colonialism and the promotion of women's education, women gradually began to document their personal lives. This practice is what we define as autobiography—it is not solely a Western concept.

Despite having to cope with numerous obstacles, many women are courageously writing autobiographies, yet their stories have not reached the public in time. Sadly, countless women's autobiographies have been left to gather dust in cupboards in their homes. Some autobiographies have not been published at all, while others have only seen the light of day years after the author's death.

One such woman experienced this unhappy fate. Although she completed her autobiography several years before her passing, it was not published during her lifetime. Written in Bengali, her life narration remained largely unpublished for two generations after her death, only to be published nearly 80 years later. Through her work, she has set an inspiring example for many.

Her autobiography narrates the story of this extraordinary woman and explores themes of self-esteem and independent thinking. She advocated for female education and emphasized the importance of making women self-reliant, boldly combating against the gender inequality prevalent in society at that time. This book holds a mirror to India in the 19th century, a time when upper-class women faced difficult circumstances due to traditional constraints. Nonetheless, her autobiography recounts her struggle to challenge these societal evils and highlights the successes of women.

"I found myself in a corner of the house. My parents fulfilled their duty towards me, but no one felt responsible or sympathetic towards this childless widow. I had to ask others for money. What had happened to my husband? He had taken a third wife."

In her autobiography, Haimavati describes the tragic circumstances and struggles of her life with profound sadness and self-respect. She was born into a landlord family in Khulna, East Bengal, and is the eldest child of her father. As a child, Haimavati had an attractive personality and remarkable talents, making her the favourite of her father throughout her life.

Although her father was generally opposed to social change, he had a particular fondness for his talented first-born. This affection allowed Haimavati the freedom to dress like a boy during her childhood, and he encouraged her to play and study alongside her cousins. Through these interactions, Haimavati learned valuable lessons and engaged in various discussions. This experience later empowered her to break down barriers and forge her own identity.

Haimavati was interested in pursuing higher education since childhood. Despite the opposition of the women of the house, her ambitious father made all arrangements to educate her.

The women's discussions in the household were very traditional, focusing heavily on customs and cultural practices. Haimavati's mother and grandmother disapproved of her father's progressive attitude towards their daughter. They believed that Haimavati should marry at a very young age. During that time, marriages in the families of Brahmins and Kayasthas of the Kulin community in East Bengal were arranged within their own castes. Consequently, Haimavati's female relatives began searching for a suitable groom from their caste. They eventually chose a 45-year-old man from a respected Kayastha family, who had already lost two wives and had two daughters around Haimavati's age. At just 9 years old, Haimavati was deemed an appropriate match, reflecting the societal norm of ignoring significant age differences in marriages during that era.

At that time in 1860, the age limit for marriage for girls was 10 years. The man, who is married to Haimavati, was a deputy magistrate in the then British-ruled territory. However, he violated the law. The age limit for girls had no effect on their marriage. That old husband of Haimavati would turn into a lascivious man at night. Despite this, the Deputy Magistrate had no hesitation in marrying a tender girl of his daughter's age. He had daughters from his former wives. Haimavati, a 9-year-old girl, was playing with her stepdaughters of the same age throughout the afternoon. As she says in her autobiography.

Haimavati vividly recounts her experiences with her elderly husband, who repeatedly attempted to have sex with her. In her autobiography, she wrote, "I felt like a piece of wood, silent and unresponsive. When I fell asleep, someone would take my clothes off. I would wake up and put my clothes back on."

One night, Haimavati found her husband having sex with a prostitute. When she saw them, she was terrified. Seeing her faint, the prostitute helped her regain consciousness by splashing water on her face. In such a situation, she could hear her telling her husband - "Haimavati is very young, she also comes from a cultured family. All this scares her. Such incidents should not recur in future. "

Her husband, however, did not respond. Instead he said, "What you say is right, probably she saw us. Look! Else how would she learn? "

After that, it happened again and again. In her autobiography, she said, "I am ashamed to say that such a person, the deputy magistrate, was my husband. "

A few months after their marriage, Haimavati's husband died of a liver and stomach infection. At the age of 10, she became a widow.

"At first my mother-in-law called me a 'cannibal demoness' who ate her husband. At that time, I was not allowed to put oil on my head. I have been cooking for myself for a long time. Gradually, I became ashamed of myself. I almost didn't get out of my room. When no one was around, I would go out and do my daily chores." Haimavati has mentioned her helplessness in this way in her autobiography.

"I was in a corner of the house, feeling abandoned. My parents had fulfilled their obligations toward me, but no one showed any sympathy to a child widow like me. I found myself having to beg for money from others."

Haimavati also mentioned how she was abused as a widow by people she knew, "They blamed me for my husband's death. They had a lot of sympathy for that perverted drunkard. But they had no sympathy for me. My mother and grandmother were responsible for my condition. That was the main reason. I heard that my relatives would say that, had I not been educated, this day wouldn't have arrived."

Haimavati's father was heartbroken to see her in such a state. In an effort to support the family, he transferred some of his property into her name. However, Haimavati was deeply saddened when her father passed away shortly after. His death left her devastated.

Child widows, in particular, symbolize the suffering faced by many widows, including social restrictions, domestic violence, hunger, and physical and sexual abuse. These women were required to wear white clothing and often had to eat alone. Their diets were severely restricted; they were prohibited from consuming meat, onions, garlic, lentils, or any other red-colored food items. They were expected to observe numerous fasts and practices austerity. Additionally, they were urged to abstain from non-vegetarian food and to exercise self-control through penance in order to suppress any sexual desires.

Haimavati later expressed her gratitude towards her mother-in-law in her autobiography, saying, "My mother-in-law was a kind-hearted woman. She allowed me to live a normal life. I was able to wear coloured clothes, adorn myself with bangles, enjoy non-vegetarian food, and keep my hair long without cutting it."

In the beginning, Haimavati helped her mother-in-law with household chores while also taking the opportunity to study in her spare time. At that point, she did not fully comprehend what life as a widow would entail.

A few years later, Haimavati's mother-in-law passed away. After this loss, Haimavati's situation at her in-laws' house changed for the worse. She faced numerous obstacles as a widow, both physically and financially. Despite these difficulties, Haimavati managed to survive by working as a servant and relying on her husband's elder brother's family for support. Unfortunately, she also had to endure considerable harassment from her brother-in-law.

As events unfolded, Haimavati moved to her mother's house and lived there for a few years. However, she found no peace. Her drunken brothers frequently got into brawls and began stealing her jewelry. Day by day, the situation deteriorated. She struggled to secure even two meals a day and often went 5 to 6 days without food. When she finally got a handful of rice, she had to eat it with just salt. She had no choice but to rely on the help of others. Despite her severe struggles and desperate condition, the people around her labeled her as an ascetic and a simple woman, unable to truly comprehend her misery.

In such dire circumstances, Haimavati concluded that countless other Bengalis like her would seek refuge in Banaras, the traditional shelter for widows. Bad as her situation was, she felt it would be better to endure an empty stomach in Banaras than to remain at home. At that time, Banaras, along with Kashi and Vrindavan, was home to many widows, most of whom were Bengali. The Dayabhaga Law School in Bengal aimed to help widows secure rights to their husbands' property. However, many widows faced coercion from their relatives, who often took their property by force and assaulted them in various ways.

As a result, many oppressed widows were compelled to relocate to Banaras their for safety. Unfortunately, they were not free from harm there either. They encountered unwanted pregnancies, were driven into prostitution, and faced the harsh realities of widowhood surrounding them. Reports of suicide were common. To survive, these widows would arrange for food and shelter by begging or singing hymns in temples and ashrams. Many spent their lives traveling on pilgrimages, seeking solace.

Widows were looked down upon in society during that time. They were primarily viewed as objects of consumption. Researchers indicate that Hindu widows faced significant harassment, indecent comments, insinuations, and even exploitation. Haimavati's experience in Banaras exemplified this treatment; her own cousin's wife refused to give her shelter, saying, "You are a widow, young and beautiful. People will call you my husband's kept woman. Who knows if there won't be a connection between you two?" This attitude and behavior were prevalent not just in Banaras but everywhere.

Even the shelters established to protect widows from sexual abuse proved unsafe, as Haimavati observed. She noticed that doubts were raised, not only by men but also by women, regarding a widow's sexual desires. Haimavati began questioning the customs and traditions of her society: "Should I tolerate all this just because I am a woman? Why are they so concerned about whose wife or daughter I am?"

Despite the harassment and injustice, Haimavati remained determined to pursue higher education, a dream she had harbored since childhood. In the 1880s, women were not expected to receive education, and she faced considerable criticism for her ambitions. Haimavati stated, "My goal in life was to attain higher education and establish myself. I ignored those who called me a Christian or anything else."

Her unwavering determination to study propelled Haimavati forward in life, leading her to make several important decisions. While teaching at a girls' school in Banaras, her urge to receive higher education drove her to the unfamiliar city of Calcutta. During this time, she confronted issues like gender discrimination, lack of education for women in a male-dominated society, child marriage, and the indifference towards widow remarriage. However , the Brahmo Samaj actively working for social change, inspired Haimavati.

After completing her higher education, Haimavati decided to go to Calcutta to connect with the members of the Brahmo Samaj, which championed women's education. The Brahmo Samaj's commitment to improving the treatment of widows, promoting women's education, and supporting widow remarriage deeply influenced her. At that point, she also identified with Brahmo Dharma, or Brahmoism.

Outraged by the orthodox ideas and gender discrimination prevalent among the Brahmins of Hinduism, Haimavati willingly embraced Brahmoism. The adoption of Brahmoism or Christianity posed a significant challenge to feminism in 19th-century Bengal. Haimavati also had conflicts with older members of the Brahmo Samaj regarding the remarriage of adult women.

The Brahmo Samaj had a multifaceted impact on the lives of

widows in 19th-century Bengal. According to Meredith Burthwick, the Brahmo Samaj established schools and shelters for widows and encouraged them to become self-reliant. She noted, "Brahmo Samaj and, to some extent, Christianity, are bringing hope to widows. They are trying their best to offer a normal life by alleviating the various rules imposed on them." As a result, many rural widows left their villages to seek refuge in widows' homes in Calcutta. Daughters from noble families were drawn to the Brahmo Samaj in large numbers. Upon joining, efforts were made to provide them with education, vocational training, and, to some extent, opportunities for remarriage.

Haimavati left Banaras with the help of a distant male companion and settled in Calcutta, where many highly educated members of the Brahmo Samaj resided. Some of the widows' homes established in Calcutta admitted highly educated people with the intention of continuing their education under their care. However, upon her arrival, Haimavati found that her expectations were not met. She observed that these so-called educated persons were primarily focused on planning trips to England. Although they were sympathetic to Haimavati, they were unable to assist her with her educational pursuits, leading her to experience failure once again. Distressed and uncertain about her next steps, she contemplated going to her brother's house. Ultimately, she decided that seeking shelter at her brother's place was not the best option, and during this time, she received some support by teaching the wife of a zamindar.

Haimavati travelled alone throughout the country for various activities, which worried some of her well-wishers. They advised her to remarry to avoid potential sexual harassment. She received four marriage proposals from the Brahmo Samaj, which is quite a lot for an older woman, but none of these proposals materialized.

In contemporary society, it is relatively easy for upper-caste widows to remarry, but this was not then widely accepted. Although the practice was legally introduced in 1856, it was rarely seen in upper-class Hindu society, and Haimavati faced many challenges regarding her remarriage.

However, with the help of some friends and supporters, Haimavati married Kunjabihari Sen in 1890. He was a humble worker at the Brahmo Samaj.

However, this union brought more problems to Haimavati's life. She encountered numerous difficulties due to her husband's irresponsible and disorganized lifestyle. Even after having four sons and a daughter, he did not earn any income or show any sense of responsibility toward the family. Haimavati herself noted, "My husband was not at all concerned about these things."

After the marriage, it became essential for Haimavati to overcome the financial crisis facing her family. She aspired to receive medical training, as many girls were enrolling in medical colleges at that time. Therefore, she decided to choose that path.

Women in Bengal historically became self-sufficient by earning a Vernacular Licentiate in Medicine and Surgery (VLMS) degree. The establishment of Campbell Medical College in 1888 opened up opportunities for women in medical education. Graduates from Campbell Medical College, Calcutta, who earned the VLMS degree were known as hospital assistants. The classes were conducted through lectures, with Indian teachers teaching in the medium of Bengali. The textbooks were available in both English and Bengali. The institute provided training in medicine and certain specialties, including dermatology. However, VLMS graduates struggled to match the caliber of students from Calcutta Medical College, where the instruction was conducted in English. This disparity was particularly evident for Indian women, who, at the time of admission, were not required to demonstrate proficiency in English or have formal academic credentials. In contrast, only those with a B.A. degree were eligible for admission to Calcutta Medical College.

Despite facing numerous social and economic challenges, these women played a vital role in the healthcare sector, especially in rural areas. Although they were not doctors, they served as health workers and were the backbone of hospitals in those regions.

The VLMS degree empowered women to be self-reliant and to support doctors. A unique advantage they had was their familiarity with the local language, which greatly aided in understanding and addressing the needs of people in rural communities.

In 1891, Haimavati was admitted to Campbell Medical College at the age of 26, bringing her baby with her. She was one of the few women present at the time. By the end of her first year, Haimavati was recognized for her outstanding performance, receiving two increments in her exam results. Her hard work and perseverance made her an exceptional student.

In her autobiography, Haimavati writes, "My memory was very sharp, so I soon began to improve in this area. There were twelve students and four teachers in the class. I wasn't afraid of making mistakes, which is why I made many of them. Others were envious of my progress."

Later, when the annual examination was done and in which the surgery,

Subjects such as surgical anatomy were included; Haimavati outperformed the students and topped the class. Even the student who was always in the lead, took 2nd place behind Haimavati by a small margin. Therefore, Haimavati was selected to receive the gold medal as she had the best position, which was a surprise for others. The protests began. There was gender discrimination at the institutional level. The students of the college did not hesitate to launch an agitation against the announcement of Haimavati's gold medal. The students boycotted classes and started throwing stones at the teachers. The saddest thing about that time was that the general public also supported the students. Articles were written for the students. It was like pouring fuel on a fire. Someone even mentioned in the reader column, "Why don't we kill that girl? This will be the end of the event. Encouraging women is our biggest mistake."

What was even more surprising was that in the end, it was the students who emerged victorious.

The protest was successful. The Inspector General and the Governor, who were assigned to resolve the case, finally persuaded Haimavati to return the gold medal in exchange for the silver medal. At that time, she needed money, so she requested to keep the gold medal and receive a monthly scholarship of 30 rupees to support her studies at Calcutta Medical College. This arrangement allowed her to continue her education.

With the financial support from the scholarship, Haimavati became more stable when she was appointed as a doctor at Lady Dufferin Women's Hospital in Chenchuraha, Hooghly, earning a salary of Rs 50 per month. There, she had opportunities to both practice medicine and provide private consultations. As the sole breadwinner of her family, she took on the role of a man who traditionally earns a living, while also fulfilling her responsibilities at home. Haimavati not only handled the financial aspects of her household but also managed the caregiving responsibilities for her children.

Haimavati was a very outspoken wife, which often led to arguments between her and her husband on various issues. Despite being influenced by her paternal instincts, she was a good wife who handed over all her earnings to her husband. She even contributed the money she earned while studying in medical college. This arrangement continued throughout her life, with her husband investing the money according to the family's needs. She wrote, "I owe everything I earn to my husband. I didn't ask him for anything. At that time, I was making a lot of money, but I needed the money, so I asked for it."

Haimavati faced harassment in her first job from her superior physician, Badrikanath Mukherjee. Initially, he was supposed to cooperate with her as the newly appointed lady doctor and explain the work. However, he began to make inappropriate comments. When it became too much for her, she turned to him and said she would read all the books herself. But the rude man ignored her and continued to speak whatever came to his mind.

After Haimavati reported this behavior to a superior English officer, he temporarily banned men from entering women's hospitals. However, this only provided a short reprieve. The doctor sought revenge and began to harass her further. He even sent goons to her house at night, who loitered around her kitchen and made various indecent comments. Unfortunately, the Sub-Inspector of Police in that district did not listen to any of Haimavati's complaints, as he was a close friend of the doctor.

Haimavati was forced to give consent to many incidents that took place during her employment. But in the male-dominated society of the time, Haimavati was vocal about the propagation of feminism and gender inequality. She was often vocal about child marriage in upper-class Hindu families and marital rape of a minor wife. Whereas in the society of that time, any discussion about the sexual desire of women was visible to everyone in the society. However, there was no open discussion on the issue then. She candidly admitted her bitter experience of child marriage over gender discrimination, describing how her twice-widowed husband repeatedly tried to force her into sex with him.

Haimavati strongly advocated for widow remarriage and actively promoted it throughout her life. She pointed out that often, the older men to whom younger girls were married were close in age to the children of their previous wives. One poignant example she shared was of a seven-year-old daughter of her husband's first wife, who expressed a desire to see her father remarry while she was bedridden. This situation caused Haimavati significant distress. After her husband's death, society placed the blame on her.

She remarked, "I feel ashamed of this tradition within Hindu society, which is so rich in heritage. A ten-year-old girl has to marry a fifty-year-old man. I pay my respects to the countless parents who choose not to condemn their daughters to a life of despair. This can only happen in India; it is not observed in any other country. My parents were neglectful and left me to depend on my husband's elder brother, abandoning me to navigate life like a servant just for two meals."

In one of the episodes, she recounts, "When she transformed into a beautiful young woman, an older man approached her with a marriage proposal. However, she declined, stating that she would rather focus on the re-marriage of her twenty-year-old widow than be interested in her own marriage. But he wasn't interested in that."

It would not be an exaggeration to say that Haimavati's story is an exception to the circumstances in pre-1900s Bengal. This 10-year-old child widow became a doctor through her own struggles and established a unique identity in society.

Haimavati was far-sighted, sharp-witted, and outspoken, enabling her to confront the immense challenges in her life with determination. She faced numerous obstacles alone to continue her education and carve out her own identity in a society that often restricted women. She successfully overcame many traditional barriers.

Regardless of the circumstances and struggles, she pursued her education at a time when it was largely inaccessible to women. At the age of 23, she married for the second time without the support of her family. Despite encountering various challenges and dangers on her path to achieving her goals, she remained steadfast in her ambitions. As a female doctor, she worked extensively outside the home while efficiently managing her responsibilities domestically. In doing so, she solidified her position in society and became an inspiration for others. Haimavati was a victim of male chauvinism within her society, but she persevered.

But she didn't accept it. Even after becoming a doctor, she raised her voice against the discrimination between men and women in the medical profession. For example, a male doctor received a salary of Rs 1,000 for maternity treatment, while a female doctor earned only Rs 180, and a female colleague received just Rs 50. Haimavati felt a deep anger about this discrimination, which compelled her to speak out against it. She believed that injustice was intolerable; why should she have to suffer simply because she was born a woman?

In many instances, Haimavati highlights the empathy women have for each other's struggles. As she journeyed through the villages of Benares, Calcutta, and even East Bengal, she found many women—divorced and widowed—who sympathized with her. Most were strangers, yet they shared a common plight. This understanding of their own situations created a bond among them. She remarked, "When I became a widow, I didn't receive much sympathy from my brother, but my sister understood me very well." One woman offered her shelter in Banaras, while another arranged for her to attend school. She would address many older women as "Didi" and received affection from them as she walked through the rural areas of East Bengal.

Haimavati assisted many women in various ways, maintaining contact through letters.

The account of Haimavati's life provides a vivid picture of the social system of her time, illustrating issues such as gender discrimination, lack of education for women, child marriage, widowhood, exploitation, and torture.

The true nature of society during that time was fully revealed only with the publication of her autobiography. This remarkable work offers a vivid portrayal of the status of women in colonial India from the 19th to the 20th centuries, highlighting their struggles against a male-dominated society, familial oppression, gender discrimination, and the challenges faced by feminism.

Haimavati's autobiography tells an extraordinary story.

It chronicles the growing opposition to the injustices faced by women and details their struggles along the way. Her narrative showcases their triumphs, demonstrating that when a woman speaks out against social evils and prejudices—regardless of the circumstances or challenges she encounters—she does not lose; instead, she achieves success. Her voice has helped chart a new direction for society, paving the way for future generations. She stands as a beacon of change.

Matangini Hazra

Memories of the freedom movement in India that will always be cherished by the people of the country. Regardless of the social atmosphere prevailing at that time, those who sought to join the struggle for independence did so in any way they could. They fought for freedom, and this fight was far from easy. It involved numerous struggles, financial losses, suffering, and, most importantly, sacrifices.

Importantly, the freedom movement was not solely a male endeavour; women were an integral part of society and played a crucial role in the struggle. Their involvement considerably strengthened the movement. Whenever women participated, they brought a new dimension to the struggle with their unique approaches.

Among these remarkable women was one whose contributions to the freedom movement and her methods of activism took the movement in a new direction. Despite lacking formal education and financial resources, she did not allow these limitations to deter her from pursuing her goal. Her unrelenting focus was on achieving freedom for her country.

In 1870 (sometimes referred to as 1869), Matangini Hazra was born on June 19 in Hogla village, near Tamluk town in the Medinipur district of West Bengal. Her father, Thakur Das Maity, was a poor farmer, and her mother, Bhagwati Maity, was a housewife. Unfortunately, due to their difficult financial situation, her family could not send her to school.

Matangini's childhood was particularly challenging. Her parents married her off at the age of twelve to a sixty-two-year-old widower, who had three children. Before she could even grasp the meaning of home, she found herself taking on the responsibilities of a homemaker. The weight of her circumstances was heavy; she had to bear the burden of adulthood far too soon. Tragically, after five years of marriage, her husband passed away, leaving her a widow at eighteen without any children of her own. Her stepchildren from her husband's previous marriage did not accept her, which led her to return to her village, where she lived alone.

Life was incredibly painful for Matangini, and she struggled to get by, often working various jobs throughout the day. Despite her hardships, she offered help to the elderly and the sick whenever she could. Over time, her spirit of service and her small acts of kindness drew her toward a greater purpose—serving her nation.

Matangini lived in a world filled with challenges, but she chose to measure up to them. She aimed to make life easier and more meaningful by confronting these obstacles. This determination inspired her to devote herself to the service of her society and country.

As a contemporary of Mahatma Gandhi, Matangini answered his call to join the freedom movement. She wholeheartedly embraced Gandhi's ideals and sacrificed her life for the nation. Even though she never met Gandhi in person, she became known as the "old Gandhi" in her community for her dedication to his principles. Matangini Hazra was a 72-year-old woman who ultimately gave her life for the country, yet her story is often overlooked in history. During India's celebration of the Amrit Mahotsav of independence, this unsung patriot emerged as a symbol of devotion to her motherland. Matangini, a childless widow who faced societal oppression, found profound meaning in dedicating her life to the country.

At the age of thirty-five, Matangini became deeply involved in the freedom movement, particularly during the heightened tensions following the partition of Bengal by Lord Curzon in 1905. The movement became particularly intense in Bengal, and Matangini was significantly impacted by it. Motivated by a deep sense of patriotism, she made independence the sole purpose of her efforts. This era saw a remarkable increase in the participation of women, and Matangini was actively engaged in the movement, inspiring others to join it alongside her. Although she was not formally aligned with any organization, her actions were deeply influenced by Gandhi's philosophy. She lived a simple life, advocated for the wearing of khadi, and dedicated herself to helping the Dalits and the elderly, even tending those afflicted by a widespread smallpox outbreak at the time.

Congress leader Ajay Mukherjee, who became the Chief Minister of West Bengal, was leading a movement in the Medinipur district that called for Purna Swaraj. Simultaneously, a procession passed through Matangini's village, chanting slogans of patriotism. Matangini, then 62 years old, began her Kranti Yatra by blowing the auspicious conch, following her Bengali tradition, and participated in the procession. From that day on, Matangini actively engaged in the freedom struggle.

In 1930, Gandhiji called for the Salt Satyagraha, or Civil Disobedience Movement, to protest against the British government's tax on salt. Protesters shouted slogans against British rule across various parts of the country. Matangini joined this movement, rallying with other agitators in her father-in-law's village, Alinen. The police arrested her and placed her in judicial custody. Due to her age and poor health, she was soon released from prison. However, despite her health issues, Matangini continued to take part in the freedom struggle, demonstrating a spirit akin to Gandhiji's. She faced repeated persecution by the British police.

When Congress was called upon to hoist the national flag at various government offices during the Purna Swaraj campaign, Matangini bravely walked through the dust to the Tamluk court and hoisted the national flag. She was arrested by the police again. Nonetheless, Matangini continued to court arrest return to jail after protesting at different times, even though she was often released due to her old age and health problems.

In 1933, Matangini participated in the Sub-Divisional Congress Conference held in Serampore. During the event, the police resorted to lathi charge when slogans were raised against the Chowkidar Tax. Matangini was injured in the lathi charge. On January 17 of that year, the then Governor of Bengal, Sir John Anderson, was scheduled to address the public in Tamluk. The local Congress opposed his visit. Seizing the opportunity, Matangini showed Anderson a black flag and shouted, "Anderson, go back!" This act was deemed a crime against the British government, leading to her imprisonment for six months.

Even while in jail, Matangini remained active. She visited other female prisoners, discussing British atrocities and the ongoing freedom struggle. Through these discussions, she became aware of the injustices perpetrated by the British and the broader context of the independence movement across the country. While still incarcerated, she was sentenced to life in prison. Her health deteriorated after her release, leaving her frailer and weaker. Yet, her patriotism never wavered.

On August 9, 1942, Gandhiji launched the Quit India Movement, leading to the arrest of many Congress leaders by the colonial authorities. Despite these arrests, protests continued. On September 29, 1942, the District Congress of Midnapore organized a plan to lay siege to all government offices in the district. The 72-year-old Matangini spearheaded this significant movement. She traveled around the village, encouraging the people to join the freedom struggle. Approximately, 6,000 individuals participated in the protest, marching toward Tamluk while shouting slogans against British rule.

The police had imposed Section 144 in the area, restricting gatherings. Matangini, holding the national flag in one hand and chanting 'Vande Mataram,' advanced despite the police's warning. She urged the officers not to open fire on the crowd. However, the police fired not once, not twice, but three times at Matangini. Even after being shot, she continued to hold the national flag and laid down her life while chanting 'Vande Mataram.' Her death brushed a life of virtue to an end.

It is hard to fathom the bravery and patriotism of a 72-year-old woman. Her unparalleled courage makes her a true martyr. Alongside Matangini, two other protesters were also killed in the police firing. In

1945, a few years after her death, Gandhiji visited the area and learned about Matangini's sacrifice. Her name resonated with the people, referred to as Old Gandhiji.

After she died, on August 15, 1947, many schools, colleges, and roads in West Bengal were named in her honor. In 1977, a statue of Matangini, the first woman martyr of West Bengal, was installed at the location where she was shot by the police. The statue was unveiled by Indira Gandhi. In 2002, during the sixtieth anniversary of the Quit India Movement, the postal department issued several postage stamps celebrating her legacy, including a 5-rupee stamp featuring Matangini's smiling face. Hazra Road is a major road in South Kolkata named after her.

We have much to learn from women like Matangini, who have left a lasting impact through their dedication. She initially did not understand the concept of freedom or the freedom movement; however, over time, she began to envision what it would be like to live in a free country and how future generations could inherit that freedom. Matangini did not simply remain lost in her dreams; she devoted herself wholeheartedly to her cause. She did not dwell on her education or her personal future; rather, driven by a spirit of service, perseverance, and determination, she tirelessly fought for freedom.

Her situation seemed hopeless. Despite her age, her health had deteriorated. However, all of her negative thoughts faded away. The idea that a woman in her situation could experience such a transformation is both surprising and uplifting. We can learn from her that there is no such thing as "I can't do this," or "it can't be done." Negativity has no place in a world defined by perseverance, determination, and truth. This has been proven time and again.

□□

Sarojini Naidu

March 8. This day is significant for everyone as we celebrate International Women's Day. It is observed with great joy and fervour. While various aspects of women's empowerment are frequently discussed, many people are unaware of another important occasion associated with this day. National Women's Day is celebrated on February 13 in honour of a remarkable woman: the freedom fighter and poetess Sarojini Naidu.

Sarojini Naidu was born on February 13, 1879, in Hyderabad to a Bengali family. Her father, Aghore Nath Chattopadhyay, was a scholar, a renowned scientist, and the principal of Nizam College in Hyderabad. He was originally from Bikrampur, Bangladesh, but the family lived in Hyderabad at that time. Her mother, Barada Sundari Devi, was a Bengali calligrapher and also wrote poetry.

Sarojini was the eldest of eight siblings. Her brother, Birendranath Chattopadhyay, was known as a revolutionary in the Indian freedom struggle, and her other brother, Harindranath, was a poet, playwright, and actor.

At that time, the family was well-established in Hyderabad, which was under the Nizam's rule, making Sarojini's education quite convenient. However, it is important to note that receiving opportunities is not enough; one's efforts and perseverance are essential. Sarojini was born and raised in a highly educated, cultured, and noble family, which greatly influenced her development.

Her talent was evident from childhood, and she excelled academically. At the age of 12, she secured the highest marks in the matriculation examination in 1891 at Madras University, standing first in her class.

It is said that when the British ruled India, Sarojini Naidu was captivated by their gait and attire. From a young age, she developed a fondness for Western food and culture. Despite her admiration for the English way of life and civilization, Sarojini was reluctant to speak English. When she informed her father of her disinterest in learning the language, he felt very upset. In his anger, he locked her in a room. At that time, English was deemed essential for success, which is why her father was concerned about her refusal to learn it. He tried various methods to make her understand the importance of the English language. Eventually, Sarojini realized her father's intentions. He hired a qualified tutor for both English and French, and gradually, she became proficient in English. She began writing in English as well.

While her father hoped she would study mathematics and become a mathematician, Sarojini harboured different aspirations. She was always more interested in literature. By the age of 12, when she matriculated, she had already written a notable play titled *Maher Munir*.

Nizam of Hyderabad was delighted to read her work, which made her path to higher education much easier. Impressed by Sarojini's skills in English poetry, the Nizam awarded her a scholarship to study abroad. At just 13 years old, she wrote a 1,300-line poem titled *Lady of the Lake*. She left school at 16 to pursue higher education and, from 1895 to 1898, she studied in London. Sarojini attended King's College, London, and Girton College, Cambridge. During this time, the Rhymer's Club in London had a significant influence on her, and receiving encouragement from Sir Edmund Gosse, her career as a poet began to flourish.

However, after three years in London, her health began to deteriorate, leading her to return to India in 1898 without obtaining a degree. At the age of 19, she married Dr. Govindaraj Naidu and became Sarojini Naidu. Their marriage was not without challenges, as they belonged to different castes and faced opposition from society. Despite these obstacles, Sarojini and Govindaraj enjoyed a happy married life together.

An important event occurred during Sarojini's three-year stay in London—she met Mahatma Gandhi for the first time. This meeting became a major turning point in her life.

During their first encounter, Sarojini was deeply impressed by Gandhi, which inspired her to join the Indian freedom struggle. She dedicated her entire life to her country. After returning to India, she invested all her talents in the fight for freedom and became an ardent disciple of Gandhi.

Sarojini drew the attention of Gopal Krishna Gokhale by engaging in the freedom struggle during the partition of Bengal in 1905. Annie Besant, a prominent woman leader, recognized her potential, and Sarojini eventually became best friends with her. From 1915 to 1918, Sarojini traveled across the country to awaken the youth and empower women. In 1916, she participated in the Champaran Farmers' Movement, for which she was jailed. She also faced imprisonment for her involvement in the Civil Disobedience movement and travelled extensively during the freedom struggle.

Sarojini played a crucial role in India's independence by resisting the British Empire and spreading Gandhi's message of freedom throughout the nation. In 1917, she founded the Women's India Association and actively participated in various satyagrahas called by Gandhiji, getting jailed a number of times in the process. Within a short span of time, Sarojini Naidu distinguished herself as an effective woman organizer. In 1925, she was elected as the President of the Indian National Congress, making her the second woman to hold this position—Annie Besant was the first. Sarojini presided over the Kanpur session of the Indian National Congress in 1925, successfully fulfilling this responsibility for a year.

Sarojini Naidu actively participated in the national movement alongside prominent leaders such as Mahatma Gandhi, Gopal Krishna Gokhale, Rabindranath Tagore, Sarala Devi, and Jawaharlal Nehru. She played a crucial role during the plague epidemic in India and was honored with the Kaisar-e-Hind award by the British government in 1928 for her remarkable contributions during this crisis. Notably, Mahatma Gandhi had received the Kaisar-e-Hind title in 1911, but both he and Sarojini Naidu returned the title following the Jallianwala Bagh massacre in 1919. In 1932, she represented India in South Africa.

After India gained independence in 1947, Sarojini Naidu was appointed the Governor of Uttar Pradesh, a position she held until her death. Her tenure as governor lasted from August 15, 1947, until March 2, 1949. Tragically, she suffered a heart attack while working in Lucknow on March 2, 1949, marking the loss of one of India's most eminent personalities.

Sarojini Naidu is affectionately referred to as the *Bulbul of India*. The bulbul is one of the most beautiful birds in the world, known for both its striking appearance and its melodious voice. In Arabian and Iranian cultures, it is called *Bulbul*, while in Europe, it is recognized as the *Nightingale*. The charm of the bulbul has been celebrated in literature by Urdu and Persian poets. Sarojini is called the *Nightingale of India* due to her eloquence, sweet speech, beautiful poetry, and impactful oratory. Such a distinction is rare for women and serves as a point of pride for the entire women's community.

Another remarkable aspect of Sarojini Naidu's personality is her writing career. From a young age, she wrote beautiful poems, and her first collection, *The Golden Threshold*, was published in 1905. Two of her best-known poetry collections are *The Bard of Time* and *The Broken Wing*. Sarojini wrote primarily in English, as her father insisted that she study in the UK. The beauty of her poetry contributed to her fame. Sarojini Naidu's contribution to literature is immense, with notable works including *The Magic Tree* and *The Wizard Master*. She gained recognition for her poetry from a very young age and was proficient in several languages, including Urdu, Persian, Bengali, and Telugu.

In honor of Sarojini Naidu, her 135th birth anniversary is celebrated as National Women's Day, a tradition that began on February 13, 2014. The Indian Coast Guard (ICG) ship named after her, *Sarojini Naidu*, patrolled the Odisha coast for 20 years before being decommissioned. This vessel was the first to start service in Goa and later served in the coastal areas of Odisha and West Bengal.

Reflecting on Sarojini's life journey, it is clear that India takes pride in being the land of the birth of a woman like her. The entire nation honors her as a source of inspiration and role model for women. She was a highly educated woman of culture, a freedom fighter, a social reformer, a literary figure, and a charismatic orator. Sarojini began writing poetry at the age of twelve and played an active role in India's freedom struggle. She spoke out against various social evils and prejudices of her time, advocating for their eradication. As an intellectual, upon returning to India, she observed that women were not participating in the freedom struggle as much as men. Consequently, she encouraged women to step out of their homes and join the movement.

Importantly, she understood the psyche of people, especially women. Through her sweet words and charming voice, she inspired women to join the cause. Her speeches were not only compelling but also attracted women to the freedom struggle, bringing a new dimension to it. Sarojini also fought for women's rights, emphasizing the importance of women understanding their rights and participating in politics and society. She not only spoke about these issues but also actively paved a new path for women through her exemplary work. It is a matter of great pride that Sarojini Naidu became the first woman Governor in independent India.

She actively participated in all the struggles alongside Gandhiji and played an inspiring role through her poetry. Women's participation in the freedom movement increased during that time, and she wrote extensively about the history of modern India. Women have always been deeply thoughtful, which is why she dedicated herself to fighting for their rights.

Sarojini had five daughters, one of whom, Padmaja, also took part in the freedom struggle. After Sarojini's passing, Padmaja published her mother's poems in a book in 1961.

Sarojini famously expressed her commitment to the cause with the words: "As long as I have breath left, as long as the last drop of blood flows in my veins, I will not give up the dream of freedom. I am a woman and a writer. As a woman, I will continue to embody strength, courage, and faith and will strive to realize the dream of raising our independent flag through the voice of my poetry."

Indeed, a country with such an influential and remarkable woman will always be a source of pride. We are proud of our nation, and women are the pride of society as a whole. A trailblazer like Sarojini will be remembered forever. Her life serves as a valuable education; her actions and ideals illuminate the essence of womanhood. India is great, and the greatness of Indian women shines through in their deeds and contributions.

□□

Muthulakshmi Reddy

This is a powerful statement from a woman, and it reflects a reality that is not often seen today. This woman, an eminent physician and legendary social reformer, dedicated years of her life to creating history through her remarkable work and mentoring many women. Despite facing numerous challenges in a society that posed many obstacles for women at that time, she tirelessly worked for their betterment, confronting these issues head-on. Among her most significant achievements was the abolition of the Devadasi tradition, a cause for which she fought relentlessly.

She faced many difficulties along the way, but she persevered in her efforts. The paragraph above discusses this legendary social reformer, who also served as the MLA for Pudukkottai in the Madras Presidency. A large programme was organized to honour her remarkable work against the Devadasi system, and she played a pivotal role in it. In her speech at this event, she expressed her thoughts with great strength and determination.

Born on July 30, 1886, in Pudukkottai, Tamil Nadu, the legendary woman was not only a social reformer but also a doctor, teacher, and administrator. She was the daughter of Narayan Swami and Devadasi Chandramal. Her father, Narayan Swami, was the Brahmin principal of the former Pudukottai Maharaja's College, while her mother was a Devadasi. In a remarkable movement for that time, Narayan Swami chose to marry Devadasi Chandramal despite fierce societal opposition.

Despite facing resistance, Narayan Swami remained committed to his love for Chandramal, resulting in them leaving their families. Although Chandramal's family did not oppose their union, Narayan Swami was estranged from his own family. Together they welcomed their first and only child, a daughter they named Muthulakshmi. As her father was distanced from his family and her mother remained close to hers, Muthulakshmi grew up connected to her maternal relatives.

Muthulakshmi was born on July 30, 1886, and was raised in her maternal uncle's house. Her family belonged to the Devadasi tradition. From a young age, she had a strong desire to study. The first school she attended was near home, but after graduating from that school, she faced the challenge of there being no school nearby for further education. She had to travel a long distance to continue her studies, and there were many challenges to overcome because, as a servant of God (Devadasi), she did not have the same rights as others in society. However, Muthulakshmi refused to be daunted by these social customs. People often taunted her, saying, "Look how Devaradiyil (the term for Devadasi in Tamil) runs after the bullock cart to go to school." For her part, Muthulakshmi simply ignored the sarcasm.

While Muthulakshmi was attending school, she encountered additional obstacles. The school she attended was for boys only, and some parents began to raise objections to her presence. They threatened to withdraw their children from the school if Muthulakshmi continued to study there, arguing that having a Devadasi's daughter in the school would corrupt their children's morals. The situation reached to the point where one of the teachers decided to resign in protest. Fortunately, at that time, the Maharaja of Pudukkottai supported Muthulakshmi and ensured that she could study alongside boys. She became the first woman from Pudukkottai to be admitted to the local Maharaja's High School. Seizing this opportunity, Muthulakshmi studied diligently.

Though her parents wanted her to marry at a young age, she rejected their proposals. They were opposed to her decision, but Muthulakshmi remained focused on her education and continued to prioritize her studies.

After graduating from high school, she decided to study medicine in her hometown. However, it was not easy for her to travel to Madras (now Chennai) to pursue her medical studies due to financial constraints. Fortunately, the Maharaja of Pudukkottai supported her education, providing the assistance she needed. She enrolled at the Madras Medical College, where the Maharaja granted her a stipend of Rs 150 per month. At that time, it was considered rare and surprising for a girl to pursue a career in medicine, especially when Muthulakshmi expressed her desire to specialize in surgery. The Madras Medical College was taken aback by her decision, as society generally believed that girls were too soft-hearted and would be scared by the sight of blood. However, Muthulakshmi proved everyone wrong. She was courageous and dedicated herself to her studies, becoming the first female student in the surgery department of the college.

After four years of hard work, the principal of the medical college walked down the corridor waving a piece of paper and announced cheerfully, "The first girl in the surgery department of our college has secured a hundred out of hundred marks!" This was a moment of joy and pride for Muthulakshmi. During her time at the college, she connected with influential figures like Sarojini Naidu and Annie Besant, whose personalities and philosophies greatly impacted her future endeavours. Additionally, she participated in various programmes and lectures organized by the Theosophical Society.

A tragic event during her studies deeply affected her when her uncle's 13-year-old daughter died during childbirth. This loss profoundly grieved her and motivated her to work against the practice of forcing underage girls into the Devadasi system, as well as to address the stigma associated with it.

After completing her studies, she then traveled to England for further studies.

In 1893, the Madras Hindu Reform Association called for an end to the Devadasis performing in public and private festivals. Similarly, in 1913, a proposed bill sought to prevent girls under the age of 16 from being assigned to the Devadasi system, but this effort was unsuccessful. In 1927, V.R. Puntulu presented another proposal to the Council of State regarding this issue. That same year, Dr. Muthulakshmi completed her medical training and was elected to the Madras Presidency Council, becoming the first woman to serve as vice-chairperson of the council.

To support this proposal, Dr. Muthulakshmi conducted interviews with hundreds of devadasis, both in and outside the Madras Presidency. In protest against the arrest of Mahatma Gandhi during the Salt Satyagraha in 1930, Dr. Muthulakshmi resigned from the Legislative Council after the motion to address the issue was defeated. Ultimately, the Madras Devadasi Bill was passed by the Madras Legislative Assembly in December 1947. On December 5, 1947, the Madras Presidency formally adopted the 1930 Bill to prohibit the dedication of underage girls as Devadasis.

While discussions about the Devadasi system were going on, two young girls reached out to Dr. Muthulakshmi, requesting her not to let them be dedicated to the tradition. She arranged for them to stay together in a hostel and attend school. Surprisingly, no one came to pick them up. Their story inspired Dr. Muthulakshmi to establish a school and hostel in Chennai.

At that time, the Devadasi system was supported by upper-class men, who thought it suited their interests. Young girls were brought into the Devadasi tradition through a religious ceremony before reaching puberty. Later, as concubines, these girls were taught dance and music, qualifying them to perform in public. They could choose their patrons, or their mothers could do that for them.

While the patron might father a child with the devadasi, he did not grant her any legal rights, surname, or inheritance. Even if the actual wife has no male heir, the son of a devadasi had no legal right to perform the last rites or rituals after the patron's death. He remained merely his mother's son. Additionally, regardless of a son's interests or skills, he was often compelled to pursue the art associated with the Devadasi tradition. If the devadasi does not have a daughter of her own, she might adopt a girl who is then forced to continue the tradition without her consent. This perpetuate a cycle where women felt like burdens to those who upheld the system.

A well-known educationist once criticized eminent lawyer and activist E.R. Krishna Iyer by highlighting a woman's dissatisfaction with her partner. Interestingly, if the concept of "Jawali" could be accepted in relation to the uniqueness of female sexuality, it might have been expressed more fully by a woman. Furthermore, it is difficult to imagine the courage a female dancer must possess to perform in front of a large audience of young men or males outside her own space. Much has been written on this subject, with numerous books and articles dwelling on the spirituality of Devadasi women, their unique sexuality, and their societal impact. Yet, these women remained largely invisible.

In *Unfinished Gestures: Devadasis, Memory and Modernity in South India*, Devesh Soneji notes that "in 1842, Dasi Annam tied a ghungroo around her legs at the age of ten, and according to records, she was entitled to one kalam of rice every month and one-and-a-half maunds of rice each day." This suggests that the Pottukkottuthal ceremony secured a woman's commitment to the local underground economy while also guaranteeing her involvement in sexual and aesthetic labour.

In her dissertation on the Tamil epic *Silappadikaram*, likely written in the late Sangam age around the 2nd century, author Sanhita Arni unveils a fascinating narrative. One part of Arni's essay recounts the story of Kanmagi and her husband Kovalan, who fell in love with the courtesan Madhavi. This tale is also referenced in *Purunuru* by Kapilar and Paranar. Kanmagi felt profound sadness because her husband had succumbed to the allure of a stranger. This suggests that even in the Sangam age, dancing girls were both feared and envied. A counter-narrative is presented to challenge the idea that the British were solely responsible for stigmatizing them. There was anxiety surrounding women's education; additionally, when these dancers performed, audiences were wary, fearing that someone's son or husband might fall under their spell. Paradoxically, despite not being married or sometimes being forced into marriage, they were often invited to partake in various household rituals to ward off evil or to bless the mangalsutra in marriage ceremonies.

In this context, the emergence and vision of Dr. Muthulakshmi changed the reality for Devadasis and women across the country forever. She believed that the practice of devadasi was a religious crime, akin to the nature of Sati, as it represented nothing more than the sexual exploitation of women in the name of the devadasi system.

About a decade after the bill was passed in 1930 to ban the submission of underage girls, a notable intellectual remarked in a speech, "Dr. Muthulakshmi, who was a devadasi herself, went abroad. For this reason, she felt ashamed of the system and invalidated it all with the stroke of a pen." One question arises from such a statement: where was the legitimacy of such a heinous practice?

Dr. Muthulakshmi was a social reformer who undertook various initiatives. She proposed the establishment of separate hospitals for women and children, leading the government to agree to open dedicated wards for children in maternity hospitals. She also advocated for medical facilities for people living in slums, particularly focusing on the construction of toilets for women.

As a physician and social reformer, she raised her voice against the wet nursing system, which involved upper-class women using lower-class women to breastfeed their infants and young children. This practice was a form of abuse, and she vehemently opposed it, seeking effective ways of putting an end to this exploitation.

Dr. Muthulakshmi introduced a bill aimed at supporting oppressed and exploited women, as well as children in brothels. Her efforts led to the establishment of a home for abused women rescued from these situations. She also founded schools for girls from marginalized and backward sections of society, including a school specifically for Muslim girls. Additionally, Dr. Muthulakshmi recommended that the government raise the legal marriage age to 21 for men and 16 for women.

She made notable contributions as a member of the Hartog Commission, an education commission. As its only female member, she travelled across the country to assess the progress of education among women. Furthermore, she established the Cancer Relief Fund, which has since grown into a nationwide institution.

In 1935, a hospital for cancer patients was opened at her request. The foundation stone for the Adyar Cancer Hospital was laid in 1952, and the hospital became operational two years later, on June 18, 1954. Today, the Adyar Cancer Institute is recognized as one of the most reputed cancer institutes in the world, treating thousands of cancer patients each year.

During her college years, Muthulakshmi regularly met with Sarojini Naidu and attended various women's meetings. She was also deeply influenced by the ideals of Mahatma Gandhi and Anne Besant, which inspired her to work for the upliftment of women and children. Through her dedication, she strived for the emancipation of women.

Women were trapped inside the house. At the request of the Indian Women's Association (IWA), Dr. Muthulakshmi Reddy resigned from her medical position and entered the Madras Legislative Council, where she was unanimously elected as its Vice-Chairman. She led the movement for women's suffrage in municipalities and legislative councils and was particularly concerned about children, providing them with food, shelter, and drinking water. To address these needs, Muthulakshmi established the Avvai Home in Chennai.

In addition to her activism, she was also a writer and authored several books on social reform. One notable work is *My Experience as a Legislator*, which details her political and legislative career. She served as the editor of *Roshni*, an important journal brought out by the All India Women's Conference (AIWC), and remained very active throughout her life. Even at the age of eight, she demonstrated her commitment to social issues. Muthulakshmi fought tirelessly for her beliefs and principles, with two of her greatest contributions being the establishment of the Avvai Home for Children and a Cancer Hospital. In recognition of her efforts, she was awarded Padma Bhushan by the President of India in 1956. She passed away on July 22, 1968.

Dr. Muthulakshmi Reddy was an independent thinker who assured her freedom regardless of the circumstances. She even arranged her own marriage to ensure that her personal freedom would not be restricted and that she would receive the respect she deserved. In 1914, at the age of 28, she married Sundar Reddy.

Dr. Muthulakshmi Reddy was a pioneer in many fields; she was the first woman to be admitted to a male college, the first female surgeon, the first woman governor of British India, the first woman chairperson of the State Social Welfare Advisory Board, and the first woman member of the Legislative Council.

Prathama, Madhyama, Uttama—these analogies have been associated with women since time immemorial. However, only a woman can truly understand the trouble that comes with such labels. She knows the struggles she must face, the problems she must overcome, and the obstacles she must navigate. Despite this, women also recognize that their journeys will never be easy; obstacles are a given. Yet, they must go beyond these challenges. This requires courage, perseverance, and determination. Women must gather these qualities to strengthen themselves and continue their fight. Because if they fight and work hard, not only will their families improve, but society as a whole will benefit, paving a new path for the next generation.

One shining example of this resilience is Dr. Muthulakshmi Reddy, one of India's first female doctors. Other pioneering women in medicine include Anandibai Joshi, Kadambini Ganguly, Rukhmabai Rawat, Haimavati Sen, and Mary Poonen Lukose. These names should be familiar to everyone in our country, yet how many of us truly know their stories?

A scrutiny of Dr. Muthulakshmi Reddy's life reveals her remarkable strength. Regardless of the circumstances, she never wavered in her commitment. She possessed immense talent and, alongside her courage and positive outlook, she aimed to uplift women. Her primary focus was to liberate women from exploitation. At a time when it was difficult for girls to pursue education, Muthulakshmi pursued higher studies tirelessly. Even when diagnosed with a respiratory illness around the age of 9 or 10, which interrupted her schooling for a year, she did not give up.

She dedicated her life to improving the health of women and children, establishing a children's development center, and participating in a conference in London in 1929 to advocate for orphans and the destitute.

Examining the life of this remarkable woman, it becomes clear that her determination to work hard and progress comes from an inner drive. Even in challenging times, support seems to emerge from various sources, leading to success that ultimately benefits society. Social attitudes are evolving, paving the way for future generations. We should remain vigilant about these changes. The life journey of Muthulakshmi Reddy serves as a profound source of inspiration. When a woman remains committed to righteousness and becomes an inspiring figure through her conduct and behavior, she truly becomes a guiding light for others.

Amrit Kaur

"I am looking for a woman who knows her own destiny. Are you that woman? The women I seek, will you be one of them?"

She received a letter that day.

As she read the letter, she felt inspired. She wrote back, "It is my sincere desire to free subjugated India from foreign power. That is why you ignited the fire in me."

She was better prepared to respond to the letter. Her goal was set. She made herself stronger and worked harder than ever before.

The two individuals mentioned here are two great personalities of our country. The person who wrote the letter was the Father of the Nation, Mahatma Gandhi, while the recipient was a remarkable woman. As Gandhiji's freedom struggle spread across provinces and engaged individuals from all backgrounds—regardless of caste, class, or gender—he aimed to involve more women in the national movement.

At that time, he was writing to a prominent woman who belonged to the Kapurthala dynasty. Born on February 2, 1887, in Lucknow, Uttar Pradesh (then part of the United Provinces), she was the daughter of Raja Sir Harnam Singh Ahuwalia, the youngest son of the royal family of Kapurthala, and her mother was Queen Priscilla Golaknath. The family later left Kapurthala following the untimely death of her father's elder brother.

As a child, she attended a Christian school and grew up in a Christian environment, as her mother was a Bengali Christian and her father had converted to Christianity. She excelled in her studies at Sherborne School for Girls in Dorset, England, becoming the head girl due to her academic achievements. She also played hockey and cricket, serving as captain of her school's cricket team. After completing her education at the University of Oxford, she returned to India in 1918.

After returning to India from England, she discovered that her father was closely associated with the Indian National Congress. They maintained good relations with leaders of the Congress, including Gopal Krishna Gokhale. Discussions often revolved around the various programs of the National Congress and the Indian freedom struggle, which greatly inspired her. Gandhiji's thoughts and vision particularly resonated with her, and although she never met Gandhi, she was captivated by his work and devoted herself to social service.

Transforming India became her life's mission. She aimed to dismantle colonialism while also addressing the prejudices and superstitions deeply entrenched in society.

As a social worker, she believed that society could not progress without confronting social evils such as purdah, child marriage, and the devadasi system. She often stated that child marriage is a grave social evil impacting national life. When girls are married off as children, they often become mothers before they are ready for the responsibilities leading to malnourished children who suffer from various health issues. Child marriage and the purdah system are significant barriers to women's progress.

She advocated for women's education and argued that the status of women in Hindu households, including marriage laws and inheritance rights, needed radical reform. To improve women's education, she emphasized the importance of making it free and compulsory from the start. Establishing many girls' schools and appointing trained female teachers were essential steps to universalizing women's education. Additionally, she called for a complete overhaul of the existing education system. She worked tirelessly to eradicate child marriage and the purdah system, aiming to reduce illiteracy among women.

The plight of Harijans plight deeply troubled her. She often remarked, "It is a matter of great shame for us that those who serve us with their whole hearts often live in poor conditions. Most of them do not have a home and reside in slums."

In 1919, she first met Gandhi in Bombay (now Mumbai) and was captivated by his personality. Following their meeting, she frequently wrote letters to him, and he wrote back. Although she wished to join the freedom struggle, she was initially unable to do so due to her parents' objections. After her father's death in 1930, she finally joined the movement.

On April 13, 1919, following the Jallianwala Bagh massacre in Amritsar, where British troops killed around 400 people, she became highly critical of British rule. She joined the Indian National Congress and became actively involved in the freedom struggle. Additionally, she strove to craft social awareness and bring about change. In 1927, she founded the All India Women's Conference, which has continuously promoted women's empowerment. She served as the editor of the journal in 1930 and later became its president in 1933.

In 1929, she dedicated herself to the Civil Disobedience Movement and traveled to Sewa village in Wadda, where Gandhi appointed her as his secretary, a position she held for 17 years. In 1930, she formally participated in the freedom movement by joining the Dandi March led by Gandhi. By 1934, she moved to Gandhi's ashram, willingly giving up her luxurious lifestyle for a life of austere simplicity.

In 1937, she relocated to Bandhu (now in Khyber-Pakhtunkhwa) as a representative of the Indian National Congress and was subsequently imprisoned by the British on charges of treason. Later, the authorities appointed her to the Advisory Board of Education, but she resigned to join the Quit India Movement in 1942, which led to her imprisonment again. During this time, she brought with her a charkha, the Bhagavad Gita, and the Bible. She was so close to Gandhi that she wrote to him every evening while in jail. This collection of letters was later titled *Letters to Princess Amrit Kaur*.

She served as the president of the All India Women's Education Fund Association and was a member of the Governing Council of Lady Irwin College in New Delhi. She represented India twice at the UNESCO Conferences in London and Paris in 1945 and 1946. Additionally, she was a member of the Board of Trustees for the All India Spinners Association.

After India gained independence in 1947, she joined the first cabinet of independent India's Prime Minister, Pandit Jawaharlal Nehru, becoming the first woman to hold a cabinet position. She was appointed Minister of Health and served in that role for ten years, during which she implemented many exemplary initiatives in the Indian health sector. In 1950, she was elected president of the World Health Assembly, becoming the first Asian woman to hold this position. Notably, in the first 25 years of the World Health Assembly, only two women were elected to this office.

As Minister of Health, she played a crucial role in establishing the All India Institute of Medical Sciences (AIIMS) in New Delhi and was its first president. She successfully raised funds for AIIMS from various countries, including New Zealand, Australia, West Germany, Sweden, and the United States. Along with her brother, she donated their extensive ancestral property in Shimla for the benefit of nurses, providing a place for nurses and other staff to spend holidays.

She also served as the president of the Indian Red Cross Society for 14 years, during which she contributed notably to development work. Furthermore, she was the president of the Indian Leprosy Association and the Chief Commissioner of the St. John's Ambulance Brigade. She initiated the National Sports Club of India and was the founder and first president of the Indian Council for Child Welfare, benefiting thousands of children. From 1954 to 1963, she was a member of the All India Motor Transport Congress.

There are numerous examples of the revolutionary role women

played in our mythology. Their strength and role in the search for truth and societal transformation extend beyond these mythologies; this journey of revolutionary consciousness among women has carried over from myth to historical reality.

When our country was enslaved, women were often veiled and faced tremendous challenges. It was difficult for them to break free from this veil. Many had to endure lack of education and suffered from various ailments. They were trapped by practices such as child marriage and sati. Yet, despite these challenges, they sought solutions to women's issues and aimed to bring them into the mainstream. They fought tirelessly, not allowing the storms of life to deter them. They persevered without patience or fear, striving to change the status of women in society. One remarkable woman who exemplified this spirit is Princess Amrit Kaur.

Princess Kaur was born on February 2, 1887, and lived until her death in February 1964 at the age of 75. She was a member of the Rajya Sabha from 1957 until her passing. After India gained independence in 1947, she became a member of the Constituent Assembly of India.

At that time, The New York Times named two Indian women among the 100 most influential women in the world: former Prime Minister Indira Gandhi and freedom fighter Princess Amrit Kaur.

The great freedom fighter Aruna Asaf Ali praised her, saying, "Princess Amrit Kaur has played a leading role in laying the foundation for many things. Despite being a princess, she left her luxurious lifestyle, stepped out of her home, followed Gandhiji, and worked inspired by his ideals. She lived a simple life."

What an incredible woman and a remarkable role model she is!

◻◻

Gulab Kaur

Since the time God created woman, he has assigned her various roles: as a daughter, a sister, a wife, and a mother. Each woman brings her own style to these roles involving specific relationships. Family is often a woman's top priority, and for a long time, her world revolved around it. Many women in my life chose not to step outside the domestic sphere, finding joy in their families. Yet, there exists a vast world beyond the confines of home, filled with possibilities that can add color and freshness to life.

Women have their own minds, hopes, and desires—something that has often been overlooked. For many, the country, the world, and their ambitions were largely confined to familial boundaries.

However, some women recognized that they had responsibilities that extended beyond the boundaries of their families. They understood the importance of stepping outside these confines to contribute to the well-being of their society and their country. They faced various obstacles in fulfilling these duties, all the while prioritizing the goal of making their country free.

Among the countless freedom fighters who participated in the struggle for independence, there was a remarkable woman who placed her country before her family. She made the difficult decision of leaving her husband and joining the fight for freedom. Ultimately, she sacrificed her life abroad for her country's cause. She became a prominent member of the Gadar Party, which pursued armed resistance rather than Gandhi's nonviolent approach.

Bibi Gulab Kaur, known for her intrepidity, was born into a farmer's family in the village of Bakshiwala, located in the Sangrur district of Punjab, in 1890. She married at a very young age to a poor farmer named Man Singh. During this time, Indians faced severe oppression under British rule, which made life extremely difficult for them. In hopes of alleviating their poverty and improving their family's situation, Gulab Kaur and her husband decided to seek work abroad.

Their journey led them to Manila, Philippines, from where they planned to travel to America. However, they encountered discrimination and inequality as Indians abroad, which deeply affected them. During this period, Indians in the United States and Canada formed Gadar Party in San Francisco. Established around 1913-14 during World War I, this revolutionary organization initially aimed to protect the rights of Indians in the US, the Philippines, Hong Kong, and Singapore. The main objective of the Party was to end British rule in India. It was founded by Sardar Sohan Singh, with prominent leaders including Baba Hafiz Abdullah (Faza), Baba Banta Singh, and Baba Harnam Singh. The party believed that an armed struggle was necessary to drive the British out of India.

While in Manila, Gulab Kaur was on her way to attend a Gadar Party meeting. The party emphasized that members should prioritize national interests over religious sentiments. Religion was to remain a personal belief, but it should not influence the organization's objectives. At that time, the Gadar Party was publishing a newspaper called *Hindustan Patra*, which highlighted the misdeeds of the British government. Gulab Kaur was impressed by the party's program and became an active member, participating in its activities and encouraging other Indians abroad to join the movement.

In 1930, a ship named the SS Korea, carrying 50 Indians including Gulab Kaur, was set to return to India from the Philippines under the leadership of Hafiz Abdullah. Their plan was to intensify the independence movement by supplying arms to the Indian armed struggle. However, at the last moment, Gulab Kaur's husband, Man Singh, changed his mind. He refused to return to India and did not allow Gulab Kaur to go either. Feeling betrayed by her husband, Gulab Kaur was furious. In her anger, she scolded him harshly, threw away her bangles, and decided to leave him to return to India with her revolutionary comrades.

Upon arriving in India with her 50 companions, all armed, Gulab Kaur continued her struggle in Kapurthala, Jalandhar, and Hoshiarpur in Punjab. One of her main tasks was to manage a printing press, and she was also involved in supplying weapons to members of the Gadar Party.

To maintain her cover, Gulab Kaur carried a media pass as a journalist. She provided arms to party members and distributed leaflets. In her capacity as a journalist, she closely monitored the printing press and the distribution of weapons. However, her activities eventually caught the attention of the British authorities. Gulab Kaur was arrested by the British police on charges of treason and was sent to Lahore Jail, where she was sentenced to two years of probation. During her time in jail, she was subjected to brutal torture by the British police, and her health deteriorated significantly. She died just a few days after her release from prison.

Gulab Kaur's contributions have been largely overlooked in books on Indian history. However, S. Kesar Singh has written a volume titled *Gadar Dhi Gulab Kaur (Daughter of Gadar: Gulab Kaur)*, which was published in 2014, that highlights her story. Regardless of how much attention she receives in historical accounts, one thing is clear: throughout history and under various circumstances, women have consistently devoted themselves to the betterment of society. Gulab Kaur is an exemplary figure, having sacrificed her husband and a comfortable life for the sake of her country.

Iqbalunnisa Hussain

Generally speaking, the attitude towards women was dismissive. It was said, "Women and animals only deserve to be persecuted." However, women have their own thoughts, and perspectives. They can think, speak, make decisions, and define themselves. Women understand the dynamics of their homes and the world; they can navigate society with confidence. They set positive examples through their actions and leave a lasting impact with their valuable contributions. This capability was often overlooked, but women accomplished tasks that exceeded everyone's expectations, proving many enhanced assumptions wrong.

Women learned to recognize their worth, voiced their opinions, and skillfully balanced responsibilities within the household while also engaging with the wider world. They managed the duties assigned to them as well as those typically allotted to men, walking side by side with men in society. They represented themselves, found their own solutions to problems, and firmly established their presence in every field, paving new paths for future generations.

However, this transformation does not happen overnight; it is a long and arduous journey for women. It is difficult to fully comprehend the struggles they face. Change occurred gradually, requiring different approaches to problems at various times. Along the way, they endured hardships to ensure that future generations do not repeat their struggles and do not succumb to obstacles.

This chapter focuses on a woman who illuminated a new path for the next generation—a social reformer dedicated to fighting for the rights and education of Muslim women. Born in Bangalore, Karnataka, in 1897, she was fortunate to come from a patriotic family that encouraged her to receive an education. Her parents motivated their daughters to learn as many languages as possible. From a young age, she had a deep interest in English. Her parents hired a female teacher to introduce her to English literature. She was a diligent student with a keen interest in higher education, but she faced setbacks when she married at the young age of fifteen.

Her husband, Syed Ahmed Hussain, worked as a government official in Mysore. Despite marrying so young, her desire for higher education remained undiminished. She explored her wishes to her husband, who readily supported her aspirations. Encouraged by him, she was able to continue her education and pursue her academic interests, furthering her journey toward empowerment.

She passed the I.A. examination in 1922 while pregnant with her child. Remarkably, when she was admitted to Maharani's College in Mysore to study for her B.A., her eldest son, Basirjaman, was also studying there. Both mother and son were awarded gold medals at the graduation ceremony.

Higher education was not her only goal; she wanted to explore how education could be applied to better the societal order. Her primary aim was to work for the empowerment of women. She was deeply concerned about how women could break free from the confines of their homes, obtain an education, and integrate themselves into the mainstream. She sought to eliminate practices like child marriage and to challenge limitations imposed on women, particularly Muslim women, who were often confined to their homes and treated like slaves.

These women faced numerous challenges due to the intersection of culture, tradition, and religion. In many Muslim families, men dominated decision-making processes, and women's lives were dictated by male preferences, which often resulted in much suffering. She recognized the many obstacles Muslim women encountered and felt that the treatment they received was deeply unfair and unjust. She believed that women should not be subjected to such harassment and that it was essential to raise our voices against these injustices.

Instead of remaining passive, she actively spoke out against social evils, including the purdah system, polygamy, and the mistreatment of women. Criticizing practices like child marriage, she pointed out that such traditions forced girls into domestic work at a young age, weakening them both mentally and physically. She continuously encouraged Muslim women to assert their rights with dignity and to fight for their financial independence.

She was fluent in Urdu, Persian, and English and worked as a teacher in a primary school. This was just the beginning of her journey. However, her true goal was not only her own education but also the education and upliftment of other women like her. She was always passionate about achieving this mission. Her life was marked by a relentless determination; she was never carefree or irresponsible.

To educate girls and inspire them to value education, she faced extreme societal resistances. Rather than being discouraged, these challenges only emboldened her to continue her quest. As a result, she established an Urdu medium school for girls. But it was more than just a school; she recognized that the existing education system made women feel mentally and physically incapable of leaving their homes or pursuing work. So she advocated for vocational education to empower women and helped organize Muslim women teachers, significantly raising the status of Muslim women within the educational faculty. Additionally, she opened a private industrial school for Muslim women in Bangalore and actively participated in the Girl Guide movement. As a strong supporter of women's education, she encouraged parents to send their daughters to school.

Even after getting married, having a child, and managing her household, she maintained her passionate commitment to education. She completed her undergraduate degree but yearned for further education in England. Nevertheless, her social work continued, as she involved women in the movement for social change.

She tirelessly worked to bring widows and women abandoned by their husbands into the societal mainstream. Despite facing widespread criticism, particularly from hardline Muslims who viewed her social service as disgraceful, she remained undeterred. Her strong feminist views fueled her commitment to uplifting women, regardless of the opposition she faced from the Muslim community.

In 1931, when she decided to stop wearing the veil, it marked a significant turning-point in her life. This bold move sparked considerable opposition from many community members, who resorted to derogatory remarks and even threats. However, these failed to demoralise her. She persevered work ethic, supported by her husband, Syed Ahmed Hussain, who was not only her friend and guide but also her mentor. He respected all her decisions, provided her with valuable guidance, and ensured her safety.

Undeterred by obstacles, she established a handicraft school for widows and orphans in 1931. She took a clever step to ease tensions by enrolling her first daughter, Malaika Hussain, in the same school.

In 1933, her husband sent her and their eldest son to the University of Leeds in England for higher education. At the time, she was the mother of seven children. Studying in England proved to be quite challenging for her, as she struggled to adjust to the new environment. Despite the difficulties, she persevered and continued her studies, ultimately earning a master's degree from the University of Leeds. Notably, she became the first woman from Karnataka to achieve this impressive feat. Her education and experiences provided her with a new perspective on the role of women in Muslim culture.

After completing her education at the University of Leeds, she worked as an assistant teacher at Vani Vilas High School in Bangalore. She later became the headmaster of an Urdu-medium school in the city. Alongside social workers Kamalama and Nanajama from the Mahila Seva Samaj in Bangalore, she traveled across the country to promote women's education and welfare initiatives. Disguised as a Hindu woman, she visited pilgrimage sites such as Benares and Haridwar.

In addition to her advocacy for social reform and the upliftment of women, she began writing about feminist issues. In her writings, she emphasized the importance of women's rights. Her work culminated in the publication of a book in 1940 titled *Changing India: A Muslim Woman Speaks*. In 1944, she wrote another book, *Purdah and Polygamy*, in which she criticized the societal and cultural discrimination faced by women and called for changes in the narrow-mindedness prevailing in society. She noted, "Discrimination against women is not a new phenomenon; it has long existed in our society." She highlighted the disparity in status between men and women, which has been evident throughout history.

While studying at the University of London, she focused on the rights of individuals and the state. Her book *Purdah and Polygamy* became one of the most widely read works of its time. Written in English by a Muslim woman in pre-Partition India, this imaginative novel is remarkable for several reasons. It received a positive response from a limited readership, which is surprising. Literary critic Munizah Shamsi describes the book as prioritizing new research and intellectual ideas over religious ones. For over a decade, the novel was available in only nine libraries worldwide.

Jessica Berman, a professor at American University, who researches gender inequality and women's rights, explores a favourable view of the book. Later, additional articles were included in the book, along with valuable comments made by eminent personalities on these articles. *Purdah and Polygamy* addresses social and practical matters, centering on an unnamed Muslim family living in Dilkusha, a neighborhood that represents many urban centers in India. Set during the twelfth year of colonial rule, the novel depicts the gender-related tensions and conflicts within Muslim families in India.

The story features a zamindar named Umar, who instructs all members of his household to watch over his wife, Zuhra. Placing her under a strict regime of purdah, he prevents her from accessing any family finances. In the opening pages, we learn that Umar has died from cancer, leaving behind his wife, daughter, and only son, Kabir. At the time of his father's death, Kabir is only 16 years old and takes charge of his father's estate. Together with her son Kabir, Zuhra gradually assumes control of the household and asserts her authority over the family. Much of the novel explores the relationship between mother and son.

The novel discusses various issues related to rights. Zuhra eventually takes on the responsibility of Kabir's four wives, highlighting Kabir's dissatisfaction with any single marriage, leading him to marry multiple times. His first wife, Nazneen, is described as extremely weak and ill, his second wife, Munira, is deemed unattractive and ordinary, and his third wife, Magboul, is portrayed as fiercely modern and independent. The narrative approaches its conclusion following Kabir's fourth marriage to Noor Jahan, allowing readers to clearly perceive his incompetence in managing relationships.

After the deaths of Kabir and his mother, his son Akram assumes his father's responsibilities, while his mother Nazni rules the family with an iron fist. Eventually, the family inherits land, which becomes significant in the story. The author's frustration with prevailing customs in Muslim society is evident throughout the novel. She uses sarcasm to highlight the privileges afforded to men in society. For instance, she explores the concepts of submission, subjection, and slavery, all of which hold various degrees of significance. Her narrative effectively critiques the male-centric view of relationships, presenting it as beneficial for both genders. As a man's self-esteem grows, so does that of a woman. In contrast, a woman who lacks this recognition suffers humiliation.

The author also portrays female characters like Magboul in her novel. As an independent-minded writer, she has consistently criticized polygamy and opposed the practice of purdah while interacting with men and relatives. In her story, Magboul emerges as more capable than Kabir's first two wives. Together with her father, she engages in a financial venture, earning a substantial income from it. A tragic turn occurs when Magboul leaves Dilkusha behind in his final moments. Her character emphasizes that women can endure and thrive through their own resilience. Additionally, the author delves into the loving relationship between Magboul and Kabir's second wife, Munira, suggesting the possibility of female unity despite their differing interests. According to the author, this bond, formed through shared experiences, signifies strength among women.

The novel in question was published more than seventy years ago, in 1940. Turkish-born scholar Deniz Kandiyoti (1988) described it as a portrayal of "classic patriarchy." One of the most tragic incidents depicted in the story involves a man living among many women, which leads to conflict among them. For example, the relationship between Zuhra and her daughters-in-law is strained. Zuhra consistently tries to prevent them from getting too close to her son, fearing that such closeness would undermine her control and authority within the family. While Zuhra's character is often portrayed with a bad temperament, her behaviour is rough and rude.

Following the publication of the novel, the practice of polygamy saw a decline in society. Purdah became less common in urban areas than in rural ones, yet within families, numerous difficulties persisted regarding women's economic status, education, mobility, and self-reliance.

During a time when women faced powerful opposition, Iqbalunnisa Hussain emerged as an ardent advocate for change through her writings. While many Muslim writers of the period expressed views supportive of women, Hussain distinguished herself by featuring female characters as the protagonists of her novels, whereas male characters were more prominent in the works of her contemporaries. Despite this focus on female heroines, their influence can still be traced in pre-independence Muslim literature.

During the pre-independence period, the growing knowledge of English literature among women was a notable trend. Many female writers contributed to the enrichment of Indian culture in English, including notable Hindu authors like Kamala Das, Kamala Markandeya, Ruth Prawer Jhabvala, and Anita Desai. However, Muslim writers did not achieve the same level of influence during this time.

Iqbalunnisa Husain holds a unique position among pre-independence Indian women writers. Unlike her male contemporaries, her writings focused on a limited range of topics, primarily detailing the status of Muslim women in society and the family. She often depicted them as captive pigeons.

During the Indian freedom movement, a time of significant societal change, writers like Iqbalunnisa recognized the need to alter the mindset of women within Muslim society. In her book *Purdah and Polygamy*, she emphasizes the necessity for change. Her perspective reflected a realistic portrayal of concrete truths, setting her apart from her contemporaries who wrote fiction. Iqbalunnisa believed that non-Muslim writers could not accurately depict the real problems faced by Muslim women. She argued that the representations of purdah and polygamy by Hindu writers were insufficiently accurate.

Her novel tells the story of three generations of a conservative Muslim business family living in one of India's most prosperous cities. The patriarch, Omar, is portrayed as a wealthy, traditionalist blindly adhering to customs. He rented out six rooms in his house, leading four families to live in cramped conditions with inadequate light and ventilation.

When Omar fell ill with cancer, his ill-equipped and illiterate son Kabir became the head of the family. This situation exacerbated the living conditions, as the number of families in the house increased. Kabir arranged her marriage with a girl from a wealthy family without consulting his mother, as he trusted his new wife. However, his mother disapproved of the marriage. When her wife gave birth to a child, Kabir sent for a doctor against his mother's wishes, who insisted that the traditional approach was sufficient and that complete rest was necessary. His mother even suggested that Kabir remarry, which caused emotional distress for his first wife.

Through her narrative, Iqbalunnisa shows how Muslim culture often undermines the power of women. The struggles faced by Kabir's first wife highlight her lack of agency. As a result of this oppressive atmosphere, Kabir's first wife endured numerous hardships. Pressured by his mother, Kabir agreed to marry a second girl chosen by her after his first wife went to Kashmir for treatment.

In a surprising twist, after marrying his second wife, Kabir took a third wife. This third wife was beautiful, intelligent, and simple, with her parents supportive of the match. Tragically, she was the third daughter of their parents, which, in Muslim culture, is considered inauspicious. Thus, the societal expectation forced the family to marry her off to Kabir.

Kabir's first wife returned home one day and was shocked to see her husband's third wife. The new wife was very proud, being a writer who had published her work in various journals. She also loved her husband's poetry, and since Kabir was a poet, he encouraged her to write. However, Kabir's mother did not appreciate his creative endeavours at all.

Time passed, Kabir grew older, and his first wife's son reached adulthood. To everyone's surprise, Kabir began a relationship with a widow. After Kabir married her, his three wives did not accept this new addition to the family.

The ignorance of women is a common phenomenon in Muslim culture, and polygamy is an inhumane practice that has caused the suffering of thousands of women. This was a frequently observed situation in society at that time. The new wife expressed her feelings through her writing, critiquing the problems affecting culture.

Kabir's third wife was a cultured, brave, and creative woman, but she struggled to confront these societal issues. Iqbal un-Nisa vividly portrayed her challenges and eventual defeat.

In his book *Nationalism in Indo-Anglian Fiction*, Govind Prasad Sharma argues that a better, happier society can be built by addressing and reforming societal systems. The writer does not shy away from discussing religion. The narrative is vibrant, and the characters are deftly crafted, providing an emotional depth that resonates with readers.

As a feminist, Iqbal un-Nisa's writings have a significant impact compared to others. In this context, her book *Purdah and Polygamy* shares themes with *Sunlight on a Broken Column* by Atiya Hussain. Both books call for social change within Muslim culture. While Atiya Hussain's book narrates the experiences of two generations, Iqbal un-Nisa's *Purdah and Polygamy* recounts the story of four women and one man, recording the dissatisfaction that has arisen regarding polygamy. Iqbal un-Nisa effectively conveys the underlying realities through her dialogues. She presents a meaningful message while maintaining her characters' discipline in a simple, accessible Indian English style.

During that time, there were very few writers in India who wrote in English. In the pre-independence era, only two Muslim women writers did so, and while their contributions to literature were significant, they were not widely recognized. However, in terms of content and literary value, their contributions to Indian literature are remarkable. In fact, it is impossible to discuss pre-independence Indian literature without analyzing the works of these two writers. In summary, Indian Muslim women novelists have effectively portrayed the status of women in politics, culture, and social dynamics. They recognized that violence against women is often a reflection of men's excessive pride and selfishness. Addressing the problems faced by women was the primary goal of writers at that time. Many believe that *Purdah and Polygamy* was not merely a novel, but an ode to the oppression faced by women.

After returning to India from England, Hussain fully dedicated herself to the task of reforming society. At that time, several contemporary reformers opposed her efforts, which fueled resentment within the Muslim community. Many men in her community felt threatened by her progressive endeavours. She faced trenchant criticism from conservative members of her community, but she remained undeterred. Despite the opposition, she successfully represented India at the 12th International Women's Conference in Istanbul, making a lasting impact on the next generation of women.

Khwaja Altaf Hussain wrote a novel titled *Voices of the Silent*, which highlighted the atrocities committed against women. Muslim scholar and human rights advocate Mumtaz Ali, along with his wife Mohammadi Begum, founded a newspaper called *Tehzeeb-e-Niswaan*, which brought attention to issues such as child marriage and advocated for proper marriage and education for women.

Iqbalunnisa Husain's writings emerged alongside other contemporary voices, but she was the only woman writer from the Muslim community at that time whose thoughts forged a unique path. Her work became a benchmark for success and merit, challenging the men of her community. Despite facing opposition, she continued to write tirelessly, leaving an indelible impact on the next generation.

In the 19th century, Muslim women lived under various social, traditional, and orthodox constraints. Iqbalunnisa devoted her time to caring for her family and fulfilling societal expectations, often being constrained by personal laws that dictated her life based on religious and moral ideals. However, she relentlessly sought to break free from these constraints.

As a strong advocate for social service, Iqbalunnisa fought for the rights of widows and other marginalized women. She also championed women's education, encouraging parents to send their daughters to school. No matter the challenges she faced, her steadfast spirit and determination allowed her to overcome obstacles.

Her strength has always been a powerful force for change. Society is evolving, creating new opportunities for women. The path that once was rough, thorny, and arduous has transformed into one that is more navigable. Today, women step forward with confidence, empowered by newfound knowledge and circumstances. Success now awaits at the top, and it is women who are leading the way.

□□

Janaki Ammal

It's the year 1970 in the state of Kerala. To provide more electricity and create job opportunities for the local population, the Government of India planned to build a hydroelectric power plant, which would require clearing approximately 8.3 square kilometers of old evergreen forests. They hoped this project would be successful; however, it posed serious threats to the region's flora.

An 80-year-old woman strongly believed that this project would harm the plant world and advocated for the preservation of the rich, biodiversity-filled forest. Despite her age, she was determined and led a movement, fighting relentlessly for her cause. Ultimately, she succeeded, and the Silent Valley National Park in Kerala was established, showcasing around a thousand species of trees, including various endangered orchids and numerous native flowers.

This national park, which was once destined for destruction, now stands as a testament to her accomplishments as a prominent botanist.

Throughout her life, she developed many hybrid crops and plant varieties. She imported different types of sweet sugarcane from abroad and cultivated local varieties through experimentation and grafting. Additionally, she researched the cytogenetics of different species of brinjal.

After returning from her studies abroad, she played a crucial role in the conservation of native plants in India and gained recognition as a leading botanist championing an indigenous approach to environmental preservation.

This woman was extraordinary, and her work has served as an example for many. Social attitudes towards women, as well as those towards girls, have evolved. There is no turning back on her journey, regardless of the circumstances or the environment that surrounds them. We have many examples of such women; no matter how difficult the struggle, the path to success can be challenging.

Born on November 4, 1897, in Tellicherry (now Thalassery), Kerala, she left a lasting legacy through her exemplary work. She was the tenth child of her parents. Her father, Edavalath Kakkavath Krishnan, served as a judge in a lower court in Tellicherry, while her mother, Goddess Karuvai (Krishnan), was highly educated. The family resided in a large house by the sea, known as Edathala House, where she grew up.

Her family's matriarchal tradition provided her with a unique and valuable opportunity, as women were encouraged to pursue higher education. Although not everyone could take advantage of such opportunities, if one possessed the desire and strong will to fulfill their ambitions, success was attainable. She had a deep interest in reading, and her supportive family encouraged her to further her education. Choosing to study botany was an unusual choice for women in her era.

An important influence on her life was her father's passion for gardening. He created a vast garden in front of their home, filled with beautiful flowers and a variety of plants, all meticulously cared for. He even authored two books on the birds of the North Malabar region. Growing up in such a beautiful environment deepened her attraction to nature and plant science. One claims of this from an article written on her by her niece, Dr. Geeta.

Although she had a matrilineal heritage and access to higher education, she could not escape gender discrimination. At that time, the presence of a single woman in academic institutions was often unwelcome. However, she remained determined to achieve her goals. The societal limitations and gender barriers she faced did not succeed in making her deviate from her aspirations. She went to London to continue her research. During the chaos of World War II, she worked as a specialist cytologist at the John Innes Horticultural Institution in London from 1940 to 1945. Afterwards, she served as a cytologist at the Royal Horticultural Society in Wisley from 1945 to 1951.

In an era when many questioned the value of a girl's education, she faced potent challenges as a student seeking opportunities abroad. Her determination and hard work were remarkable, yet sadly, her story remains unknown to many. She was an extraordinary Indian woman whose passion for reading and learning defined her.

Dr. Edavaleeth Kakkath Janaki Ammal was the first Indian woman botanist and the first woman to earn a doctorate in botany from the United States. A victim of gender discrimination, she set an example for others by overcoming various social barriers to realise her dreams.

As Ammal's siblings grew up and got married, she was expected to follow suit. However, when her turn came, she chose a different path. Despite pressure from others, she refused to marry and instead committed herself to higher education. She graduated from Queen Mary's College, Madras, and obtained a degree in Botany from Presidency College in 1921, earning a scholar honors degree in the process.

After graduating with an honours degree in botany, Janaki Ammal received a unique opportunity in the field of education. Prior to this, she taught at the Women's Christian College in Madras for three years. A significant opportunity arose when she was awarded a scholarship in 1917, provided by philanthropist Levi Bagwora, specifically for the higher education of Asian women. In 1924, she was able to study botany at the University of Michigan through the Barbour Scholarship. Despite being a prestigious student and traveling to the U.S. for higher education, Ammal, like many travelers, was detained at Ellis Island until her immigration status was cleared, as noted by her niece, Dr.

Geeta. Interestingly, her long hair and traditional Indian silk attire led to her being mistaken for an Indian princess. When asked about it, she playfully did not dispel the impression.

While at the University of Michigan, she focused on plant cytology, genetic composition, and gene variation, specializing in interspecies and intergeneric hybrids. Ammal completed her Master of Science in 1925 and received her doctorate in 1931, becoming the first Indian woman to earn a science degree in the U.S.

In 1940, Ammal moved to Norfolk, England, to work at the John Innes Institute. There, she collaborated with C. D. Darlington on plant genetics. At that time, Darlington was researching how chromosomes influenced heredity. Together, they significantly contributed to the Chromosome Atlas of Cultivated Plants, which remains an important resource for plant scientists. This atlas documented the chromosome numbers of about 100,000 plants, helping to reveal the reproductive and evolutionary patterns of various botanical groups.

Janaki Ammal worked with Darlington from 1940 to 1945, during World War II, when London was being bombed by German forces. Reflecting on her harrowing experiences, Ammal recounted how she sought shelter under her mattress during the blasts. Afterward, she cleaned up the broken glass and debris from damaged walls, and despite these challenges, she continued her research with unwavering determination.

In 1946, the Royal Horticultural Society at Wisley offered Dr. Janaki Ammal a position as a cytologist. She left the John Innes Institute and joined the Royal Horticultural Society as its first paid female employee. During her time there, she focused on the botanical applications of colchicine, a medicine that can double the number of plant chromosomes and help plants grow faster. One of the notable results of her research is the hybrid 'Magnolia Cobus Janaki Ammal', which features white or pale pink flowers. Though Ammal returned to India in 1950, the flowers blooming from the seeds she planted at Wisley serve as a lasting reminder of her contributions. She is honored in the famous garden at Wisley, where flowers bloom every spring, and a delicate white magnolia flower has been named in her memory.

In addition to this, a newly developed yellow hybrid rose at the John Innes Centre in England has also been named after her to honour her life and work. This rose is called E.K. Janaki Ammal.

During her lifetime, India faced several famines, including the devastating Bengal famine of 1943, which resulted in a terrible loss of life. In response to the looming agricultural crisis, Prime Minister Jawaharlal Nehru sought the expertise of Dr. Janaki Ammal, India's first woman botanist. She accepted his request and returned to India in 1950 as an officer on special duty for the renovation of the Botanical Survey of India (BSI). Nehru played a crucial role in this endeavor, and Ammal's work significantly impacted agriculture in post-independence India, where she made substantial contributions during her three-decade-long career in various government sectors.

Dr. Ammal identified several hybrid varieties of high-yielding sugarcane suited for the Indian climate and conducted research on plant varieties for cross-breeding.

Nehru entrusted her with roles, including directing the Central Botanical Laboratory in Lucknow. In these positions, Ammal worked diligently to reorganize the BSI, which was established in 1890. However, she expressed concerns about certain measures implemented by the Indian government to increase food production. In 1940, the government reclaimed 25 million acres of land for food production, primarily for cereals. Ammal's correspondence with Darlington was noted by historian Vinit Damodaran, who remarked on the negative impact of deforestation on local ecosystems. Sadly, during her travels, she found only one tree, Magnolia Griffithii, remaining in Assam after traveling 37 miles from Shillong, highlighting the environmental challenges she was passionate about addressing.

Since then, Ammal's career has taken a different turn. After spending decades applying her techniques to improve the commercial use of plants, she began to focus on preserving perishable native plants. One of her main goals for the Botanical Survey of India (BSI) was to collect and preserve plant specimens from all corners of the country. She envisioned a BSI that would be run by Indian scientists and aimed to protect endangered plants in India.

When the government took over the BSI from the British for the first time, they appointed a European, Hermenegild Santapu, as the director. This decision left Ammal feeling unfairly overlooked. In a letter to Darlington, she expressed her anger and anguish over the appointment. Historian Damodaran quoted her saying, "I bring to you the news of a great defeat for botany in India. The government has chosen a man of Kew tradition as the Chief Botanist of India, and I have to take instructions from him even though I am the Director of the Central Botanical Laboratory. This time, we won and we lost. Despite India's independence from British rule, we are still subjugated."

Ammal believed that if specimens were collected by foreign botanists and studied solely in British herbaria, no genuine systematic study of Indian plants could be conducted. "How do you create revitalized botanical surveys, both in terms of collection and research, that can enable new discoveries?" she pondered. With this in mind, Ammal submitted a memorandum stating, "In the last thirty years, plants collected in India have mainly been gathered by foreign botanists and often tested in institutions outside India. They are now found in various gardens and herbaria across Europe, making modern research on the flora of India more intense outside the country than at home. And this remains a problem."

To preserve Indian plants, Ammal recognized the necessity of valuing indigenous knowledge. As an expert, she was particularly interested in the Imperial Sugarcane Institute (now a sugar factory) in Coimbatore. This institution aimed to cultivate the indigenous sugarcane crop, specifically the sweet variety (Saccharum officinarum), which was being imported from Java. However, with Ammal's interest and assistance, the institute shifted its focus to developing its own sweet cane varieties instead of relying on imports. This change significantly increased both the quantity and sweetness of sugarcane cultivation in India.

Ammal's research on hybrid crops enabled the institute to develop new varieties of plants by combining native species with other breeds.

She consistently experimented with different types of grasses to create better hybrids and sweeter sugarcane. Through this process, she developed several grass species using hybrid techniques, including Sakram-Jia, Sakram Arians, Sakram Imorata, and Sakram Sorghum.

In 1955, Ammal was the only woman to attend an international conference in Chicago, which helped to shift perceptions of women among men worldwide. The conference covered a variety of topics, including how human activities alter the environment and influence our evolutionary process, either knowingly or unknowingly. In a room full of foreign men, she spoke about India's supportive economy, the significance of tribal culture, the cultivation of indigenous plants, women's access to higher education, and the importance of the Indian matrilineal tradition that values women as stewards of family and wealth.

As a scientist, Janaki Ammal was a pioneer in restoring forest land and addressing the gender gap.

In her later years, Ammal lent her voice to the environmental campaign 'Save Silent Valley,' which aimed to halt a hydropower project that would inundate a valuable forest area. By the time she joined the protesters and activists, she had already established herself as a prominent figure in Indian science and held the title of scientist emeritus at the Centre for Advanced Studies in Botany at the University of Madras. Her scientific career and passion for indigenous natural plants ultimately brought her back to India after her time abroad. In a letter to Darlington, she wrote, "I am about to embark on an adventure. I have decided to conduct a chromosome survey of the trees in the forests of Silchap Valley, which will be turned into a lake by the release of water from the Kunti River."

Using her scientific expertise, Ammal led a chromosome survey of the valley's plants to preserve the botanical knowledge of the area. In the 1970s, she spearheaded a powerful environmental movement.

Thanks to her tireless efforts in environmental activism, the government eventually abandoned its project in the region, and the forest was declared a national park on November 15, 1984. Sadly, Ammal did not live to see this outcome; she passed away on February 7, 1984, just nine months before her 87th birthday.

In 2015, Dr. Geeta wrote in an article, "Dr. Ammal never liked to talk about herself. She believed that her work would live on forever." Indeed, she was right—her contributions, from the sweetness of sugarcane to preserving biodiversity of Silent Valley and the blooming magnolias of Weasly, bear eloquent testimony to her unique achievements.

After her retirement, Ammal continued to do research which focused on medicinal plants and ethnobotany, and she conducted her studies at the Centre's Film Laboratory in MaduraVoyal, near Madras, until her death in February 1984.

Ammal received numerous awards and honors for her work. She was elected to the Indian Academy of Sciences in 1935 and the Indian National Science Academy in 1957. In 1977, she was awarded the Padma Shri by the Government of India. In 2000, the Ministry of Environment and Forests established a National Award for Plant Taxonomy, named the 'Janaki Ammal National Award' in her honor. Additionally, the Janaki Ammal Herbarium at the Indian Institute of Integrative Medicine in Jammu serves as a tribute to her legacy.

Ammal led a highly organized professional life, while her personal life was also well-structured. She lived simply, and her colleagues often described her as "quiet, unobtrusive," with actions that were "active and dynamic." Throughout her life, she had a deep love for animals and an enduring fascination with all types of plants—be they crops, medicinal plants, or wild flora.

When asked about her life, she simply says, "My work will tell about my life and it will live forever." She approached everything with diligence. In fact, it is her work that endures and has earned her considerable praise and public recognition. With her achievements, Ammal has undoubtedly become a guiding light for women in the 21st century.

Dr. Janaki Ammal's life story is compelling, particularly given her position as a woman in the 20th century, during a time of visible gender disparity in education. In 1913, female education in India was limited; the female literacy rate was less than 1%.

She stands as a guiding light for the entire nation, consistently demonstrating that India is great and that women from this great country are equally remarkable.

Vijaylakshmi Pandit

Woman! Although the word is made up of a few letters and is small in size, it is not possible for anyone to fully understand its meaning and importance. It's amazing how the word encompasses! Words, like mind, heart, happiness, laughter, sadness... Maybe small words but they have a depth of meaning. The small word 'woman' has such a depth that women possess rare qualities of perseverance, truthfulness, and extraordinary efficiency. If we sit and discuss this word, its meanings will keep ramifying endlessly. A woman is beautiful in her own way. She has broadened her horizons with the passage of time; her work, responsibilities, duties are acquiring greater significance with the passage of time.

Women have created a special place for themselves in society. However, a woman's life is never easy. She faces many challenges. But the woman continues to do her work. Once a woman is strong, she continues to grow stronger. Continue to be more patient. No matter what obstructs her, she never fails. The most important thing is that her success is not only hers, it ensures the success of her next generation. Looking at the entire journey of a woman's life, even if she walks on the thorny path herself, she always tries to make the path of the next generation easier.

Let's turn our attention to a great woman who forged a new path for generations to come. She was born in Allahabad, India in 1900. Her father was a famous barrister. Her mother was a Kashmiri who lived in Lahore. Born in such a family, this woman was attracted to politics from a very tender age. At the age of 16, she attended her first public meeting. Organised by one of her cousins, Rameshwari, the political meeting was supposed to discuss the oppression of workers in South Africa. The girl actively participated in the discussions. In 1921, at the age of 21, she was married to Ranjit Sitaram Pandit, a well-known barrister from Kathiyawad in Gujarat. Ranjit Sitaram Pandit originally hailed from Bambuli village in Ratnagiri district of Maharashtra. He belonged to the Saraswat Brahmin community of Maharashtra. Ranjit Sitaram Pandit was a great scholar of Sanskrit literature. He translated Kahlan's famous play *Rajatarangini* from Sanskrit into English. He participated in India's freedom struggle and was arrested. Not only the husband, but the wife was also arrested for taking part in the independence movement. Sitaram, however, was not arrested once. He was arrested three times in 1932-1933, 1940 and 1942-1943. Both he and his wife were arrested by the British government in 1942 at the height of the Quit India Movement. However, she did not receive much support from her husband. Born in 1893, Pandit died in captivity in Lucknow in 1944.

She was deeply saddened. She had to face many difficulties. She was responsible for all three of her daughters. However, she didn't lose heart. She continued her work. She was released from prison after her husband's death in 1944. With H. N. Kunju and B. Shibarao, she represented India at the United Nations Conference on Foreign Relations. She presided over the Indian Women's Conference held between 1941 and 1943. She spoke out against gender inequality and women's rights.

Her work didn't stop there. She was the first woman prime minister of independent India. She was a candidate in the provincial elections of 1937, conducted under the Government of India Act 1935. And she won. She was elected as the Minister of Local Government and

Health and became the first female cabinet minister. She opposed the Government of India Act, 1935. She called for the establishment of a new Constituent Assembly. He remained in office until 1938. In 1939, during the Second World War, when the British took India into the world war without any discussion with its elected representatives, she and her fellow ministers resigned from the cabinet. She served again as a minister from 1946 to 1947. In 1946, she was elected to the United Nations Constituent Assembly.

She was the mother of three daughters. Two of them in the US. In July 1944, she went to America to meet the. When she applied for a visa to visit the United States, alarm bells rang throughout the British Empire. The purpose of the visit was stated in the visa application. She wished to spend a few days with her daughters in America and forget the pain of losing her husband. However, the British were suspicious and apprehensive. She was a prominent anti-colonialist. The British Empire understood that if she was allowed to go to America, she would undoubtedly bring the inequities of British rule and the missteps of colonial rule to the attention of the American people. A senior official in Delhi commented: "We must watch Mrs. Pandit carefully. Because an enemy will misrepresent Her Majesty's Government and will criticise India in front of the American Govt.

"For all these reasons, her visa application had put the British government in a dilemma. They feared that if she was allowed to go to America, she would preach to the American people in favour of the Indian freedom struggle in America and draw the attention of the American public to the injustices of colonial rule. The United States was helping the British Empire in the war against Hitler. If she is able to do all this, the American people may support Indians. The U.S. won't help Britain. Without the help of the US, they would find it difficult to win the war against Hitler.

Then there would be pressure on the British rulers to end British rule in India. On the other hand, if they rejected her visa application to go to America, then they would be subject to severe criticism. There were many other reasons for which the British Empire was worried. Her husband had died in prison as a political prisoner. The British government was deeply disturbed by the unnatural death of her husband. Not only that, he was imprisoned a year ago for opposing colonial rule. After discussing all this in detail, the British government came to the conclusion that these women were definitely a cause of concern for British rule. Her role as a fierce anti-colonialist was very effective. They decided to arrest her.

Her passport / visa application was approved after a week's deliberation by the British. Her views on a widow's right to visit her daughters allayed fears of anti-colonial propaganda in the United States. But she didn't give up and neither remained quiet. During her visits, she spoke eloquently about the flaws of colonial rule. Emphasizing the issues of the helplessness of common people and sufferings of prisoners under colonial rule, she ensured the rights of Indians to be free. She was well aware that social disparities were being created due to colonialism. Therefore, she always emphasized the need for equality.

A meeting was held in Virginia to discuss the post-World War II world. At that meeting, in 1945, she attended the United Nations Conference in San Francisco as a non-governmental delegate. In that meeting, she was of the opinion that the Indians who were present in the meeting as official representatives were no better than wooden puppets in the hands of the British rulers. They have no idea about colonial rule. "The Indian delegates present at the meeting were only the handpicked candidates of the British rulers, who had neither the correct understanding of facts nor the authority to do so," she said. They've just been elected. Therefore, they will not have any strong opinion for the betterment of Indians. "

On her return to India in 1946, she again took charge of her health department and local system of administration. She was elected to the Constituent Assembly of India the following year. While there had been a lot of discussion about male members of the Constituent Assembly, there was very little discussion about the role of women members. Of the 299 members of the Constituent Assembly, and 15 were women. These 15 women members of the Constituent Assembly of India were accomplished lawyers, freedom fighters and politicians. They emphasized the importance of equality in the formulation of the Constitution based on their experience. At the Constituent Assembly, she greatly advocated for human rights and equality.

She spoke in the Assembly on the protection of fundamental rights. Even after the independence was won, she gave an insightful speech on imperialism. According to her, "Although imperialism has been abolished, its influence has not ended. The biggest challenge is to fight for our survival. We have already seen the post-liberation situation in countries like Burma and Indonesia. And it has taught us a lot. "

She cared not only about her country, but about the world. Significantly, she considered the sacrifice of a few for the good of many to be justified. She used to say, "If the rights of a few are being violated, they should not forget that their progress is worthless without the progress of all."

This extraordinary woman is Vijayalakshmi Pandit.

She was born in 1900 to father Motilal Nehru and mother Swarup Rani Nehru. Vijayalakshmi's father, Motilal Nehru (1861 - 1931), was an eminent barrister. Born into the Kashmiri Pandit community, Motilal became the president of the Indian National Congress twice during India's freedom struggle. Vijayalakshmi was the daughter of Motilal Nehru's second wife. Vijayalakshmi's mother Swaroop Rani (1868-1938) was a daughter of the Kashmiri community settled in Lahore. She became the second wife of Motilal after the death of his first wife. Vijayalakshmi was the second of three siblings. Pandit Jawaharlal Nehru the first Prime Minister of independent India was her elder brother. He was 11 years older than Vijayalakshmi. Vijayalakshmi's younger sister Krishna Hothisingh (1907-1967) was a well-known writer and publisher. She has written many books on her elder brother and our first Prime Minister Jawaharlal Nehru.

With her extraordinary personality, she introduced India to the world before and after independence. She represented India at the 1946 United Nations Conference and was the only woman representative at the conference. This is an honor for all women. She was the first woman president of the United Nations General Assembly. Not only this, as a well-known Indian politician and diplomat, Vijaylakshmi Pandit became the sixth and first woman Governor of Maharashtra and the eighth President of the United General Assembly.

After India gained independence from colonial rule in 1947, her brother Jawaharlal Nehru sent Vijaylakshmi Pandit, who had represented the Soviet Union, the United States, and the United Nations, to London as an Indian diplomat. Beginning her career as a diplomat, she served as Ambassador to India, the Soviet Union (1947-1949), the United States and Mexico (1949-1951), and Ireland (1955-1961). In one of her speeches in 1946, she emphasized the need for women in every country of the world to contribute to every sphere of society by becoming the equal partners of men in a better developing world organization. She also served as India's High Commissioner to the United Kingdom and as India's Ambassador to Spain (9848-9979). She publicized the state of India-Britain relations across the world and drew global attention to the situation arising out of the nationalisation of the Suez Canal in 1956.

On her return to India, she served as the Governor of Maharashtra from 1962 to 1964. Later, she was elected to the Lok Sabha from her brother's constituency Phulpur during 1964-1968. After Mrs. Indira Gandhi imposed emergency rule in India, Mrs. Pandit severely criticized Indira who was her niece. According to her, Indira made a mockery of democracy in a democratic country like India. She compared the incarceration of Jayaprakash Narayan, Morarji Desai and many others to decisions taken in the totalitarian regime in Hitler's Germany forty years ago. As a result, the relationship between the two soured. She retired from active politics after this conflict.

After retirement, she settled in Dehradun in the Himalayan foothills. In 1977, she joined the Janata Party's election campaign against Indira Gandhi.

Many believe that Nehru helped bring his sister to the forefront. But there's no truth to it. "My love for my brother has hurt me a lot in my political life. Once Sir Girija Shankar Vajpayee alerted me saying that Nehru would be more helpful than her as the backbone of her other allies. So keep your emotions under control. "When people regularly criticised her for being a woman, she didn't mince words. "As a politically empowered woman, does she feel any different? "I don't think I've ever been different. When a helping hand is extended to me unnecessarily in Parliament, I do not want such help at all; rather, I expect help from their minds. "This kind of thinking about women in politics is seen all over the world.

In their first meeting, Churchill said to Vijaylakshmi"Just because I have accepted you doesn't mean that my thinking about women has changed." So I don't want you to fill any idea in women's heads. "

This shows what obstacles Vijayalakshmi had to face. She had to struggle a lot to secure equality for herself and ensure that other women got equal rights. She was an exception in a male-dominated society. Despite all the difficulties, despite many negative feelings, she was able to establish herself in different fields. In an interview, she said, "Women are doing much more than what I was doing in my time. But I got a lot of appreciation for my work because when I was working, women had no rights. "

Vijaylakshmi Pandit was not only a politician but also a writer. Her works deserve admiration. These include *The Evolution of India* (1958) and *The Scope of Happiness: A Personal Memoir* (1979). In her essay 'So I Became a Minister', she describes her duties and responsibilities. "As Minister of Local Self-Government and Health, when I entered my office room on July 18, 1937, I had a strange feeling." A young man came and introduced himself as my personal assistant and said something to me. And then I understood what he was saying. There was an old man in our family who loved to fight. Maybe it's the blood running through my body. Now I have got the opportunity to prove the fighting qualities of our generation. I was a minister. "At one point in her memoirs, she mentions that when her brother (Jawaharlal Nehru) suggested that she should become India's ambassador to Moscow, she initially could not accept it. Because she felt that to join such a post, proper training was needed. She also realized that at that time, the eyes of the whole world were on independent India. In such a case, no error will be accepted. She discussed it with her brother Nehru. With Nehru's advice, she discussed the matter with Sardar Patel.

In this context, she said, "I went on a morning walk with him for three days, about 5 km. I wanted some information and guidance. I discussed with him the world's view of India based on governance, the four problems of the world and India's political attitude towards Moscow. When my brother used to inform us about this in the UN, Sardar Patel used to talk about truth, morality, friendly relations with other countries and avoiding war. I said these were just words of hope and hope. Sardar ji, you are not saying any policy based on reality. We must focus on a realistic and rational plan. After some discussion, I reminded him of Kautilya's *Arthashastra*, one of India's most famous treatises on political planning for nation-building. That is why Kautilya emphasized on pragmatic thinking to build a well-organized empire.

"In response, Sardar said," "It is not appropriate to give the example of Kautilya because a country whose military power is weak should not be hostile to powerful countries." He was a wise man, but always preferred to wait for the right moment. He believed that our foreign policy would always give importance to morality. "

As a trailblazer, when it comes to India Vijayalakshmi Pandit realized her responsibility as a path-finder . In her autobiography, she says, "When I see my next generation ahead, my mind is filled with joy. Because today's girls can do a lot in life by walking on the path that my colleagues have built. In 1884, she attempted to write a book titled *Forgotten Women* on the contributions of women who played a significant role in nation-building but have no mention in history.

However, it should not be supposed that Mrs. Pandit accomplished what she did without facing any hindrance. She had to face a lot of opposition. A lot of hard work had to be put in. Verinder Grover, one of the two leading ladies of modern India, Ranjana Arora, mentions how an extraordinarily courageous woman like Vijayalakshmi had to face opposition from some narrow-minded leaders of the Congress. Throughout her life, she emphasized on the important role of both men and women in nation-building and worked tirelessly against gender discrimination.

"Today, the rights of women that we are talking about are not just a matter of discussion; the rights of men also need to be discussed. Men and women cannot be separated. Men and women cannot be treated differently. We cannot discuss it separately."

The important thing is that at a time when society was not so open about women, a woman boldly discussed such an issue. She fought for women's rights. She has certainly succeeded. Otherwise, today's women would not have been able to assert themselves in society and make their mark on so many spheres of life. From this, it can be easily understood that our women are always worried about their problems, their lifestyle. They are always working to change the social situation, how they can bring change in their life and society. And that change always leads to betterment of self and society. When a woman understands her responsibilities towards her family, her society, her caste, and herself, then her progress as well as the progress of everyone is possible.

Sucheta Kriplani

A society cannot exist without politics. It seems as if society and politics are so closely intertwined that in the absence of one, the other ceases to exist. Without politics, no society can progress.

Although the Creator at the time of creation gave the same rights to both men and women and sent them to the earth from the beginning, man has claimed certain things as his sole right. Some of it was directed towards women. Men are responsible for all the outside work. They go out and they go to work. When they get home, the women do all the housework. They don't work outside. Their world remains confined in the four walls of a house. A man can say whatever he wants. But a woman has no right to have an opinion. If she could not voice her opinion within the four corners of the house, how could she go beyond the four walls of the house?

Where there is no right or opportunity to speak about oneself or one's own rights, how can one express one's opinion about others? Where one could not have an opinion on general issues, how can one have an opinion on a particular policy? Where it is difficult to step out of the house, how is it possible to step into the path of politics and express your opinion about yourself, about others, about the state, about the country?

But nothing is impossible for a woman. She can do the impossible. The situation is serious. However, it was very difficult to move forward in politics. No one ever thought that a woman can work effectively in politics or can have a strong opinion by choosing a political career. Once a woman is strong enough to do something, nothing is impossible. No matter how long it takes, a river always breaks the rock and makes its own way. Forward...! And in different places, it creates its own unique identity. In the same way, a woman, like a river, overcomes all the difficulties and obstacles in its path and creates forges own path. She is an inspiration for others as well as for herself.

She was born on 25 June 1908 in Ambala, Punjab (now in Haryana) to a Bengali Brahmin family. Her father, Surendranath Majumdar, worked as a government medical officer and got transferred to various places. So she studied at various schools in different parts of the country. Her father, who worked as a government doctor, was a passionate patriot, fully committed to serving the country. Her father's actions instilled a sense of patriotism in her.

She says that, as a child, she had these qualities rather than something else. She was a self-aware child. However, the circumstances of that time, the environment in which she was growing up, influenced her personality. Not only this, from childhood, her father taught her the *Bhagavad Gita*, which helped her understand Hindutva and Hinduism. When someone gave her wrong information, she strongly opposed it. Her sister was her partner in all of this. She loved her very much. The two sisters had been together since childhood. When she was a student at Kinnaird College in Lahore, her Bible teacher made some derogatory remarks about Hinduism. She and her sister felt very upset. She returned home and went to meet her father. She insisted on father explain Hinduism to her. Her father also taught her about Hinduism and other religions. He explained the gist of the *Bhagavad Gita* very well. The next day, the two sisters went to the school and confronted the teacher who had made derogatory remarks about Hinduism. They had an argument with the teacher about Hinduism. Not only that, she also taught some portions of the *Bhagavad Gita* to the teacher. Since then, the teacher stopped commenting on Hinduism in the class.

When she was ten, she and her siblings heard her father and his friends talking about the brutal massacre at Jallianwala Bagh. This angered her and her siblings so much that they could not suppress it. They used to tease some Anglo-Indian children playing with them by calling them names.

In her book *An Unfinished Autobiography*, she describes the Jallianwala Bagh massacre that she heard of at the age of 10. Here, she describes an interesting event in her life. The Prince of Wales came to Delhi after the Jallianwala Bagh massacre. The students of her school were taken to the Dacia garden to pay their respects to the Prince. But she and her sister refused to go. But she had to go, despite her own reluctance. The two sisters were very angry at their own cowardice. They felt sad. "According to our conscience, it was a shameful incident. We both felt very small. "

She was a very bright student. She completed her schooling from Indraprastha College, New Delhi and graduated from St. Stephen's College, New Delhi. She then joined the Banaras Hindu University as a lecturer in constitutional history.

This was a time when the atmosphere was charged with the spirit of national unity and that of the freedom struggle. Not only in India, the fight for freedom was being fought in many parts of the world.

All of this had a profound effect on her. She was drawn into the fight for freedom. She was most impressed by Gandhi. She was aware of Gandhiji's every move and followed it. She also came to describe herself as a Gandhian.

Two sisters could see India's freedom struggle unfolding before them. Inspired by Gandhi's ideals, they strongly desired to join the rapidly growing freedom movement in India. Her father supported them. Although he was a government doctor he shared the patriotism of his two daughters. However, both of them could not participate in the freedom struggle. They were disappointed. Sadly, in 1929, her father and older sister both passed away, leaving her forever. After their death, she joined the Banaras Hindu University as a lecturer to take care of her family.

Although she was offered a highly-paid job at the University of Lahore, she did not take it up. Despite the low salary she was offered at the Banaras Hindu University she joined it because here she could talk about the freedom struggle among her students.

In those days, universities supplied soldiers for the freedom movement. She instilled patriotism in students. Who is this woman that has been talked about for so long? Was the woman who was so much attracted to the freedom struggle able to join the freedom struggle?

She was also a member of the Constituent Assembly, which was tasked with drafting key documents needed to govern the newly independent country. She was one of the 15 women in the 299-member Assembly. Other women members included Sarojini Naidu, Vijayalakshmi Pandit, Purnima Banerjee and Ammu Saminathan.

From teaching history to creating history, she led an eventful life. She remained an active political figure till the end of her days. She was the first woman 'prime minister' of India and was Chief Minister of Uttar Pradesh from 1963 to 1967. When Indira Gandhi came to power in 1966, she became the first woman Prime Minister of India. Although much has been written about Indira Gandhi, not many know that India already had its first woman chief minister three years ago. She became the Chief Minister of Uttar Pradesh in 1963.

The name of their extraordinary woman is Sucheta Majumdar. She was the daughter of Surendra Nath Majumdar and Sulekha Majumdar was her elder sister. In 1934, Sucheta met freedom fighter Acharya Jivatram Bhagwan Das Kriplani. Acharya Kriplani was a renowned Gandhian leader. Born on November 11, 1888, Acharya Kriplani was a very strong-minded persona.

Acharya Kriplani was greatly influenced by Gandhiji. Though he had known Gandhiji earlier, he used to see him from a distance, but never got an opportunity to meet him from close quarters. However, during the Champaran Satyagraha in 1917 he had a chance to meet Gandhi personally. He helped Gandhi in many ways during the Champaran Satyagraha. He quit his job as a teacher and joined the

Satyagraha. Gandhiji was very fond of him, strong personality, ideology and patriotism. He regarded him as one of his closest friends.

This was the beginning of the second part of his life. This was an important time in his life. After the Champaran Satyagraha, he again returned to teaching and joined the faculty of the Banaras Hindu University in 1919. In 1920, Acharya Kriplani again left the Banaras Hindu University and joined the Satyagraha.

Acharya was the general secretary of the Congress when he met Sucheta in 1934. He became president of Congress in 1946. He also served as the President of the Indian National Congress at the time of independence.

Acharya Kriplani, a very idealistic leader, remained with Gandhiji throughout his life. He also played an important role in drafting the Constitution of India. As a four-time MP, he raised the voice of the people in Parliament and sought to make sure they got justice. In 1950, due to ideological differences, Acharya broke away from the Indian National Congress and formed his own Kisan Mazdoor Praja Dal, which later merged with the Samajwadi Party to become the Praja Socialist Party and he became its president. In 1951, he formed another party, the Kisan Mazboot Prajapati Party. He felt that the Congress had drifted away from Gandhi's ideas. That's why he formed his own party. He was the only opposition leader who moved a no-confidence motion against Nehru in 1963. After Nehru's passing, he also opposed Indira. After some time, Sucheta also felt the need to join the Praja Socialist Party. After the Indian National Congress announced its Samajwadi side and steps in the Avadi conference in 1957, he realised that he was an active member of the organisation for a long time and there was no need to stay out of its fold. He not only returned to the INC but also became its general secretary.

Acharya Kriplani remained in the opposition for the rest of his life. Acharya Kriplani and Sucheta remained cordial to each other, maintaining tolerance and honesty in politics.

After developing a relationship with Acharya Kriplani, Acharya introduced Sucheta to Gandhiji as a staunch Gandhian and encouraged her to join the freedom struggle. Sucheta, who was already inspired by

Gandhi's ideals and had already identified herself as a Gandhian, was actively engaged in various activities of the freedom struggle.

In 1942, the political atmosphere of India became charged. Demonstrations and rallies demanding independence have been held. Mahatma Gandhi was fasting at Aga Khan's palace in Pune. At one point, he was in critical condition. Many freedom fighters, including 34-year-old Sucheta Kriplani, were issued arrest warrants and forced to work underground. Distraught over Gandhi's declining health, she decided to visit him soon.

"I am Mrs Kriplani and I want to meet Gandhiji at his residence. I should be allowed to see him. You can arrest me when I go out. You have to do this for me. "

The Home Secretary, in consultation with the Governor, advised her to leave the city within 24 hours of her meeting Mahatma Gandhi. However, she was not arrested.

Gandhi was very pleased with her work. She dedicated her entire life to the country. In the meantime, she developed a love affair with Acharya Kriplani. The two decided to get married. However, no one liked the marriage of Acharya and Sucheta. The families did not accept the marriage proposal. Gandhi himself was not in favour of the marriage. He thought that Acharya Kriplani might leave the freedom movement after his marriage and he would lose his closest and most important friend, his right hand. He thought that his two trusted and hardworking lieutenants bury themselves in family responsibilities. So he said, if Sucheta wants to get married, she should marry someone else instead of Acharya.

But Sucheta did not give up the decision to marry Acharya. She was determined to marry Kriplani. She finally went to Gandhiji. She explained how close she was to Acharya Kriplani. There's a deep connection between them. If she married, she would marry him. If she doesn't marry him, and no one else. She also said that the suspicion that Kriplani would withdraw from the freedom movement after marriage was unfounded. Sucheta argued that Gandhi would get two workers instead of one after marriage.

Thus, Sucheta Majumdar became Sucheta Kriplani. After their

marriage, both of them got very busy fighting the freedom struggle and helping others. They stayed away from each other most of the time.

She had her husband's support in everything she did. Under his guidance and influence, Sucheta began actively participating in the Satyagraha. Sucheta, along with Aruna Asaf Ali, Usha Mehta and other women leaders, came to the fore during the Quit India Movement and was imprisoned by the British. She was sent to prison for a year. "I wanted to start a political career. Before going to jail, I used to feel small in front of the person who had gone to jail, because I had not graduated from prison life. Kriplani wanted me to do whatever I liked, not necessarily politics. "His advice to Sucheta at the beginning of his life was' Apna daman saaf rakhna '," he said in his autobiography.

Later that year, the Partition of Noakhali (now in Bengal) triggered violent communal riots. Along with Gandhi and Acharya Kriplani, she visited the riot affected areas and served the victims of the massacre. She worked closely with Mahatma Gandhi. Gandhiji was deeply impressed by her political commitment, and appointed her as the founding secretary of the Kasturba Gandhi National Organization. Gandhiji wrote, "A woman of rare courage and character, who would raise the dignity of Indian womanhood. "

The year 1946 proved very eventful for Sucheta. By the end of the year, she was elected to the Legislative Council. She was a member of the sub-committee entrusted with the responsibility of drafting the Constitution of India. Sucheta Kriplani was one of the few women elected to the Constituent Assembly. On August 14, 1947, when India was about to be born as a nation, the Constituent Assembly began its proceedings at 11 pm. When Sucheta sang Vande Mataram in that historic session just before Jawaharlal's Tryst with Destiny speech, everyone present in the council rejoiced. That was a historic moment for Sucheta. Because she not only opened the study with singing; but also ended it by singing 'Saare Jahaan Se Achha' and the national anthem. Sucheta's voice was sweet, rich and heartwarming! Her bhajans were a regular feature at Gandhi's prayer meetings in 1946-47. Behind her gentle voice, however, was a strong-willed and courageous woman who, despite being deeply influenced by the wisdom and philosophy of her political mentor, Mahatma Gandhi and his wife, never gave up her independent thinking. She never shied away from expressing her opinions.

When independence was won, both Sucheta and Acharya were assigned the task of rehabilitating the refugees. When Sucheta and others were distributing relief materials at a camp in Noakhali, Gandhiji told them, "People should work for the help they are getting. "

Hearing this from Gandhiji, Sucheta was deeply hurt. Gandhiji understood this.

Gandhiji said, "Don't take away their self-respect. Don't make them beggars." In the book *Understanding Gandhiji: Gandhians in Conversation with Fred J Blum*, Sucheta says, "While working with Gandhiji in other fields, I realised that it is not enough just to help people by giving things from above. What we should try to do is to create energy among people to help themselves."

One thing that everyone felt - educated, uneducated, people from all walks of life who were in touch with him had immense love for Gandhiji. Everyone felt that he was mine and we wanted to do something for him. Every human being was precious to him and he kept everyone in a circle of love. That was his number one quality. He was also a teacher. We have had many great leaders in the past, but I don't think anyone else has the quality to develop the best in us. He evaluated us, gave us that kind of work and always guided us. That is why he was able to create a permanent division of labour. "

She remained active in politics even after independence. Sucheta Kriplani was elected to the United Nations General Assembly in 1949. In 1952, due to differences between Nehru and the Congress, Acharya Kriplani broke away and formed a new party called Krishak Mazdoor Praja Party (now defunct). She joined the group for a short time. She eventually returned to the Indian National Congress.

She was elected from the New Delhi constituency in the first general elections held in 1952.

She contested from the short-lived party founded by her husband KMPP. She defeated Congress candidate Manmohini Sehgal and served as Minister of State for Small Scale Industries. Five years later, Sucheta returned to the Congress and was re-elected from the same constituency.

With her sharp intellect and brilliant oratory, she managed to cement a special place for herself as a distinguished parliamentarian.

She was also the first woman president of the Congress. She founded the All India Mahila Congress in 1940. In an interview in 1974, she said, "Thousands of women have participated in various struggles of the Congress; but women have not yet been properly organized and there is no women's organization parallel to or as part of the Congress organization. "She also said," I had to go from state to state to set up small women's wings in every state. "

She was a member of the Uttar Pradesh Legislative Assembly. From 1960 to 1963, she was the Minister of Labour, Community Development and Industries in the Government of Uttar Pradesh. In October 1963, she became the Chief Minister of Uttar Pradesh, the first woman to hold that position in any Indian state. The highlight of her tenure was her firm handling of the state government employees' strike. Kriplani had a reputation as a strong administrator, rejecting demands for pay increases for state government employees.

She was last elected to the Lok Sabha in 1967 from Gonda constituency in Uttar Pradesh. When the Congress split in 1969, she left the party to form the NCO along with Morarji Desai. But in 1971 she lost the election. She retired from politics that year. Around the same time, her health began to deteriorate. In 1972, she suffered two heart attacks. Two years later, she suffered a third heart attack and died on 1 December 1974 at the age of 66.

Sucheta Kriplani was a highly qualified parliamentarian and a brilliant orator in Lok Sabha debates. She was very intelligent, hardworking and a good teacher and perseverance. She was an honest and sincere person. Under different circumstances, the Uttar Pradesh Congress party was divided into two factions, one led by Kamalapati Tripathi and the other by C.B. Gupta. She became involved in local politics. In opposition to their power, C.B. Gupta impressed upon Sucheta that she should go to Delhi and ensure she became the Chief Minister of Uttar Pradesh, as he himself had lost the election. She did a great job as Chief Minister. The old-timers still remember her as the best chief minister of Uttar Pradesh. Her lifestyle was also very simple and very impossible for a chief minister. After retiring from active politics, she and her husband built a beautiful house for themselves in New Delhi's Sarcomata Enclave. Later, Sucheta performed her duties as a very efficient and caring housewife. In her frugality and pomp, Sucheta always prepared sherbets, jams and a variety of food items at home.

At the same time, she was writing three or four autobiographical articles for *the Illustrated Weekly of India*. Unfortunately, she was unable to complete her autobiography. Since they were childless, the Kriplani couple donated all their wealth and resources to the Public Welfare Fund, which was set up to help the economically disadvantaged groups in the national capital.

Both husband and wife were loyal to different political parties but this did not affect their normal lives. On a visit to the United States in 1960, Sucheta Kriplani and her husband were asked by some people, "What happens to India when husband and wife are in opposed political parties?"

"Peaceful coexistence. "They both said yes. "If we had lived in America, we would have divorced twice. "

The Government of India has renamed one of the two hospitals attached to Lady Hardinge Medical College, New Delhi as Sucheta Kriplani Hospital in her honour.

Her extraordinary life teaches us that when a woman wants to do something and goes out to do it fearlessly, God is there to help her.

Begum Aijaz Rasool

It was in 1935. With the introduction of the Government of India Act, a woman in India joined politics with her husband. And it wasn't an easy thing to do. In 1937, when only a small number of women were involved in politics she was contesting the election. She contested the election from an unreserved seat. But she won the election and was elected to the Uttar Pradesh Legislative Assembly. She served as Deputy President of the Council from 1937 to 1940 and as Leader of the Opposition from 1950 to 1952-54. She was the first woman in India and the first Muslim woman in the world to reach such an important position.

As the only Muslim woman to be elected to the constitutional body, she gave up the practice of purdah from the time she was elected from an unreserved seat in Uttar Pradesh in 1937. In her autobiography *From Purdah to Parliament*, she said, "Islamic clerics or commentators had issued a fatwa against me that voting for a woman who is not on purdah is not religious at all."

However, the purdah system could never stop her. Of course, her family stood by her. She inherited her love of freedom from her father. He made her accustomed to both traditional and modern lifestyles. She has mentioned in her autobiography that her lifestyle was based on the old / traditional and was moving towards modernity.

Qudsia Begum was born into a royal family in the 20th century in the Muslim-dominated state of Melar Kotla in Punjab, India. Her father was Zulfikar Ali Khan and mother Mehsuda Sultana. She was born on April 2, 1909. Her father Zulfikar Ali Khan was a descendant of the royal family of Malerkotla in Punjab, while her mother Mehsuda Sultana was the daughter of Nawab Alauddin Ahmed Khan, the Nawab of Lahore. Her father created a special place for her in the political, social and intellectual circles. At a very young age, she joined her father in various political meetings and started working as her personal assistant. Like her father, she continued to pursue her political career for many years. She is well known for her legislation on the abolition of the landlord system. She was also opposed to separate electorates.

In 1929, she married Nawab Aizaz Rasool, a zamindar of Sandila in Hardoi district of present-day Uttar Pradesh (Oudh). The wedding was arranged by Malcolm Hailey. After marriage, she changed her name to Begum Aizaz Rasool. She later became known by this name. Qudsia's father died in 1931, two years after their marriage. A few days after her father's death, her mother came to visit her. She remained there till her last breath.

She was elected to the Constituent Assembly of India in 1946. She was one of the 28 Muslim women elected to the Muslim League. She was the only Muslim woman in the Parliament. And it wasn't just that. Begum Aizaz Rasul delivered her inaugural speech at the Constituent Assembly of India in 1946 at a young age.

The Muslim League in India was dissolved in 1950. Begum Aziz Rasul joined the Congress. She was elected to the Rajya Sabha in 1952 to 54. She was a member of the Uttar Pradesh Legislative Assembly from 1969 to 1989 and served as the Minister of Social Development of the Minorities during 1969-1971.

She held many important positions as a member of the Parliament. She was Leader of the Opposition from 1950-1952 and Deputy President of the Council from 1933-1940. She was the first Indian woman to hold this position. When many positions at the political level were usually occupied only by men, Aizaz Rasul, as a woman, had the opportunity to do many things in such positions. In her long political career in Uttar Pradesh, Qudsia Aizaz Rasul built a special identity for herself. She gave more importance to the unification of India to resist colonial rule than to separate electorates on the basis of caste or racism.

In her autobiography she recalls her meeting with Indian Muslim League leader M. A. Jinnah in the summer of 1941. She recalled that Jinnah had asked her why she was not joining the Muslim League. When thousands of people were eager to join Muslim League, why was she not eager? But she refrained from joining the league. She was against the creation of Pakistan. At the time of partition, she raised her voice against the provision of reservation for minorities in the Constituent Assembly. She was against the colonial government's plan to hold special elections for minorities in 1909. "My view of the rights of minorities in a democratic country is that reservation is a suicide weapon for minorities, which will forever keep them apart from the majority. Such a system will never allow them to occupy a special place in the minds of the majority. This will create a different, contradictory attitude in their minds forever." She expressed this view at a meeting held in December 1948 on behalf of Sardar Vallabhbhai Patel.

Much later, when Rasul wrote her autobiography, she mentioned the violence that took place over this incident in her autobiography. "I strongly opposed the reservation system, it seemed like suicide to me. I didn't think it was right to protect religion. Another contradictory situation arose when Begum Rasul was invited to a discussion in April 1999 to discuss the 'status of Muslims, reservation in law and jobs'. "As a religious sentiment grows and Hindutva becomes popular, it is time to rethink how the social, economic and educational conditions of Muslims have improved," she said."

Rasul faced a lot of opposition from her community for her views, so she finally spoke in favor of her community. In favour of one of these rights, she opined that "any minority community people can live anywhere in India. Even if there is a particular script or language, their children will not be deprived of primary education."

She was married to Nawab Aijaz Rasul, the zamindar of Oudh State, but Begum Rasul opposed the zamindari system. As a member of the Tenasi Committee, she was committed to abolishing the zamindari system in Uttar Pradesh. In 1939, when this law was discussed in Parliament, she gave her thoughtful opinion about the rights of farmers. The law has been amended nearly 1,000 times. In which emphasis was laid on the ancestral rights of the taxpayers.

"This Act shall not be challenged and the landlords shall scrupulously follow the written law and give their rights to the hard-working taxpayers. If they do not comply, their land will be forcibly taken away."

Rasul spoke in a very strong voice in the Lok Sabha. While many opposed India's participation in the Commonwealth, Rasul supported it. She said that one should not think that one would only give, and the others would only take. According to her, "When a person claims his rights, he must also perform his duties properly." Rasul advocated the rights of ministers irrespective of their party affiliations. She had in-depth knowledge of the law and the constitution of other countries. She argued that we need a strong and stable cabinet, which would work every day without the influence of party workers.

Rasul was able to attract everyone's attention for her remarkable role. and she instructed Muslims to abolish the special electoral system.

After the partition of India, a number of Muslim League members joined the Indian Constituent Assembly. When the head of the Chaudhry Khaliquzzaman Party moved to Pakistan, Begum Aizaz became the leader of the Muslim League, becoming a member for the drafting subcommittee of the minority.

In her autobiography, Rasul has given many photographs depicting her journey in Indian politics in which she is seen wearing cotton and silk sarees and standing next to the top leaders of the Congress in many political gatherings. She has been photographed with several leaders including Jawaharlal Nehru, Sardar Vallabhbhai Patel, Sarojini Naidu, Vijayalakshmi Pandit and Rajiv Gandhi. It is no exaggeration to say that these photographs bear testimony to her presence and role in Indian political history. She has cleverly avoided the situation of presenting herself as a woman from a different community in her autobiography. However, her remarkable work as a leading local Muslim woman is evident. Sidonien Smith notes that "attempts to harmoniously integrate themselves have failed, in part, because the events mentioned in the autobiography have been somewhat forgotten. They are not on the ground. Many personalities have been discussed in his autobiography and they are mentioned in a conversational style."

However, many secrets of pre-independence Indian political history can be found in her autobiography. The changes in Agra and Oudh Uttar Pradesh, the decline in the popularity of the Urdu language, the internal squabble in the Congress in the 1960s, the creation of regional parties, the growth of Hindutva, the social status of Muslim women under State 54, etc., are discussed in her autobiography. Rasul's autobiography notes an admirable state of affairs in the post-1960s. She also highlighted the rifts in the Congress, especially during the time of Indira Gandhi. As a Muslim woman in politics, Rasul has never been particularly biased in favour of Muslim women. In her own autobiography she did not confine herself to any particular community. In 1986, she kept quiet to end her differences with the Congress in the Shah Bano case.

The proposal for a separate constituency for Muslims and reservation in the Council of Ministers was rejected. There is no provision for political protection in the Constitution. In particular, Rokona Vajpayee argued that political reservation for both religious minorities, the Scheduled Castes and the Scheduled Tribes would be like a self-liquidation mechanism for them that would create some conditions for their presence. The policies designed for minorities in the national policy can bridge the gap between other classes and them. "Rasul's expression created a dilemma in the Constituent Assembly for a long time. It was the time when the democratic rule of independent India was introduced, secularism was absolutely necessary for the good management of democracy. Communalism was being removed from India. Therefore, the framers of the Constitution had to face many obstacles in establishing a secular democratic regime. Two groups opposed the proposal. One group was of the opinion that in a secular state, no one should be allowed to use religious symbols, clothes, etc. On the other hand, the second group was of the opinion that in a country like India where religion is given so much importance, such a rule should not be implemented. According to the Constitution of India, all religions should be treated equally."

Later, the interview was published in various newspapers and magazines.

She worked on language rights. She emphasized that no matter where a minority lives in India, their children should be given primary education in their own language. She was not the only one who spoke in favour of the Urdu language, but the head of Anjuman-e-Taraki-Eurdoo, Zakir Hussain, had also raised his voice for the promotion and protection of the Urdu language before independence. After partition, there was a need to show the depth of Muslims' relationship with Urdu language for the protection of Muslim culture and language in North India. There was a lot of controversy in the Constituent Assembly over the adoption of Urdu as a regional language. Ardent champions of Hindi opposed it.

It may be mentioned that Rasul was the president of the Indian Women's Hockey Federation for 20 years and president of the Asian Women's Hockey Federation. The Indian Women's Hockey Cup was named after her. For her immense interest in sports, she presented the men's jersey to the Prime Minister's XI team for a friendly match against the President's XI. It was a proud moment for the Indian women's hockey team to be established and recognised internationally. Elvira Britto, who captained the Indian women's hockey team from 1960 to 1967, said, "Begum Rasul's election as the president has brought recognition to the Indian women's hockey team at the international level. Under her guidance and with the cooperation of other members, the Indian women's hockey team has improved a lot. She formed various committees with various personalities related to hockey and took steps to improve it. It was under her guidance and inspiration that the Indian women's hockey team excelled at the national level and played Test series against Japan, Sri Lanka and other countries. "

She was awarded the Padma Bhushan in 2000 for her outstanding social service.

Begum Rasul was a travel enthusiast. She accompanied the Prime Minister during her friendly visit to Japan in 1953. She visited Turkey in 1955 as a member of the Indian delegation. She was also very interested in literature. Rasul published a book titled *3 Weeks in Japan*.

In the chapter 'The Road to Partition' in her autobiography, Rasul later explained her decision to stay back in India. "I have received several letters from the Prime Minister of Pakistan, Liaquat Ali Khan, in which he was ready to accept any of my demands in exchange for my leaving India." But my husband and I decided that we will not leave our country under any circumstances and we were firm in our decision. My mother, brother and sister, who live in Lahore, naturally wanted us to move there. My mother was worried about my safety. " However, during her long stay in India, she contributed to the betterment of the country and society through her work, thoughts and writings. Begum Qudsia died on 1 August 2001 at the age of 92. This woman will always be remembered for the remarkable work she did by rising above caste and religion.

Women have the strength to overcome all the barriers and circumstances placed on their way. If a stone blocks the progress of a slow-moving stream of water, it may stop for a while. But the stream erodes and flows on. A woman's journey through life reminds one of the irresistible movement of a stream.

□□

Bina Das

It was 1932, and she was only 21 years old. She was supposed to receive her bachelor's degree on that same day. However, this did not happen. In the conference hall of the University of Calcutta, she fired at the Governor of Bengal, Stanley Jackson, who was the chief guest at the event. It was a shocking moment—an unexpected act from a young student! She committed a serious crime and, most importantly, showed no fear while shooting at the chief guest in front of an audience.

She was born in 1911 in Krishnanagar, Bengal. Almost all of her family members were actively involved in the struggle for India's independence. Maa Sarla Devi dedicated herself to this cause by establishing a hostel. Here, bombs were stored and distributed among the freedom fighters.

Her father, Benimadhab Das, was a well-known teacher and social worker associated with the Brahmo Samaj. He taught at Ravenshaw Collegiate School in Cuttack for several years. One of his most famous students was the great freedom fighter Subhas Chandra Bose.

Benimadhab Das did not limit his contributions to education; he also actively participated in the Brahmo movement, which aimed to reform Hindu society and its prevailing religious traditions at the time.

Her elder sister, Kalyani Das, was also a freedom fighter. Growing up in a family devoted to the Indian freedom struggle, she naturally absorbed rebellious thoughts from her environment. As a result, her rebellious nature manifested itself from a young age.

Bina Das was deeply inspired by the love for their country felt by her family members and their dedication to social service. She was not only fascinated by this passion but also became a leader in her own right, leaving a lasting impact and serving as an example for others. Along with her elder sister, Kalyani Das, Bina participated in various rallies and protests against the British government during their school days.

While pursuing her high school education, Bina Das became increasingly aware of political issues by joining the Student's Union. At that time, the union played a crucial role in fostering a rebellious spirit among women participating in India's freedom struggle. It organized various acts of defiance and aimed to educate girl students in self-defense skills, including lathi-wielding, sword-fighting, bicycle riding, driving, and shooting. Through these efforts, 100 female students received training from various revolutionaries to prepare them for the freedom struggle. Notably, the ashram supporting this initiative was run by Sarala Devi, Bina Das's mother.

The movement began in Calcutta in 1928 and played a significant role in training freedom fighters at the grassroots level. This institution provided women from across the country with the opportunity to participate in the freedom struggle. Arrangements were made for students to stay in a hostel called Punya Ashram. Bina Das's elder sister, Kalyani, served as its secretary. Like other insurgent groups, it was actively engaged in various resistance activities in West Bengal. The members of this organization assisted other rebels and worked under the guidance of leaders like Deshsukh Majumdar.

Women played a crucial role in the freedom struggle, and Bina was inspired by her family to take part in the resistance. Her first act of defiance against the British Raj occurred when she and a group of female students protested against the Simon Commission, effectively forcing English women to remain in college past their term.

In 1928, various revolts aimed at expelling British Commissioner Simon were underway. Bina and Kalyani, two sisters, were actively involved in the rebellion. Bina planned to shoot and kill a high-ranking British officer. In 1932, Kalyani was sentenced to nine months in jail for her rebellion against the British, which ignited a fierce resolve in Bina's heart. Determined to resist the British government, Bina sought the help of Kamala Dasgupta, the warden of the women's residence. However, Kamala was more than just a warden; she was the mastermind behind providing arms to the revolutionaries.

Bina became a close friend of Kamala Dasgupta, who provided her with a gun when Bina requested for one. She now awaited the right moment and opportunity to act.

In her memoir, translated from Bengali by Dhira Dhar, Bina Das reveals how Subhas Chandra Bose (Subhas Babu) was greatly influenced by her father and often visited their home. She recounts a remarkable incident from her school days that illustrates her rebellious spirit.

"One day, we heard that the wife of the British Viceroy was scheduled to visit our school. The day before her visit, we were called out of the classroom to rehearse the welcome program. We were instructed to stand flowers in hand in the canopy. When she entered the school premises, we would welcome her by placing flowers at her feet. Hearing this made me furious, and I walked away. It felt very insulting. Tears filled my eyes as I sat in a corner of the classroom, and the other girls joined me. The situation was more serious than it seemed. Most importantly, we all pledged to dedicate our lives to the freedom of our motherland. I often remember this childhood vow later in life, and it gives me courage and strength in my weakest moments." This incident highlights Bina's fierce patriotism.

In 1926, Sarat Chandra Chattopadhyay published a novel titled *Pather Dabi*, which the British authorities banned. However, Bina Das managed to obtain a copy of the novel and read it day and night.

Although she was an excellent student, she did not do well in the English exam because she spent so much time reading the banned novel.

During the English test, she was asked to write about her favorite novel. Bina Das chose *Pather Dabi* and not only wrote about it but quoted extensively from the novel in her answer sheet. However, despite her efforts, she lost marks because her paper was evaluated by English teachers who noticed that she had written about a banned book. As a result, she could not receive the marks she deserved. This was a difficult situation for Bina Das. She reflected, "This is my country. The author of the novel is also from this country. Yet, he does not have the freedom to write novels that educate the people of his nation!"

Bina was deeply upset. This marked the beginning of her struggle for freedom. "This piece, which I wrote in English for 'Deshmatruka,' is my first tribute to the country."

The Bengal Revolutionary Party was founded by Subhash Bose in 1928. It was there that Bina Das met Suhasini Ganguly. When Bina first expressed to Suhasini her desire to join the party, Suhasini asked her, "You joined this party to engage in the freedom struggle. So tell me, how far are you willing to go for the freedom of your country?"

"I can go to any extent for the freedom of my country," Bina replied immediately.

Suhasini welcomed Bina into the Bengal Revolutionary Party. The group operated in such secrecy that its members did not even know each other. Bina worked tirelessly for the independence of the country, and it was during this time that she learned to shoot.

On the morning of February 6, 1932, Bina discovered that Governor Stanley Jackson, the then Governor of Bengal, would be the chief guest at the convocation ceremony of the University of Calcutta. Bina was also set to receive her degree that day, but her mind was filled with turmoil. She decided that this was the perfect opportunity to raise her voice against British rule. Bina shared her feelings with her friend Kamala, and a discussion ensued. After much deliberation, they arrived at the decision: the governor would be shot. Kamala Dasgupta agreed with Bina's course of action.

However, her parents were not happy with her decision. They were distraught and terrified, but they also understood the revolutionary spirit of their daughter. They were convinced that she would face severe consequences for her actions. Radha Kumar, in her book *History of Durang*, mentions that Dasgupta collected money from other associates, and a male comrade purchased the gun. Das recounts her feelings when she decided to take this plunge, and her horror when her parents learned of her plan. Yet, being a freedom fighter from a young age, she recognized the sacrifice that daughters make for their motherland. A girl can do anything for her country.

Imbued with revolutionary ardour, Bina made the bold decision to assassinate Sir Stanley Jackson, the Governor General of Bengal. Unfortunately, she failed in her attempt. Although she bravely fired at Stanley, she missed her target because of the distance between them. Despite having learned how to shoot, she had not gained the necessary skill to hit a target from afar. When Bina first fired two shots, Jackson moved back just in time, preventing the bullets from hitting him. Undeterred, Bina continued to shoot, and one bullet grazed Jackson's ear, but he remained unharmed. Eventually, she was captured by the Lieutenant-Commander.

During the incident, a teacher was also injured. Bina was arrested and sentenced to nine years in prison. Her sister, Kalyani Das, narrated the events that transpired. The Glasgow Herald reported on February 6, 1932, that Bina entered the conference hall with a revolver loaded with five bullets, intending to fulfill her goal. She concealed the gun in her clothing and seized the opportunity as Jackson was about to give his speech.

She approached him and fired two shots, but Jackson had already moved away from her line of fire. When she fired a third shot, it went past Jackson's ear, but he remained unscathed.

Stanley Jackson was an English cricketer who was also an army officer and a politician. He played 20 Test matches for England between 1893 and 1905. Jackson was born on November 21, 1870, in Lyft. His father, William Jackson, was the first Baron Allerton. While attending Harrow School, Jackson was accompanied by Winston Churchill, who was a Member of Parliament and later became Prime Minister. In 1889, he entered Trinity College, Cambridge, where he played cricket for Cambridge University, Yorkshire, and England.

Jackson captained England in five Test matches in 1905, scoring a total of 492 runs and taking 13 wickets across all games. This was during his final appearance in Test cricket. He was notably the first batsman to make his Test debut in the 1890s. In 1921, he served as the president of the Marylebone Cricket Club. Following the death of Lord Hawke in 1938, Jackson succeeded him as President of Yorkshire County Cricket Club, holding this position until his own death on March 9, 1947.

In addition to his cricketing career, Jackson was a lieutenant in the Harrow Volunteers. He was appointed captain of the 3rd (Militia) Battalion on January 16, 1900, and served with his battalion in the Second Boer War, arriving in South Africa in March of that year. In 1914, he was transferred to the West Yorkshire Regiment as a lieutenant colonel. He was elected as a Member of Parliament in February 1915, and from 1922 to 1923, he served as Economic Secretary in the War Office. In 1927, he was appointed Governor of Bengal and became a Grand Commander of the Most Eminent Order of the Indian Empire (GCIE).

While serving as Governor of Bengal in 1928, Jackson inaugurated the Malda District Central Co-operative Bank Limited in Malda district to promote the cooperative movement.

While waiting for the hearing in the Calcutta High Court, Bina Das strongly opined that it was God's judgment. Her religious views always made her aware that the influence of Christianity could never bring freedom to India. In one of her comments, she interestingly compared Stanley Jackson to a common man. Her response wasn't personal. "She fired at the man who was the governor of Bengal. She protested against British rule by shaping the spirit of vengeance of countless men and women of his kingdom. "

Bina Das once said, "I will die one day, but if I die, I will die fighting against British rule." This statement encapsulates her entire personality and the depth of her convictions.

Bina was released from prison in 1942 after serving a nine-year sentence. That same year, she joined the Quit India Movement. During this movement, she was attacked by a British police officer, leaving her severely injured and in need of hospitalization. However, this did not deter her; she went to jail again for her beliefs.

Later, she continued her involvement in the struggle for India's independence. Her dedication and sacrifices will always be remembered. The life story of Bina Das, including her fight against the injustices of British rule, inspired many. Her courage inspired numerous women to leave their homes and actively participate in the freedom struggle. From 1946 to 1951, she served as a member of the Bengal Legislative Assembly. In 1947, she married fellow revolutionary Jatin Bhowmik. In recognition of her social service, Bina Das was awarded the Padma Shri in 1960.

After her husband's death, she moved to Rishikesh but rejected the pension given to freedom fighters by the government.

Bina Das worked tirelessly for nine long years to resist the expansion of the British Empire in her homeland. Unfortunately, among the few women from Bengal who are remembered for their significant contributions to the freedom struggle, Bina Das has not received much recognition. On December 26, 1986, an unidentified body was discovered on the roadside in Rishikesh. It took nearly a month to identify the body, which was ultimately revealed to be Bina Das. The circumstances surrounding her death remain a mystery.

Despite her lonely and mysterious death, Bina Das will always be remembered for her contributions to India's freedom struggle. She was one of the most prominent women freedom fighters from Bengal, and her actions were so courageous that she was often referred to as the "Tigress of Bengal." It is hoped that in the coming years, a detailed account of her life will be included in the history books on the Indian freedom struggle.

In examining Indian society and the social conditions of that time, it is evident that both the Bengal and Indian freedom struggles were initiated and led by men. Women, despite the societal constraints they faced, were inspired to join the freedom movement and contribute to the movement aimed at liberating the country. Although women participated in these struggles amid considerable social challenges, they were often handicapped by male dominance and were often controlled by the upper castes and elite.

Even as they worked hard to achieve their goals within the freedom struggle, many women from marginalized backgrounds found their identities in this fight. Unfortunately, there was minimal discussion about women's perspectives, practices, and cultural consciousness. It raises concern as to why the political leaders of the time didn't fully recognize or understand the mentality of women.

The stories of these unsung women revolutionaries hold great significance in India's freedom struggle. When we reflect on their sacrifices, it evokes deep emotions that impact our mental and moral sensibilities. It is undeniable that throughout history, no significant progress in society has been achieved without the collaboration of women. Whenever women have faced humiliation, they have rallied to fight for the nation's betterment. They have fought valiantly, achieved success, and left a lasting impact on future generations.

☐☐

Kamala Sohonie

Time! It moves at a steady pace, never stopping or rushing. Our experiences—sad, happy, good, or bad—reflect our actions and thoughts. No one can halt time. However, if we take the time to plan and act, we can definitely achieve significant results.

For many years, science and technology were predominantly seen as male domains. Women faced numerous challenges and barriers in these fields, including social norms, family expectations, and traditions.

Although the country was not independent and still bore the burdens of oppression, modern education had begun to take root. The introduction of modern science education created an opportunity for individuals to contribute to society. In this context, one woman aspired to promote science education in her community. However, she encountered formidable social barriers. While many of her family members pursued studies in science and entered related careers, her journey was fraught with challenges.

Despite the obstacles, including gender discrimination, she remained resolute in her desire to work in science. She persevered, dedicating herself to her studies and efforts. Ultimately, she succeeded in overcoming these hurdles, becoming a renowned scientist. Although gender discrimination created numerous barriers in her pursuit of her dreams, she triumphed and became the first woman in her country to earn a PhD in science.

For many years, women were underrepresented, underpaid, and often overlooked for their scientific achievements and expertise, a trend observed worldwide. Women scientists frequently faced gender discrimination, which was particularly severe during the colonial rule in India. Despite the tireless efforts of notable figures like Raja Ram Mohan Roy, Ishwar Chandra Vidyasagar, Savitribai Phule, and others to promote girls' education, the number of women pursuing careers in science remained very low. Amidst such challenging circumstances, one woman made history by becoming the first Indian woman to earn a Ph.D. in biochemistry in 1939. Her remarkable achievements opened doors for other women at the Indian Institute of Science (IISc), Bangalore.

Born on June 8, 1912, in Indore, Madhya Pradesh, she was raised in a highly educated family. Her father, Narayan Rao Bhagwat, and her uncle, Madhavrao Bhagwat, a chemist, shaped her educational journey. She studied at the Tata Institute of Science and the Indian Institute of Science in Bangalore, following the family tradition. In 1933, she graduated from the University of Bombay with a degree in chemistry and physics, achieving the highest marks in her class.

She later joined the Indian Institute of Science (IISc), which not only honored her family's legacy but also helped her fulfill her dream of becoming a scientist.

At that time, she faced a significant obstacle: she applied to work with Prof. C.V. Raman, the first Indian Nobel Prize winner in Physics, but her application was rejected because he believed that women were not qualified to conduct research. This dismissal was particularly disheartening for her, considering her top scores. Her father and uncle were equally distressed by the situation, prompting her to repeatedly appeal to Prof. Raman. Unfortunately, he maintained his stance, stating, "I don't take girls in my institute."

Refusing to give up, she became more determined to enter the Indian Institute of Science. She insisted on receiving a detailed written explanation for her rejection from IISc and organized a protest at the institute. This unusual event left Prof. Raman with no justification to provide in writing, ultimately forcing him to enroll her at IISc. However, although he accepted her, he set three conditions for her admission.

The first was that she would not be allowed to attend the campus as a regular first-year student.

The second was that, according to the institute's rules, she would have to study and conduct research work until late at night.

The third rule prohibited her from disrupting the lab environment or interacting with male classmates.

This was very disappointing for a 22-year-old woman, but due to her determination to study and her strong desire to move forward, she accepted all the conditions and began her studies at the Indian Institute of Science (IISc). Some data suggest that gender discrimination has existed at IISc from its inception. In 1909, there were plans to build housing for workers, which in 1911 was converted into two blocks for staff and students. Despite this, many years passed before a hostel for women was constructed. Nevertheless, several steps have been taken to enhance women's education.

Professor C.V. Raman did not make things easy for his students. At that time, there were three female students enrolled at IISc, and he had strict instructions that these students should not talk to any male classmates. Noted author and scientist Abha Sur, in her book *Depressed Radiance*, discusses caste, gender, and modern science in India. In the late 1930s and 1940s, a few more female students were admitted to IISc, resulting in gradual improvements in hostels, toilets, and other facilities for women. For the first time, the construction of hostels for girls was mentioned in the IISc budget in 1942, with the IISc President, M. Visvesvaraya, highlighting the importance of this development in one of his speeches.

She became the first woman admitted to IISc in 1933. Although there is no specific information about the first women enrolled, the 1920 annual report of the institute mentioned a student named M. Mehta who enrolled that year. Two years later, in 1922, Miss R.K. Christy's name appeared on the list. Eleven years later, in 1933, the student who enrolled was Miss K. Bhagwat, later known as Kamala Sohonie.

However, the treatment she received left her deeply hurt. At a felicitation event organized by the Indian Women Scientists Association (IWSA), she remarked, "Although Professor C.V. Raman was a great scientist, he was very narrow-minded. I'll never forget the way he treated me. It was a great insult to me. At that time, discrimination against women was rampant. If we receive such treatment from a Nobel laureate, what more can we expect from others?"

As a child, Kamala was very quiet and modest. At first glance, one might assume that her life as a woman was calm, simple, and easy. However, her life was far from straightforward. She faced numerous obstacles along her journey. Despite eventually becoming a renowned scientist, she had to confront many challenges, although she was fortunate to have the full support of her family. Through her perseverance, willpower, and hard work, Kamala has become a source of inspiration for many, overcoming the problems and obstacles in her path. She became a prominent female scientist.

Kamala studied at the Indian Institute of Science (IISc), where she met a teacher who profoundly influenced her life—M. Srinivasaya. He was a pioneer in microbiological research in India and was known for his strict adherence to rules. He emphasized punctuality and encouraged his students to work diligently. While working with Professor Srinivasaya at IISc, Kamala researched the properties of proteins in orange peels, milk, and pulses. In 1935, he published an article in which he first described the characteristics of non-protein nitrogen in nine types of pulses. This research highlighted the importance of easily digestible nutrients for improving children's nutrition. In another study, Kamala demonstrated that orange milk was exceptionally nutrient-rich, which set the foundation for her master's research in 1936. Her tireless work and dedication inspired Professor C.V. Raman to believe that women could excel in scientific research. Initially, she was not allowed to stay on campus as a regular student during her first year. However, after performing well in her first-year examinations and demonstrating her dedication, Professor Raman permitted her to continue her studies on campus.

Kamala's success encouraged many girls to pursue studies at IISc in the years following her enrollment, leading to greater acceptance of women in the academic field.

Guided by her teacher, M. Srinivasaya, she excelled in her research on proteins in milk, pulses, and nuts, focusing on crucial aspects of nutrition. In 1936, she became the first Indian woman to earn a master's degree with distinction.

Later, Kamala received an opportunity to work at Frederick G. Hopkins Laboratory at the University of Cambridge, England, under Dr. Derek Ridger. It was a significant honor for her to study Biological Natural Science as a student of Newnham College, Cambridge University, in 1937. After working with Dr. Ridger, she studied plant tissue under Dr. Robin Hill. During this research, she examined potatoes and discovered the enzyme cytochrome c in oranges, which plays a vital role in the electron transport chain found in plants, humans, and animals. Through her hard work and determination, Kamala completed her research in just 14 months and prepared a comprehensive 40-page research paper. Her PhD dissertation was more extensive and detailed than those of her contemporaries, making her the first Indian woman to receive a doctorate from the prestigious Cambridge University.

Despite her generally quiet nature, Kamala gradually forged her path to success. Her research caught the attention of many scientists, leading her to apply for a fellowship at the Friedrich G. Hopkins Laboratory. In 1939, she applied for and secured the fellowship, joining the lab where she made groundbreaking discoveries regarding the historical significance of vitamins in food, which transformed nutrition in the field of biochemistry.

Later, her dream of working with great scientists was fulfilled. She received two scholarships from the Sir William Dunn Institute of Biochemistry at the University of Cambridge, as well as one from a university in the United States, allowing her to meet eminent scientists from Europe.

Notably, during the 1930s, the struggle against colonialism in India evolved into a mass movement. This was a time when Jawaharlal Nehru sought input from technocrats and scientists like Meghnad Saha and M. Visvesvaraya to create a blueprint for a modern, science-guided nation. This appeal resonated with Kamala. After earning her Ph.D. in 1939, she returned to India to fulfill her duty to her country and joined the fight alongside the people as a supporter of Mahatma Gandhi. She sacrificed a promising career abroad to demonstrate her deep commitment to India. Upon her return, she was appointed Professor and Head of the Department of Biochemistry at Lady Hardinge Medical College in New Delhi. She later worked as an assistant director at the Nutrition Research Laboratory in Coonoor, where she researched the effects of vitamins.

While studying at the University of Cambridge, Kamala met Madhav Sohonie, a brilliant student of Octrial Science from the University of London. The two became close friends after their initial meeting. After returning to India, she married Madhav in 1947, changing her name from Kamala Bhagwat to Kamala Sohonie. When asked if it was a love marriage, Kamala's son later stated, "It was not an arranged marriage, but it was done with the consent of both families. My mother was a beautiful and loving person. At home, she cooked for everyone and always prioritized our education. She was beloved for her kind heart and generous nature." After marriage, Kamala became a Professor of Biochemistry at the Royal Institute of Science in Mumbai.

She joined the department as a professor and conducted research on nutritional aspects of various nuts. It is said that she was appointed as the director of the institution four years later due to gender discrimination. During this time, Kamala and her students conducted significant research on three categories of food commonly consumed by the poor in India.

A meeting with the then President of India, Dr. Rajendra Prasad, had a profound impact on Kamala. At his suggestion, she conducted research on toddy (palm juice), which was a popular drink at the time known locally as "Neera." Her research on Neera (juice from the flowers of various palm species) revealed significant amounts of vitamin A, vitamin C, and iron in the drink, which could help preserve the concentrations of vitamins when produced into palm jaggery. She discovered that the sulfhydryl compound in Neera helps protect the vitamins.

This is one of the most important aspects of research. Subsequent surveys conducted by her demonstrated that the inclusion of 'Neera' in the diet significantly improved the health of children and pregnant women, effectively eliminating malnutrition in tribal society. Kamala sent her students to various parts of the country to analyze the vitamins and nutrition in the local drinks. However, her efforts did not stop there. She continually worked to popularize 'Neera' because it was both inexpensive and readily available, and she aimed to diversify the quality of tallgud. Her dedication paid off, as Kamala was awarded the President's Award for her unique research.

Later, Kamala joined the Aarey Milk Project Factory in Bombay as a consultant, where she developed a protocol to prevent milk from curdling too quickly. Praising her groundbreaking research, extraordinary work, and scientific achievements, scientist Derek Ridger once stated, "She has already made history." This is indeed a fitting and eloquent tribute.

In addition to her scientific pursuits, she was also an accomplished writer. Kamala authored numerous books for children and young adults, as well as several on consumer rights. She was a founding member of the Consumer Guidance Society of India (CGSI), which was started by nine women in 1966. CGSI is India's premier organization dedicated to the protection of consumer rights.

Even after retiring in 1969, Kamala remained engaged in research, which was far from complete. This work led to new analyses of enzymes such as glutamate decarboxylase and deamylase, as well as the detection of hemagglutinin. While both she and her husband enjoyed a comfortable life in retirement, Kamala did not wish to live a passive and silent life. She continued to work with the Consumer Guidance Society of India, where she and her colleagues played a key role in championing consumer rights and raising awareness against various injustices. She later designed a kit for testing the purity of household food items.

In other words, Kamala led a fruitful life and found success in all her endeavours. In 1997, she received the National Award for Excellence in Science, and on June 28, 1998, the Indian Council of Research Centres, in whose official journal she regularly published articles, organized a special function to honor her. Kamala received a standing ovation for her achievements. Tragically, she collapsed at the event and passed away shortly after.

The life and journey of this remarkable woman exemplify what it means to be great. Her work is a true reflection of her greatness. If she had given up after being insulted by Prof. Raman, it would have taken many more years for girls to gain access to I.I.S.C. There is no doubt about this. She successfully broke the gender barrier for women at that time, paving the way for the emergence of many female scientists. Through her struggles, she climbed the ladder of success with unwavering patience and perseverance.

Kamala's philosophy of life strongly emphasizes merit. She didn't just dream of success; she faced numerous obstacles and endured humiliation to achieve her goals. It is clear that she is a symbol of inspiration for all women. The nation owes her a debt of gratitude for her ideas, ideals, and unparalleled contributions to science. Society as a whole is indebted to women like her. Despite the challenges she faced and the pain she endured, she kept moving forward. She forged a path for herself and left a legacy for future generations.

Her light continues to shine. When a woman achieves success through perseverance, it represents not just her personal progress, but also serves as a beacon of hope for her family and community. She becomes a source of inspiration, illuminating even the darkest paths.

□□

Dakshayani Belayudhan

In the early 20th century, Indian princely states under British rule, such as Travancore and Cochin, were heavily influenced by the caste system. Within this social hierarchy, Dalits faced significant humiliation and persecution. One such community was the Pulaya, who were regarded as an untouchable caste and positioned at the bottom of the caste hierarchy. They experienced not only racial oppression but also social harassment, as upper-caste individuals imposed strict rules on them, leaving them with little recourse.

Both Pulaya men and women were forbidden from covering the upper part of their bodies with clothing, resulting in them being half-naked. Some were even compelled to cover themselves with grass, and they could not cut their hair. Additionally, they were prohibited from having contact with high-ranking individuals, and their children were barred from attending school. They were not allowed to enter the main roads and market areas of Ernakulam city, effectively isolating them from hospitals and the broader society.

As this oppression continued, a significant social change began to take shape. Voices were raised against the prevailing injustices, culminating in a historic meeting. At that time, there were strict rules forbidding Dalits, particularly those belonging to the Pulaya caste, from assembling in any public place. King Ramavarma had enforced a law that prohibited them from sitting together on the ground. In response to this unjust rule, the Dalits expressed their outrage and resistance. The situation escalated into a notable confrontation.

In their determination, they decided that if they could not gather on land, they would step into water to hold meetings. They would reach the middle of a lake in small boats to convene. This gathering was called the "Meeting on the Backwaters," which allowed them to avoid breaking any rules while sending a powerful message of rebellion to the upper castes.

This struggle deeply impacted a young girl from the Pulaya community who witnessed the discrimination against her people and the severe atrocities they faced. Inspired by her community's efforts to resist oppression, she learned about their fights led by members of her family. Her uncle, Kalachamuri Krishnadi Asan, and her brother, K.P. Valon, were prominent figures in this movement, advocating for the rights of the Pulayas. In 1934, they presented a report highlighting the conditions faced by the Pulayas, further fueling the fight for their rights.

Dakshayani was born on July 4, 1912, in a Dalit community in Mulavukad village, located in the Kanayannur region of Ernakulam district. During that time, the naming rituals for the Dalit community were peculiar; they did not have the right to give their children names that were considered respectable, unlike the upper castes. As a result, parents in the Dalit community often chose unusual names for their daughters, such as Azhaki, Pumala, Chaki, Kali, Kurumba, Thara, and Kilipakta. However, Dakshayani's parents chose to name her 'Dakshayani,' which means "daughter of Daksha" and is another name for Durga. Her daughter, Meera, reflected on this by saying, "Maa has mentioned it very well in her book that in those days, Pulaya women would criticize her for being given such a name."

When Dakshayani was born in 1912, it was common for a Dalit

woman to face discrimination for various reasons. Such social norms were prevalent at that time, but Dakshayani refused to accept them. From a young age, she sought to challenge these traditions and live independently, aiming to liberate her community from the constraints of the caste system. As she grew older, she began to resist, but it was not easy. She faced numerous obstacles and humiliation, yet she confronted every challenge in her life.

Before Dakshayani's birth, two prominent social reformers, Sree Narayana Guru and Ayyankali, vocally opposed the severe caste system that dominated Kerala society at the time. They organized movements to advocate for the Dalit community's right to access education and public spaces. Through satyagrahas and marches, they encouraged both men and women to fight against the feelings of inferiority brought on by caste discrimination. At that time, there were strict regulations regarding their movement; many roads were designated exclusively for upper-caste individuals. Additionally, Dalits were required to bow down and wait for upper-caste individuals to pass. Dakshayani's early awareness of these injustices inspired her to become a rebel.

Dakshayani was the first educated woman from the Pulaya caste, completing her Bachelor of Arts degree in 1935 at Madras University, studying at the Government College in Kochi. Between 1935 and 1945, she worked as a government high school teacher in Trichur and Tripunithura. She was not only the first Dalit woman in India to pass the 10th grade but also the first Dalit woman to graduate from college. Furthermore, she became the first Scheduled Caste woman graduate, science graduate, member of the Cochin Legislative Council, and one of only nine women in the Constituent Assembly of India.

There have been several movements focused on how women could cover the upper part of their bodies. Between 1813 and 1859, a significant movement known as the Maru Marakkal Samaram emerged, aimed at addressing the issue of Dalit women's right to cover their bodies. Later, Dakshayani actively fought for social change, protesting against the practice of forcing women to keep the upper part of their bodies uncovered. As a result, she achieved great success and made history by asserting her right to do so at a time when Dalit women faced restrictions on covering their breasts.

Recalling her early days, Dakshayani said, "During my graduation, I was the only science graduate in that college. The upper-caste teachers did not show me any experiments in the laboratory; I was merely watching from a distance." She completed her graduation in 1935 and joined a high school as a teacher on April 2, 1935, in Peringothikara, located in the Trichur district. Following this, she went to Madras for training. This clearly demonstrates Dakshayani's determination to achieve her goals.

After completing her training, she joined the government school at Peringottukara in Trichur, where a majority of the population belonged to the Ezhava caste. The upper-caste individuals in the area could not accept a Dalit woman as a teacher in the classroom. The owner of the house she was staying in did not allow her to draw water from the well but permitted her to do so because her mother had converted to Christianity. As a result, she had to stay with her mother. At that time, Dakshayani remarked, "Large seas do not have a caste system, but the water of a small well probably recognises the caste system." In 1942, she moved to a school in the upper-caste dominated Tripunithura area.

In 1941, Dakshayani was transferred to an upper-caste region in Tripunithura. In her book, she recounts an incident when she was walking along a road, and a woman from the Nair community confronted her, demanding that she step off the road. This was a common practice directed towards the Pulaya community. With mud on both sides of the road, Dakshayani refused, stating, "I will not get down from the road. If you want to pass, you should step off the road and go into the field." The field was four to five feet lower than the road, which forced the woman to step down but she did not walk on the road beside Dakshayani. Such superstitions, prejudices, and societal distinctions that Dakshayani faced while working in the school compelled her to challenge these norms and seek their removal from society. She desired policy changes that would rationalize and provide justice to her community while aiding in the collective development of the country.

Dakshayani was married to R. Velayudhan, a leader from a Scheduled Tribe. In the presence of Gandhiji and Kasturba, they were married by a leprosy-afflicted priest in the village of Seva, located in Wardha. Dakshayani later became the first Dalit Member of Parliament and the first woman leader of the Dalit community. In 1945, she was nominated to the Cochin Legislative Council by the state government. She was also elected to the Constituent Assembly in 1946, becoming the first and only Dalit woman member of that assembly. Dakshayani served as a member of the Constituent Assembly and the Provisional Parliament from 1946 to 1952. As a Member of Parliament, she emphasized the importance of educating Dalit women. Influenced by Ayyankali, a prominent social activist, Dakshayani began to raise her voice against social evils prevalent in society.

She was a Gandhian and a staunch supporter of Gandhi. During the drafting of the Constitution, she addressed many issues concerning the Dalit community and supported Dr. B.R. Ambedkar, agreeing with his views. On November 8, 1948, when Dr. Ambedkar presented the draft of the Constitution, Dakshayani backed him and advocated for the approval of the draft. She expressed her opinions on the centralized rule of the British and the role of the Governor, suggesting that the draft constitution should be chosen by the common people through a general election. She questioned why these principles were not being followed and emphasized the importance of realizing the dream of a clean, democratic nation.

On November 29, 1948, during the discussion on Article 11 of the Constitution, she reiterated her concerns about discrimination in society based on caste. The Deputy Chairman of the Constituent Assembly allowed her extra speaking time, saying, "Because you are a woman." In response to the issue of caste discrimination, she stated, "Caste discrimination can be removed if people are educated. The Constituent Assembly should pass a special resolution on racial discrimination. The focus should be on how people behave and change themselves in the future; that should be the main goal of the Constitution."

She highlighted that the members of the Constituent Assembly were exceptionally talented, far-sighted, and energetic. As the only woman from the Dalit community among them, Dakshayani sought to bring about change in society by contributing valuable opinions in various deliberations. She aimed to challenge prevailing social customs and make strides for her community.

Dakshayani was elected to a reserved seat for Scheduled Castes in the Cochin Legislative Council. Following in the footsteps of her brother K.P. Vallon, she was elected to the Cochin Legislative Assembly in 1945 and to the Constituent Assembly of India in 1946 from the Madras constituency. At the age of 34, she not only became the first and only Dalit woman to. Be elected to the Constituent Assembly but also played a significant role in decision-making for the public interest of the nation, proving that a person from a minority community has the right to express her opinion.

Speaking at a meeting of the Cochin Legislative Assembly, Dakshayani expressed her anguish over the plight of the backward castes. She said, "As long as the practice of untouchability is not legally abolished, and various programs for their revival are not undertaken, merely calling them 'Harijan' will be like addressing a dog as 'Napoleon'." Furthermore, she emphasized her commitment to ensuring that the Dalit community can make decisions for themselves based on their safety and convenience.

She opposed the separate appointment of Governors by both the Centre and the States. Additionally, she believed that the draft constitution should be approved through a general vote. During the discussion on Article 11, which aimed to abolish the caste system and make it a criminal offense, Dakshayani stated, "We can never have a Constitution which does not have a law on untouchability." Her aims aligned closely with Gandhi's ideals and vision for India. Her primary goal was to restore the status of Untouchables in the country, advocating for their rights and addressing the miserable conditions in their society.

Dakshayani's views created a stir in Parliament. After Sardar Patel's Minority Report was presented on August 28, 1947, she expressed her thoughts in a speech, saying, "Call them Scheduled Castes or Harijans or whatever, but as long as they are treated as servants of other classes, there is no point in having separate constituencies or elections. Personally, I am not in favor of reservation. The true progress of these backward classes will only be possible after we achieve freedom from British rule and actively participate in the collective development of the country."

Beyond her political stance, Dakshayani was vocal about the neglect of Dalits and the need for their enjoying rights in terms of economic and social security. She envisioned a strong, united India rather than a system with different electoral frameworks and constituencies.

In her speech, she said, "The Constituent Assembly needs to go beyond the conventional ideas and adopt an approach that provides a new way of life for the people. Untouchability must be criminalized and genuinely eradicated from society." According to her, social evils and differences could only be eliminated in a democratic nation through moral force. In another speech, Dakshayani said, "I believe that a Constituent Assembly not only creates the rules of the Constitution but also offers a new perspective on life for the citizens of that democratic nation. While it may be easy to draft a Constitution by using other countries as examples, protecting your citizens, granting them their rights, and establishing a new foundation rooted in a new consciousness is far more challenging. It is our moral responsibility to eradicate social discrimination from our society. Our freedom will come from within India, not from the British government." All these speeches made by Dakshayani in the Constituent Assembly were influenced by the thoughts of Gandhi and Ambedkar.

Reflecting on her personal experiences of caste discrimination and social dynamics, Dakshayani stated at the Pulaya Mahasabha: "Two of my elder brothers and my father Kunjan's younger brother, Krishnethi, along with Pandit Karupad (a professor at Maharaja's College) and T.K. Krishna Menon (from a prominent Dewan family), formed the Pulaya Mahasabha, electing Krishnethi as its president. At that time, we were not allowed to sit together in my native place. However, the meeting took place on water, using small boats, thanks to the fishermen. By doing this, we aimed to challenge the caste system; this land may be marked by caste discrimination, but there is no caste in the water of the sea."

Dakshayani was the mother of five children: Dr. Reghu (Indira Gandhi's doctor), Prahladan, Dhruvan, and Bhagirath (Secretary General of the Indian Ocean Rim Association - IORA). She was deeply involved with her family and wrote many letters to her daughter, filled with advice and counsel that served as beacons in her daughter's life. "I am proud of my family. I have confidence in my abilities and never feel inferior."

Dakshayani's daughter, Meera, has been profoundly influenced by her mother's fearlessness and has expressed it in many places. For example, she recounts, "I began my menstruation when I was in the ninth grade. I asked my father about this change in my body and requested her to bring some sanitary products."

Dakshayani found it easier to work at the social level than in the realm of traditional politics. She was particularly fond of working with women sanitation workers in Delhi's Munirka slum and founded the 'Mahila Jagriti Parishad' in 1977 to organize a national convention of Dalit women in Delhi.

Along with her associates, she sought to uplift Dalits. Although untouchability was abolished in the Constitution, she observed that it persisted in society for nearly a decade.

Dakshayani was unsuccessful in her last political campaign in 1971. Notably, her husband's relative, K.R. Narayanan, later became the first Dalit president of India. Dakshayani passed away in 1978 at the age of 66.

Examining the life of Dakshayani reveals both the struggles she faced and the strength she exhibited. Her tenacity in fighting against the deeply entrenched caste system, particularly during a time when social perspectives lagged far behind, is nothing short of remarkable.

Terms such as backward class, Dalit, and Harijan, which have been coined at different times, remain sensitive. While it may seem that Dalits no longer need to struggle for their place or education, as seats in government schools are reserved for them, caste-based discrimination and atrocities still exist in many parts of the country. Recent incidents in Uttar Pradesh have shaken public consciousness. Nonetheless, the enduring struggle of women against these abhorrent practices will always be remembered, as their sacrifices and relentless passion for positive change have propelled many societal transformations.

Meera recalls, "Mother used to say that long ago, when my people and I walked with our heads down in Mulavukad, I never lost the will to walk with my head held high." Sharing with us a poignant memory, Meera writes, "One night while studying for an exam, I sat with my head bowed, waiting for a cup of coffee. When my mother saw me, she patted me on the back and said, 'Sit up straight.' It reminds me of the past and how we had to lower our heads in front of upper caste people. Despite this, I still can't shake the confidence to face the world."

Dakshayani Velayudhan fought vigorously against the caste system. Her immense contributions were meant not only for the Dalit community but also for the fundamental rights and dignity of every citizen in the country. Later, she served as the editor of *Jai Bhim*, a publication founded by Ambedkarites. As the first Dalit couple, Dakshayani and her husband, R. Velayudhan, were leaders of two opposition parties in the Provisional Parliament, with R. Velayudhan representing the Socialist Party and Dakshayani representing Congress. She died on July 20, 1978, at the age of 66.

□□

Amrita Shergill

There is a saying: "Martya mandaly deha nahi, debata hoile marayi." Even a deity born as a human being on the earth is subject to mortality.

Life is simple yet profound. As with all beings, there is birth and there is death. Humans are mortal; they embody the cycle of life and death. For some, the time between birth and death is long, while for others, it is short. Humans possess a variety of talents. Some individuals leave a lasting impact on the earth during their long lives, while others, despite leading brief lives, leave an indelible mark. The talented among us manage to create a legacy that renders them immortal, regardless of their lifespan. Here, we focus on the life of a remarkable artist.

Painting plays a crucial role in challenging and decentralizing the prevailing stereotypes about women's status in society, their progress, and their concerns. When a woman artist explores these ideas through her work, the significance of her art becomes even more pronounced in discussions of these themes.

Among many artists in our country, she was one of the most talented women painters who uniquely represented Indian culture through her artwork. Her achievement as a woman painter extends beyond the range of other female artists; each of her pieces serves as a milestone in the world of contemporary painting. By artistically presenting the subtle and complex elements of life, she expressed the bonds and relationships shared by individuals in a way that is rarely seen among her contemporaries. In her paintings, she captured the dynamics between women, portraying scenes of women at the marketplace, at marriage ceremonies, and reflecting on women's roles within the household. These enhance the emotional depth of her work, and in some instances, her paintings echo the silent rebellion or protest of women. At a time when society often depicted women as defenseless, this artist stood out as an exception.

We are discussing such a great woman artist, who once said this about her paintings, "The paintings of Europe mean Picasso, Matisse, Braque, and many others; but the paintings of India mean only me." This ambitious and indomitable artist elevated Indian painting to new heights during her brief but illustrious career. Her unique style not only gave a new direction to Indian art but also established a distinct identity for it. Undoubtedly, she secured a prominent place among the leading artists of the 20th century.

Amrita Shergil was born on January 30, 1913, in Budapest, Hungary, to a Hungarian-Indian family. Her father, Umrao Singh Shergill Majithia, came from an aristocratic Jat family and was well-versed in Sanskrit and Persian. Her mother, Marie-Antoinette Gottesman, hailed from a middle-class Hungarian Jewish family and was an opera singer.

Marie Antoinette had visited Lahore in 1912, where she met Umrao Singh Shergill. After deciding to marry, they moved to Hungary, where Amrita was born. Amrita spent her childhood in Hungary, learning to play the piano and violin. She began drawing at the age of five and underwent formal training in painting by the age of eight. In 1921, the family relocated to Summerhill, Shimla, India. At nine, Amrita began performing with her younger sister, Indira, at the Shimla Gateway Theatre on Mall Road. She was enrolled at St. Mary's Convent School in Shimla but struggled with the Catholic teachings, which led to her growing rebelliousness. Eventually, her discontent with school resulted in her dropping out in 1924.

At the age of 16, she travelled to Europe with her mother to study formal painting in Paris. While studying under Lucien Simon, she was greatly influenced by renowned European painters such as Paul Cézanne and Paul Gauguin.

Amrita had gained fame in Paris for her exceptional painting skills. She dedicated most of her time to drawing, playing the piano, and reading books, all while nurturing her secret ambition to become a painter.

Reflecting on her artistic journey, she once said, "I don't remember ever starting to paint, but I've always had a natural inclination to paint. I've always believed I would just be an artist."

Recognizing her talent, Amrita's uncle, Irwin Bacatte, a painter himself, encouraged her to study at the College of Fine Arts in Paris. In 1929, she joined the Académie de la Grande Chaumière, where she embraced her own painting style instead of conforming to conventional classroom teaching. Gradually, she lost interest in formal education, though she continued her studies at the École Nationale des Beaux-Arts under Lucien Simon's guidance. Amrita developed a strong interest in drawing and painting human figures, producing many nude images of both men and women.

Between 1930 and 1932, she created over sixty paintings that captured the essence of life and various symbolic landscapes through oil. In 1930, she held an exhibition of her work in Paris. After returning to India in 1935, she sought to explore new directions in painting, particularly drawing inspiration from the art of the Ajanta and Ellora Caves, which she incorporated into her work.

Amrita's mother wanted Amrita to marry and lead a happy life, without wandering aimlessly. However, Amrita had a different perspective on marriage. She did not view it as the cherished goal of a woman's life. Due to circumstances, she ended up marrying her childhood friend, Victor Egan, who was a cousin on her uncle's side and had gone to medical school. Although Amrita's mother did not approve of the marriage, Amrita refused to marry anyone else. They were married in court on July 16, 1938. Even after her marriage, Amrita continued to paint. The couple moved to Shimla when the war broke out in Europe. Over time, Amrita experienced feelings of depression, during which she created two significant artworks titled "Ancient Storyteller" and "The Swing." She was honored by the Indian Academy of Fine Arts in Amritsar. In addition to her painting, she wrote letters to many prominent personalities, which were later compiled by artist Bibhan Sundaram. Her independent thinking and outlook on life are evident in this collection.

Amrita's personal thoughts, along with her emphasis on women's emancipation and self-respect, are reflected in her artwork. She laid emphasis on the dignity of marginalized and destitute people in society through her art. For example, in her 1937 painting "The Bride's Toilet," she depicted the status and behavior of women in society. Each of her paintings carries a voice for justice, artistically portraying the despair in women's lives. Moreover, she ensured that each character in her artwork respected others, which garnered her considerable praise. She experimented with both Indian and European styles, and her talent as a painter emerged naturally. It is said that when she was only seven years old, she would paint the stories she heard. Amrita recalled, "I remember as a child I used to draw with pencils and colors, using picture books and so on. I've been experimenting with different colors since I was a kid. I presented myself in different ways." One notable painting features Amrita dressed as a Tahitian woman, freely presenting truth and reality. The symbolic reflections of life are especially evident in her works.

Shergill used an original artistic style in her paintings that others struggled to succeed with, even after many attempts. She created art for the sake of art, not for entertainment. Her creativity ran deep, making it impossible for her to see art as merely a means to earn money. Any negative comments about her art would deeply affect her. Throughout her lifetime, Amrita gained both social and financial prestige, but she eventually fell into depression.

Amrita Shergill's early works and her post-apocalyptic painting style were significantly influenced by Western artistic movements. In the 1930s, she created many pieces that focused on the bohemian culture of Paris. Her 1932 oil painting "Young Girl" brought her considerable fame, earning her a gold medal and making her the only Asian artist selected as a delegate to the prestigious Grand Salon in Paris in 1933.

During this time, her paintings gained widespread publication. She painted numerous works depicting the Parisian way of life, including portraits of her friends and students, self-portraits, and explorations of the symbolic nature of gender and identity. The National Museum of Modern Art in Delhi described her self-portraits as a montage of the creator's melancholic, contemplative, and ecstatic moods.

The first half of Amrita's life was spent abroad, while the second half was spent in India. With an Indian father and a Hungarian mother, Amrita naturally absorbed the traditions and characteristics of her diverse cultural background. She presented the hidden essence of Indian culture at an exhibition in Paris, where she attended a social function wearing a saree. She consistently distinguished herself in a male-dominated society, earning the title of the 'Frida Kahlo' of India.

In 1936, Amrita's paintings received widespread acclaim in the Indian media, establishing her as an exceptional artist. At the fifth annual exhibition of the Lalit Kala Akademi in New Delhi, she received two awards. Another exhibition of her works was held in Bombay on November 20, 1936. Her major paintings often featured groups of young women, brides, hillbillies, portraits of her father, and villagers. Her travels to Ajanta and Ellora significantly influenced her art, and upon moving to South India, she felt that her true artistic voice could finally be expressed freely in her own country. Even her teachers recognized that the "hidden painter" in Amrita would be greatly inspired by India.

Colors can be even more vibrant. The lifestyles of the poor and marginalized communities in India, as well as the lives of women, were powerfully reflected in her paintings. She was opposed to conventional painting techniques, choosing instead to depict the harsh realities of life, including the social conditions of the impoverished. Personally, she was against colonialism, which was evident in both her artwork and her writings.

Furthermore, she strongly opposed the social injustices and discrimination prevalent in Indian society. She was greatly influenced by

Gandhi's philosophy and way of life. Jawaharlal Nehru held her in high regard, and they exchanged letters. In one of his letters to Amrita, Nehru wrote, "I love your works of art, for they express the vitality of life." Amrita's 'South Indian Trilogy' is considered her greatest collection of artworks, which includes "Bride's Toilet," "Brahmachari," and "South Indian Villager Going to Market." These pieces were regarded as some of the most significant works of art of that era.

Amrita had a unique way of expressing her thoughts in her paintings and also showed the ability to convey them poignantly. She gave new dimensions to her work by blending both Indian and Western artistic styles. Additionally, she critiqued the Indian painting style of her time, feeling that, apart from artists like Rabindranath Tagore and Raja Ravi Varma, most were not doing justice to the purpose and direction of art. She believed that the poor expressed a unique beauty in their lives, contrasting with the elite class she depicted in her artwork. In her paintings, she captured both the dark and bright sides of life.

Her 1930 painting, "Portrait of a Young Man," won the École des Beaux-Arts award in 1931. In 1932, she painted a portrait of her friend and colleague Maria Luisa, titled "Young Girl," which earned her a gold medal at the Grand Salon in 1933. In 1931, Amrita created a piece named "Torso," using the surface of her fingernails as a model. The tradition of using a woman's body as a model in Indian painting began in 1930. She adopted a modern and free-thinking lifestyle while in Paris, which is reflected in her artwork. Her experimentation with color significantly influenced her paintings.

As a woman, she often featured female subjects in her works to convey her unique perspective. She beautifully illustrated the happiness, sorrow, and strength of women in her paintings. In her 1934 piece, "Tahitian," she depicted the buttocks of a woman, influenced by Paul Gauguin, using gray-brown hues to portray the body.

It is said that Amrita had several female lovers throughout her life. She found it a sweet experience to form relationships with women, so she distanced herself from men. During her time in Paris in the 1930s, she reportedly had a romantic relationship with her close friend and associate, Marie Louise Chasny. Although both later denied this relationship, Amrita mentioned in a letter to her mother, "Whenever the opportunity arose, I had something special to share with a woman."

By doing this, she did not sever her relationships with men; instead, she sought to cultivate meaningful connections with them. She viewed her body as a topic worthy of discussion, both physically and mentally. Throughout her life, she encountered many men and believed that sexual desire is a natural human tendency, asserting that there is nothing unusual about the environments people come from.

She openly expressed her bisexual thoughts in her personal reflections and artwork. In a letter to her mother in 1934, she wrote: "You are very clever, faithful, and realistic. That's why I can share so much with you. Like you, I too struggle with my feelings about men. However, I now find it increasingly difficult to suppress my physical sexual desires. I believe it is utterly impossible for such feelings to be confined solely to a painting; only the unintelligent would think otherwise. So, whenever I have the opportunity, I will pursue a relationship with a woman." She is regarded as the first woman to articulate such views about her own body, aiming to challenge insignificant traditional practices, a theme reflected in her work.

Her creations often showcased a blend of ideas from both genders as well as the hidden thoughts of men.

In an article published in *The Hindu* in November 1936, Amrita wrote, "Indian painting does not accurately represent myth and romance. Personally, I feel the need for a new style that embodies Indian philosophy." She was selected as a representative at the Grand Salon in Paris in 1933 as a young artist, and during her trip to South India in 1937, she painted works such as "Bride's Toilet," "Brahmachairis," and "South Indian Villagers Going to Market." After visiting the caves of Ajanta, she demonstrated a return to Indian classical painting. Her artworks vividly represent the diversity of Indian culture, traditions, customs, and colors. Through her canvas, she not only conveyed her artistic vision but also illustrated the philosophy of life in India. Notably, she often used her domestic help as models.

Influenced by Rabindranath Tagore and Jamini Roy of Bengal, she began a new phase of her painting career after moving to her ancestral home in Saraiya, Sadarnagar, Gorakhpur, Uttar Pradesh. This shift marked the beginning of an experimental phase in Indian painting with the Calcutta Group of Artists. Alongside them, the "Progressive Artist Group," which included Francis Newton Souza, Ara, Bakre, Gade, M. F. Husain, and S. H. Raza, aimed to broaden the horizons of Indian painting. Amrita drew significant inspiration from Rabindranath and Abanindranath, the two central figures of the Bengal School of Painting. While depicting women, she emulated Tagore's style of black and white silhouettes and Abanindranath's use of dark colors. During her stay in Saraiya, she created "Village Scene," "In the Ladies Enclosure," and "Siesta," offering a genuine portrayal of Indian rural life. In her paintings "Siesta" and "In the Ladies' Enclosure," she applied artistic techniques from the miniature school of painting, while employing the style of the Pahari school in "Village Scene."

Upon returning to India, she was driven to depict herself as a unique painter. Many of her works reflect the despair of Indian women, including "Three Girls" from 1935, "Hill Women," "Red Verandah" from 1931, and "Two Girls" from 1935, addressing themes of personal freedom, social status, and sexual desire. Shergill did not perceive women as mere victims of tradition; instead, she believed they should possess the freedom to express themselves fully. She is considered the first female painter with such progressive views in modern Indian art, demonstrating courage in defying conventional norms.

Shergill's contribution

Amrita Shergill passed away in Lahore on December 5, 1941, at the age of 28. After her death, her work achieved enormous fame. It would be no exaggeration to say that she was a unique figure in the realm of modern Indian painting and provided a new direction for the art form. Despite coming from an affluent family, she raised her voice against many unethical practices prevalent in society. Instead of dwelling on the challenges she faced in life, she focused on advancing her lifestyle, often moving beyond the contemporary thinking of her time. She took pride in this.

Her paintings reflect deep emotional expressions rather than mere intellectual thoughts. Amrita not only set a precedent in the world of painting but also opened up many new avenues for artistic expression. In 1976, she was named "the nation's most valuable asset," signifying that the Indian way of life will always embrace its distinctive painting style. Her works embody both beauty and reality, revealing her life's mission as a flame that connected her to the world. Her purpose brought her back to her homeland, and her love shaped her understanding of life. Amrita's artistry is notable for its fusion of Eastern and Western influences.

From Syed Haider Raza to Arpita Singh, many artists have drawn inspiration from Shergill's work. Her commitment to expressing the positions, hopes, and disappointments of women has earned her recognition both in India and abroad. Many of her pieces are preserved in the National Art Museum in New Delhi, which has declared them a national treasure. Some of her works are also displayed in the Lahore Museum.

The art of a woman is often instinctive. She effortlessly beautifies her home and family with her unique touch. Alongside decorating each item in her household, she nurtures every family member, skillfully preparing and serving food. However, the scope of a woman's artwork can vary based on time, environment, and circumstances; some women's creativity remains confined within their homes, while others break through those barriers. Amrita Shergill was one of the fortunate few who could establish her reputation herself through her art. Although she did not enjoy a long life, she lived her brief years beautifully, traveling to many places, experiencing diverse cultures, and reflecting these experiences in her paintings. Amrita lived a life full of love and remained acutely aware of her beauty. She embraced love fully, often forming new connections as previous ones ended, and she strived to befriend everyone. In her last three years, she provided a new direction for Indian painting and influenced many prominent writers such as Amrita Choudhury, author of the novel "Faking It," and Salman Rushdie, who was inspired by her painting "The Moor's Last Sigh."

Most of the paintings Amrita created during her lifetime vividly depicted the lives of women. As a woman herself, she had a profound understanding of a woman's body, mind, and psyche, shaped by her own experiences and significantly influenced by her mother, who was the daughter of an artist and encouraged Amrita's pursuit of art. As a woman artist, Amrita beautifully captured various phases of a woman's life through her use of cotton and color, reflecting the experiences of women in a captivating manner. Her artwork remains a topic of discussion even today, illustrating that, although time has passed and her life has ended, Amrita continues to live on through her paintings.

□□

Gaidinliu Pamei

Gaidinliu was born on January 26, 1915, in the village of Nangko (Longkou), which is now part of the Tamenglong subdivision in Manipur. She was the daughter of the Kabui, or Rangmei, Naga tribe and the fifth of eight children in her family, having six sisters and one brother. Her parents were Lothong Pamei and Kalaklenlou, who were part of the ruling family in the village. Unfortunately, Gaidinliu could not receive formal education, as there was no school in her village.

Despite her lack of formal education, Gaidinliu exhibited leadership qualities from an early age, as it was inherent in her. During her teenage years, she became influenced by her grandfather's son, Hariso Jadonang, who was engaged in an armed struggle to drive the British out of India.

Jadonang believed that to strengthen the political movement against British colonial rule, the existing religious practices would need to be reformed. As a result, he announced a new belief system called the Herakka movement.

Jadonang was ten years older than Gaidinliu, and his religion represented a fusion of Christianity, Hinduism, and Naga animism. The propagation of this new religion increased his popularity. The Herakka movement aimed at the upliftment of the tribal people and led to a growing number of followers. Within six years of its inception, the British saw Jadonang as a threat to their control in the eastern region.

By 1915, the British had been extending their reach in Northeast India for nearly fifty years. Their goal was to subjugate the Naga tribes, as these tribes were obstructing tea production in Assam, which was a prized commodity for the British. Consequently, the colonial government set up factories in Assam to create an alternative to imported sugar, which was crucial for the United Kingdom. Military campaigns in the region facilitated the British administration's political expansion and economic interests. Alongside the Naga Hill Administration, the British invited the American Baptist Foreign Mission Society from Burma to evangelize the Nagas. By the time Gaidinliu was born, various mission stations had already been established by American missionaries, who focused on conversion and education.

The Zeliangrong community exhibits a complex pattern of leadership, power dynamics, competition, and legitimacy. Not all Naga tribes participated in the civilizing mission introduced by the British. Jadonang, in particular, was a prominent opponent, working to raise awareness among the local population about the British rulers and missionaries. By the mid-1920s, Jadonang's movement was gaining significant traction, and this was when Gaidinliu became his closest associate. Her interactions with him provided her with profound insights.

In 1927, at the age of 13, Gaidinliu joined the Herakka movement under Jadonang's guidance, becoming his first follower. Her early life was marked by notable events, including a sacred pilgrimage to Bhuban Hill, where Jadonang believed he received a divine sign to preach the new religion.

He advocated the Herakka religion for the Zeliangrong people, leading to the construction of temples and places of worship. In Kambiron, he built two temples, creating spaces for communal worship and connecting the community to their deities. Many people visited Rahkai to pray to their deity, Tongkao Ragwang, through verses and dance music. Jadonang oriented his temple slightly to the east to align with the sunrise and sunset, signifying its importance to him. He taught the worship of Tingwang as the sole deity, deemphasizing the local gods and goddesses while stating that prayer did not always require sacrifice.

This new faith marked an important period in the religious history of the Zeliangrong people. The temple included two bathrooms, and it saw devotees flocking to offer prayers. Jadonang sought to dispel numerous local superstitions and introduced new prayers, shlokas, devotional music, and dances. Following her mentor's example, Gaidinliu established a Tarangkai in her village, Lungkai, where various religious ceremonies were held.

As he emerged as a new leader, Jadonang sought to collect taxes from the people, consequently abolishing the heavy colonial house tax and rejecting the Pothang system of feudal labor. The colonial authorities accused him of orchestrating attacks against the Kukis, traditional enemies of the Zeliangrong, with the intent of driving out the British and establishing Naga rule.

The colonial authorities did not view Jadonang as a person with supernatural or paranormal mental abilities. Instead, he was accused by innocent villagers into believing that he was a god, prompting them to worship him. Ursula Graham Bower, a contemporary psychologist of Gaidinliu, referred to him as the center of the "Money Spinning God Racket."

In 1931, Jadonang and Queen Gaidinliu spread the religious and spiritual movement in the Bhuban Hills. This was their last trip together.

Jadonang was arrested while returning from that trip and was executed by the British Army on August 29, 1931, for allegedly sacrificing humans to appease his gods.

At the time of Jadonang's execution, Gaidinliu was only 16 years old. As his successor, she was responsible for leading Jadonang's movement. Although she was ten years younger than her brother, she continued his work and was accused of inciting communal unrest against the Kukis and the British authorities. The British police sought to arrest her, but she operated in secrecy, organizing protests against British rule. The residents of Zeliangrong were pressured not to pay taxes to British officials, and local Nagas provided financial support for Gaidinliu's movement. Many joined her organization as volunteers. The British authorities initiated a manhunt for her, but each time they caught her, she managed to escape. She travelled extensively across Assam, Manipur, and Nagaland.

While in hiding, Gaidinliu intensified the Herakka movement. Herakka means sacred, with 'Hera' referring to minor deities and 'Ka' indicating fence or sacrifice. The movement promoted the worship of only Tingwang, rejecting sacrifices to minor deities. The term "sacred" here signifies that there should be no blood sacrifice. It was believed that those who embraced the Herakka religion would find their destinies brightened and their souls welcomed into heaven. Herakka believers wore a specific type of earring, and Queen Gaidinliu shared the teachings of her religion with her people.

In response to her growing influence, the Governor of Assam dispatched the 3rd and 4th battalions of the Assam Rifles, overseen by Naga Hills Deputy Commissioner J.P. Mills, to arrest her. A financial reward was offered for information leading to Gaidinliu's capture, with the promise that villagers who provided such information would be exempt from taxes for ten years. Gaidinliu's group engaged in guerrilla warfare with the Assam Rifles in North Cachar Hills on February 16, 1932, and at Hangaram village on March 13, 1932.

In October 1932, Gaidinliu was in need of a safe place to stay, so she traveled to Pulomi village and constructed a wooden fort there. However, on October 17, 1932, while the fort was being built, her group was ambushed by the Assam Rifles, led by Captain Macdonald. Gaidinliu and her supporters were caught off guard and had no chance to resist. She was arrested near Kenoma village, where she insisted, "They are not responsible for the attack on the Assam Rifles at Hungram Post," but her words went unheard.

Veera Ramani was only 16 years old when she joined the freedom struggle alongside Gaidinliu. The courageous Gaidinliu managed to keep the British soldiers out of Manipur for an entire year before her capture in 1932. Following her arrest, she was sentenced to life. Due to fears that Gaidinliu could incite another rebellion if she remained in one location, the British transferred her to various jails throughout the region.

In December 1932, supporters of Leng and Bepungwemi killed the Kuki chowkidar, and Gaidinliu's followers suspected that a Kuki had informed the British about her whereabouts, leading to her arrest. Many of her supporters were either imprisoned or killed during this time.

From 1933 to 1947, Gaidinliu spent time in several jails located in Guwahati, Shillong, Aizawl, and Tura. The rebels, inspired by Gaidinliu and her mentor Jadonang, refused to pay taxes to the British government. Her movement eventually came to an end with the arrest of her last remaining followers, Dikeo and Ramjo, in 1933.

In 1937, Jawaharlal Nehru visited Gaidinliu in Shillong Jail and promised to advocate for her release. Following this visit, a statement was published in the Hindustan Times, where Gaidinliu was referred to as a "mountain girl," and Nehru bestowed upon her the title of 'Queen' of her people. Nehru also wrote to British MP Lady Astor, requesting her release, but his plea was denied due to concerns that Gaidinliu would cause further unrest.

After meeting her in prison, Nehru recognized Gaidinliu as a fighter for Indian independence and linked her struggle to the Civil Disobedience Movement of 1932. He published an account of her life in prison, titled "Gaidalorani: Queen of the Nagas," in the newsletter of the All India Congress Committee. Gaidinliu gained national recognition during this time, and the article was later republished in the American fortnightly magazine *The Living Age* in 1938.

Nehru poignantly expressed his sentiments about her situation: "What kind of anguish or repression will they bring to her who, in her youth, dared to challenge an empire? She can no longer walk freely on forest roads or sing in the fresh air, the mountains, and the forests. This innocent young woman sits in a dark room, perhaps looking at the sky, while loneliness and confinement consume her burning heart. And yet, India still does not know this brave mountain girl. The day will come when India will remember her, celebrate her work, and bring her out of jail." As a result of Nehru's support, she became known locally as 'Rani Gaidinliu'.

When the interim government was established in India in 1946, Gaidinliu's release was ordered immediately. After her release, she dedicated herself to the welfare of her people and lived with her younger brother Marang in the village of Bhimrap in Tuensang until 1952. In 1953, she returned to her village in Langkow. During a visit to Manipur, Prime Minister Jawaharlal Nehru met with Gaidinliu in Imphal to discuss the development and progress of the Zeliangrong people.

Gaidinliu opposed the rebels of the Naga National Council (NNC) because they were promoting division and terrorism in India. The NNC aimed to create a separate state outside of India, while Gaidinliu demanded a separate Zeliangrong region within India. As a result, the Naga National Council strongly opposed her. Naga activists criticized Gaidinliu's efforts to integrate the Zeliangrong tribes into a single administrative framework, viewing her work as an obstacle to their own movement.

Additionally, Baptist leaders considered the Herakka revival movement as anti-Christian and warned Gaidinliu to change her stance, threatening dire consequences if she did not comply. Consequently, she went into hiding in the 1960s to protect the Herakka culture and solidify her position. In 1965, her supporters killed nine Naga leaders, which sparked heated discussion at the time. The Indian government urged her to abandon violence.

In 1966, after reaching an agreement with the Government of India and at an advanced age, Gaidinliu emerged from hiding and began working for the betterment of her people in a peaceful and democratic manner.

Despite her heroism, Gaidinliu's actions were not well accepted among the Nagas due to the Herakka movement's hostility towards Christianity, especially since many Nagas converted to Christianity in the 1960s. As a result, Naga nationalist groups did not recognize Gaidinliu as a leader, viewing her as too close to the Indian government.

On January 20, 1966, she traveled to Kohima and met with then Prime Minister Lal Bahadur Shastri on February 21, where she demanded the establishment of a separate administrative unit for the Zeliangrong. On September 24, 320 of her followers surrendered at Hennema, with some being recruited into the Nagaland Armed Forces.

In the late 1960s, as she embarked on a path of non-violence, she was invited to major events by the Rashtriya Swayamsevak Sangh (RSS) and the Vishwa Hindu Parishad. According to Jagdamba Mal, during her speech at the Hindu Conference in Jorahao, Assam, in 1966, Gaidinliu stated that conversion to Christianity posed a threat to Naga culture. She called for enhanced activities from Hindu society to curb the influence of the Nagas and also met RSS chief Mohan Bhagwat.

Gaidinliu was not only recognized as a national figure but also emerged as a spiritual leader. In 1979, she was invited to attend the second World Hindu Conference in Allahabad. Gaidinliu's meeting with Ashok Singhal was documented, and a photo of her standing in front of the Kashi Vishwanath temple appeared on the cover of several magazines (Veliang 2012).

Queen Gaidinliu's personality was carefully constructed to fit into the context of the Sangha. The offices of Kalyan Ashram, an organization working for tribal people, as well as hostels and offices of the Vishwa Hindu Parishad, bookstores, homes, and calendars featured her alongside other prominent Hindu leaders. The Sangh Parivar has consistently referred to Gaidinliu as a Hindu in various writings. She stated, "I am Indian, all Nagas are Indian, and Nagaland is part of India."

Gaidinliu's biography, written by Jagdamba Mal, claims that she was a member of the Sangh Parivar and served as its spokesperson in the Northeast, advocating for Hindutva. She opposed the Anti-Conversion Freedom Religion Act in Arunachal Pradesh in 1978 and criticized the visit of Pope John Paul II in 1986. Gaidinliu, along with other tribal leaders in Kohima, issued press releases supporting the construction of a Ram temple in Ayodhya. Additionally, she wrote a letter to the central government supporting the demolition of the Babri Masjid and advocating for Hindu society to be allowed to build the Ram temple.

Jagadamba notes that as the Rani Maa, Naga Hindus held her in high regard, and she inspired many. Her home in Kohima became a popular tourist destination, where visitors often met her.

People took photographs and collected autographs, and she became a symbol of Indianness, beloved by all. From children to the elderly, everyone referred to her as the Queen Mother. Numerous articles in various magazines depicted her as a Hindu. However, this portrayal raised questions among some Zeliangrongs, who felt uncomfortable with how the Sangh Parivar was presenting Gaidinliu. The organization characterized her as a symbol of Mother India in the Northeast, which led to feelings of inclusion within India.

During her time in Kohima, she received the Tamrapatra from the government of Indira Gandhi in 1972, marking the 25th anniversary of India's independence for her role as a freedom fighter. She was honoured with India's then highest civilian accolade, the Padma Bhushan, in 1982, and also received the Vivekananda Seva Samman in 1983.

Gaidinliu returned to her native Langkow in 1991 and passed away on February 17, 1993, at the age of 78. After her death, she was honoured with the title of Birsa Munda. In 1996, the Government of India issued a postage stamp in her memory, and in 2015, a commemorative coin was released to celebrate her birth centenary.

Throughout her life, Gaidinliu was dedicated to reviving the traditions of her Zeliangrong people, which include the Liangmei and Rongmei ethnic groups now residing in Assam, Nagaland, and Manipur. She was critical of Naga Christian nationalists and missionaries for promoting foreign religions among local communities. Gaidinliu's views contrasted sharply with those of Naga nationalists, as she believed, "To lose religion is to lose culture, and to lose culture is to lose identity."

◻◻

Ismat Chughtai

If writers, journalists, and thinkers ignore the current social situation and turn away from pressing social problems to focus solely on their own interests, their work will reflect that shift. Their writings will lack strength and authenticity. An article that deviates from reality is lifeless and holds no significance.

One can imagine the kind of person who made such an important observation. Thankfully, one of the authors remarked on this.

She was an Indian writer, poet, and journalist. In the early 1930s, influenced by Marxist thought, she penned stories and novels that addressed social inequality, the struggles of the middle class, and women's desires and issues. Her writings dwelt on the despair, hopelessness, and oppression faced by women in society at that time. She pointed out how families and society often remained silent despite witnessing such suffering. She also noted that many writers of her era ignored these realities and felt compelled to remain silent. Yet, some writers courageously spoke out against the prevailing social evils.

Ismat Chughtai was one of those writers. Fearlessly, she addressed the customs, traditions, injustices, and inequities of her time. She skillfully articulated the experiences of women, highlighting their sorrows and struggles throughout her body of work. Chughtai was born on August 21, 1915, in Badayun, Uttar Pradesh, as the ninth child of Nusrat Khanum and Mirza Qasim Baig Chughtai. She had six brothers and four sisters. Chughtai received her education at the Women's College of Aligarh Muslim University and earned her B.A. in Arts from Isabella Thoburn College in 1940. Despite facing opposition from her family, she persevered to complete her B.Ed at Aligarh Muslim University.

During this time, she became associated with the Progressive Writers' Movement and met Rashid Jahan, another influential writer, at a meeting in 1936. Rashid Jahan inspired Chughtai to write about the realities of life and women's issues. Impressed by this meeting of the Writers' Association, Chughtai began to focus her writing on women's rights and issues. While women were often portrayed as weak and helpless in the literature of that era, Chughtai sought to give women a different role and identity in her stories. Each character she created was distinct, and she wrote different stories featuring various characters.

For instance, in her story "Lihaaf," the heroine, Begum, develops a deep bond with her masseuse, showcasing a close and intimate relationship. Similarly, in "TIL," the protagonist Rani is a village woman who openly expresses her sexual desires without shame. Other stories by Chughtai include "Gainda," "Gharwali," and "Khidmatgar." In "Gainda," she narrates the love affair between a poor widow working as a maid and an upper-caste Hindu man. In "Gharwali," Lajjo, an orphan, regards her body as her most valuable possession and takes pride in her sexual desires without feeling ashamed.

At the time Chughtai was writing, it was considered morally and socially irresponsible for women to address women's issues in their writing. However, this societal pressure did not deter her. She published several books focusing on feminism and women's issues, challenging the prevailing mindset of a male-dominated society and the emphasis placed on men's views regarding sexual relations. Chughtai also spoke out against the dominance of men in the religious sphere and how it impacted women's sexual desires.

Like her contemporaries Rajendra Singh Bedi, Krishnan Chander, and Saadat Hasan Manto, Chughtai was greatly influenced by 19th-century Western writers, which led her to give considerable importance to sexual desire in her works. Her writings reflect the unvarnished truths of middle-class Muslim families and upper-caste households.

In her story "Gainda," she addresses the caste system by portraying a housemaid who defies caste restrictions and falls in love with someone outside of her caste. Additionally, in her first novel, "Ziddi," she vividly depicts the sexual abuse of a teenage housemaid by her landlord's son.

Chughtai began writing early on, but her works were not published until later. She wrote a play titled "Fasadi" (The Troublemaker), which was published in the Urdu magazine "Sakuyi" in 1939 and is considered her first play.

She later published her columns and articles in various newspapers. Her early writings include "Bachpan" (an autobiography), "Kafir" (her first collection of short stories), and "Dhit," among others. Although she faced criticism for an article published in a magazine, claiming she disrespected the Quran, she did not address the criticism and continued to write in her unique style, presenting her ideas in her own way.

However, during that time, many voices criticized her women-centric works, claiming they negatively impacted society in various ways. She faced substantial criticism but remained committed to distinctive style. When her stories were deemed vulgar by society, she stated, "I choose my stories objectively. If someone thinks they're vulgar, I cannot change their feelings. I believe the experience of human life can never be vulgar as long as it reflects the true reality of life."

She joined the Progressive Writers' Movement and embraced a collaborative writing style, working alongside Jehan, Sajjad Zaheer, Sahibzada, Mahmood Zafar, and Ahmed Ali. She was also influenced by other writers, including William, Sandy Pooter, George Bernard Shaw, and Anton Chekhov. Among her early works are two short story collections, *Kalyan* and *Koten* published in 1941 and 1942, respectively.

Chughtai opposed the idea of partition and wrote about it in her book *Jadin*. In many of her writings from that period, she depicted the violence surrounding the partition and advocated for the safety of both men and women. Her use of satire and a rebellious narrative style distinguished her works from those of Manto and Krishan Chander. Through her efforts, Urdu literature took a new direction and gained a broader readership, enabling literature to transcend societal boundaries and explore new dimensions.

In her book *Yahan Se Wahan Tak*, Chughtai discusses painting, freedom of expression, and transparency. She stated, "If writers, journalists, and thinkers detach themselves from the present and reflect on their achievements, their writings will lose power." She emphasized that articles devoid of reality lack significance.

Strengthening her focus on women's issues, she wrote extensively on previously unexplored aspects of women's lives, including gender inequality and homosexuality. Her novel *Tedhi Lakeer* is a semi-biographical work and is considered one of her unique contributions to literature. In it, she sensitively addresses themes such as child sexual abuse and the societal position of homosexuals, as well as the mental state of individuals affected by these issues.

Her first novel, *Ziddi* was published in 1941, and she began writing at the age of 20. This novel narrates the love affair of a teenage girl who works as a maid in an affluent family, focusing on her relationship with the son of the housekeeper. Later, Chughtai chose themes similar to those of the novelist Hijab-Lamitaz Ali, emphasizing emotional and romantic elements in her narratives. Critics have commended her distinctive style and her nuanced depiction of the female psyche compared to that of men. In 2015, critic and lyricist Amar Hossain remarked that "Chughtai has not only articulated the voice of conservative ideas in her unique linguistic style, but she has also presented them in a highly poetic manner." Her novel *Ziddi* was translated into English as "Wild at Heart" by American author Toni Morrison and adapted into a film in 1948.

Ismat Chughtai's short story "Lihaaf" was published in Lahore in 1942 in the journal Adab-i-Latif. The story quickly gained popularity. Influenced by public discourse, Chughtai crafted a narrative around the relationship between the Begum of Aligarh and her masseuse. "Lihaaf" explores how the Begum's life is affected after marrying the Nawab, and how she becomes both physically and emotionally attached to her masseuse.

Following the publication of "Lihaaf," Chughtai faced considerable criticism. At that time, writing about such topics was largely unacceptable. The story not only highlighted women's sexual desires but also laid the groundwork for discussions about women's roles in society. Chughtai addressed prevailing societal attitudes and also touched upon themes of bisexuality. Through her work, she demonstrated how a woman could fulfill her sexual desires and find satisfaction despite the constraints imposed on her by a patriarchal society. This was articulated in great detail within the narrative.

After "Lihaaf" was released, Chughtai was heavily criticized for portraying same-sex relationships among women. The story challenged the authoritarian views of a male-dominated society. As a result, she was summoned to court over accusations of obscenity related to "Lihaaf" and was presented before the Lahore High Court.

In an interview, when asked about the alleged obscenity of her stories, Chughtai replied, "I shape the reality of life in my stories. If some people find it vulgar, I don't care about their feelings. I believe that the experiences of life can never be vulgar because they are based on real life. Such people think that if they close the door to their homes and do whatever they like, then everything is fine. I would argue that these people are ignorant. I talk about women's loneliness, illustrating the anxiety and depression faced by women who seem to have everything, yet lack the companionship of their husbands."

Saadat Hasan Manto, a fellow member of the Progressive Writers' Movement, also faced criticism for his short story "Odour" and appeared in a Lahore court as well. Both Chughtai and Manto were charged but later acquitted. This incident, which stirred public interest starting in 1945, garnered widespread media attention. Other members of the Progressive Writers' Movement, such as Majnun Gorakhpuri and Krishan Chander, supported them during this challenging time.

Reflecting on her experiences and the story "Lihaaf," Chughtai shared, "I felt very weak about life. I wrote what I experienced. But it felt like this was a protest against me."

In many of her stories, Ismat Chughtai addresses the chauvinistic attitudes toward women prevalent in the male-centric society of the East. She illustrates how men often view women as mere accessories or tools for their own sexual gratification, treating them as disposable playthings. This notion was something Chughtai vehemently rejected. She argued that society has conditioned men to see women solely as objects for their enjoyment.

Through her works such as "Lingering Fragrance," "Apna Khoon," "Neera," "Gainda," "Tinis Grani," "Is Par Zor Nahin Hai," and "Ganga Behti Hai," she delves deeply into the issue of patriarchy. Additionally, her story "Badan Ki Khusboo" explores the sexual exploitation that occurs within Nawab families. In contrast, "Til" addresses women's sexual desires in a society where marriage is often viewed as the only means of social acceptance for women. With her story "Chautika Jora," she voices her opposition to the societal belief that women are commodities.

Chughtai presents the realities of life in a dramatic fashion that resonates with many readers. Living in a society where women are often confined to the roles of wife and mother, she fiercely challenged this limitation through her writing, forging a distinct identity as a writer.

Using a variety of metaphors and comparisons, Chughtai's unique storytelling style continues to captivate feminists today. In her autobiography, she emphasizes, "The most important thing in today's world is that we strengthen our self-confidence, and progressive literature plays a crucial role in doing so. It is disheartening that if our writers and journalists focus solely on their personal advancement, neglecting the betterment of society and failing to expose its realities and flaws, their literature becomes lifeless and meaningless."

Another story of Chughtai 'Gharwali' gives ample evidence of the author's feminist thinking. In the story 'Gharwali', the author describes in a sharp satirical style how marriage has been accepted as the main purpose of women's life in a patriarchal society. The orphaned Lajjo character of this story considers her body as the most valuable asset and has adopted it as the main means of earning money. The story not only describes sex work, but also accurately depicts a woman's sexual desire. 'Lajjo 'enjoyed sex without any hesitation. Over time, the owner of the house Mirza where Lajjo worked marries her, and he throws Lajjo out of the house in protest against Lajjo's relationship with other men. Through this' Gharwali 'story, the singer has described how marriage was imposed on women and how it was felt as a huge burden. And how it controls their sexual desire is also explained. In a very independent and conscious way, the artist has given shape to the secret sexual desire of women through this story, which was considered taboo for women. On the other hand, Chughtai describes the lifestyle of sex workers, their social status. At a time when writers and filmmakers used to describe these sex workers as unethical, Chughtai describes their morality and good qualities. To describe a teenage sex worker, she quietly mentions that she is also a human being like you and me. A very bold, open-minded character, Lajjo has expressed her sexual desire very openly.

In her essay 'Woman', Ismat Chughtai presents a social conception of women's liberation. She highlighted the ill-treatment of women in the society. According to her, why is there so much emphasis in the society on the motherhood of the woman, but not about the fatherhood? She asked why all the rules and regulations of the society are only meant for widows. In the story 'Gainda', the young widow quietly describes how she is oppressed by society, how she is forbidden to wear make-up, colorful clothes. Although the tender girl wanted to wear vermilion and colorful clothes, social constraints did not allow her to do so. She was told that she could do this only if her husband was alive. Ismat Chughtai has strongly protested against these practices prevailing in the society. She wondered why there are different rules for men and women in society. Why is it that while society has made various rules for a widow, there is no such rule for a widowed husband? In her story, she explains why she was so upset. Ismat Chughtai has raised her voice against the dowry system in her short story 'Chauthika Jora'. She described how young women from poor middle-class families are being oppressed by this dowry system. Kubra's parents could not arrange a dowry for her marriage. Parents have to pay enough dowry in return for the girl to be able to secure food, clothing and shelter in future. Dowry is one of the most abominable practices in Indian society. Ismat Chughnatai describes the ill-effects of this dowry system and how it has affected

Kubra's life and family. She said that women should be empowered to eradicate gender discrimination from society.

Kubra was just a burden on her poor parents. Getting her married was the only goal of her parents' life. Questions about her marriage were bothering her. That's why Kubra was never happy. A poor girl's heart was grieving. There came Rahat as a ray of hope in their lives. Poor Kubra's family was always hungry. They hoped that one day he would ask Kubra to marry him. But all their dreams were shattered the day Rahat told them that his marriage had already been fixed. Kubra eventually died of tuberculosis.

In the early 1960s, Ismat Chughtai wrote eight novels. Her first, *The Innocent Girl*, was published in 1962. The story, which was later adapted into a movie, follows a young actress who is forced into prostitution after her father abandons her family. It depicts the ups and downs of Bombay's social life, including themes of sexual abuse and economic decline in the 1950s.

One of her novels, *Saudai*, which was based on the 1951 film *Buzdil*, was published in 1966 and co-written with Latif. Critics argue that this collaboration would not have been possible without Chughtai's permission. Although she faced some criticism after the release of *Masooma* and *Saudai*, she received praise for her fifth novel, *Dil Ki Duniya* (The Heart Breaks Free). Critics believe this novel is a second adaptation of her earlier work, *Tedhi Lakeer*. *Dil Ki Duniya* addresses the harsh social customs that women from Muslim families in Uttar Pradesh had to endure. The novel shares many similarities with *Tedhi Lakeer*, written in an autobiographical style. According to Hussain, he was impressed by *Tedhi Lakeer*, noting the courage with which Chughtai raised her voice against societal injustices. He mentioned that *Dil Ki Duniya* would resonate with him for the rest of his life and that he found reflections of his writing style in these two novels.

When discussing Chughtai, it is impossible to overlook her friendship with Sadat Hasan Manto, one of the most prominent writers in Urdu literature. Although they were contemporaries and competitors, their friendship remained strong and unaffected. Both were celebrated for their writing and their relationship was defined by mutual respect.

A fan of Manto from Hyderabad once asked him in a letter, "Why aren't you and Chughtai married?"

In response, Manto wrote in his essay "Ismat Chughtai": "If we had thought about marrying, we might have surprised ourselves even more than we would have surprised others. When we become aware of this, our wonder might turn into sadness instead of happiness. The idea of marriage between Ismat and Manto is quite strange."

Ismat Chughtai's journey as a writer is a testament to the strength of femininity. She has drawn upon her personal experiences and the societal environment around her to convey her insights through her literary works. Chughtai explored the hidden desires and mental struggles of women, addressing issues such as dowry, the caste system, education, and health. Her writing reflects not only her experiences but also the political climate of her time, capturing the political upheavals and changes she lived through. A firm believer in Marxism, Chughtai aimed to illuminate the complexities of society through her literature, examining relationships between men and women and gender differences.

Chughtai resisted the constraints often placed on women; she was a strong proponent of female autonomy. She posed critical questions about how a woman could live freely without succumbed to societal pressures, how she could navigate life on her own terms, and how she could express her opinions openly. Despite facing substantial criticism and overcoming many obstacles, she never backed down. She powerfully articulated the thoughts and feelings of women, asserting the belief that "a woman is the master of her own will." Throughout her life, she fought for women's emancipation from conservative societal norms and passionately communicated this through her writing.

There is no doubt that Chughtai's choice of subjects and her fearless style make her a distinctive writer. She forged a unique identity within a conservative society, fearlessly voicing the thoughts of women that had often been suppressed in Indian society. Her works reflect influences from both leftist and rightist ideologies. Chughtai examined the struggles of women in both pre-independence and post-independence Indian society in her literary works and films.

A prominent figure in Indian Urdu literature, she depicted the realities of life, which earned her several prestigious honors, including the Soviet Land Nehru Award, Filmfare Award, and the Padma Shri from the Government of India in 1976. Ismat Chughtai passed away on October 24, 1991, at the age of 76.

Chonira Belliappa Muthamma

Women have to struggle, but they can still achieve their goals. Whenever a woman ventures out to work, she faces obstacles. This has been true throughout history. In today's world, women still encounter struggles as they strive to make a difference in society and take bold decisions. Balancing time, societal expectations, and family responsibilities while forging their paths is not easy. When a woman first steps onto an uneven road, the extent of her struggle cannot be underestimated. Yet, despite the storms and obstacles she faces, women have not faltered. They have not turned back; they are determined to move forward.

The focus here is extraordinary women who have entered various fields in our country for the first time. Not only did they take the initiative, they also found success, paving the way for many others who followed. However, their journeys were not without difficulties.

They encountered various challenges that sometimes hindered their education and progress. Yet, they persisted and never gave up.

According to a 2019 report, women in India are paid 19% less than men. Additionally, women are 26% less likely than men to be employed in a workplace, and only 9% occupy senior leadership positions. Gender discrimination, objectification, and workplace harassment remain common issues, with many women facing significant risks in their lives.

C.B. Muthamma experienced a similar struggle in her life. She was the first woman ambassador of India and the first woman to join the Indian Foreign Service (IFS) as an officer. Muthamma was also the first Indian woman to serve as an ambassador. Born on January 24, 1924, in Kodagu, Karnataka, a coffee-growing region in South India, her father was a forest officer who passed away when she was only nine years old. As a single parent, Muthamma's mother raised her four children with strong emphasis on education. After completing her schooling at St. Joseph's Girls School in Madikeri, Muthamma continued her education at Women's Christian College in Chennai and graduated from Chennai University.

She completed her master's degree in English and, a year after India's independence in 1948, she cleared the UPSC exam.

Muthamma became the first woman in India to join the Indian Administrative Service. However, her journey was not easy; she faced significant struggles along the way. Her challenges began when she passed the UPSC exam and entered the workforce as the country's first female officer. Although Muthamma's first choice was the Indian Foreign Service (IFS), the examiners of the UPSC board of examiners attempted to pressure her into changing her mind. Despite this, she topped the Foreign Service list and became India's first IFS officer in 1949.

When she joined her position, she was forced to sign a declaration that stated she would have to resign if she got married. "It was totally undemocratic, but at that time, I found it impossible to resist," she recalled.

During that period, there was a vindictive attitude among men, who were encouraged to maintain strong positions. Muthamma later addressed this issue in many of her articles.

This rule applied to Muthamma was not unique; similar restrictions were prevalent for women at the time. Other women, such as Meera Sinha Bhattacharjee and Rama Mehta, also lost their jobs due to this peculiar policy of the Ministry of External Affairs, as highlighted by Kissen Rana in the Indian Foreign Affairs Journal. The situation for women in Indian society at that time mirrored what was occurring in the Ministry. Many ambassadors resented Muthamma's position, as they found it unacceptable to have a woman as their equal. Muthamma later recognized that this was not just an issue for India's civil servants and diplomats, but a broader problem within the diplomatic community. She subsequently served as India's Ambassador to Myanmar, the UK, Pakistan, and the United States.

Muthamma was deeply upset because she recognized the unfair treatment of women in her field. She was not someone who would tolerate injustice or stand by while others suffered. Muthamma was well-known for her fight against gender discrimination within the Indian Foreign Service.

Despite being eligible for a promotion, the Ministry of External Affairs did not elevate her to the position of Foreign Secretary or even to Grade 1. In response to this discrimination, Muthamma took legal action against the government, arguing that the promotion process was biased against her.

Following her legal complaint, the Ministry finally promoted her. However, they hoped that her petition would be dismissed by the court. Contrary to their expectations, the Supreme Court did not dismiss her appeal; instead, it delivered a landmark judgment. In 1979, Muthamma's case set an important precedent in the Indian judicial system. A three-judge bench headed by Justice V.R. Krishna Iyer stated, "There is an urgent need to change the contradictory aspects of the recruitment process regarding gender discrimination. These changes should be implemented immediately without waiting for further pro-gender comments."

Additionally, Muthamma referenced another decision made by the Ministry of External Affairs, which stated that "women officers who take advantage of cohabitation with their husbands can be suspended at any time." This information was included in her 2003 book *Slain by the System*.

In Muthamma's case, Justice Krishna Iyer highlighted the misogynistic nature of the rules governing the Foreign Service. He pointed out the gender gap, particularly concerning Rule 8 (2) of the Foreign Employment Procedure, which mandated that "a female employee is required to obtain government consent before her marriage and can be dismissed at any time afterward if the government believes her family background is affecting her performance." The Supreme Court ultimately rejected this rule.

The Supreme Court stated that it is not mandatory for a woman Indian Foreign Service (IFS) officer to seek government permission to marry. She was subsequently promoted to a higher IFS position in the Government of India, in addition to Grade-I. In 1979, she filed a lawsuit against the Appointments Committee of the Cabinet (ACC) and the Ministry of External Affairs under Article 14 (Equality before the law) and Article 16 (Equality of opportunity in matters of employment) of the Constitution of India. Earlier, on August 2, 1961, she had protested against the appointment of IFS officers and Article 18(4), which stated that no married woman could be appointed to the IFS.

The judges of the Supreme Court, led by V. R. Krishna Iyer, noted that under Articles 14 and 16, any examination of a subject should be based on reality rather than superstition. However, Solicitor General Soli Sorabjee, arguing against the case, contended that it was reasonable to exclude women from ambassadorships. He claimed that appointing a woman to such a position could compromise the confidentiality of sensitive information and suggested that the issue concerning Muthamma should be disregarded.

Despite C. B. Muthamma having passed the Grade-I examination and being appointed as India's Ambassador to Hungary, the legal process was still ongoing. The judges, led by V. R. Krishna Iyer, delivered a strong judgment in favor of the rights of Indian women in this case.

They stated, "In many instances, women face numerous challenges. Article 15 of the Constitution asserts that there shall be no discrimination against any citizen on grounds of religion, race, caste, sex, or place of birth. Article 14 guarantees equal protection of the laws to all."

The judges added, "If there is some truth to the allegations, if there is unconstitutional coercion, if there is a display of male arrogance, or if there is genuine gender bias, then the complainant must be held accountable."

"If it is mandatory for a woman to seek permission from the government before getting married, then the same requirement should apply to men. If a woman's family responsibilities might hinder her choices, it is only fair to recognize that men may face similar challenges. Understanding the current system of monogamous families, inter-caste marriages, and the spirit of non-cooperation is difficult.

If a married man has rights, then a married woman should also have rights. The misogynistic attitudes of a male-dominated society only serve to weaken the vulnerable sections of our community. It's important to remember that one of the goals of our freedom struggle was to liberate women from oppression.

Like justice, freedom is often invisible. Unfortunately, Articles 14 and 16 of the Constitution have been largely overlooked. There is a significant gap between the protections offered by the Constitution and the existing laws concerning women's rights."

In the competitive world of Indian bureaucracy, promotions are often influenced by religious sentiments or social status. It is important to consider the Solicitor General's perspective. Based on the arguments and evidence he has provided in his defense, we direct that the complainant's case be reconsidered and that the existing inter se policy be abolished.

This hearing later assisted many women advocating for equal rights in securing their claims. During her career, she was appointed as the first woman ambassador of India. She subsequently served as India's Ambassador to Accra, Ghana, and to Hengku, Netherlands. She retired in 1982 after 32 years of dedicated service.

Foreign Secretary Nirupama Rao highlighted C. B. Muthamma's impact, stating, "She is a role model for Indian women."

Muthamma was the first Indian woman civil servant and once stated in her speech, "I have been in the first place for many days; now the time has come to become another first."

India's Arundhati Ghosh, who represented the country at the Nuclear Talks in Geneva, spoke highly of Muthamma, saying, "She was a true feminist who always cared about her subordinates. For instance, she pointed out that the Joint Secretary used two air conditioners in her room, while not a single air conditioner was available in the office rooms of common employees."

Muthamma didn't just speak about this disparity; she took action. With great enthusiasm, she installed one of her air conditioners in the general staff room. Arundhati Ghosh highlighted this act to emphasize Muthamma's greatness.

After her retirement, Muthamma continued her social work. She was appointed as the Independent Palme Commissioner and represented India at the Commission on Disarmament and Security Issues, a non-governmental organization that reports directly to the United Nations. Even in her late teens, she was involved in social reform, exhibiting no restrictions on her thoughts or actions. She helped victims and supported people from all walks of life. Her generosity knew no bounds.

Muthamma was not only the first woman in the Indian Foreign Service; she also authored numerous articles on contemporary social issues and politics. In her 2003 essay, "Slain by the System," she critically examined Indian politics and its class divisions. Reflecting on her career, she once said, "In hindsight, I could not have helped anyone, but during my tenure in the Ministry of External Affairs, my work against the anti-women mindset was very combative." Additionally, she co-authored the *Kodava Cookbook*, published in 2000, which features elaborate recipes from Coorg.

Muthamma passed away on October 14, 2009, in Bangalore at the age of 85.

C.B. Muthamma demonstrated that as long as social equality is not regarded as an integral part of the Indian Constitution, the Gender Equality Act will remain merely a symbolic gesture. She brought to the attention of the Hon'ble Supreme Court the necessity for parity in foreign employment and many other areas. Through her efforts, she advocated for women's rights to equality in the Indian Foreign Service (IFS) appointment process and sought to create a more comfortable work environment by removing various obstacles.

In the 20th century, women were often discouraged from pursuing higher positions within the government or the administrative sector. In England, women were not permitted to work until 1946, and the Foreign Office and the Commonwealth viewed the appointment of women as civil servants or their collaboration with male counterparts as an affront to the British Empire.

Some held the belief that "it is not possible to love a clever woman, while a beautiful woman cannot be easily trusted." Both in England and America, strict regulations mandated that women civil servants resign upon marriage.

The situation in India during the 20th century mirrored these challenges, as exemplified by the experience of India's first woman IFS officer, C.B. Muthamma. She raised her voice against the gender discrimination present in the oral examination conducted by the Union Public Service Commission (UPSC) and strongly protested the discrimination she faced in promotion during her long tenure.

Muthamma passed the UPSC examination in 1948. However, during her oral examination, she was profoundly hurt when the chairman of the UPSC refused to allow her to join the IFS. He misused his authority to give her low marks in the oral test. Even more surprisingly, she was forced to resign from her position after her marriage.

In 1979, she appealed to the Supreme Court, leading to two significant judgments regarding Indian Foreign Service (IFS) jobs. During the hearings, the government realized that the Court's ruling would likely favor them, and the decision was subsequently published in the Official Gazette.

However, when Muthamma rejected her promotion and voiced her concerns against the government, they claimed she was unqualified to be appointed as an ambassador. Despite this, following the court's decision, she was appointed as the Ambassador to The Hague, where her performance was praised. Nonetheless, this recognition resulted in a delay in her promotion. Eventually, while the case was ongoing, the government agreed to reassess its previous decision.

Muthamma perceived the patriarchal attitudes within the Ministry of External Affairs as dismissive of women. Consequently, she urged the government to eliminate such biases from all recruitment processes.

Her story highlights the establishment of constitutional rights in the face of anti-women attitudes. Her petition resulted in reforms in the recruitment process in the Ministry of External Affairs, and the Supreme Court's ruling abolished gender discrimination in government recruitment.

Muthamma has become an inspirational figure for future generations, earning the respect of many. Achieving one's goals requires determination, hard work, and resilience in overcoming obstacles, and she exemplified this tenacity. By challenging societal norms, she not only succeeded but also paved the way for many other women. Her journey underscores the importance of steadfastness, firmness, and patience in claiming one's rights.

It is undoubtedly challenging for women to step out and establish their presence in society, yet she did so with strength and determination. She broke through existing barriers and set a powerful example. As a mentor to many, she demonstrates that strong-minded women can make significant contributions to society and become role models for others.

Kanaklata Barua

Time and circumstance are inextricably linked, creating a situation we must live with. However, humans are not only adapting to this reality; they are also constantly striving to change it. We don't just try; we succeed. Considering the context of time and circumstance, we see that we are now citizens of a free country. We are all born free. In expressing our opinions, making decisions, and taking action, we are ultimately the masters of our own lives, able to pursue what we desire. Life may seem comfortable today, but a century ago, that was not the case.

During British rule, many children born in subjugated India dreamed not of personal gain but of making their country independent. They were ready to sacrifice their lives for this cause. Millions fought for India's independence, and thousands lost their lives. On Gandhi's call, numerous women from every corner of the country participated in the struggle for freedom.

While we often remember a few well-known names among the women freedom fighters, many more made significant contributions, even if their stories aren't as widely discussed. One such brave individual was from the eastern state of Assam in India. She displayed extraordinary courage from a young age and participated in the freedom struggle. At just 17 years old, she took a bullet to the chest while fighting for her country. This age is typically when life begins, yet she chose to sacrifice her life for her homeland. Despite her short time on earth, her name has been etched in golden letters in history.

As Martin Luther King, Jr. said, "It's not how long you live that matters, but how well you live." This quote reflects the life of a remarkable woman who has etched her name in the pages of history. At the young age of seventeen, she became an inspiration to many through her significant contributions. She has made her nation proud with her work and taught people the art of living. The way she accomplished so much in such a short time is truly inspiring.

Kanaklata Barua was born on December 22, 1924, in Barangbari village, located in the Ghorpur subdivision of Sonitpur district in Assam. Her father, Krishnakanta Barua, was a farmer, and her mother was Kameswari Barua. Unfortunately, Kanaklata lost her mother when she was only five years old. Her father remarried, but tragedy struck again when he passed away when Kanaklata was just thirteen. After her father's death, she assumed the responsibility of caring for her stepmother, her sisters, and three step-siblings, leaving her childhood behind. A few years later, her stepmother also passed away, and Kanaklata took full responsibility for the household. This situation made it impossible for her to continue her education, bringing her formal schooling to an end as she focused on supporting her younger siblings.

At the age of seven, Kanaklata attended a meeting that ignited her patriotic spirit. In 1931, a raiyat meeting was held in the village of Gemri, which she attended with her uncles, Debendranath Bose and Jadunath Bose. The meeting was presided over by renowned Assamese poet Jyoti Prasad Agarwal, whose powerful poetry resonated deeply within her. It was at this meeting that Kanaklata's heart was imbued with a strong sense of patriotism. From that moment, she resolved to contribute to her country's struggle for freedom.

By the age of thirteen, Kanaklata was determined to join the Azad

Hind Fauj. However, due to her young age, she was not considered eligible for participation in any party activities or memberships. Nonetheless, she was inspired by the stirring poetry of Jyoti Prasad Agarwal, Gandhi's call for independence, and Bishnu Prasad Rabha's passionate speeches. The young Kanaklata was prepared to lay down her life in the fight to drive the British out of India.

Kanaklata did not feel frustrated for not being a member of the Azad Hind Fauj. Despite her young age, she was determined to take part in the freedom struggle. Adhering to Gandhi's principle of non-violence, she was always prepared to sacrifice her life for her country. In 1942, when Kanaklata was just 17 years old, Mahatma Gandhi launched the Quit India Movement, urging people with the powerful call "Do or Die." This stirred the nation and inspired many, including Kanaklata, who took the lead as part of the young generation known as the "Death Army," always ready to sacrifice their lives for the cause. Despite being under eighteen, she was recognized for her patriotic devotion and elected as the president of the women's wing of this group, all the while keeping it a secret from her family.

At that time, Kushal Kunwar served as the president of the Assam Congress and followed Gandhi's philosophy of non-violence. He was falsely accused of derailing a train that resulted in the deaths of several British officers, leading to his conviction and death sentence. This news incited anger among the people of the Gohpur subdivision, prompting protests where demonstrators sought to remove the British flag from key locations and hoist the national flag instead. As the leaders were arrested, police brutality escalated. In these turbulent times, secret meetings led by Jyotiprasad Agarwal were held, which Kanaklata frequently attended.

On September 20, 1942, the Death Army positioned itself to hoist the national flag at the local police station. Participants marched with national flags in hands, chanting slogans such as "English, leave India," "Vande Mataram," and "Swaraj is our birthright." Despite police warnings to halt, Kanaklata pressed on. Tragically, the police opened fire, and she fell but did not let go of the flag she held.

Before reaching her eighteenth birthday, Kanaklata sacrificed her life and became immortal in the hearts of her fellow countrymen. Another member of the Death Army, Mukund Kakoti, also lost his life in the police shooting. This incident intensified the resolve of protesters across Assam, some of whom were injured during the firing. Ultimately, Rampati Rajkhwani succeeded in hoisting the flag at the police station.

The freedom fighters brought Kanaklata's body back to her village, Barangabari, where she was cremated.

Following the Quit India Movement, British influence began to decline. The country finally achieved independence on August 15, 1947. However, the sacrifice of young martyr Kanaklata was not forgotten. The first patrol vessel commissioned into the Indian Coast Guard in 1997 was named ICGS Kanaklata Barua in her honor. Additionally, in 2011, a full-fledged statue of her was erected in Gauripur. Her courage, patriotism, and inspiring speeches continue to motivate many. A film based on her life, directed by Assamese filmmaker Chandra Mudol, was made. It was titled "Epah Phuil Epah Joril," with the Hindi version released as "Purab Ki Aawaz."

Kanaklata Barua's life's journey demonstrates that a woman's strength can overcome any obstacle, regardless of age. No matter what circumstances or challenges she faces, once a woman sets her mind to something, she is determined to achieve it. At the tender age of 17, Kanaklata encountered daunting difficulties, but her response to those challenges was exemplary. Rather than confine herself solely to family matters, she addressed problems while remaining focused on her life goals. Although she passed away before she could fully realize her dreams, her contributions have made her immortal in the eyes of future generations. This is the essence of India's womanhood!

Anna Rajam Malhotra

The Creator is magnificent in His creations, and all of them are wonderful. Among these, women hold a particularly important place in God's creation. A woman embodies strong character, and her life revolves around her goals.

When a woman sets her goals in life, she embraces her individuality and perseverance. Her journey consistently aligns with these aspirations. Although she faces obstacles, she possesses the strength to confront and overcome them. This resilience is a natural progression for women, empowering them to navigate challenges effectively. Not only does this ability help her overcome various problems, but it also allows her to make the best use of her time.

Throughout history, women have been associated with many admirable qualities, such as patience, tolerance, honesty, simplicity, faithfulness, generosity, nobility, kindness, and more. These virtues are essential to womanhood and they enable women to give their best.

A woman takes pride in these qualities, which are often referred to as femininity. Ultimately, a woman's strength lies in her courage.

The woman we are discussing here exemplifies bravery. She was determined to achieve her goals and was resolute in her pursuit of life. Despite the circumstances, she never backed down. At a time when most women in India were hesitant to enter the administrative field, she not only aspired to this direction but also actively fought against gender discrimination. She is none other than Anna Rajam Malhotra, who became India's first IAS officer and the first woman secretary under the Government of India. While many may be familiar with Kiran Bedi, India's first female IPS officer, few know about Anna Rajam Malhotra.

Born on July 17, 1927, in Niranam, Kerala, Anna Rajam was the daughter of Ottavellil O.A. George and Anna Paul. She spent her childhood in Calcutta, where her education began. After completing her schooling at Presidency Women's College, she graduated from Malabar Christian College in Calicut and earned a master's degree in English literature from the University of Madras.

Anna passed the Indian Administrative Service (IAS) entrance examination in 1950, unaware that she was the first Indian woman to do so. However, during her preparation for the second phase in 1951, she faced significant opposition. A four-member committee chaired by R.N. Banerjee, the head of the UPSC board, recommended that Anna should be assigned to the Ministry of External Affairs or another department deemed more suitable for women, rather than being considered for IAS.

But she was resolute in her decision and never wavered. She opposed the ruling of the UPSC board members and stood firm in her choice. She defended her position vigorously and ultimately succeeded in her efforts, being appointed to the Madras Cadre. However, her appointment letter contained a troubling clause: "She will be dismissed from service after she gets married." Thankfully, the rules have changed over the years.

Anna was first appointed under Rajagopalachari, the Chief Minister of Madras, who was strongly opposed to the appointment of women in civil service roles. He even canceled new appointments of women in this sector, believing that they were not capable of managing law and order in the workplace. Rajagopalachari suggested that Anna be placed in the secretariat rather than being appointed as the sub-collector of a district. However, Anna rejected this suggestion, confident in her abilities. She possessed skills like horseback riding, sharpshooting, and the handling of a revolver, which reinforced her belief that she was not inferior to her male counterparts. She fought tirelessly to prove herself once again and demonstrated that she could hold her own in any field, regardless of workplace challenges.

Her determination paid off, and she was later appointed as the first female Sub-Collector of Hosur district. However, this achievement marked just the beginning of her remarkable journey. She faced numerous obstacles along the way, with gender inequality being one of the largest challenges. In the early years of her career, she encountered substantial resistance.

On one occasion, Anna learned that the women of a village in her district wanted to meet her. It was her first visit to the village, traveling in a tonga. When she arrived, the women surrounded her, and some elderly women exclaimed, "Hey, she looks like us." Anna understood their sentiments; they likely never expected that a woman who appeared so ordinary could achieve such a prestigious position.

Later, Anna reflected on her experiences, highlighting how men often questioned women's competence and doubted their ability to manage situations, resorting to aggressive actions like lathi charges or gunfire to control law and order.

Instead of blaming men for these perceptions, Anna focused on changing the mindset surrounding gender roles. She committed herself to combat these biases and worked tirelessly to eradicate gender discrimination, using her position to advocate for change.

As India's first woman IAS officer, Anna faced many adversities but also received praise for her performance. She learned that Rajaji (Rajagopalachari) commended her work in his official report and at a public meeting in Trichirapalli, describing her as a representative of progressive women.

The Chairman of the UPSC also praised her contributions, stating, "It is Anna's work that is encouraging more and more women to join the civil services."

Anna Rajam served as the Managing Director of India's Ministry of External Affairs during Indira Gandhi's tenure as Prime Minister. When her husband, R.N. Malhotra, returned to India and became the Governor of the Reserve Bank of India, Anna was entrusted with a significant responsibility: overseeing the construction and supervision of India's first computerized transport facility at Nhava Sheva, Maharashtra.

In the 1970s, there were growing concern about operational difficulties due to overcrowding at Indian ports. Policymakers in the field of port management began to address these challenges, focusing on improving transportation management along northern land routes and waterways. At that time, the Bombay port was the main port in India, but it was unable to cope with the increasing demand. Consequently, the government designated Nhava Sheva as India's first container port.

Anna had no prior experience in such a role, and the site was essentially a muddy water body. Each day, she would leave her home on Carmichael Road in South Bombay by 7 a.m. to catch a boat to Nhava Sheva near the Gateway. Prime Minister Rajiv Gandhi visited the state several times, praised Anna's work, but humorously remarked that she could not arrange for delicious food. Throughout her career, Anna had the opportunity to work with seven Chief Ministers and two Prime Ministers: Indira Gandhi and Rajiv Gandhi.

In May 1989, the port was inaugurated, and Anna was awarded the Padma Bhushan that same year. Despite her remarkable achievements, Anna humbly attributed her success to the villagers in the area with whom she spent her time.

India's first woman IAS officer, Anna Rajam Malhotra, passed away on September 17, 2018, at the age of 91.

Many people still do not know about this outstanding woman, her remarkable work, and her contributions to society. Administrators like her are rare. Hardworking, strong-minded, and honest women like Anna Rajam Malhotra have served as a source of inspiration for countless individuals and have encouraged women to pursue careers in civil services throughout history. She achieved her goals through determination, overcoming the social barriers of her time. Her success has made her a role model for many.

We must honor her fortitude, integrity, and, above all, her sense of patriotic responsibility. Through her dedication, she not only fulfilled her duties to her country but also to society as a whole. Despite facing numerous obstacles, she worked tirelessly to achieve her goals and paved the way for future generations of women. She showed new horizons to women everywhere.

Women have the right to exist and thrive in society, and they often do so on their own. Their struggles are not just for themselves but also for future generations.

◻◻

Bibliography of data Reference:

- Wikipedia
- India Today
- The Indian Express
- Women in Economics and Policy
- Youtube
- Feminism in India
- Free Press Kashmir
- Wikipedia, Wikimedia Foundation
- Encyclopædia Britannica
- SheThePeople
- The Print, 24 June 2023
- SOAS Library Special Collections Blog
- Jehan Numa: Queens of Bhopal Blog
- Azadi Ka Amrit Mahotsav
- Historic Royal Palaces – Tower of London
- Feminism in India
- Stree Shakti – The Parallel Force
- Banglapedia: National Encyclopedia of Bangladesh
- Women's History Network
- History of Missiology – Boston University
- The High-Caste Hindu Woman
- Dictionary of Women Worldwide: 25,000 Women Through the Ages
- International Institute for Asian Studies
- PWOnlyIAS
- Asia Research News
- STEM Pioneers

Bibliography

1. Queen Prabhavati Gupta (443 CE)
- *Prabhavatigupta* — the Wikipedia article provides a concise summary of her life, regency period (~390–410 CE), family lineage, and later years up to around 443 CE Indiethink+2Wikipedia+2Docslib+2.
- Hans Bakker (ed.), *The Vakatakas: An Essay in Hindu Iconology* (1997) — includes a detailed discussion of her iconographic significance and political role Wikipedia.
- Upinder Singh, *A History of Ancient and Early Medieval India* — situates her regency within the broader Gupta–Vākāṭaka political system Wikipedia.
- *The VakatakaGupta Age* (Motilal Banarsidass, 2007) — explores material culture, inscriptions, and grants associated with her period granthsouthasia.wordpress.com+4Wikipedia+4Docslib+4.
- Ajay Mitra Shastri, *Vakatakas: Sources and History* (1997) — provides primary-source analysis and genealogical data relevant to her rule Wikipedia+1Docslib+1.

Journal & Archaeological Reports
- "Prabhavati Gupta – The Regent Queen of the Vakataka Dynasty" (IJISSHR, Vol. 2, Issue 3, July–Sept 2015) — article references and bibliography include works like Gupta (1970), Banerji (1933), Majumdar, Altekar, Mookerji, Upadhyaya, Smith, and others reddit.com+4scribd.com+4Docslib+4.

2. Queen Sugandhadevi (883 – 914 CE)
- **Kalhaṇa**, *Rājataraṅgiṇī* — the primary chronicle detailing Kashmir's history, including Sugandha's regency (902–904 CE), rule as sovereign (904–906 CE), her exile and final campaign in 914 CE Reddit+15Wikipedia+15Bharatpedia+15.
- **P.N.K. Bamzai**, *Cultural and Political History of Kashmir*, Vol. 1 — offers context on Utpala dynasty kings Sankaravarman and successors, including Sugandha's rise and fall Wisdom Library+7Wikipedia+7ResearchGate+7.
- **Mark Aurel Stein**, *Kalhaṇa's Rājataraṅgiṇī: A Chronicle of the Kings of Kaśmīr* — a critical modern edition and commentary, essential for primary narrative and numismatic references Wikipedia.
- **Premnath Bazaz**, *Daughters of the Vitasta* — includes appraisal of Sugandha as "loved by the people, trusted by the courtiers, and admired by the army" and her reign as golden era of Kashmir Reddit+11Feminism in India+11Wikipedia+11.
- **Feminism in India** article "Sugandha Devi: The Queen of Kashmir's Golden Era" — surveys her temple-building initiatives, urban development (Gopalapura, Sugandhapura), and religious patronage ResearchGate+6Feminism in India+6LinkedIn+6.
- **Krishna Swaroop Saxena**, *Political History of Kashmir (600–1200 AD)* series (Part 6) — political analysis of Sugandha's reign, her struggle between Tantrins and Ekangas, succession conflicts, and final defeat in 914 CE ResearchGate+8Wisdom Library+8LinkedIn+8.
- ResearchGate study "Status of Women in Ancient Kashmir (South Asian Studies)" — examines Sugandha's role, personal relationships (e.g. with minister Prabhakara), her regency, seizure of rule, dethronement, exile, and demise ResearchGate+3ResearchGate+3LinkedIn+3.

- **Scroll.in**, "Five extraordinary Indian queens…" — overview of Sugandha in broader frame of women's rule in India; mentions her accompaniment on military campaigns, façade during the death of Sankaravarman and coinage evidence Scroll.in+1Wikipedia+1.
- **Indica Today** article on *Rājataraṅgiṇī study* — insider detail on factions (Ekangas vs Tantrins), Kushan-era coinage, and rapid succession post906 CE LinkedIn+5Indica Today+5Wikipedia+5.
- **Wisdom Library** essay *Political history of Sankata and Sugandha (904–906 CE)* — timeline including her regency, brief kingship, deposition, exile, and failed military comeback EverybodyWiki Bios & Wiki+2Wisdom Library+2Bharatpedia+2.
- Pandey, Sugandhaa. *"Sugandha Devi: The Queen of Kashmir's Golden Era."* **Feminism in India**, 2 Aug. 2022. *Feminism in India*, feminisminindia.com/2022/08/02/sugandha-devi-kashmir-queen/. (Profile of Queen Sugandha of 10th-century Kashmir, with historical context from Kalhana's *Rajatarangini*.)

Secondary Sources:
- Stein, Mark Aurel. *Kalhaṇa's Rājataraṅgiṇī: A Chronicle of the Kings of Kaśmīr*. (Translation and commentary, includes coins of Sri Sugandha Deva.)
- Bamzai, P.N.K. *Culture and Political History of Kashmir*, Vol. 1. (Contextual & political history including Sugandha's monarchy.)
- Bazaz, Premnath. *Daughters of the Vitasta*. (Biographical insight into Sugandha's reign and popularity.)
- Saxena, Krishna Swaroop. *Political History of Kashmir 600–1200 AD*, Part 6. (Detailed analysis of Sugandha's rule, court factions, downfall.)
- "Status of Women in Ancient Kashmir." *Journal of South Asian Studies*. (Gendered analysis of Sugandha's ascent, relationships, regency, and politics.)
- "Sugandha Devi: The Queen of Kashmir's Golden Era." *Feminism in India*. (Temple-building, urban foundations, legacy of rule.)

Early life & marriage to Sankaravarman (883–902 CE); her presence in campaigns and avoidance of Sati Indica Today+2Wikipedia+2ResearchGate+2Bharatpedia+1EverybodyWiki Bios & Wiki+1
- **Regency** (902–904 CE), including administration under Gopalavarman and influence of minister Prabhakara, whose affair and alleged involvement in regicide undermined her rule ResearchGate+6Wikipedia+6Bharatpedia+6
- **Monarch in her own right** (904–906 CE): proclamation as Sri Sugandha Deva by her subjects, founding of towns and temples (Sugandhapura, Gopalapura, Gopalkesava, Gopalamatha monastery) Bharatpedia+5Feminism in India+5Wikipedia+5
- **Dethronement & exile**: Tantrin coup, installation of Partha (10-year-old ruler) in 906 CE and her retreat to Haskapura (Ushkur) Wisdom Library+4Wikipedia+4LinkedIn+4
- **Attempted restoration & death** (914 CE): military effort via Ekangas, final defeat near Srinagar, imprisonment and execution at Nispalaka Vihāra EverybodyWiki Bios & Wiki+5Feminism in India+5LinkedIn+5

3. Queen Didda of Kashmir (924 – 1003 CE)
- **Kalhaṇa**, *Rājataraṅgiṇī* — the foundational 12thcentury chronicle of Kashmir; offers detailed account of Didda's regency (958–980 CE) and reign (980–1003 CE), including family dynamics, court intrigues, and political consolidation Reddit+15Wikipedia+15Feminism in India+15.
- **Stein, Mark Aurel**, *Kalhaṇa's Rajatarangini: A Chronicle of the Kings of Kaśmīr* (Motilal Banarsidass) — critical modern edition and translation cited extensively by secondary literature Dhaara Magazine+9Wikipedia+9Feminism in India+9.
- **Bamzai, Prithivi Nath Kaul**, *Cultural and Political History of Kashmir* — includes the

chapter "Didda The Dominating Queen," characterizing her as powerful, ruthless, and politically astute Feminism in India+1sringeribelur.com+1.
- **Ganguly, Dilip Kumar**, *Aspects of Ancient Indian Administration* — discusses Didda's governance and administrative reforms during her regency, cited in various bibliographies kashmirlife.net+10Feminism in India+10Wikipedia+10.
- **Kaw, M.K.**, *Kashmir and Its People: Studies in the Evolution of Kashmiri Society* — offers socio-political contextualization of her rule and lineage from Lohara and Shahi families Wikipedia+3Feminism in India+3Wikipedia+3.
- **Kaul, Ashish**, *Didda: The Warrior Queen of Kashmir* (Rupa, 2025) — popular non-fiction biography of Didda's rise from disabled princess to sovereign, highlighting her strategic rule and legacy Reddit+5Rupa Publications+5Rupa Publications+5.
- **"Didda – A Critical Examination of the Career of the Controversial Queen of Kashmir"** by Shanmukh, Saswati Sarkar, Kirtivardhan Dave & Dikgaj — analytical article dissecting her rule using verse-by-verse translations of *Rājataraṅgiṇī*, contrasting interpretations of Stein and Kalhaṇa, and including perspectives of Bamzai, Bazaz, Majumdar, etc. sringeribelur.com.
    - Articles in **Feminism in India** series:
    - *Queen Didda: The Woman Monarch of Kashmir* — feminist reinterpretation of Didda's political persona and legacy Indica Today+12Feminism in India+12Feminism in India+12.
    - *Queens of Kashmir: How History Depicted Them as 'Immoral' & 'Power Hungry'* — critiques gendered bias in portrayal of queens, including Didda, drawing on Bamzai and Kalhaṇa's narrative framings Feminism in India.
- **Achakzai, Khawar Khan.** *"Queen Didda: Between Facts and Fantasy."* **Free Press Kashmir**, 18 Jan. 2021, freepresskashmir.news/2021/01/18/queen-didda-between-facts-and-fantasy/. (Account of Queen Didda of Kashmir (r. 958–1003 CE) based on historical chronicles like *Rajatarangini*.)
- **Madras Courier / The Daily Guardian** articles — general public overviews of Didda's life, highlighting her reputation as the "Catherine of Kashmir," her consolidation of power, coinage legacy, and temple patronage The Daily Guardian.
- **Indica Today** longread "Rajatarangini and the Study of Kalhaṇa's History" — includes commentary on Didda's coinage (DiKshema coins), court purges, and rebellion management Wikipedia+9Indica Today+9Reddit+9.
- **Regency Period (958–980 CE):** Didda ruled as regent for her son and successive grandsons—Abhimanyu II, Nandigupta, Tribhuvanagupta, Bhimagupta—eliminating royal rivals to consolidate power The Daily Guardian+6Wikipedia+6Wikipedia+6.
- **Reign as Sovereign (980–1003 CE):** Ruled Kashmir directly, founding the Lohara dynasty, maintaining authority with advisor Tunga, and instituting administrative and artistic patronage Feminism in India+4Wikipedia+4Dhaara Magazine+4.
- **Personality & Gendered Portrayals:** Historians depict her as shrewd, powerful, ruthless—and sexualized in narrative; feminist re-evaluations question biases in such depictions Feminism in Indiasringeribelur.com.
- **Coinage & Epigraphy:** Coins jointly bear her name ("DiKshema"), temple and religious endowments, assertion of masculine titles such as 'Deva' / 'Rajan' in inscriptions Dhaara Magazine.

4. **Queen Rudrama Devi** (c. 1223–1289 CE
Major epigraphic records mentioning Rudrama Devi include the Potugallu inscription of Karimnagar (1235 CE) and the Yeleshwar inscription (1246 CE), which mention her name and role during her father King Ganapatideva's reign. Reddit+15Ancient Pages+15dharmayudh.com+15Reddit+1Reddit+1
- **Contemporary traveler accounts** Marco Polo, who visited the region around 1289–1293 CE,

noted the enlightened rule under Rudrama Devi, praising her justice, prosperity, and the longevity of her reign. Reddit+9Wikipedia+9Wikipedia+9
- **Bolla Sravanthi**, "**Rudrama Devi: The Warrior Queen of the Kakatiya Dynasty**" (*International Journal of History*, 2023, Vol. 5(2):29–31) — a concise peer-reviewed study on her administrative innovation, military campaigns, and gendered leadership. historyjournal.net
- *Rudrama Devi: The Queen Who Wore a King's Image* (Feminism in India, 2019) — examines how Rudrama Devi adopted male attire and regal titles ("Rudradeva") as a symbolic strategy to legitimize her sovereignty. Reddit+15Feminism in India+15historyjournal.net+15
- *Forgotten lioness of the Deccan* (Sunday Guardian Opinion) — highlights her military strategy, agrarian reforms, and the Nayankara system, underscoring why her reign remains underrecognized in mainstream historical narratives. Sunday Guardian Live
- *Rudrama Devi: The Warrior Queen of Warangal* (The Jaipur Dialogues, 2022) — elaborates her early life, accession after her father's death, key military victories, fortification projects, patronage of temple architecture, and circumstances of her death. Andhra Portal+3The Jaipur Dialogues+3historyjournal.net+3
- *Rudrama Devi: The Brave Warrior Queen* (Dharmayudh, online history blog) — discusses her rule, gender role dynamics, agrarian policies, and reaction to rebellion by nobles and regional kingdoms. dharmayudh.com Rudrama Devi was named heir by her father Ganapatideva and began joint rule around c. 1261–1262 CE, ruling independently from c. 1269 after his death. She adopted the title "Rudradeva" and male attire to reinforce political legitimacy. Feminism in India+4The Jaipur Dialogues+4Wikipedia+4
- Rudrama strengthened the Warangal fortification—raising stone walls, moat systems, bastions—and commissioned irrigation works and tank construction to support agrarian productivity. Wikipedia

5. **Khanzada Begum** (c. 1478 – 1545 CE)

Babur, *Baburnama: Memoirs of Babur, Prince and Emperor* — Khanzada features prominently as "Jaanam," her brother's beloved elder sister, especially during her marriage to Shaybani Khan, exile, and return to him Reddit+15Wikipedia+15Geni+15.
- **Mukhoty, Ira**, *Daughters of the Sun: Empresses, Queens & Begums of the Mughal Empire* (2018) — includes a full chapter on Khanzada, detailing her sacrifices, marriages, exile, return, and later influence in the imperial household Hindustan Times+2ResearchGate+2Garhwal Post+2.
- "Women and Religious Patronage in the Timurid Empire" — discusses Khanzada Bigum's contribution (e.g. commissioning a khānqāh in Herat) and her aristocratic status within the wider Timurid network .
- **Newstrack Network**, "Khanzada Begum … the First Lady of the Mughal Empire and Babur's 'Jaanam'" (June 2025) — popular summary of her life: sacrifice in marrying Shaybani Khan, suffering and exile, return via Shah Ismail, second marriage to Mahdi Khwaja, and legacy of service to her brother and nephew Humayun .
- **Navbharat Times (in Hindi)**, article "Khanzada Begum: popular Hindi profile focusing on her sacrifice, marriage to Shaybani Khan, exile of a decade, and eventual homecoming .
- **Political Sacrifice & Marriage Alliances**: Allowed her brother Babur's survival by marrying Shaybani Khan, the Uzbek conqueror, thereby becoming a political pawn—but she maintained loyalty to her Timurid lineage and spirit throughout Newstrack EnglishRedditResearchGate.
- **Court Position & Influence**: Crowned *Padishah Begum* by Humayun, she continued to play a mediating role in family conflicts long after Babur's death, including riding on horseback to reconcile Humayun and his brothers even in her sixties Reddit+1Garhwal Post+1.
- **Cultural & Literary Significance**: Through Gulbadan Begum's *Humayunnama*, she is

presented not just as a familial figure but a model of female virtue, agency, and power—the basis for the genre of "mirror for princesses" texts in Mughal court culture Cambridge University Press & Assessment.

6. **Gulbadan Begum** (1523–7 February 1603)
- **Gulbadan Begum**, *Ahwali Humāyūn Badshah* (commonly known as *Humāyūnnāma*) Written ca. 1587 at the request of her nephew Akbar, this is the sole surviving memoir by a woman of the Mughal court, offering a vivid eyewitness account of life under Babur, Humayun, and early Akbar. The manuscript ends abruptly around 1552 CE, following Kamran Mirza's blinding, and is incomplete. A single, battered copy survives in the British Library, rediscovered by Colonel G. W. Hamilton and translated into English by Annette S. Beveridge in 1901 under the affectionate title "Princess Rosebud." The Bengali translation by Pradosh Chattopadhyay appeared in 2006 Rekhta+15newbritannicaencyclopedia.blogspot.com+15Wikipedia+15The Hindu+1The Asian Age+1.
- **Annette S. Beveridge (transl.)**, *The History of Humāyūn-Badshah* (*Humāyūnnāma*) (Royal Asiatic Society, 1902) — the first and authoritative English translation, with scholarly commentary. Also discussed in *Life and Writings of Gulbadan Begam (Lady Rosebody)* (1898) Wikipedia+2Wikipedia+2Wikipedia+2.
- Malhotra, Shrishti. *"Gulbadan Banu Begum: Mughal Historian & Author of Humayun-Nama."* **Feminism in India**, 25 Jan. 2018, feminisminindia.com/2018/01/25/gulbadan-banu-begum-womens-history/. (Discusses Gulbadan Banu Begum (1523–1603), daughter of Emperor Babur and author of the memoir *Humayun-Nama*. Notably, Gulbadan's Persian chronicle is the only surviving historical account written by a woman in 16th-century Mughal Indiafeminisminindia.com.)
- *"Gulbadan Begum (1523–1603)."* **Stree Shakti – The Parallel Force**, n.d., streeshakti.com/bookG.aspx?author=14. (Summarizes Gulbadan Begum's life as Babur's daughter and Humayun's sister, her education in Persian, and her writing of the *Humayun Nama* around 1587 at Akbar's request. Also details her pilgrimage to Mecca in 1575 and her legacy as a Mughal historian.)
- **Pradosh Chattopadhyay (transl.)**, *Humayunnāma* (Bengali, Chirayata Prokashan, 2006) — accessible regional-language translation Wikipedia+2Wikipedia+2newbritannicaencycloped ia.blogspot.com+2.
- **Tuhina Islam**, "The Literary Contributions of Gulbadan Begum: A Mughal Court Lady's Influence on Persian Literature and History." *Frontline Social Sciences & History Journal*, Vol. 4, No. 10 (2024), pp. 12–21. An openaccess peer-reviewed study exploring the historical and literary importance of Gulbadan's memoir, her style, and their broader Persianate context newbritannicaencyclopedia.blogspot.com+9frontlinejournals.org+9jhss-uok.com+9.
- **Tuhina Islam**, "Literary Contribution of Mughal Court Lady Gulbadan Begum." *Journal of History and Social Sciences*, examining her role as the first Persian prose writer in the Mughal royal household and her narrative of everyday life under Humayun and Akbar jhss-uok.com+1The Hindu+1.
- **Ruby Lal**, *Vagabond Princess: The Great Adventures of Gulbadan* (Juggernaut, 2024) — the first full-length biography of Gulbadan, based on her memoir and extensive archival and travelrecord research. Lal reconstructs the missing parts of the pilgrimage to Mecca, exile in Aden, and court life behind the Zenana walls, weaving feminist historical insight that centers female experience in Mughal society Hindustan Times+5Scroll.in+5The Hindu+5.
- **Ruby Lal**, "What a Mughal Princess Can Teach Us about Feminist History," *Time Magazine*, March 2024 — highlights Gulbadan's unique contribution to feminist historiography as the only known female prose memoir from an Islamic royal court, and describes the dismissal of her work by traditional historians TIME.

- **Feminism in India**, article "Gulbadan Banu Begum: The Mughal Historian We Don't Know Of" (2018) — underscores how Gulbadan's narrative diverges from male-authored chronicles and portrays the harem as a complex social structure with relationships based on age and hierarchy, rather than pure sexualized seclusion The Hindu+3Feminism in India+3Karwaan: The Heritag+3.
- **First female prose historian** of the Mughal court, offering an intimate portrait of royal life—from exile to pilgrimage to palace intrigues.
- **Pilgrimage & Public Life**: Leads the first female hajj by a Mughal royal over four years (1576–1580)—only to end up exiled by Ottoman Sultan Murad III; survives shipwreck and months in Aden, chronicled in Lal's biography with primary document evidence from the Ottoman archives Wall Street Journal.
- **Feminist historiography**: Her memoir illuminates daily experiences of women, eunuchs, and children—challenging androcentric narratives of Mughal history and revealing the richness of female social-worlds TIME.
- **Literary style**: Unlike the elevated prose of Abul Fazl or other chroniclers, her Persian is simple, direct, influenced by Baburnama, and grounded in lived experience rather than royal glorification Hindustan Times+2Feminism in India+2Wikipedia+2.

7. **Rani Abbakka Chowta** (16th century)
- **Inscriptions & Local Chronicles**: While no surviving royal inscriptions by Abbakka herself are known, oral histories, temple records, and later local chronicles from Tulu Nadu preserve her memory and deeds. Ullal's matrilineal Chowta dynasty followed Aliya Santana inheritance.Reddit+15Wikipedia+15Jain Heritage Centres+15
- **European Narratives**: Portuguese chroniclers like Gaspar Correia and Italian traveler Pietro Della Valle provide external perspectives—Correia notes her naval resistance, calling her opponents "fighting like a man," and Della Valle describes her appearance and character. Satesh Vasu+1Swarajyamag+1
- **Feminism in India**, "Rani Abbakka Chowta: The Queen Who Made Portuguese Colonisers Miserable" (2018) — feminist reinterpretation of her resistance, alliances, politics, and status as India's first woman freedom fighter.Feminism in India
- **Swarajya Magazine**, "Rani Abbakka: An Untold Legacy" (2019) — contextualizes her naval and land campaigns, and critiques inadequate modern recognition.Feminism in India+15Swarajyamag+15Satesh Vasu+15
- **Swarajya Magazine**, "The Admiral Queen" by Archana Garodia Gupta (2015, updated 2016) — personal accounts, folklore, and narrative of multiple queens named Abbakka across decades including encounters with European visitors.Swarajyamag+1Wikipedia+1
- **The Better India**, "The Forgotten Story of Rani Abbakka Chowta, the Fearless Warrior Queen of Tulu Nadu" (2017) — detailed regional history, regency context, and popular legacy.Reddit+13The Better India+13Feminism in India+13
- **The Federal**, "Rani Abbakka Chowta: The Tulu queen of Karnataka who took on the Portuguese" — explores her cross-communal alliances, women's battalion, strategies, erosion and martyrdom.Hindu Janajagruti Samiti+5The Federal+5Wikipedia+5
- **Jain Heritage Centres**, "Rani Abbakka Chowta | Jain Heritage Centres" — narrative summary of her lineage, reign from Ullal (port of Mangalore), naval battles, administration, and alliances across faiths.Jain Heritage Centres
- **Colours of Glory / Remembering Abbakka** by D. P. Ramachandran (2019) — nationalist commemoration, highlighting her symbolic importance and modern reinterpretations.Colours of Glory
- **Historified**, "Rani Abbakka Chowta – The Fearless Queen" (2022) — overview of her military career, alliances, folk legend, and memorialization initiatives in Karnataka.Historified

- Following Aliya Santana tradition, Abbakka was crowned Queen of Ullal by her uncle Tirumala Raya in 1525 and trained in warfare from childhood.Colours of Glory+8Jain Heritage Centres+8Wikipedia+8
- **Resisting Portuguese expansion (1555–1568 and beyond)** Key confrontations: Admiral Dom Álvaro da Silveira (1555), defense of Mangalore and Ullal, victory killing of General João Peixoto, death of Admiral Mascarenhas (1568), followed by alliances with Zamorin and Bijapur. Betrayal by husband and eventual capture.The Federal+8Jain Heritage Centres+8Wikipedia+8
- **Socially inclusive administration & Women warriors** Abbakka's forces included Hindus, Muslims, Jains, Mogaveera seamen; she even organized a women's "Ponnule pade" battalion using agricultural swords.Wikipedia+1Feminism in India+1The Federal+1Wikipedia+1
- **Legacy & Modern Commemorations** Remembered in Yakshagana, Bhuta Kola folk theatre; annual Veera Rani Abbakka Utsava; postal commemoratives 2003 & stamp 2023; Indian Navy patrol vessel and public statues in Ullal and Bengaluru.WikipediaJain Heritage Centres+8asian+8Reddit+8

8. **Hamida Banu Begum** (1527 – 29 August 1604),
- **Humayun-nama** by Gulbadan Begum Though written by her sister-in-law, this account offers key personal details about Hamida's life, her marriage to Humayun, her pregnancy, and her influence at court Wikipedia+15Wikipedia+15ResearchGate+15.
- **Muni Lal**, *Humayun* (Vikas Publishing House, 1978/1986)Includes analysis of Hamida's early life, marriage, motherhood of Akbar, and her role in consolidating his rule ResearchGate+1Wikipedia+1.
- **Neeru Misra & Tanay Misra**, *The Garden Tomb of Humayun: An Abode in Paradise* (2003) Discusses Hamida's commissioning of Humayun's Tomb and her role in Mughal funerary patronage ResearchGate+1Reddit+1.
- **Abraham Eraly**, *Emperors of the Peacock Throne* (Penguin)Offers broader context on her marriage and impact on Humayun's exile and empire building Wikipedia+15Wikipedia+15Reddit+15Wikipedia+7The Indian Express+7The Times of India+7.
- **Audrey Truschke, Marika Sardar & John Seyller**, *The Ramayana of Hamida Banu Begum: Queen Mother of Mughal India* (2020) Scholarly edition presenting her Persian-translated Ramayana manuscript, with detailed essays on courtly culture and art patronage Wikipedia+15qm.org.qa+15shulphink.com+15.
- **ResearchGatearchive**,"TheStatusofWomenduringtheMughalPeriod…"(Misra&Misra,2003) Explores Hamida's life span, influence in Akbar's court, her interventions (e.g. removal of Bairam Khan), and filial authority as *Maryam Makani* digital.library.ucla.edu+2ResearchGate+2Wikipedia+2.
- **Islamic World Journal**, "The Islamic World" (John Seyller et al.) Analyzes Hamida's personal seal-stamped manuscripts, her library, and cultural engagements across Persianate literary networks ResearchGate+1ResearchGate+1.
- **Times of India**, "Akbar's mother read Ramayan, her copy is in Doha's museum now" (2024) Highlights Hamida's Persian Ramayana manuscript and her patronage of Sanskrit-Persian translation projects The Times of India.
- **Times of India trending story**, "5 most powerful women in Mughal era" (June 2025) Includes Hamida among elite women who shaped Mughal politics, noting her role in Akbar's consolidation of power The Times of India.
- **Indian Express**, "The Begum Will See You Now" (Dec 2018) Uses anecdotes from *Humayun-nama* to illustrate Hamida's personality, wit, and standing in the Zenana court life The Indian ExpressWikipedia+2Karwaan The Heritage+2Wikipedia+2.
- *"Hamida Banu Begum."* **Wikipedia**, Wikimedia Foundation, last edited 4 Mar. 2025, en.

wikipedia.org/wiki/Hamida_Banu_Begum. (Biography of Hamida Banu Begum, wife of Mughal Emperor Humayun and mother of Emperor Akbar, including her title Maryam Makani and role in Mughal history.)
- *"Humāyūn's Tomb."* **Encyclopædia Britannica**, 14 Mar. 2025, www.britannica.com/topic/Humayuns-Tomb. (Discusses the Mughal mausoleum in Delhi, noting it was commissioned in 1569 by Hamida Banu Begum in memory of her husband Humayun, an example of Mughal architecturebritannica.com.)
- **Marriage & Dynastic Role** Married to Humayun in 1541 despite initial resistance, bore Akbar in exile, and emerged as a central stabilizing figure in the early Mughal era ResearchGate+1commons.wikimedia.org+1.
- **Court Influence & Regency** Served as regent during Humayun's absence; instrumental in political decisions such as the dismissal of Bairam Khan in 1560 on Akbar's accession qm.org.qa.
- **Cultural Patronage & the Ramayana** Commissioned the Persian-translated *Ramayana*, richly illustrated, now known as the "Doha Ramayana," reflecting cultural synthesis and cross-religious exchange in Akbar's court qm.org.qa+1The Times of India+1.
- **Legacy & Mourning** Widely revered during her life; upon her death on 29 August 1604, Akbar famously shaved his head in mourning twice in his life only for her and his foster-mother Jiji Anga. She was given the posthumous title *Maryam Makani* ("dwelling with Mary") ResearchGate+1The Times of India+1.

9. **Sultana Chand Bibi (1550–1599 CE)**,
- **Ferishta**, *TarikheFerishta* (GulshaniIbrahimi): the main Persian chronicle documenting Chand Bibi's political life, regencies, and death in 1599 Reddit+15NJA PASTIC+15 dewalghatdiaries.com+15.
- **South Asia Journal: "Whatever Happened to Chand Bibi Sultan? Narratives of a Deccan Warrior Queen"** (Sarah Waheed, July 2024): analyzes multiple historical narratives of her demise (murder, suicide, escape), using Persian, Urdu, Dakhnī, and Marathi sources Madras Courier+3Taylor & Francis Online+3khidki.hydlab.co.in+3.
- **Manu S. Pillai**, *Rebel Sultans* (2018/2019): chapter on Chand Bibi highlighting her agency in defending Ahmednagar, her multiple languages, court presence, and the circumstances of her tragic death while brokering peace talks Reddit+3Manu S Pillai+3mint+3.
- **Pushkar Sohoni**, *The Architecture of a Deccan Sultanate* (2018): details Ahmadnagar's material and architectural setting during Chand Bibi's era, giving context to her rule and fort defences NJA PASTIC+15Wikipedia+15Taylor & Francis Online+15.
- **Sarah Waheed**, essay "Chand Bibi, a queen from the multiethnic medieval Deccan" (Khidki/NewsMinute): explores her distinct Deccani identity, multilingualism, mobility in crisis, court culture, and nuanced historiography beyond nationalist frames khidki.hydlab.co.in+1Taylor & Francis Online+1.
- **Uzma Perveen & Muhammad Zubair**, "Chand Bibi Sultan: Legendary Person" (Pakistan Journal of Gender Studies, Vol. 10, No. 1, 2015): reconstructs Chand Bibi's life from scattered materials, including *Ferishta*, evaluating her leadership and strategies Taylor & Francis Online+3NJA PASTIC+3tehqeeqat.org+3.
- **Madras Courier**, "Chand Bibi: The Deccan's Warrior Queen": widely accessible profile emphasizing her 1595 defense of Ahmednagar, legendary mythologization, and enduring folk status Madras Courier+1mint+1.
- **Dewalghat Diaries**, "Sultana Chand Bibi of Bijapur": overview of her regencies at Bijapur (1580–1590) and Ahmadnagar (1595–1600), and historical memory of her military leadership khidki.hydlab.co.in+2dewalghatdiaries.com+2Wikipedia+2.
- **Regency & Political Agency** Served as regent of Bijapur (for Ibrahim Adil Shah II, 1580–

1590) and of Ahmadnagar (for her nephew Bahadur Shah, 1595–1599), exercising real executive power in both courts Manu S Pillai+3Wikipedia+3dewalghatdiaries.com+3.
- **Military Leadership & Defiance** Defended Ahmednagar fort in 1595 with personal bravery—wore armour, rode into battle, rallied troops during broken defenses—earning formal respect from Mughal generals as "Chand Sultan" mint.
- **Death & Divergent Narratives** Historiography records three competing versions of her death—assassination, suicide, escape—revealing how her memory has been shaped by politics and legend Taylor & Francis Online.
- **Cultural Mobility & Identity** Spoke multiple tongues (Arabic, Persian, Turkish, Marathi, Kannada), practiced artistic hobbies (sitar, painting), and refused purdah norms—portrayed riding horses and hawking publicly in contemporary representations Madras Courier+1Wikipedia+1.
- **Ethnic & Regional Complexity** Chand Bibi embodied the pluralism of Deccani society—her lineage, linguistic cosmopolitanism, and alliances with various Deccan Sultanates underscore a rich cultural milieu outside the Mughal northcentric narrative khidki.hydlab.co.inThe Caravan.

10. **Nur Jahan** (MehrunNissa; 1577–1645 CE)
- **Tūzk-e-Jahangiri (Memoirs of Jahangir)** – Jahangir's autobiography records his reflections on Nur Jahan's political influence, military leadership (e.g. rescuing him from coup), patronage, and strategic control over governance Wikipedia+15Wikipedia+15Prepp+15.
- **Persian Sultanate Chronicles**, notably **Intikhab-i-Jahangir Shahi** by Shaikh Abdul Wahab (d. 1622/23) – a nowpartially preserved source cited by later historians, documenting court events and Nur Jahan's role in Jahangir's reign Wikipedia.
  - "Nur Jahan." *Wikipedia*, 2025. https://en.wikipedia.org/wiki/Nur_Jahan.
  - "Nur Jahan | Empress, Accomplishments, & History." *Encyclopædia Britannica*, 2025. https://www.britannica.com/biography/Nur-Jahan.Encyclopedia Britannica
  - Lal, Ruby. *Empress: The Astonishing Reign of Nur Jahan*. W. W. Norton & Company, 2018. https://www.amazon.com/Empress-Astonishing-Reign-Nur-Jahan/dp/0393239349. Amazon+1Wikipedia+1
- **Findly, Ellison Banks**, *Nur Jahan: Empress of Mughal India* (Oxford University Press, 1993) – authoritative scholarly biography detailing her rise, the "Junta," cultural influence, religious policy, arts and architecture. It includes a select annotated bibliography for further reading Wikipedia+2Google Books+2Oxford Academic+2.
- **Lal, Ruby**, *Empress: The Astonishing Reign of Nur Jahan* (Norton & Company, 2018) – a vivid modern biography that recenters her as de facto ruler, entrepreneur, and artistic innovator. Praised in major international media Reddit+15Wikipedia+15Wikipedia+15.
- **Lal, Kishori Saran**, *The Mughal Harem* (Aditya Prakashan, 1988) – situates Nur Jahan within harem politics, female authority, and their portrayal in colonial historiography Wikipedia.
- **Youth Ki Awaaz**, "Politicisation of Indian Medieval History" – critiques European and colonial portrayals of Nur Jahan, exposing narrative biases and emphasizing local perspectives on her equal status in court politics Youth Ki Awaaz.
- Historical discussions and Redditbased commentary further highlight her strategic and entrepreneurial skills—for trading, fashion design, and controlling royal patronage networks; as well as her direct military command riding a war elephant to rescue Jahangir in rebellion Reddit+2Reddit+2Reddit+2.
- **Political Partnership & Junta Politics** After marrying Jahangir in 1611, Nur Jahan wielded de facto authority alongside her brother **Asaf Khan**, forming a powerful court faction. Jahangir himself relied on her decisions in governance and diplomacy Google BooksReddit+2Reddit+2Prepp+2.

- **Military Leadership** She personally led forces to rescue Jahangir during Mahabat Khan's rebellion in 1626, riding atop a war elephant—marking one of the most dramatic female military interventions in Mughal history Wikipedia+5Reddit+5Reddit+5.
- **Cultural Patronage & Innovation** Commissioned her father's mausoleum (ItimadudDaulah's tomb), which inspired Mughal architecture; was a trendsetter in fashion, garden design (e.g. Achabal Gardens), and abroad commercial ventures (jagirs, trade ships) Reddit+2Reddit+2Reddit+2.
- **Literary Identity & Poetry** An accomplished poet writing under the pen-name *Makhfi*, Nur Jahan's linguistic skills (Persian, Arabic) and courtly wit are frequently celebrated in memoirs and poetry anthologies Prepp+2Reddit+2Reddit+2.
- **Decline & Legacy** After Jahangir's death in 1627, Nur Jahan attempted to elevate her son-in-law Shahryar but was eclipsed by Prince Khurram (Shah Jahan). She lived her last years in Lahore, dying in December 1645 aged 68. Her mausoleum bears her self-crafted epitaph emphasizing humility Reddit+1Prepp+1.

11. **Jahanara Begum** (23 March 1614 – 16 September 1681)
- **Jahanara Begum**, *Risāla-ye-Sahibiyyah* — her own devotional autobiography and Sufi treatise (circa 1640), now in manuscript form, reflecting her spiritual identity and self-representation as a female subject in public religious discourse Reddit+15Equinox Journal+15The Sunday Guardian+15.
- **Mughal court chronicles**, notably *Shahjahannama* and other Persian historical records, include references to her commissioning of public works and her active role in succession politics during Shah Jahan's reign Wikipedia.
- **Ashna Hussain**, "Jahanara Begum: Self-representation in the Public Space," *Islamic Studies Collection* (2021). Explores Jahanara's public religious persona and governance of visibility in Mughal society Equinox Journal.
- **Afshan Bokhari**, several essays (2008–2015), including *The 'Light' of the Timuria* and *Masculine Modes of Female Subjectivity*, examining her Sufi affiliations, poetic identity, and gendered authority through literary lens Equinox Journal.
- **Shadab Bano**, "Piety and Princess Jahanara's Role in the Public Domain," *Proceedings of the Indian History Congress* 74 (2013), pp. 245–250. Focuses on her status as a patron of Sufism and her institutional presence in public space Brill Reference Works+6Equinox Journal+6wikipedia77.en-us.nina.az+6.
- **Andrea Butenschon**, *The Life of a Mogul Princess: Jahanara Begum* (Delhi, 2004). A dedicated biography offering insights into her upbringing, court influence, spiritual life, and architectural patronage Wikipedia+15Brill Reference Works+15Equinox Journal+15.
- **Kathryn Lasky**, *Princess of Princes: The Story of Jahanara Begum of India* (New York, 2002). A biography for younger readers emphasizing her political and spiritual journey Brill Reference Works.
- **Renuka Nath**, *Notable Mughal and Hindu Women in the 16th and 17th Centuries A.D.* (Inter-India Publications, 1990); includes a chapter on Jahanara's architectural projects and family history wikipedia77.en-us.nina.az+1Wikipedia+1.
- **Ruby Lal**, *Domesticity and Power in the Early Mughal World* (Cambridge University Press, 2005). While covering broader domestic politics, offers key interpretive commentary on Jahanara's role in the imperial family and spatial politics The Sunday Guardian+1Equinox Journal+1.
- **Jami Masjid, Agra (1648)** — built by Jahanara using her personal allowance; an important example of Mughal female patronage in sacred space and urban planning Wikipedia+3Wikipedia+3BDC TV+3.
- **Chandni Chowk Caravanserai and Bazaar Complex** — Jahanara commissioned the

original caravanserai and bazaar in Shahjahanabad in the mid17th century, laying foundations for Old Delhi's central commercial axis along with gardens and caravanserai structures Wikipedia+2BDC TV+2Brill Reference Works+2.
- **Spiritual Authority & Sufism** A devoted disciple of the Chishti Silsila, Jahanara authored *Risāla-ye-Sahibiyyah*, founded khānqāhs, and fostered Sufism as state culture alongside her brother Dara Shukoh The Sunday Guardian+3Equinox Journal+3Brill Reference Works+3.
- **Political Influence & Succession Dynamics** As Padshah Begum, she mediated court politics—stabilizing Shah Jahan's reign, managing sibling rivalries, and later preserving favor under Aurangzeb while sheltering her father in imprisonment Reddit+6Brill Reference Works+6The Times of India+6.
- **Architectural & Urban Legacy** She directly shaped early Shahjahanabad through construction of Chandni Chowk, caravanserai complex, and Jami Masjid Agra; of eighteen buildings commissioned by women, five were hers, indicating her rare public presence in architecture and commerce Wikipedia+1BDC TV+1.
- **Literary Voice & Self-Representation** A poet in Persian and Arabic, Jahanara maintained an authorial voice rarely seen among Mughal princesses—her manuscript and letters reflect both interior spirituality and outward political persona RekhtaEquinox Journal.

12. **Rani Ahilyabai Holkar** (31 May 1725–13 August 1795)
- **Malcolm, John**, *A Memoir of Central India, including Malwa and adjoining provinces* (1st ed. 1823; 3rd ed. 1832). The British officer interviewed eyewitnesses of Ahilyabai's reign and remains a foundational source for her political and administrative history Amazon India+15Wikipedia+15Reddit+15.
- **Burway, Mukund Wamanrao**, *Devi Ahilyabai Holkar* (Indore State Press, 1920; rev. ed. 1922). Early biographical account drawn from Holkar state records and oral histories Ahilyabai Holkar+2Ahilyabai Holkar+2Wikipedia+2.
- **Thakur, V. V.**, *Life and Life's Work of Shree Devi Ahilya Bai Holkar* (Indore, 2007). Reportedly commissioned by local administration, richly documents her public works, temple construction, and social policies Encyclopedia Britannica+4Wikipedia+4Ahilyabai Holkar+4.
- **Jahagirdar, Vijaya** (trans. Sangita Soman), *Karmayogini: Life of Ahilyabai Holkar* (Mehta Publishing House, English trans. 2017/2022). Modern narrative biography celebrating her political craft as a ruler and philanthropist .
- **Kibe, M. V.**, "Fragments from the records of Devi Shri Ahilyabai Holkar," *Indian Historical Records Commission Proceedings*, Vol. 13 (1930), pp. 132–139. Extracts from archival state records .
- **Thakur, V. V.**, "A Short Note on the Charities of Devi Shri Ahilya Bai Holkar," same proceedings, pp. 139–143. Focused on her ghats, dharmashalas, and temple construction .
- **Dighe, V. G.**, in *Provincial Maratha Dynasties*, vol. 8 of *History and Culture of the Indian People* (Bharatiya Vidya Bhavan, 1977/2001), pp. 270–272. Synthesizes her reign within broader Maratha politics .
- **Gordon, Stuart**, *The Marathas, 1600–1818* (Cambridge Univ. Press, 1993). Offers analysis of Ahilyabai's reign within Maratha military-administrative evolution .
- **Encyclopaedia Britannica**, "Ahilyabai Holkar" (updated June 2025). Concise summary of her reign, temple patronage, and impact on Malwa and wider India .
- **Reddit tribute threads**, e.g. r/Indore and r/IndiaSpeaks (2022)—celebrating her philanthropic legacy and temple-building across pilgrimage sites from Varanasi to Dwarka, and noting how she ruled from the front and ruled with compassion .
- **Wikipedia**, "Ahilyabai Holkar". Quick overview referencing her charitable architecture, textile industry in Maheshwar (Maheshwari sarees), public infrastructure, and reforms .**Regency & Governance**: After the deaths of her husband and son, Ahilyabai was appointed

manager of Malwa by the Peshwa in 1767. She ruled wisely for nearly three decades until her death in 1795, establishing Indore and Maheshwar as stable centers of Maratha power Reddit+1Reddit+1.
- **Philanthropy & Temple Patronage**: She rebuilt iconic shrines—Kashi Vishwanath Temple, Somnath, Dashashwamedh Ghat in Varanasi, Gaya, Omkareshwar, Dwarka, Badrinath—and established dharmashalas, wells, roads, and ghats across India Reddit+3Wikipedia+3Reddit+3.
- **Culture & Economic Revival**: Revived handloom weaving in Maheshwar by bringing in Gujarati, Mandu weavers and launching the renowned Maheshwari sari tradition; regarded as a cultural renaissance in her reign WikipediaReddit.
- **Public Orientation & Accessibility**: Broke purdah norms, held daily durbars, remained open to all subjects, prioritized just and efficient rulership—earning widespread reverence Encyclopedia Britannica+2Reddit+2Reddit+2.

13. **Rani Kittur Chennamma** (23 October 1778 – 21 February 1829)
- **Wodeyar, Sadashiva Shivadeva**. *Rani Chennamma of Kittur*. National Biography Series, National Book Trust, 1974. A foundational biography drawing on British India Office archives, local oral histories, and correspondence between East India Company officials and Kittur court sources.Wikipedia+15Exotic India Art+15Reddit+15
- **Kalburgi, M. M.** *Khare Khare Kitturu Bandaya*, and *Kitturu Samsthana Sahitya* (Vol. III)— Kannada-language key works documenting Kittur's revolt and sociocultural context. Wikipedia
- **Tammanagoudar, Sangamesh**. *Kitturu Rani Chennamma* — regional biography, also listed in Kannada literary corpus.Wikipedia
- **Naikar, Basavaraja**. *Queen of Kittur* — regional narrative biography celebrating her valor and historical significance.Wikipedia+14Wikipedia+14Exotic India Art+14
- **Chandana A**. *Kittur Rani Chennamma* — a brief children's biography (~45 pages) emphasizing her resistance against British colonial demands.Wikipedia+15BriBooks+15Exotic India Art+15
- **Kapil**. *Rani Chennamma: Warrior Queen of Kittur* (Hindi edition, Inspir. Biographies for Children series, 2017). Simple narrative for young readers tracing her courage and moral leadership.Amazon India
- **Wikipedia**, entry *Kittur Chennamma* — gives a general historical overview of her life, armed struggle (1824 against the East India Company), adoption of an heir, and legacy as a symbol in Karnataka's independence memory.Reddit+3Wikipedia+3Reddit+3
- **Reddit / IndianHistory subreddit**, e.g.: "Kittur Chennamma (23 October 1778 – 21 February 1829)… led an armed force against the East India Company in 1824… One of the first female rulers to rebel… She has become a folk hero."RedditReddit+1Wikipedia+1
- **Resistance against British expansion** After the death of her husband (1816) and only son (1824), she adopted Shivalingappa as heir. The British refused to recognize the adoption (prefiguring later Doctrine of Lapse logic) and attempted to annex Kittur. Chennamma led military resistance in 1824 and again, ultimately falling during captivity in 1829.Reddit
- **Military leadership & cultural memory** Learned martial arts early; commanded Kittur's forces personally. Remembered in Karnataka as a symbol of female valor, in folk songs, plays, and annual festivals—especially during the Kittur Utsava.Reddit
- **Sources & historiography** Wodeyar's 1974 biography remains the most scholarly and archival-supported account. Local Kannada histories like Kalburgi's and Tammanagoudar's offer rich context but rely on local narrative traditions. Wikipedia and popular narratives help illustrate her legacy and modern perception.Wikipedia

14. **Qudsia Begum** (1801 – 17 December 1881)
Sultan Jahan Begum (Ruler of Bhopal), *HayatiQudsi: Life of the Nawab Gauhar Begum*

(Qudsia Begum), translated by W. S. Davis (London: Paul, Trench, Trübner, 1918; 160 pp.) A first-hand biographical memoir authored by her descendant and ruler Sultan Jahan Begum—covering Qudsia's early life, regency, piety, and statecraft. Wikipedia+15South Asia Commons+15Wikipedia+15

- **Shaharyar Khan**, *The Begums of Bhopal: A Dynasty of Women Rulers in Raj India* (IB Tauris, 2000) Secular political history of the Bhopal Begums, with a key chapter on Qudsia's accession, reforms, and her role as founder of the female-led dynasty. Wikipedia+1Reddit+1
- **Jadunath Sarkar**, *Fall of the Mughal Empire, Volume I: 1739–1754* (1927; various editions) Includes context on Qudsia's reign during Muhammad Shah's weakness, her de facto regency, and interactions with Maratha, Rohilla, and Sikh powers. My Heritage Walks+1Wikipedia+1Wikipedia
- Studies of **Qudsia Bagh** and the **Golden Mosque (Sunehri Masjid)** in Old Delhi Qudsia Bag was built in 1748 in her honor; the adjacent Sunehri Masjid was commissioned ca. 1747–1751 by her near the Red Fort. These memorialized her public presence and gave her lasting architectural legacy. Reddit+15Wikipedia+15Sahapedia+15Profil Baru+1Wikipedia+1
- *Times of India*, "The begum of Bhopal" (11 July 2003) Overview article highlighting her rise to power at 17, state reforms (waterworks, mosques, rail link), and eventual abdication in favor of her daughter in 1837. Wikipedia+9Reddit+9timesofindia.indiatimes.com+9Reddit+3Wikipedia+3timesofindia.indiatimes.com+3
- **Founding the Women's Dynasty of Bhopal** At the age of just 17 (in 1819), Qudsia Begum became ruler on the death of her husband, rejecting male claimants and installing her daughter Sikandar Begum—with legal support from ulema and nobles—to begin a dynasty of female rule that lasted over a century. BookswagonWikipedia+2Reddit+2timesofindia.indiatimes.com+2
- **Administrative Reforms & Public Works** During her 18-year regency, she improved tax collection, built piped water systems, funded rail links from personal funds, and supervised major architectural projects like the Jama Masjid (built 1835–1857) and Gohar Mahal palace. Wikipedia+1timesofindia.indiatimes.com+1
- **Architectural Patronage & Delhi Legacy** Even after her retirement, her Delhi monuments (Qudsia Bagh garden palace and Sunehri Mosque) testified to her imperial influence; part of her palace complex survives and serves as a heritage landmark. WikipediaSahapediaThe Indian Express
- **Dynastic Influence Post-Abdication** Although she formally abdicated in 1837 in favor of her daughter, she continued to remain politically active behind the scenes during the reigns of her daughter and granddaughter. Wikipedia

15. Sikandar Begum (10 September 1817 – 30 October 1868)

- **Sikandar Begum**, *A Princess's Pilgrimage: Nawab Sikandar Begum's A Pilgrimage to Mecca* — originally written in Urdu and translated into English (London, 1870); this first-hand memoir, edited by Siobhan LambertHurley in 2007, provides insight into her experiences as the first Indian ruler to perform Hajj, her perceptions of Mecca and Jeddah, and her views on Ottoman Arabs and Turks Reddit+15Wikipedia+15Wikipedia+15.
- **Shaharyar M. Khan**, *The Begums of Bhopal: A Dynasty of Women Rulers in Raj India* (I.B. Tauris, 2000) — a detailed political and social history of the four generations of female rulers, including an indepth chapter on Sikandar's reforms, loyalty to Britain, and court policies Feminism in India+1TwoCircles.net+1.
- **Dictionary of Indian Biography**, entry "Bhopal, Nawab Sikandar Begam of (1816–1868)" — concise biographical overview emphasizing her regency, British recognition, knighthood, Hajj, and administrative vigour Wikisource+1The Hindu+1.

- **TwoCircles.net**, "Nawab Sikandar Begum's Hajj memoir" — popular summary of her pilgrimage account with critical reflection on her colonial-era observations and identity as a Muslim-woman-traveler abebooks.de+9TwoCircles.net+9CiNii+9.
- **Feminism in India**, "Sikandar Begum: The Begum Who Was The 'Star Of Colonial India'" (2019) — feminist reinterpretation highlighting her reformism, educational initiatives, female visibility, and formal recognition as a British knight Feminism in India.
- **Wikipedia / Bhopal State and Nawabs of Bhopal** — covers Sikandar Begum's institutional reforms: establishment of district administration, modern judiciary, secretariat, postal and customs systems, language shift to Urdu, architecture including Moti Masjid and Moti Mahal, and her revival of Delhi's Jama Masjid post-1857 Wikipedia+5Wikipedia+5Homegrown+5.
- **Regency & Sovereignty**: Regent for her daughter, Shah Jahan Begum, from 1844–1860. Recognized by the British as Nawab Begum in her own right in 1860; ruled until her death in 1868 Reddit+5Wikipedia+5Wikipedia+5.
- **Loyalty & British Recognition**: Supported the British during the 1857 Rebellion—banned rebel pamphlets, strengthened intelligence—and was awarded GC SI (Grand Commander of Star of India) in 1861 (only other female to receive it was Queen Victoria) Wikipedia+1TwoCircles.net+1.
- **Administrative Reform**: Introduced modern institutions—secretariat, judiciary, mint, postal services, intelligence network, district and sub-district divisions, revenue reforms, and replaced Persian with Urdu as court language in 1862 Wikipedia+1Homegrown+1.
- **Education & Public Works**: Founded Victoria School for Girls and Urdu/Hindi schools across districts. Designed and built major structures—Moti Masjid (1860), Moti Mahal, Shaukat Mahal—and reopened Delhi's Jama Masjid in 1862, personally cleaning it and leading prayer after Restoration Feminism in India+2Wikipedia+2Homegrown+2.
- **Religious Piety & Self-Representation**: First Indian ruler to perform Hajj (1863), travelled with around 1,000 women, and authored critical memoir in Urdu; her later English memoir contests colonial and Orientalist discourses Homegrown+4TwoCircles.net+4Wikipedia+4.
- **Public Persona & Gender Role**: Rejected purdah, performed martial activities—hunting, polo—and maintained direct public engagement with justice and governance; depicted as a powerful, handson ruler breaking conventional gender norms Feminism in India+1Homegrown+1.

16. **Sultan Shah Jahan Begum** (29 July 1838 – 16 June 1901)
- **TajulIkbal: TarikheBhopal** (*The History of Bhopal*), by Shah Jahan Begum, translated from Urdu by H. D. Barstow (Calcutta: Thacker & Spink, 1876) — a three-part chronicle she authored detailing the history of Bhopal, its rulers, and her own reign. Printed in refined Nizami Press style everydaymuslim.org+14Everything Explained Today+14Wikipedia+14.
- **HayatiShahjehani: Life of Her Highness the Late Nawab Shahjehan Begum of Bhopal**, translated by B. Ghosal (Bombay: Times Press, 1926) — her posthumous memoir compiling personal reflections and state events ResearchGate+2Everything Explained Today+2Wikipedia+2.
- **Shaharyar M. Khan**, *The Begums of Bhopal: A Dynasty of Women Rulers in Raj India* (I. B. Tauris, 2000) — political and cultural history that places Shah Jahan's reign in the longer tradition of female leadership in Bhopal Everything Explained Today+3Wikipedia+3artikel.siakadpt.com+3.
- **Barbara Daly Metcalf**, "Islam and Power in Colonial India: The Making and Unmaking of a Muslim Princess," *American Historical Review* (2011) — addresses Shah Jahan's role in Muslim reform and literary endeavors, including her linguistic projects and court influence everydaymuslim.org+2Taylor & Francis Online+2Turkiye ve Hindistan+2.
- **Muhsin Ramazan İşsever**, "Sultan Jahan Begum of Bhopal: Legacy & Linguistic

Contributions," *Audodilder* (Vol. 10, Issue 1, April 2025) — highlights her Urdu literary works (e.g., *GauhariIqbal*, *AkhtariIqbal*) under the penname "Shirin," and her cultural patronage in Ottoman Indian context internationaljournalcorner.com+6DergiPark+6Wikipedia+6.

- **"Sacralizing the City: The Begums of Bhopal and their Mosques"** (author and journal unspecified) — traces the architectural and religious patronage of Qudsia, Sikandar, and Shah Jahan Begums, including the construction of TajulMasjid during her reign ResearchGate+1Wikipedia+1.
- **Enroute Indian History**, "The Jewel in the Crown: Shah Jahan Begum" (2022) — discusses her progressive educational reforms, founding of girls' schools, patronage of Aligarh Muslim University, and constructing the Taj Mahal Palace at Bhopal Enroute Indian History+1internationaljournalcorner.com+1.
- **Everyday Muslim**, "A female ruler and her literary legacy" — details her literary output (*Tahzib un-Niswan wa Tarbiyat ul-Insan*), architectural projects (Ali Manzil, Benazir and Taj Mahal), and state modernization efforts everydaymuslim.org+1Turkiye ve Hindistan+1.
- **Literary & Reformist Accomplishments**: Shah Jahan Begum compiled the state history (*TajulIkbal*), authored manuals for women's education (*Tahzib un-Niswan wa Tarbiyat ul-Insan*), and produced UrduPersian poetry under her penname "Shirin." Her Qur'anic lexicon (*Khizanatul Lughat*) offered lexicon entries in Urdu, Persian, Arabic, Sanskrit, English, and Turkish—reframing social taboos like widowhood with neutral terms Turkiye ve Hindistan.
- **Architectural Patronage**: Commissioned the massive **Taj-ul-Masajid** mosque, initiated its construction, and built the famous **Taj Mahal Palace** (1871–84) in IndoSaracenic style—modeled after Agra's monument—marking her architectural legacy in Bhopal WikipediaEnroute Indian History.
- **Educational & Social Reforms**: She was a patron of girls' schooling, founding several institutions; served as Chancellor of Aligarh Muslim University; sponsored public buildings, libraries, and civic projects; and supported modern sanitation, postal, and healthcare systems in Bhopal Wikipedia.
- **Political & Religious Diplomacy**: Promoted Sunni Hanafi practice in state affairs, banned certain Sufi orders, and maintained ties with the Ottoman court—giving and receiving honors, including Ottoman medals—highlighting her transnational Muslim identity Turkiye ve Hindistan.
- **Succession & Legacy**: After her death in June 1901 (aged 62), she was succeeded by her daughter Sultan Jahan Begum. Her reforms were continued by subsequent Begums, establishing Bhopal as a model of socially and religiously progressive Muslim princely state Wikipedia.

17. **Sultan Jahan Begum** (9 July 1858 – 12 May 1930)
- **Sultan Jahan Begum**, *An Account of My Life* (Original title: *GauhariIqbal*), translated by C. H. Payne in three volumes (London: John Murray, 1910, 1920, 1927) — her own autobiography, chronicling her statecraft, reforms, personal reflections, and public engagements Reddit+15Sotherans+15Wikipedia+15.
- **Sultan Jahan Begum**, *The Story of a Pilgrimage to Hijaz* (Calcutta: Thacker, Spink & Co., published 1909) — detailed memoir of her 1903–04 hajj to Mecca and Medina, documenting geography, religious sites, public receptions, and administrative correspondence The Library of Congress+1The Hindu+1.
- **Shaharyar M. Khan**, *The Begums of Bhopal: A Dynasty of Women Rulers in Raj India* (I.B. Tauris, 2000) — provides an in-depth chapter on Sultan Jahan's rule, her reforms in education, health, municipal governance, and literature Youlin Magazine+1Wikipedia+1.
- **Siobhan LambertHurley**, *Muslim Women, Reform and Princely Patronage: Nawab Sultan Jahan Begam of Bhopal* (Routledge, 2007) — academic monograph analyzing her roles in

reform movements, literary culture, and women's empowerment Wikipedia+15Wikipedia+15Wikipedia+15.
- **Muhsin Ramazan İşsever**, "Sultan Jahan Begum of Bhopal: Legacy & Linguistic Contributions" (*Audodilder*, Vol. 10 Issue 1, April 2025) — discusses her extensive Urdu literary output (41+ works) and her influence on Urdu reform and culture DergiPark.
- **"Sacralizing the City: The Begums of Bhopal and their Mosques"** (ResearchGate article) — analyzes her architectural patronage, particularly the partial completion of the **Taj-ul-Masjid**, and its significance in civic identity Wikipedia+2Wikipedia+2Youlin Magazine+2.
- **The Indian Express**, "The last Begum of Bhopal: How Begum Sultan Jahan fought patriarchy and educated a generation of women" (May 2021) — profile essay emphasizing her educational initiatives, public health missions, and pioneering identity as a female chancellor of AMU indianexpress.com+1Wikipedia+1.
- **Youlin Magazine**, "Sultan Jahan: The Last Ruling Begum of Bhopal" (July 2022) — narrative portraying her reforms, writing career, personal discipline, and global presence at events like the 1911 Delhi Durbar Youlin Magazine.
- **Literary & Educational Leadership** Authored approximately 41 Urdu works on child-rearing (*Bachchon ki Parwarish*), health (*Tandurusti*), women's guidance (*Hidayat uz-Zaujan*), and biographies (*GauhariIqbal*), playing a central role in Urdu literary culture and women's education reform Wikipedia+3Google Arts & Culture+3Wikipedia+3.
- **Public Health & Education Reforms** Instituted free compulsory primary education (1918), founded women's hospitals like Sultania Zenana Hospital, led vaccination programs, and oversaw municipal modernization and irrigation projects The Hindu+2Wikipedia+2Sotherans+2.
- **Governance & Institutional Foundations** Established state legislative and executive councils, reformed taxation, judiciary, and police; chaired women's educational organizations; served as founding Chancellor of Aligarh Muslim University — the only woman to do so to date Wikipedia.
- **Architectural Patronage** Commissioned the **Taj Mahal Palace** (1871–1884) and initiated **TajulMasajid**, one of the world's largest mosques; these structures symbolize her synthesis of imperial vision and urban planning Wikipedia.
- **International Presence & Honors** Attended the 1911 Delhi Durbar; received British imperial honors (GCSI, GCIE, GBE); engaged in international women's committees and state diplomacy Wikipedia+1mr.kuchewar.com+1.

18. **Jindan Kaur** (1817–1 August 1863)
- **Jind Kaur** (Rani Jindan) is not known to have authored memoirs herself, but British colonial correspondence—especially letters by GovernorGeneral Dalhousie chanting her as a rallying symbol—and Sikh Army petitions repeatedly referenced her public importance and defiance, highlighting her centrality to Sikh leadership chitradivakaruni.com+15sikhmuseum.org.uk+15Wikipedia+15.
- **M. L. Ahluwalia**, *Maharani Jind Kaur* (Singh Brothers, 2001) — one of the first full biographical studies drawn from Punjab government records and her life in exile Wikipedia.
- **Priya Atwal**, *Royals and Rebels: The Rise and Fall of the Sikh Empire* (Hurst, 2020) — includes detailed chapters on Rani Jindan's regency, political maneuvering, and conflicts with the British Wikipedia+1jaipurliteraturefestival.org+1.
- **Christy Campbell**, *The Maharajah's Box* (2010) — biographical account of Duleep Singh but gives important context to Jindan's influence and the later Hapsburg exile period Reddit+13Wikipedia+13theguardian.com+13.
- **Chitra Banerjee Divakaruni**, *The Last Queen* (HarperCollins, 2021) — historical novel narrated by Rani Jindan herself; though fictional, it revived popular awareness of her life and struggles ResearchGate+8Wikipedia+8Goodreads+8.

- **Surbhi Saraswat**, "The Lost World of Rani Jindan" (*International Journal of Religion*, 2024) — critical essay analyzing how Divakaruni's novel renegotiates history and challenges colonial-era erasure Ijor.
- Singh, Aamna. *"Maharani Jindan Kaur (Lady Jinda)."* **Azadi Ka Amrit Mahotsav** (Ministry of Culture, Govt. of India), 6 Feb. 2023, amritmahotsav.nic.in/district-reopsitory-detail.htm?12523. (Official profile of Maharani Jind Kaur (1817–1863), regent of the Sikh Empire and mother of Maharaja Duleep Singh, including British depictions of her as the "Messalina of the Punjab" due to her resistanceamritmahotsav.nic.in.)
- *"Duleep Singh."* **Historic Royal Palaces – Tower of London**, n.d., hrp.org.uk/tower-of-london/history-and-stories/duleep-singh/. (Contains the story of Maharani Jind Kaur's later life: her exile and reunion with her son Duleep Singh in 1861, and accompanying him to England where she died in 1863, as documented by the Tower of London historical narrative.)gu
- **The Guardian**, "Rebel Queen – a thorn in the crown" (2010) — profile of Jindan as a symbol of resistance to British power and colonial vilification campaigns calling her the "Messalina of the Punjab" Reddit+4theguardian.com+4Wikipedia+4.
- **Sikh Museum Initiative**, "The Queen with the 'only manly understanding in the Punjab'" (2019 blog post) — features Dalhousie's infamous letter and outlines her political symbolism in Sikh resistance sikhmuseum.org.uk.

Themes & Historical Legacy
- **Regency & Political Agency** Appointed regent (1843–1846) for her five-year-old son Duleep Singh, Jindan Kaur reconstituted the Khalsa Council, resisted British claims, and ruled with notable assertiveness and visibility—holding court without purdah and asserting sovereignty openly Wikipediasikhmuseum.org.uk.
- **British Opposition & Exile** Following the First AngloSikh War (1845–46), the British marginalized her politically, imprisoned her in Sheikhupura and Chunar Fort, seized her pension, then exiled her. She escaped in 1849, traveling disguised to Nepal where she lived with dignity until permitted to see her son in 1861 Reddit+4sikhmuseum.org.uk+4Wikipedia+4.
- **Separation & Reunification** Separated from Duleep Singh for over thirteen years, she only reunited with him in Calcutta in 1861 and subsequently lived in England until her death in August 1863 in Kensington; cremation was performed posthumously in Bombay and later reinterred near Ranjit Singh's samadhi in Lahore Reddit+3Wikipedia+3The Pioneer+3.
- **Colonial Smear Campaigns** British narratives portrayed Jindan Kaur as immoral and dangerous—a "Messalina of the Punjab"—to justify sidelining her influence. She became a lightning rod for colonial stereotypes about female rulers challenging patriarchal norms theguardian.comReddit+1Reddit+1.
- **Modern Reappropriation & Heroism** Recent scholarship, historical fiction, and cultural projects (e.g. Sikh Museum, literary festivals) celebrate Jindan as a figure of courage, maternal sacrifice, and anti-colonial martyrdom. Works by Divakaruni, Atwal, Campbell, and others aim to reclaim her narrative from marginalization Ijorjaipurliteraturefestival.org

19. **Begum Hazrat Mahal** (c. 1820 – 7 April 1879)
- **Widely referenced in British colonial correspondence and Indian rebellion narratives**—though she left no known memoirs, official memos from GovernorGeneral Dalhousie and British registry documents repeatedly mention her as a pivotal figure in Awadh's antiBritish leadership Jafri Library+10Wikipedia+10Goodreads+10.
- **Kenizé Mourad**, *In the City of Gold and Silver: The Story of Begum Hazrat Mahal* (1992, reprinted) — a biographical narrative combining archive-based research and descendant oral history, introducing her dramatic transformation from court dancer to rebel queen Amazon+1Goodreads+1.
- **Malathi Ramachandran**, *Begum Hazrat Mahal: Warrior Queen of Awadh* (Niyogi Books,

2023) — a vivid historical novel portraying her rise, command of the rebel army, siege of the Residency, and exile in Nepal; based on extensive research yet dramatized for popular readership Amazon+5Niyogi Books India+5Wikipedia+5.
- **Dr. Kirti Narain**, *Begum Hazrat Mahal* (Giri Institute / ICSSR, 2016) — a research monograph based on field interviews, archival studies in Lucknow, and socio-historical reconstruction of 1857's events, highlighting women's martial roles and symbols of resistance (e.g. lotus code) Wikipedia+10Docslib+10Everand+10.
- **Wikipedia**, "Begum Hazrat Mahal" — authoritative overview of her life: origins in Faizabad, marriage to Wajid Ali Shah, leadership making her son Birjis Ali ruler in 1857, regency during rebellion, and exile to Nepal where she died in 1879 Goodreads+3Wikipedia+3Goodreads+3.

20. **Jhalkari Bai** (22 November 1830 – 1890)
- **Bhawani Shankar Visharad**, *Veerangana Jhalkari Bai* (1964) – the earliest standalone biography, based on Bundeli oral traditions, community histories, and references to Rani Lakshmi Bai's battle accounts Reddit+12samyuktajournal.in+12Wikipedia+12.
- **Badri Narayan**, *Women Heroes and Dalit Assertion in North India: Culture, Identity and Politics* (2006) – analyzes Jhalkari's symbolic status in Dalit cultural movements and narratives of resistance Wikipedia+1Bharatpedia+1.
- **Srikrishna Sarala**, *Indian Revolutionaries: A Comprehensive Study, 17571961* (1999) – includes Jhalkari as part of the 1857 insurgent milieu Bharatpedia+1Wikipedia+1.
- **B. L. Varma**, *Jhansi Ki Rani* (1951) and **Ram Chandra Heran's** *Maati* – historical novels and Bundeli fiction that popularized her legend in post-colonial narratives Wikipedia+3Taazakhabar News+3Wikipedia+3.
- **Swati Sengupta**, *The Incredible Life of Jhalkari Bai: The Braveheart Warrior* (2022) – a concise biographical account for younger readers, emphasizing her martial skill, origin, and sacrifice Wikipedia+13speakingtigerbooks.com+13Goodreads+13.
- **The Better India**, "The Other Jhansi Ki Rani: The Woman Who Took on British Forces Disguised as Laxmibai" (2017) – widely circulated online summary of her bravery and historical legacy swatisengupta.com+6The Better India+6The Jaipur Dialogues+6.
- **The Avenue Mail**, "Jhalkari Bai: The Incognito Twin of Rani Laxmibai" (May 2025) – retrospective opinion column emphasizing her Dalit identity and historical erasure Reddit+10The Avenue Mail+10The Jaipur Dialogues+10.
- **The Jaipur Dialogues**, "Jhalkari Bai–Valor Unparalleled" (2022) – profile piece positioning her as a forgotten hero and champion of Dalit visibility The Jaipur Dialogues.
- **Military Loyalty & Tactical Decoy** As head of the "Durgavahini" women's brigade, she used her uncanny resemblance to Rani Lakshmi Bai to impersonate the queen during the Siege of Jhansi—sacrificing her identity to secure the Rani's escape under British assault The Better India+3samyuktajournal.in+3Wikipedia+3.
- **Marginalized Heroism & Postcolonial Recovery** An uncrowned hero of the 1857 revolt, her narrative was largely omitted by mainstream colonial and early nationalist histories; only after the 1960s did Dalit activists, folk singers, and community scholars begin reclaiming her legacy as a symbol of castebased resistance Goodreads+2samyuktajournal.in+2The Avenue Mail+2.
- **Contested Death Date & Legacy** While many sources record her martyrdom during the siege (5 April 1858), alternative accounts—cited by Dalit folklorists—suggest she survived and lived until 1890 in obscurity samyuktajournal.in.
- **Contemporary Recognition** Celebrated today through Jhalkari Bai Jayanti ("Shahid Diwas"), state commemorations, a dedicated museum at Jhansi Fort, and a postage stamp. The Kori community and Bundelkhand Dalits promote her as a foundational figure of self-respect and regional pride samyuktajournal.in+4Taazakhabar News+4Wikipedia+4.

21. **Uda Devi Pasi** (19th Century)
- **Bhawani Shankar Visharad**, *Veerangana Uda Devi* (1964) — one of the earliest dedicated biographies drawing from Bundeli oral traditions, caste-community narratives, and regional historical memory.Reddit+14Wikipedia+14Feminism in India+14
- **Badri Narayan**, *Women Heroes and Dalit Assertion in North India: Culture, Identity and Politics* (SAGE, 2006) — contextualizes Uda Devi within Dalit socio-political movements and historic feminist reclamation of caste identities.Wikipedia
- **Charu Gupta**, *The Gender of Caste: Representing Dalits in Print* (2016) — examines representation gaps in mainstream historiography and how figures like Uda Devi have been marginalized.Wikipedia
- **Crispin Bates & Marina Carter (eds.)**, *Mutiny at the Margins: New Perspectives on the Indian Uprising of 1857* (SAGE, 2017) — includes archival documents and references to underrepresented figures including Uda Devi.Reddit+15Wikipedia+15Feminism in India+15
- **"Uda Devi: Dalit Freedom Fighter in the 1857 Uprising"**, *Feminism in India* (2017) — highlights her background in the Pasi caste, her enlistment under Begum Hazrat Mahal, and her ultimate martyrdom from a pipal tree sniper's perch.Wikipedia+10Feminism in India+10Ambedkarite Today+10
- **Kayva Gokhale**, *Uda Devi: A True Veerangini*, *Amar Chitra Katha* (2021) — illustrated narrative emphasizing her role in the women's battalion, the death of her soldier husband, and her sniper action at Sikandar Bagh.The Theorist+8Amar Chitra Katha+8Amar Chitra Katha+8
- **ThePrint**, "Don't Remember the 1857 Mutiny with Rani of Jhansi Alone…" (July 2025) — profiles Uda Devi as a Dalit icon of resistance, recounting British accounts of her sniper role and her symbolic erasure by caste-centered narratives.ThePrint
- **SheThePeople.TV**, *Dalit History Month: Remembering Uda Devi* (April 2021) — connects Uda Devi's martyrdom to contemporary Dalit memory and activism, noting her commemoration by the Pasi community.SheThePeople
- **Dalit resistance hero**: Belonging to the Pasi caste, Uda Devi defied both caste and gender norms by organizing a Veerangini battalion under Begum Hazrat Mahal's authority. Her martyrdom at Sikandar Bagh serves as a symbol of marginalized agency in the 1857 uprising. Feminism in IndiaSheThePeople
- **Guerrilla sniper strategy**: British accounts—including Commander Campbell and William Forbes-Mitchell—note sniper shots from a pipal tree that felled multiple soldiers before revealing a female Dalit rebel, demonstrating her lethal sharpshooting and battlefield presence.Wikipedia+2Amar Chitra Katha+2Amar Chitra Katha+2
- **Postcolonial erasure & recovery**: Colonial and nationalist historiography has largely erased her role. Her rediscovery in Dalit feminist scholarship, community commemorations, and public statues (notably at Sikandar Bagh), challenges dominant caste-based narratives. ThePrintSheThePeople
- **Ongoing legacy**: Each November 16, the Pasi community gathers in Lucknow to remember her martyrdom. The Uttar Pradesh government in 2022 also announced a women's battalion named in her honour.Wikipedia

22. **Azizan (Azizun) Bai**—also known as Azizun Nisa/Azeezan Bai—(the 19th-century)
- **Poonam & Tripuresh Tripathi**, *Azizan Bai's Contribution to the Freedom Struggle: With Special Reference to Kanpur* (RESEARCH REVIEW Int'l Journal of Multidisciplinary, Vol. 10, No. 4, 2025). Focused, peer-reviewed article that uses archival, regional, and oral sources to document her espionage, logistical support to rebels, and ultimate sacrifice Awaz The Voice+12rrjournals.com+12tornosindia.com+12.
- **Sugandhaa Pandey**, "Azizun Nisa: The Courtesan & Strategist Who Played a Crucial Role In The Revolt of 1857" (*Feminism in India*, Sept 2021). A concise narrative of her transition

from performer to spy activist, and leadership of "Mastani Toli" women's group in Kanpur The Federal+2Feminism in India+2Wikipedia+2.
- **Tornos India (TornosAwaz)**, "Azizan Bai – Contribution of a Beauty to the Struggle of 1857" (*Lucknowledge*, July 2021). Contextualization of her relationship with Nana Sahib, intelligence gathering, arms distribution, and folk memory alongside references to Savarkar's *Indian War of Independence 1857* tornosindia.com+1dharmayudh.com+1.
- **Dharmayudh.com**, "Azizan Bai: Incessant Struggle of a Courtesan… in the First War of Independence 1857". Detailed portrayal of her spy network, female soldiery, and battlefield courage during the Siege of Kanpur DNN24+11dharmayudh.com+11fairgaze+11.
- **Times of India**, "Azizan Bai: Courtesan who took up sword for motherland" (2023). Recounts her upbringing, kotha legacy from Lucknow to Kanpur, formation of "Mastani Sena" women brigade in male attire, and defiant execution refusing collaboration with the British The Times of India.
- **FairGaze / The Federal Review**, "Dance to Freedom: From Ghungroos to Gunpowder" (May 2024). Features AK Gandhi's recent biography highlighting Azizun Bai along with other tawaifs who contributed to the 1857 struggle The Federal.
- **Espionage & Resistance** Born around 1832 or 1824, Azizan Bai—once a Lucknow courtesan—moved to Kanpur and allied with Nana Sahib's rebellion leadership. She ran a spy-network, sheltered revolutionaries, distributed arms, and led a female auxiliary group called "Mastani (Mastani Sena)," dressed in male uniform and riding into action with pistols and medals tornosindia.comIndian Liberals.
- **Martyrdom & Refusal to Betray** British accounts note Havelock personally offered her pardon if she revealed rebel names. She refused, replying: "I want the destruction of the British… take my life; you cannot make me bow" before being executed—her defiance became legend DNN24+1The Times of India+1.
- **Marginalization and Rediscovery** Though colonial and mainstream nationalist histories largely ignored her, Dalit feminist scholarship and local memory have revived her legacy. Today she's commemorated in Kanpur by statues, commemorative events, and her name is increasingly featured in feminist narratives about the 1857 uprising rrjournals.comFeminism in IndiaThe Federal.
- **Cultural Identity & Symbolic Resistance** As a courtesan (tawaif), she used public performance spaces to network and support revolutionaries. Her story challenges caste, class, and gender hierarchies in both historical analysis and postcolonial remembrance Women Chapter.

23. **Manikarnika Tambe – Rani Lakshmibai of Jhansi** (19 November 1828 – 18 June 1858)
- **Dattatray Balwant Parasnis**, *Maharani Laxmibaisaheb Yanche Charitra* (1894) — one of the earliest detailed biographies of Lakshmibai, based on interviews with her adopted son Damodar Rao and eyewitnesses Wikipedia+15Wikipedia+15The Bio Diary+15.
- **DR M. S. Renick**, *A New Light upon the History of Rani Laxmibai of Jhansi* (2004) — offers revisionist insights into her upbringing and political formation, with critical evaluation of earlier sources Exotic India Art+1copsey-family.org+1.
- **Tapti Roy**, *Raj of the Rani: Bundelkhand in 1857* (Oxford University Press, 1994) — analytical exploration of Jhansi's uprising, Lakshmibai's leadership, and the social dynamics of Bundelkhand copsey-family.org.
- **Tapti Roy**, *The Politics of a Popular Uprising* — situates Rani Lakshmibai's role within the broader context of people's revolt rather than mere military insurgency copsey-family.org.
- **S. N. Sen**, *1857* (Government of India, 1957) — government-commissioned overview; while noted for bias toward British sources, still a key mid-century reference copsey-family.org+1Reddit+1.

- **Joyce Lebra (Chapman Lebra)**, *The Rani of Jhansi: A Study in Female Heroism in India* — historical monograph exploring Lakshmibai's symbolic status in Indian nationalism and feminist history The Bio Diary+9indianexpress.com+9Wikipedia+9.
- **Zahied Rehman Ganie & Shanti Dev Sisodia**, "The Unsung Heroines of India's Freedom Struggle," *AIJSSR* vol. 5 no. 2 (2020) — includes Rani of Jhansi as part of women's contributions to India's independence movement Grafiati+1Grafiati+1.
- **Tapti Roy**, *Rani of Jhansi* (Penguin India, 2006) — popular biography grounded in scholarly rigor recounting Lakshmibai's life details and rebellion-era decisions copsey-family.org.
- **Mahasweta Devi**, *Jhansi Rani* (1956, Bengali) & *The Queen of Jhansi* (English translation, 2000) — a literary reconstruction blending historical records, G. C. Tambe's archives, and folk narratives Wikipedia.
- **Harshita Murarka**, "A Closer Look at Rani Lakshmibai's History & the Manikarnika Row," *The Quint* (2018) — revisits historical controversies and representation of Lakshmibai in popular culture Journals of India+3TheQuint+3indianexpress.com+3.
- **Grafiati bibliography** on Rani Lakshmi Bai — an annotated academic catalog of journal articles, theses, and books useful for further research Reddit+5Grafiati+5Grafiati+5.
- Community posts on r/IndiaSpeaks and r/IndianHistory recount her childhood, training, and heroic escape with Damodar Rao, while capturing popular memory of Lakshmibai's bravery Reddit+1Reddit+1.
- **Symbolic Legacy**: Celebrated as India's 'Joan of Arc of the East', she inspired nationalist iconography, literature, poetry (e.g. Subhadra Kumari Chauhan's "Jhansi ki Rani"), and continues as a feminist and Dalit-symbol in modern narratives indianexpress.com.

24. **Savitribai Phule** (3 January 1831 – 10 March 1897)
- **Savitribai Phule**, *Kavya Phule* (1854) — her own poetry collection, addressing gender and caste oppression, published in her lifetime Wikipedia+15Wikipedia+15Reddit+15.
- **Letter by Savitribai**, referencing her colleague Fatima Sheikh—used in debates on Muslim women educators with Phule in school founding Reddit+1Reddit+1.
- **Dhananjay Keer**, *Jyotirao and Savitribai Phule: Their Year 1851 to Death* (1964/1992) — early authoritative biography documenting her life and contributions Vajiram & Ravi+4Wikipedia+4Wikipedia+4.
- **Ganesh and Bhalerao (eds.)**, *A Forgotten Liberator: The Life and Times of Savitribai Phule* — critical essays and letters, recommended on Reddit Reddit+15Reddit+15Reddit+15.
- **Bidyut Chakrabarty**, *Savitribai Phule: The Firebrand Intellectual* (upcoming, c. 2024) — political science analysis underlining her anti-caste feminist thought in prophetic detail Wikipedia+1Reddit+1.
- **Gail Omvedt**, *Jotirao Phule and the Ideology of Social Revolution in India* and *We Will Smash This Prison!: Indian Women in Struggle* — foundational social-movement context to Savitribai's activism Reddit+4Wikipedia+4Wikipedia+4.
- **Articles on Satyashodhak Samaj**, the reform society founded in 1873 (Savitribai led the women's wing), pivotal in women's education and Dalit rights Wikipedia+3Wikipedia+3Vajiram & Ravi+3.
- **Charu Gupta**, *The Gender of Caste: Representing Dalits in Print* (2016) — historiographical critique noting the erasure of Dalit women like Savitribai in mainstream scholarship Wikipedia.
- **Feminism in India**, "Remembering Mai Savitribai Phule…" (Jan 2023) — highlights her struggles founding the first girls' school in Maharashtra in 1848, the barbers' protest, and work with widows and victims of infanticide Wikipedia+3Reddit+3Reddit+3.
- **Vajiram & Ravi UPSC summary**, "Savitribai Phule Biography, Contribution in Education" (Mar 2025) — concise yet informative, covering her reforms (schools, social uplift, grief care shelters) Vajiram & Ravi.

25. Fatima Sheikh (c. 9 January 1831 – 9 October 1900)
- A crucial **letter by Savitribai Phule**, dated 10 October 1856, references Fatima by name — indicating her involvement with Phule's schools even during times of Adversity ("Fatima could be struggling… but she will not complain") Reddit+15ThePrint+15The Indian Express+15.
- A **century-old photograph**, published by the Maharashtra State Bureau for Literature and Culture (Savitribai Phule – Samagra Writings, 1988), shows Fatima Sheikh seated next to Savitribai and two students — confirming her real presence and role The Indian Express+3Reddit+3ThePrint+3.
- **ThePrint**, "Fatima Sheikh: the woman who reshaped Indian education…" (2025) — traces her founding role in Pune's Indigenous Library (1848), her status as a trained teacher alongside Savitribai, and her important but overlooked legacy The Indian Express+8ThePrint+8Wikipedia+8.
- **The Indian Express**, article (2023): "Who was Fatima Sheikh: India's oftforgotten feminist icon" — profiles her origins, collaboration with Phule, and reasons for historical marginalization .
- **The Better India**, "How India's first Muslim woman teacher started a 'Beti Padhao' movement…" (2018) — celebrates her outreach among marginalized communities and her radical role in girls' education .
- **TRT World**, "The forgotten legacy of Fatima Sheikh" (2020) — contextual analysis of her contribution to anti-caste feminist education alongside Phule, and her current invisibility in mainstream historiography .
- **Writing Women (Vijaya Chikermane)** — essay on the deep friendship of Savitribai and Fatima, working together to defy gender and caste exclusion through education .
- **Educational Pioneer & Alliance Builder** Fatima Sheikh trained as a teacher alongside Savitribai at Cynthia Farrar's institute in Ahmednagar. She cofounded the first school for girls in India (1848) in her home — later named *Indigenous Library* — teaching children from marginalized castes and religions alongside Savitribai The Indian Express+3ThePrint+3TRT World+3The Financial Express+8Wikipedia+8The Hindu+8.
- **Social Resistance & Inclusion** Despite harsh social opprobrium—from both patriarchal Hindu and conservative Muslim circles—Fatima persisted, delivering doortodoor advocacy and education despite being pelted with stones, dung, and insults while walking to school ThePrint+1The Better India+1The Second Angle.
- **Under-Documented Legacy & Recovering History** Modern scholarship and media have revived recognition of her contributions, but Fatima's life and work remain poorly documented in mainstream historical literature. A single letter, photo, and mentions in Marathi sources represent almost all available evidence RedditThePrint.
- **Symbol of Marginalized Feminism** Her life symbolizes early solidarity across community lines—DalitBahujan and Muslim women working together for progressive causes—and represents a foundational figure in intersectional feminist and anticaste history TRT Worldwritingwomen.co.
- Savitribai Phule. *Letter, 10 October 1856* (published in *Samagra Writings*, 1988). (Primary.)
- ThePrint. "Fatima Sheikh: The woman who reshaped Indian education…" 6 July 2025.
- The Indian Express. "Who was Fatima Sheikh: India's oftforgotten feminist icon." 10 January 2023.
- The Better India. "How India's first Muslim woman teacher started a 'Beti Padhao' Movement…" 19 September 2018.
- TRT World. "The forgotten legacy of Fatima Sheikh, India's first Muslim teacher." 29 May 2020.
- Chikermane, Vijaya. "The Revolutionary Friendship of Savitribai Phule and Fatima Sheikh." *Writing Women* blog.

26. **Muktabai "Mukta" Salve** (19th century)
- **Muktabai Salve**, *"Mang Maharachya Dukhvisayi"* ("About the Grief of the Mangs and Mahars"); an autobiographical essay published in *Dnyanodaya* fortnightly journal on 15 February and 1 March 1855, when she was around 14 and a pupil at Savitribai Phule's school in Pune. It critiques Brahminical patriarchy, untouchability, and caste oppression from a Dalitfeminist perspective dalitweb.org+11decodingthecodes.blogspot.com+11Velivada+11.
- **Aishwarya Javalgekar**, "Mukta Salve: The First Female Dalit Writer," *Feminism in India* (2017). A concise profile emphasizing her radical early critique of caste/religion and recognition as a feminist pioneer Feminism in India+1ShethePeople+1.
- **Ambedkarite Today blog**, "Mukta Salve—the first Dalit feminist," highlighting her historical significance, family background (granddaughter of Lahuji Raghoji Salve), and the revolutionary importance of her essay Velivada+2Ambedkarite Today+2Wikipedia+2.
- **Velivada.com**, "Mukta Salve: the first female Dalit writer and student of Savitribai Phule," an analysis of her life, historical erasure, and legacy in anticaste feminist scholarship .

Themes & Historical Significance
- **Dalit Feminist Courage**: As a young Mahar/Mang Dalit girl with limited education, Mukta boldly published her critique of Vedic hegemony and caste violence, including graphic accounts of atrocities under Peshwa rule ShethePeople+4Ambedkarite Today+4Velivada+4.
- **Earliest Dalit Woman Writer**: Her 1855 essay is widely recognized as one of the first published works by a Dalit woman, predating much of modern Dalit literature and signaling early anti-caste feminist consciousness Velivada+2Feminism in India+2Velivada+2.
- **Influence of Phule Movement**: Mukta was one of the earliest students at Savitribai and Jyotirao Phule's girls' schools; her essay demonstrates the impact of inclusive education in generating critical voices from marginalized communities Feminism in India.
- **Erasure and Rediscovery**: Despite the radical clarity of her writing, Mukta's life and legacy were almost completely forgotten until feminist historians and Dalit scholars reclaimed her as a foundational figure in Maharashtra's anti-caste and women's emancipation movements HCGProgressive Students' Forum TISS.

27. **Tarabai Shinde** (1850–1910)
- **Tarabai Shinde**, *Stri Purush Tulana* ("A Comparison Between Women and Men"), Marathi, Shri Shivaji Press, Pune, 1882 (first printing of 500 copies at nine annas). This bold essay responded to a conservative newspaper's vilification of a widow and rigorously critiqued patriarchal, caste, and religious norms. It enjoyed no contemporary readership and was widely condemned. Jyotirao Phule endorsed it in Satyashodhak Samaj's *Satsar*. The pamphlet vanished from public view until republished by S. G. Malshe in 1975 Reddit+15Indian Liberals+15Wikipedia+15.
  o "Tarabai Shinde." *Wikipedia*, 2025. https://en.wikipedia.org/wiki/Tarabai_Shinde. LinkedIn+2Wikipedia+2Google Arts & Culture+2
  o "Tarabai Shinde: The Woman Credited with Writing India's First Feminist Text." *The Indian Express*, 2025. https://indianexpress.com/article/research/tarabai-shinde-the-woman-credited-with-writing-indias-first-feminist-text-9867557/.The Indian Express+1JETIR+1
  o "Tarabai Shinde." *Google Arts & Culture*, 2025. https://artsandculture.google.com/story/tarabai-shinde-zubaan/VwWxmlfRaYmiLw?hl=en.
- **Rosalind O'Hanlon (transl.)**, *A Comparison Between Women and Men: Tarabai Shinde and the Critique of Gender Relations in Colonial India* (Delhi: Oxford University Press, 1994). A scholarly English edition with analysis of the text and historical context Wikipedia+7Tarabai Shinde+7Reddit+7.
- **Ramachandra Vasant Kumbhar**, *Feminist Historiography and Feminist History Writing of Tarabai Shinde* (Aayushi International Interdisciplinary Research Journal, Special Issue

No.68, February 2020). Examines Tarabai's social and feminist historiography roots and her textual significance ResearchGate.
- **Joshi P. S.**, *Tarabai Shinde: The woman feminist who protested patriarchy and caste discrimination in India* (conference paper, 2012). A historical overview of Tarabai's context and significance .
- **Prarthana Puthran**, "The Unwavering Feminism of Tarabai Shinde", *Indian Liberals* (2020). Profile summarizing her life, motivations, and the existential courage behind her writing .
- **Forward Press**, "Savitribai and Tarabai Shinde: Rising Against a Conspiracy of Silence" (2013). Discusses Tarabai's overlooked role in Indian feminist history alongside Savitribai Phule .
- **Mainstream Weekly**, "Tarabai Shinde... protest patriarchy and caste discrimination" (review essay). Explores her use of religious iconoclasm and literary satire in challenging Hindu social values .
- **Wikipedia**, entry *Tarabai Shinde* (updated recently). Provides biographical sketch, summary of *Stri Purush Tulana*, its reception, rediscovery, and Phule affiliation. Recognizes her as an early feminist advocate in India .
- **Knowpia / Tarabai Shinde profile**. Includes selected sources: O'Hanlon's edition, Gail Omvedt's *Dalit Vision*, and edited collections like *Shadow Lives* (Kali for Women); notes Tsunde Shinde's essay was cited by Susie Tharu & K. Lalita .
- **Kalahut.com**, article "Tarabai Shinde: A Pioneer of Feminist Thought in India" (2024). Highlights her critique of Hindu scriptures and her advanced ideas concerning women's emancipation in colonial India
- **First Modern Feminist Critique in Colonial India** *Stri Purush Tulana* is recognized as the earliest explicitly feminist work in modern India, combining critiques of caste, patriarchy, widow oppression, child marriage, sexual double standards, and religious hypocrisy often backed by shastras Wikipedia+1Wikipedia+1.
- **Context & Consequence** Written in response to the Vijayalakshmi case (1881), Tarabai directly challenged the misogynistic discourse found in Pune newspapers and Hindu orthodoxy; she was publicly attacked and largely disappeared from discourse after publication despite Phule's public support Indian LiberalsWikipediaKnowpia.
- **Rediscovery & Legacy** After being lost for nearly a century, the pamphlet was rediscovered in 1975; its English translation appeared in 1994. Since then, feminist historians have reclaimed Tarabai's central role in shaping intersectional feminist thought in India WikipediaWikipediaTarabai ShindeForward Press.
- **Influence on Feminist Historiography** Tarabai's critique extended beyond individual injustices to ideological foundations of gender inequality, situating her as a pivotal voice in feminist historiography and social resistance in colonial India Fundación MenteClaraResearchGateForward Press.

28. **Pandita Ramabai Sarasvati** (23 April 1858 – 5 April 1922)
- **Ramabai Sarasvati, Pandita:** *The High-Caste Hindu Woman* (London: Bell & Sons, 1887) – first English-language book by an Indian woman, critiquing widowhood, caste hierarchy, and patriarchal norms. CiNii+5Encyclopedia+5Open University+5
- **Pandita Ramabai Sarasvati:** *Strī Dharma Nīti* ("Morals for Women", 1882) – Marathi tract on women's education and reform. Goodreads+2Encyclopedia+2The New Historia+2
- **Ramabai, Pandita:** *United Statesci Lokasthiti āṇi Pravasavṛtta* ("Life in the United States", 1889) – travelogue reflecting American social life and feminist observations. indianchristianwritings.blogspot.com+2The New Historia+2Goodreads+2
- **Ramabai, Pandita:** *A Testimony* (Kedgaon: Mukti Mission, 1917) – personal reflections and letters detailing her mission experience. reddit.com+15indianchristianwritings.blogspot.com+15Open University+15

- **Ramabai, Pandita:** *Famine Experience in India* (1897) – inspired by her relief work during the Great Famine in Maharashtra. indianchristianwritings.blogspot.com+1The New Historia+1
- **Kosambi, Meera (ed.).** *Pandita Ramabai through Her Own Words: Selected Works* (New Delhi: Oxford University Press, 2000) – bilingual anthology of her writings, including unpublished texts and translations, plus contextual essay. Fundación MenteClara+7Bagchee+7CiNii+7
- **Dyer, Helen S.** *Pandita Ramabai: The Story of Her Life* (London: Morgan & Scott, 1900; reprints) – early biography covering her orphanhood, scholarship, widowhood, life in England, and mission-building. Wikipedia+3Goodreads+3Open University+3
- **Sengupta, P. S.** *Pandita Ramabai Saraswati: Her Life and Work* (Bombay: Asia Publishing House, 1970) – comprehensive historical biography emphasizing reformist and social work contributions. The New Historia+3Wikipedia+3Open University+3
- **MacNicol, Nicol.** *Pandita Ramabai* (Calcutta: Association Press, 1926) – devotional/Christian missionary perspective on her life. indianchristianwritings.blogspot.com+2Open University+2Encyclopedia+2
- **Underhill, Barbara; Fuller, Mary L.; Butler, Clementina.** Collaborative biographical commemorations in *Women Who Have Worked and Won* (late 19th century), featuring Ramabai among reformist women leaders. The New Historia+2indianchristianwritings.blogspot.com+2Goodreads+2
- **Bhagabati Dikshit Sarma, Prithvi Sinha & Sneha Garg**, "Baptising Pandita Ramabai: Faith and religiosity in the social reform movements of colonial India," *Indian Economic & Social History Review*, Vol. 58, Issue 3 (2021) – explores her controversial conversion and interfaith diplomacy. SAGE Journals
- **Uma Chakravarti**, *Rewriting History: The Life and Times of Pandita Ramabai* (Delhi: Kali for Women, 1998) – feminist historiographical portrait, including her ideological evolution. Wikipedia+1Wikipedia+1
- **Kosambi, Meera**, "Indian Response to Christianity, Church and Colonialism: The Case of Pandita Ramabai," *Economic and Political Weekly* (1992) – detailed examination of her religious journey and its political impact. Wikipedia
- **Feminist & Social Reform Pioneer**: Ramabai challenged child marriage, widow oppression, caste restrictions, and campaigned for women's education well before the broader reform movement. EncyclopediaThe New Historia
- **Cross-Cultural Identity & Global Advocacy**: A multilingual devotee of Sanskrit, later Christian convert, lectured in Britain and America, helped found Mukti Mission to rescue child widows and educate women. Open UniversityThe New Historia
- **Institution Builder**: Founded Arya Mahila Samaj in Pune and Mukti Mission near Poona (founded 1889), which sheltered, educated, and trained thousands. Her work was honored by Kaiser-i-Hind medal in 1919. Wikipedia+2The New Historia+2Encyclopedia+2

29. **Dr. Kadambini Ganguly (née Bose)** (18 July 1861 – 3 October 1923)
- Kadambini Glass-microscopy sources show her life: **she left no known autobiography**, but her educational journey, medical career, and social interventions are documented in her speeches, letters, and public appearances, notably within **Brahmo Samaj archives** and **Indian National Congress records** India Today+15Wikipedia+15Reddit+15.
- Chakrabarty, Roshni. *"Kadambini Ganguly, India's First Female Doctor Who Made Calcutta Medical College Start Admitting Women."* **India Today**, 18 July 2019, indiatoday.in/education-today/gk-current-affairs/story/kadambini-ganguli-india-s-first-female-doctor-1570858-2019-07-18. (Biography of Dr. Kadambini Ganguly (1861–1923), one of the first two female graduates in the British Empire and the first Indian woman to practice Western medicine. Notes that she was also the first woman to address an Indian National Congress session (1890) and a pioneer for women's education and healthcare.)

- *"Ganguly, Kadambini (1861–1923)."* **Banglapedia: National Encyclopedia of Bangladesh**, Asiatic Society of Bangladesh, 2014, en.banglapedia.org/index.php?title=Ganguly,_Kadambini. (Details Kadambini Ganguly's achievements: graduating from Bethune College in 1883 alongside Chandramukhi Basu, overcoming prejudice to earn a medical degree in 1886, and later obtaining further medical training in Britain. Also covers her social activism, including legal action against a newspaper that disparaged her qualifications.)
- **Nikhil Verma et al.**, *Dr. Kadambini Bose Ganguly (1861–1923): First Indian woman to practise Western medicine in India.* International Journal of Historical Studies (2024). This peer-reviewed paper analyses her educational excellence and role in empowering women through medicine Science Museum Blog+2SAGE Journals+2Wikipedia+2.
- **Behar Herald**, *Kadambini Ganguly: First Hindu Bengali Female Physician in India* (2020). Offers a biographical overview, contextualized with anecdotes such as her discriminatory experiences and campaign for women's rights Behar Herald+1Wikipedia+1.
- **India Today**, "Meet Kadambini Ganguly: The woman who rewrote the rules of Indian medicine" (2019). Summarizes her pioneering path to Calcutta Medical College and her legacy in women's medical education history.rcplondon.ac.uk+15India Today+15The Times of India+15.
- **Times of India / NDTV**, "Google honors India's first woman doctor on her 160th birthday" (2021). Highlights her groundbreaking graduation in 1886 and her global recognition in 2021 via Google Doodle Wikipedia+3www.ndtv.com+3The Times of India+3.
- **Science Museum Blog (London)**, "Honouring Kadambini Ganguly" (2022). Chronicles her journey for medical education, including overseas diplomas, and frames her life as emblematic of women's emancipation in colonial India Science Museum Blog.
- **Banglapedia**, biography of Kadambini as a pioneering figure from East Bengal who gained first entrance to University of Calcutta, fought social prejudice, and became a medical professional and activist Science Museum Blog+2Banglapedia+2Wikipedia+2.
- **Wikipedia**, entry *Kadambini Ganguly*—summarizes her education, career, activism, and personal life, with bibliography including secondary academic sources like Kopf's *The Brahmo Samaj and the Shaping of the Modern Indian Mind* Wikipedia+4Wikipedia+4Banglapedia+4.
- **First Indian Female Physician & Colonial Trailblazer** In 1886 Kadambini became one of the two first female graduates in South Asia (alongside Chandramukhi Basu) and the first Indian woman to practice Western medicine in India RedditReddit+13Wikipedia+13The Times of India+13. She earned her medical credentials from Calcutta and later from Edinburgh, Glasgow, and Dublin in 1893—a rare triple diploma feat at that time PMC+3Behar Herald+3Indiatimes+3.
- **Champion of Women's Rights & Social Reform** Kadambini actively challenged patriarchal norms. She filed a successful libel suit in 1891 against conservative media that had vilified her, and she fought for coal miners' welfare, workers' rights, and women's participation in medical conferences Science Museum Blog+2PMC+2The Times of India+2. She was also among the first women delegates and first female speaker at Indian National Congress sessions in 1889–90 Reddit+4PMC+4The Times of India+4.
- **Advocate for Women's Education & Institutional Change** Her enrollment at Calcutta Medical College in 1884 challenged institutional bans on women; her graduation influenced the university and national reforms opening higher education to women in the Indian Empire India Todayfeminisminindia.comBanglapedia.
- **Enduring Legacy & Inspiration** Kadambini's story remains a powerful narrative in feminist and medical history. She has been honored in popular culture (e.g. TV series *Prothoma Kadambini*, Google Doodle) and reverberates across generations in Bengal and beyond India times+2Wikipedia+2Wikipedia+2.

30. **Bhikaji Rustom Cama** (commonly known as *Madam Bhikaji Cama*; 24 September 1861 – 13 August 1936)
- **Saha, Panchanan**, *Mother of Indian Revolution: Madam Bhikaji Rustom Cama* (Parul Prakashani, 2015). A narrative biography based on archival records and lesser-known primary sources, tracing her international activism from London to Paris, flaghoisting incident, and revolutionary patronage ClearIAS+14Readersend+14Wikipedia+14.
- **Laursen, Ole Birk**, "*'I Have Only One Country, It Is the World': Madame Cama, Anticolonialism, and IndianRussian Revolutionary Networks in Paris, 1907–17*," *History Workshop Journal*, Vol. 90 (2020), pp. 96–114. Detailed academic study of her global alliances and international socialist network connections southasianbritain-demo.rit.bris.ac.uk.
- **Sethna, Khorshed Adi**, *Madame Bhikhaiji Rustom Cama* (Government of India, Ministry of Information & Broadcasting, 1987). Official biography curated by the Indian state, covering life phases, activism, and return to India mid1930s Wikipedia+6southasianbritain-demo.rit.bris.ac.uk+6Wikipedia+6.
- **Visram, Rozina**, *Asians in Britain: 400 Years of History* (Pluto Press, 2002) & *Women in India and Pakistan* (Cambridge University Press, 1992). Contextual essays that explore expatriate Indian women activists including Cama, their struggles, and networks ClearIAS+15southasianbritain-demo.rit.bris.ac.uk+15Wikipedia+15.
- Founder of the nationalist periodical ***Bande Mataram*** (Paris, 1909) and editor/cofounder of ***Madan's Talwar***. These revolutionary publications distributed Indian nationalist literature covertly into British India despite being banned Reddit+5Wikipedia+5ClearIAS+5.
- **Flag of Indian Independence**: In 1907 at the International Socialist Congress, Stuttgart, Cama unfurled one of the earliest tricolor flags with Lotuses and **"Vande Mataram"**, co-designed with Savarkar and Shyamji Krishna Varma—an iconic act immortalized in nationalist history Wikipedia+13Reddit+13Reddit+13.
- **Narang, Gaurvi**, *Bhikaji Cama—Parsi revolutionary who plotted Savarkar's escape, raised 1st Indian flag abroad*, *ThePrint* (July 2025). A richly detailed profile on her international activism, flag incident, and ties with Savarkar's escape planning Reddit+2ThePrint+2dharmayudh.com+2.
- **"Bhikaiji Cama"**, entry in *Encyclopaedia Britannica*. Authoritative overview noting her early education, exile, international speaking tours, and contributions to women's rights movements alongside anti-colonial activism Wikipedia+3Encyclopedia Britannica+3ClearIAS+3.
- **"Madam Bhikaji Cama: Migrant Parsi Women who hoisted the First Flag of Indian Independence…"**, *Dharmayudh.com*. Highlights her role in famine relief, revolutionary propaganda, and expatriate activism in Europe lucknowdigitallibrary.com+4dharmayudh.com+4Reddit+4.
- **Wikipedia**, *Bhikaiji Cama* entry — precise life data, overview of India House, Paris Indian Society, flag hoisting, exile and legacy details with full bibliography references (e.g. Sethna, Visram, Forbes) WikipediaWikipedia.
- **South Asian Britain** profile — lists secondary sources on her network, India House links, and archival collections (India Office Records at British Library) southasianbritain-demo.rit.bris.ac.uk.

Historical Themes & Significance
- **Exile Activism & Revolutionary Publishing** In London and Paris from 1902–1935, Cama cofounded Indian Home Rule Society and Paris Indian Society, became a link between Indian revolutionaries and global socialist networks, and financed/published banned nationalist literature smuggled into India Wikipedia.
- **Flag Iconography & Symbolic Nationalism** Designing/hoisting the tricolor flag in 1907 symbolized India's quest for sovereignty internationally—a precursor to the modern flag and internationally recognized act of protest dharmayudh.com.

- **Global Feminist Nationalism** Cama advocated women's rights within the nationalist framework; visited international forums from Germany to Egypt, urging inclusion of women in nation-building—even as she prioritized independence over suffrage for immediate activism ClearIASThePrint.
- **Legacy & Commemoration** Granted return to India in 1935; bequeathed her estate to Avabai Petit orphanage for girls. Honored through India Post stamp (1962), Indian Coast Guard ship ICGS Bhikaji Cama (1997), Bhikaji Cama Place in Delhi, and public memorials in Gujarat/Mumbai Reddit+5Wikipedia+5Wikipedia+5.

31. **Ramabai Ranade** (25 January 1862 – 25 January 1924)
- **Ramabai Ranade**, *Amchya Aayushyatil Kahi Athavani* ("Some Memories of My Life," 1910, Marathi) — the **first autobiography by an Indian woman in Marathi**, recounting her childhood, early marriage, self-education, and decades of activism Wikipedia+15Wikipedia+15ThePrint+15.
- *Himself: The Autobiography of a Hindu Lady* (English translation of her Marathi memoir, Longmans 1938) — published posthumously, it offers intimate insight into her personal and public life Wikipedia+1Indian Liberals+1.
- Contributor biography entries such as **Wikipedia**'s *Ramabai Ranade* article — comprehensive overview including her work with Seva Sadan and feminist activism Wikipedia.
- Profiles in Feminism in India and Indian Liberals describe her leadership in women's reform, Seva Sadan, and the women's suffrage movement Feminism in IndiaIndian Liberals.
- **Seva Sadan Society** founding and expansion — Ramabai founded Seva Sadan in Pune in 1909 to train nurses and teachers, support widows, and empower women economically. Multiple branches across Maharashtra emerged due to its popularity Al Jazeera+15ThePrint+15SheThePeople+15.
- **Huzurpaga Girls' High School** in Pune — Ramabai played a key role launching this as one of the first Indian-run girls' high schools in 1885 with the Maharashtra Girls Education Society Indian Liberals+4Wikipedia+4Wikipedia+4.
- **ThePrint profile** "Meet 19th century India's 'new woman'—Ramabai Ranade…" (2025) — highlights her blend of tradition and modernity, leadership in the women's conference of 1904, and her public interventions Indian Liberals+2ThePrint+2Al Jazeera+2.
- **Feminism in India**, "Ramabai Ranade: The Unparalleled Force" (2017) — portrays her social reform activism, support of women's rights, and speech training initiatives Feminism in India.
- **Indian Liberals**, "Women and Liberalism: Life of Ramabai Ranade" — detailed overview of her founding of literary/social clubs, public speaking training for women, and liberal social spaces created under her guidance Indian Liberals.

Themes & Historical Significance
- **Self-Education & Transformative Partnership** Married at age 11 to Justice Mahadev Govind Ranade, she overcame illiteracy—learning Marathi, English, and Bengali—and became an active social reformer trained by her husband in a deeply transformative mutual partnership Wikipedia+6Reddit+6Wikipedia+6.
- **Women's Education & Training** Ramabai co-founded *Huzurpaga* (Poona Native Girls High School) in 1885, enabling girls' matriculation in Pune. She also led women's training societies in Bombay and Pune, teaching sewing, public speaking, weaving, and nursing to women across castes and classes Indian Liberals+1Wikipedia+1Wikipedia+1Indian Liberals+1.
- **Seva Sadan Movement (1909–)** Ramabai launched Seva Sadan in Pune as a women's welfare institution offering homes, vocational training, and medical care for destitute and widowed women. Its inclusive mission transformed social service in Maharashtra and remains active today ThePrintNCRI Women Committee.
- **National Women's Movement & Suffrage Advocacy** Chaired the first India Women's

Conference in Bombay (1904), and endorsed women's franchise campaigns in the 1920s. She also advocated for labor rights of indentured Indian women in Fiji and Kenya Indian Liberals+2ThePrint+2Al Jazeera+2.

- **Legacy & Memory** Honored with an Indian postage stamp on her birth centenary (1962), and memorialized via the popular Marathi TV series *Unch Majha Zoka*. Her life inspired widespread recognition as a feminist pioneer and social reformer Wikipedia+3ThePrint+3Wikipedia+3.

32. **Dr. Rukhmabai** (also known as Rakhmabai Raut; 22 November 1864 – 25 September 1955)
- **Dadaji Bhikaji v. Rukhmabai** (1885–88) – this Bombay High Court suit on "restitution of conjugal rights" challenged child marriage and consent, triggering public debate and influencing the passage of the Age of Consent Act, 1891 Wikipedia+15www.ndtv.com+15Wikipedia+15.
- **Enslaved Daughters: Colonialism, Law and Women's Rights** by Sudhir Chandra (Oxford University Press, 1998; 2024 edition) – detailed biographical and legal analysis of Rukhmabai's case and its consequences pascal-theatre.com+2Wikipedia+2Wikipedia+2.
- Trained at the **London School of Medicine for Women** and obtained the **Triple Qualification** (Edinburgh, Glasgow, Dublin) in 1894; served as Chief Medical Officer in Surat and Rajkot hospitals, and was awarded the **KaiseriHind medal** for public health service pascal-theatre.com+3The Better India+3Royal College of Physicians of Edinburgh+3.
- She may not have published major works, but in **1929 she authored a pamphlet: "Purdah – The Need for Its Abolition"**, advocating widow rights and rejecting purdah intervention pascal-theatre.com+2Wikipedia+2Royal College of Physicians of Edinburgh+2.
- **Shivani Bahukhandi**, "Rukhmabai: From Child Bride to India's First Practising Female Doctor" (*Feminism in India*, August 2017) – feminist narrative covering her legal struggle and medical path Wikipedia+15Feminism in India+15pascal-theatre.com+15.
- *The Better India* profile "India's First Practising Lady Doctor" (2017) – overview of her legal victory, medical education abroad, and decades-long medical service The Better India.
- **FeminisminIndia.com** essay (2017) – similarly traces her protest of child marriage and career following legal emancipation Feminism in India+1pascal-theatre.com+1.
- **Wikipedia**, entry *Rukhmabai* – detailed life summary, key court case, medical career, and legacy; cites Sudhir Chandra's biography and others pascal-theatre.com+3Wikipedia+3library.imsc.res.in+3.
- **Royal College of Physicians of Edinburgh** heritage profile – outlines her medical education, feminist activism, and public health service Royal College of Physicians of Edinburgh.
- **Pascal Theatre Company** overview – summarises her life journey as rebel-bride and doctor, and lists this bibliography's key works pascal-theatre.com.
- **Social Reform Voice**: Through writings under pseudonym and later the 1929 pamphlet, she advocated against purdah and child marriage, foregrounding women's right to public life and education Feminism in IndiaRoyal College of Physicians of EdinburghWikipedia.
- **Impact on Legislature**: Her court case helped catalyze passage of the **Age of Consent Act 1891**, raising statutory consent age and initiating women's legal rights discourse in British India Feminism in India+6www.ndtv.com+6library.imsc.res.in+6.
- **Legacy of Feminism**: Rukhmabai's life inspired national consciousness about marriage, education, and women's bodily integrity. She is commemorated via Google Doodle (2017), ongoing literature, and the film *Doctor Rakhmabai* starring Tannishtha Chatterjee (2016) AnyTV News+4Wikipedia+4Feminism in India+4.

33. **Dr. Haimabati Sen** (born Haimabati Ghosh; 1866–5 August 1933)
Haimabati Sen, *The Memoirs of Dr. Haimabati Sen: From Child Widow to Lady Doctor*, translated by **Tapan Raychaudhuri** and edited with an introduction by **Geraldine Forbes**

Illustrious Daughters of the Land | 445

(New Delhi: Roli Books, 2000). This is Sen's original Bengali notebook memoir—discovered and translated—detailing her early marriage, widowhood, struggle for education, medical training at Campbell Medical College (Calcutta), and career in Hooghly as a medical officer. It offers rare insights into gendered oppression and social mobility in late19th/early20th century Bengal Reddit+14Wellcome Collection+14Wikipedia+14.

- **Indrani Sen**, "Resisting patriarchy: Complexities and conflicts in the Memoir of Haimabati Sen" (*Economic & Political Weekly*, March 2012). A thorough examination of gender, caste, familial dynamics, and colonial attitudes reflected in Haimabati's text ResearchGate+1Wikipedia+1.
- **Wikipedia**, article on *Haimabati Sen*, which provides a biographical summary, career highlights, and references to key works including the memoir and scholarly studies Wikipedia.
- Born in Khulna district (now Bangladesh) to a conservative Kayastha family in 1866, Haimabati was married before age 10 and widowed within a year. She eventually escaped oppressive family conditions, seeking education in Benares, Calcutta, and East Bengal before remarrying at 23 Roli+11Wikipedia+11The Tribune+11.
- The memoir—written in Bengali school notebooks during the 1920s—remained unpublished until its translation in 2000. The recovery of her voice has allowed scholars to reconstruct lives of elite women in colonial Bengal who defied convention through education and profession vedamsbooks.com.

34. **Dr. Matangini Hazra** (1870 – 29 September 1942)
- **Wikipedia**, entry *Matangini Hazra* — detailed life summary of her birth, early life, activism in Salt Satyagraha and Chowkidari Tax Bandha, her leadership in Quit India, martyrdom with the flag held high, and her legacy through stamps, statues, and local memorials Shopizen+11 Wikipedia+11midnapore.in+11.
- **Banglapedia**, "Hazra, Matangini (1870–1942)" by Sonia Amin — authoritative regional biography detailing her peasant origins, widowhood, Gandhian inspiration, and final martyrdom at Tamluk Banglapedia+1Wikipedia+1.
- **Feminism in India**, "Matangini Hazra: The Supreme Sacrifice" (Nov 2017) — describes her leading a procession of 6,000 women volunteers in Tamluk, her refusal to retreat under Section 144, and her final steps into police fire while chanting *Vande Mataram* Bengal Chronicle+4Feminism in India+4Reddit+4.
- **Aranyascope**, "Matangini Hazra – The Unsung Revolutionary" (2019) — chronicles her transformation from a child widow laborer to a Gandhian social worker, her village-level activism, multiple imprisonments, humanitarian deeds during epidemics, and eventual martyrdom .
- **Bengal Chronicle**, "Matangini Hazra: A Benevolent Patriot of Bengal" (Feb 2022) — overview of her early social work, Salt Satyagraha involvement, later activism in Chowkidari tax protests and protest flag incident with the Governor of Bengal's visit .
- **Shahid Matangini Hazra Government College for Women** (Tamluk website) — outlines her life narrative, valor, posthumous commemoration in her home region, and the college's naming in her honor .
- **Reddit / r/IndianHistory**, user account of Matangini leading her final procession at age 72, shot three times yet virile until the last moment — capturing her unyielding courage as "Gandhi Buri" .
- **Legacy of Commemoration** Since independence, Matangini has been honored via statues in Kolkata and Tamluk, the naming of Hazra Road, a postal stamp (2002), and the establishment of a government college in Tamluk bearing her name in 2015 Wikipediamatanginicollege.ac.inmatanginicollege.ac.in.
- **Womanhood, Rural Origin & Revolutionary Zeal** Born to a peasant Mahishya family, widowed very young, she overcame systemic hardship with selfless service—nursing the

sick during smallpox epidemics and leading local women in nationalist struggle, thereby challenging gender and ageist stereotypes of political leadership Wikipedia

35. **Sarojini Naidu** (13 February 1879 – 2 March 1949)
- **Sarojini Naidu**, *The Golden Threshold* (London, 1905) — her debut poetry collection blending lyrical imagery, Indian folklore, and emerging nationalist sentiment Reddit+10Testbook+10Reddit+10Wikipedia+2Wikipedia+2Next IAS+2.
- **Sarojini Naidu**, *The Bird of Time: Songs of Life, Death & the Spring* (London & New York, 1912) — includes major poems like *"In the Bazaars of Hyderabad"* and *"The Village Song"*; this collection marked her turn toward nationalist and cultural themes Next IAS+7Wikipedia+7Wikipedia+7.
- **Sarojini Naidu**, *The Broken Wing: Songs of Love, Death & Destiny* (London, 1917) — continues her poetic trajectory with more introspective and political resonance Testbook+5Wikipedia+5ThriftBooks+5.
- **Sarojini Naidu**, *Speeches and Writings of Sarojini Naidu* (Madras, 1918) — collected works showcasing her political and feminist voice.
- **Sarojini Naidu**, *Mohammad Ali Jinnah: An Ambassador of Unity – His Speeches & Writings 1912–1917* (Madras, 1919) — essayistic tribute highlighting her commitment to unity.
- **Sarojini Naidu**, *The Sceptred Flute: Songs of India* (New York, 1928) — posthumous anthology consolidating her poetic legacy.
- **Sarojini Naidu**, *The Feather of the Dawn* (Bombay, 1961; edited by Padmaja Naidu) — posthumously published, containing unpublished and previously scattered works.
- **Padmini Sengupta**, *Sarojini Naidu: A Biography* (first ed. 1966) — the first full-length biography of Naidu, tracing her literary and political trajectory.
- **Mushirul Hasan**, *Sarojini Naidu: Her Way with Words* (Niyogi Books, 2006) — literary-critical study focusing on her poetic style and political engagement.
- **Britannica Editors**, *Sarojini Naidu* entry (6 June 2025) — authoritative summary of her life, activism, and literary output.
- **NextIAS**, "Sarojini Naidu: Biography, Literary Journey, Political Activism & Legacies" — overview of her early talent, education in England, and fusion of literary romanticism with nationalist fervor.
- **Reddit commentary** (user on r/india / r/Poetry), reflecting admiration for her poem *"In the Bazaars of Hyderabad"* and its vivid imagery as a quintessential Indian lyric.
- Naidu's legacy lives on via institutions (Sarojini Naidu School of Arts & Communication, Golden Threshold building in Hyderabad), stamps, musical compositions, and even an asteroid named in her honor Wikipedia.

36. **Dr. Muthulakshmi Reddy** (30 July 1886 – 22 July 1968)
- **Devika, V. R.**, *Muthulakshmi Reddy: A Trailblazer in Surgery and Women's Rights* (New Delhi: Niyogi Books, 2022) A richly detailed biography celebrating her numerous "firsts"— from being the first girl admitted to a boys' school in Pudukkottai, to becoming India's first woman surgeon and first female legislator in British India Wikipedia+13Grafiati+13Wikipedia+13tehelka.com+4Niyogi Books India+4books.jgu.edu.in+4India Today+4tehelka.com+4Wikipedia+4.
- **India International Centre (ed.)**, *Muthulakshmi Reddy: A Legend Unto Herself* (New Delhi, 2012) Essays commemorating her life, reforms, and legal victories Grafiati.
- **Madras Institute of Development Studies (ed.)**, *The Manifesto and the Modern Self: Reading the Autobiography of Muthulakshmi Reddy* (Chennai, 2008) A critical reading of her unpublished autobiography and reflections on identity, modernity, and feminism Grafiati.

- **Basu, Aparna; All India Women's Conference (eds.)**, *The Pathfinder: Muthulakshmi Reddi S.* (New Delhi, 1986) A commemorative anthology published on her centennial Wikipedia+15Grafiati+15Wikipedia+15.
- **Reddi, Muthulakshmi**, *My Experience as a Legislator* (Triplicane: Current Thought Press, 1930) Memoir of her time in the Madras Legislative Council, including her introduction of the Devadasi Abolition Bill and advocacy against child marriage and brothels PMC+4encyclopedia.com+4ChakraFoundation.Org+4Wikipedia+7PMC+7Frontline+7.
- **Reddi, Muthulakshmi**, *Autobiography* (Adyar: Avvai Home, 1964) A first-person account of her early life, education, and public service India Today+9encyclopedia.com+9Frontline+9.
- **"The Pioneers: Dr. Muthulakshmi Reddy"**, *Frontline* (The Hindu, 2008) A tribute outlining her medical achievements, legislative contributions, and founding of Avvai Home and Adyar Cancer Institute Wikipedia+9Frontline+9Wikipedia+9.
- **"Dr. Muthulakshmi Reddy: The Unsung Feminist"**, *India Today* (July 2018) Highlights her fight for women's rights, her leadership in WIA, and her legislative victories including abolition of the Devadasi system India TodayNiyogi Books India+6PMC+6Wikipedia+6.
- **"Dr. Muthulakshmi Reddy: Beacon of Women's Liberty"**, *Indian Liberals* (2023) Biography describing her defiance of gender barriers and contributions to education, health, and legal reform Indian Liberals.
- **"The Incredible Story of India's Revolutionary Feminist"**, PMC (peer-reviewed article) Captures her childhood, academic excellence, alignment with Annie Besant and Gandhi, and her institutional legacy PMCChakraFoundation.Org+1Indian Liberals+1.
- **Wikipedia entry**, *Muthulakshmi Reddy* Summarizes her life, pioneer roles in surgery and politics, and major reforms and awards (Padma Bhushan 1956) Wikipedia+1tehelka.com+1.
- **Encyclopedia.com**, "Reddi, Muthulakshmi" Lists her writings and outlines her suffrage activism, legislative career, and reformist milestones encyclopedia.com.
- Honored with the **Padma Bhushan** in 1956; remembered through commemorative institutions, government schemes, and naming of landmarks; her birthday celebrated by Google doodle (2019) in recognition of her trailblazing life WikipediaWikipedia.

37. **Amrit Kaur** (2 February 1887 – 6 February 1964)
- **Amrit Kaur (Rajkumari)**, *Selected Speeches and Writings of Rajkumari Amrit Kaur* (Delhi: Archer Publications, 1961) — a collection displaying her reflections on Gandhi, women, public health, and nation-building Reddit+15Wikipedia+15Wikipedia+15Google Books.
- **Amrit Kaur**, *Woman in India* (1935); *Challenge to Women* (1946); *To Women* (1948); and *Gandhi and Women* (date unspecified) — essays reflecting her feminist and social-political philosophy Constitution of India+1iastoppers.in+1.
- **Amrit Kaur**, *Letters to Rajkumari Amrit Kaur by Mahatma Gandhi* (Navajivan Publishing House, 1961) — correspondence revealing her close working relationship with Gandhi Constitution of India.
- **"Rajkumari Amrit Kaur: The princess who built AIIMS"**, *ThePrint* (3 July 2025) — detailed profile of her tenure as Health Minister and founding of All India Institute of Medical Sciences Wikipedia+15ThePrint+15Constitution of India+15.
- **"Meet Rajkumari Amrit Kaur: India's First Health Minister"**, *Feminism in India* (2018) — covers her freedom struggle involvement and advocacy of women's rights, health, and social reforms Feminism in India+1Constitution of India+1.
- **Health Issues India**, "Amrit Kaur: Woman of the Year" (2020) — analysis of her campaigns against malaria and welfare programs, and her global public health influence healthissuesindia.com+1TIME+1.
- **Time**, "1947: Amrit Kaur" (2020) — featured in TIME's "Women of the Year", summarizing her life, influence, and legacy in global health TIME.

- **Wikipedia**, entry *Amrit Kaur* — biographical summary including her constitutional role, ministerial office, and organizational leadership (Tuberculosis Association, Red Cross, AIIMS) docmode.org+7Wikipedia+7Wikipedia+7.
- **Constitution of India website**, biography profile — covers her early life, education, AIWC leadership, Constituent Assembly membership, and health ministry achievements Constitution of India.

38. Gulab Kaur (1890 – 1941)
- **Kesar Singh**, *Gadar Di Dhee Gulab Kaur* (Punjabi, 2014) — the most dedicated biography available, reconstructing her life and activism based on oral testimony and archival sources. The Better India+8Counterview+8Feminism in India+8
- **Feminism in India**, "Gulab Kaur: The Sikh Woman Who Fought For India's Freedom From Manila" (May 2022) — highlights her recruitment by the Ghadar Party in the Philippines, her arms distribution under a journalist disguise, and bold public speeches onboard ships. Wikipedia+3Feminism in India+3The Sikh Encyclopedia+3
- **The Sikh Encyclopedia**, "Gulab Kaur (1890–1941)" — concise historical outline of her origins in Sangrur, Ghadar involvement, frontline organizing across Punjab, capture and prolonged imprisonment in Lahore Fort. The Tribune+2The Sikh Encyclopedia+2SikhiWiki+2
- **The Tribune**, "Rebel we forgot: Ghadar icon Gulab Kaur, 100 years on" (Aug 2024) — documents how villagers rediscovered her photograph and commissioned a library and memorial in her honour. The Times of India+15The Tribune+15The Times of India+15
- **OneIndia News**, "Gulab Kaur: A brave woman who returned from Philippines to India to fight British" — profiles her dramatic decision to sail alone and work with Kartar Singh Sarabha before arrest in the Lahore conspiracy case. Wikipedia+6https://www.oneindia.com/+6The Times of India+6
- **The Better India**, "The Forgotten Woman Who Left Husband & a Safe Life to Fight The British" (Jul 2019) — contextualises her sacrifice and revolutionary resolve. amarujala.com+3The Better India+3Feminism in India+3
- **Arms Smuggler, Organizer & Motivator** Disguised as a journalist with a press pass, Gulab Kaur ran revolutionary printing operations, distributed arms and propaganda on ship routes, recited patriotic poetry, and inspired Ghadar volunteers. When men faltered, she dramatically stripped her glass bangles and declared: "We women will take your place." Wikipedia+1The Sikh Encyclopedia+1Wikipedia+2Feminism in India+2The Sikh Encyclopedia+2
- **Regional Mobilizer & Martyr of Punjab** Traveling across Kapurthala, Hoshiarpur, and Jalandhar districts, she mobilized rural Punjabis for insurrection, liaised with Kartar Singh Sarabha, maintained underground press cells, and coordinated conspiratorial action. Her capture in Lahore led to two years of harsh imprisonment and torture in Shahi Qila. She succumbed to illness in prison or within a few years of release (accounts conflict between 1925 and 1941). Feminism in India+3https://www.oneindia.com/+3The Times of India+3
- **Legacy of Rediscovery** Forgotten for decades, her life resurfaced when villagers in Bakshiwala recognized a photograph from 1973. Literary, architectural, and commemorative efforts—including naming buildings and libraries—have since worked to honor her revolutionary service. The Tribune

39. Iqbalunnisa Hussain (1897)
- **Iqbalunnisa Hussain**, *Changing India: A Muslim Woman Speaks* (original essays compiled in 1940; republished by Oxford University Press 2015) — reflections on Muslim women's education, purdah, polygamy, and Muslim personal laws Goodreads+12Tertulia+12Feminism in India+12.
- **Iqbalunnisa Hussain**, *Purdah and Polygamy: Life in an Indian Muslim Household* (first

published 1944; Sahitya Akademi edition 2018) — a trenchant critique of oppressive social practices and religious conservatism+6Wikipedia+6ojs.plhr.org.pk+6.
- **Mumtaz Rehman**, "Iqbalunnisa Hussain: A Pioneer In The Education Of Muslim Women In India" (*Feminism in India*, May 2021) — outlines her life story, educational breakthroughs, schooling reforms in Bangalore, and posthumous legacy Wikipedia+2Feminism in India+2Feminism in India+2.
- **Pakistan Languages and Humanities Review**, Munnzza Noreen & Muhammad Asif, "Muslim Women's Agency and South Asian Literature: A Postcolonial Feminist Analysis of *Purdah and Polygamy*" (Vol. 7 No. 2, 2023) — academic critique using postcolonial feminist theory to analyze her writing as pioneering Muslim anglophone literature.
- **Indian Liberals**, "Iqbalunnisa Hussain: A Stalwart of Muslim Women's Education" (profile) — emphasizes her school founding, university excellence, and public activism.
- **Wikipedia**, entry *Iqbalunnisa Hussain* — provides life dates, education (BA gold medal, MA from Leeds 1933), career as educator/headmistress in Bangalore, activism in girls' school reform, international participation, writings and lobbying for Muslim women's rights.
- **Feminism in India (Hindi edition)** profile by Kirti Rawat — outlines her pioneering role in Muslim education and resistance to community backlash in Hindi-language context.
- Her writings in *Changing India* and *Purdah and Polygamy* were among the earliest Anglophone Muslim feminist critiques: she directly challenged child marriage, polygamy, seclusion, and religious patriarchy. These works are considered landmark texts in South Asian feminist literature TertuliaGoodreadsojs.plhr.org.pk.

40. **Dr. Edavalath Kakkat Janaki Ammal** (4 November 1897 – 7 February 1984)
- **Savithri Preetha Nair**, *Chromosome Woman, Nomad Scientist: E. K. Janaki Ammal, A Life 1897–1984* (Routledge, 2023) — the first full-length biography of Janaki Ammal, exploring her groundbreaking work on plant chromosomes, her global scientific travels, and her activism—from Nazi-era Britain to India's Silent Valley movement scientificwomen.net+14Routledge+14Wikipedia+14.
- **Nirmala James**, *E. K. Janaki Ammal: Life and Scientific Contributions* (Enview Research, 2023) — a richly contextual biography highlighting her scientific accomplishments and social milieu, drawing on archival materials and family memoirs adda247.
- **Darlington, C. D. & Janaki Ammal, E. K.**, *The Chromosome Atlas of Cultivated Plants* (Oxford/Botanical Society of UK, 1945) — monumental, multi-thousandspecies cytogenetic catalogue, co-authored with C. D. Darlington, considered a bible for plant cytologists shethoughtit.ilcml.com+11The Wire Science+11scientificwomen.net+11.
- **Selected journal articles** (Decade of 1930s–1960s), including:
- *Intergeneric hybrids of Saccharum* (Journal of Genetics, 1940),
- *Adaptive isochromosomes in Nicandra* (Annals of Botany, 1945),
- Cytological studies in *Solanum*, *Datura*, *Mentha*, and *Asparagus* species, published in leading journals like *Cytologia*, *Current Science* and *Proceedings of the Indian Academy of Sciences*.
- **The Hindu**, "The First Indian Woman Botanist, E.K. Janaki Ammal" (March 2025) — retrospective celebrating her contributions to sugarcane breeding, cytogenetics, and environmental activism, including her role in the Silent Valley movement.
- **The Biotalk Magazine**, "Let's Appreciate: Janaki Ammal (1897–1984)" — detailed exposition of her plant-breeding innovations, polyploidy research, role at the Botanical Survey of India, and tributes including the Padma Shri awarded in 1977.
- **Wikipedia**, *Janaki Ammal* (2025 edition) — overview of her educational trajectory, key research positions (Michigan, John Innes Centre, Royal Horticultural Society), major scientific contributions, and honors including Nehru's invitation and Padma Shri.
- **Global Scientific Collaboration** Spent World War II years conducting cytogenetic research

in London at the John Innes Centre; co-authored *Chromosome Atlas* and worked at Royal Horticultural Society in Wisley; one of the few South Asian scientists of her era with global institutional recognition Wikipedia+2The Hindu+2scientificwomen.net+2.
- **Institution-builder in India** Invited by Prime Minister Nehru in 1951 to reorganize the Botanical Survey of India; served in leadership roles at Allahabad, Jammu, BARC Trombay, and University of Madras as Emeritus Scientist @mathrubhumi+4The Indian Express+4thebiotalkmagazine.com+4.
- **Environmental Leadership & Ethnobotany** A pioneer advocate for botanical conservation; instrumental in protests to save Kerala's Silent Valley forest through biodiversity assessments and activism The Indian Express.
- **Legacy & Honors** Awarded **Padma Shri** in 1977. Honored by naming botanical scholarships, a magnolia cultivar (*Magnolia kobus Janaki Ammal*), and a herbarium collection after her scholarsquare.in+3thebiotalkmagazine.com+3The Indian Express+3.

41. **Vijaya Lakshmi Pandit** (née Swarup Kumari Nehru; 18 August 1900 – 1 December 1990)
- **Vijaya Lakshmi Pandit**, *So I Became a Minister* (Indian edition published ca. 1938) — a personal account of her tenure as Minister for Local SelfGovernment and Public Health in the United Provinces from 1937–39 infinite-women.com+15Wikipedia+15Encyclopedia Britannica+15.
- **Vijaya Lakshmi Pandit**, *Prison Days* (1945) — reflections on her multiple imprisonments during the Freedom Struggle (1932–33, 1940, and Quit India, 1942–43) Constitution of India+2Goodreads+2dvda.in+2.
- **Vijaya Lakshmi Pandit**, *The Evolution of India* (Oxford University Press, 1958) — a political commentary on independent India's development and global role WikipediaIndian National Congress.
- **Vijaya Lakshmi Pandit**, *The Scope of Happiness: A Personal Memoir* (Crown Books / Navjivan, New York, 1979) — reflective autobiography spanning her personal life, diplomacy, and family legacy Reddit+15Wikipedia+15Encyclopedia Britannica+15.
- **Anne Guthrie**, *Madame Ambassador: The Life of Vijaya Lakshmi Pandit* (Harcourt, Brace & World, 1962) — one of the earliest biographies documenting her political and diplomatic path Constitution of India.
- **Vera Brittain**, *Envoy Extraordinary: A Study of Vijaya Lakshmi Pandit and Her Contribution to Modern India* (Routledge Revivals, 1965) — richly researched portrait blending interviews, archival records, and political analysis Routledge+1Wikipedia+1.
- **Manu Bhagavan**, *Vijaya Lakshmi Pandit* (Allen Lane, 2023) — a newly acclaimed, definitive biography based on research across archives in multiple countries Penguin Random House India.
- **Ranjana Arora & Verinder Grover**, *Vijaya Lakshmi Pandit: A Biography of Her Vision and Ideas* (Deep & Deep/Royal Publications) — in-depth study of her political ideas and international stature regalpublications.com.
- **Britannica**, *Vijaya Lakshmi Pandit* — an authoritative encyclopedia entry summarizing her life, political career, and major accomplishments; confirms her roles as India's first female minister, first UNGA president, and diplomatic envoy Wikipedia+2Encyclopedia Britannica+2Penguin Random House India+2.
- **Constitution of India website**, biographical profile — tracks her role in the Constituent Assembly, diplomatic appointments, governorship, Lok Sabha service, and writings including *The Scope of Happiness* Constitution of India.
- **Dangerous Women Project**, "The Dangerous Career of Vijaya Lakshmi Pandit" — examines her political courage, surveillance by British intelligence, and her public-private tensions Dangerous Women Project.

42. **Sucheta Kripalani** (25 June 1908 – 1 December 1974)
- **Sucheta Kripalani**, *Sucheta: An Unfinished Autobiography* (Ahmedabad: Navajivan Publishing House, 1978) Cut off around India's independence, this memoir captures her early activism, roles in government, and close work with Mahatma Gandhi Reddit+15Google Books+15Wikipedia+15dvda.in.
- **Ranjana Arora & Verinder Grover**, *Sucheta Kripalani: Her Contribution to Political, Economic and Social Development* (Deep & Deep Publications, 1998/1999) An in-depth portrait framed around her feminist vision and policy leadership regalpublications.com+1regalpublications.com+1.
- *The Better India*, "Meet India's First Woman CM…" (2018) Highlights her path from freedom fighter to first female Chief Minister, her work in refugee rehabilitation and founding the All India Mahila Congress The Indian Express+5The Better India+5The Indian Express+5.
- *The Indian Express*, "Who was Sucheta Kripalani…" (June 2024) Offers detailed coverage of her political ascent to Chief Ministership of Uttar Pradesh (1963–67) and her reformist governance regalpublications.com+11The Indian Express+11The Indian Express+11.
- *Journal of Research Administration*, "Sucheta Kripalani: An Inspiring Personality…" (2022) Academic article reflecting on her transformational role in Indian nationhood and women's leadership regalpublications.com+4journlra.org+4Wikipedia+4regalpublications.com.
- **Wikipedia**, "Sucheta Kripalani" (updated Dec 2025) A reliable overview summarizing her education, Constituent Assembly membership, political offices, and tenure as CM Wikipedia.
- **Constitution of India** website biography Documents her role in drafting the Constitution, participation in global delegations, and public service record Constitution of Indiadvda.in.

Themes & Historical Highlights
- **Freedom Struggle & Gandhi Collaboration** A committed Gandhian, she actively participated in the Quit India Movement (1942), was imprisoned in 1944–45, and worked with Gandhi during post-Partition relief in Noakhali and Bihar WikipediaThe Indian Express+4dvda.in+4The Better India+4.
- **Constituent Assembly & National Symbolism** She was among the 15 women members of the Constituent Assembly (1946–50) and famously sang *Vande Mataram* as India's first flag was unfurled on 14 August 1947 Wikipedia+2Jagranjosh.com+2dvda.in+2.
- **Women's Political Advocacy** In 1940 she founded the *All India Mahila Congress*, advocating women's representation, education, and empowerment in politics The Indian Express+3dvda.in+3Jagranjosh.com+3.
- **First Female Chief Minister (Uttar Pradesh, 1963–67)** Elected Leader of the Congress Legislative Party in UP, she led the state government through significant administrative reforms and employee strikes, pioneering women's leadership at the state level The Indian Express+1Jagranjosh.com+1.
- **Legacy & Governance Style** Known for her integrity, resolve during crisis (e.g., handling the 62-day UP employees strike), expansion of girls' education, infrastructure, and reservation policies for scheduled castes and women's welfare The Indian ExpressJagranjosh.comThe Indian Express.

43. **Begum Qudsia Aizaz Rasul** (also known as Begum Aizaz Rasul; born 2 April 1909 – 1 August 2001)
- **Begum Aizaz Rasul**, *From Purdah to Parliament: A Muslim Woman in Indian Politics* (Delhi: Ajanta Publications, 2001) — her autobiography recounting her journey from princely household through electoral politics, the Constituent Assembly and reform debates. The first-person narrative is an invaluable source for understanding her political courage and personal growth Organiser+12National Library of Australia+12Wikipedia+12Feminism in India+2Wikipedia+2Constitution of India+2.

- **T. P. Saxena**, "Aizaz Rasul, Begum," *Women in Indian History: A Biographical Dictionary* (1979) — concise biographical entry in a landmark reference on women leaders cbw.iath.virginia.edu.
- **Christina George**, *The Indian Express*, "Begum Aizaz Rasul: The only Muslim woman to oppose minority reservations in the Constituent Assembly" (Feb 2018) — outlines how she opposed religious-based reservations, her constitutional advocacy, and public backlash from ulemas Constitution of India+4The Indian Express+4Wikipedia+4.
- **Ekata Lahiri**, *Feminism in India*, "Begum Qudsia Aizaz Rasul: The Only Muslim Woman in India's Constituent Assembly" (Feb 2019) — highlights her electoral breakthrough in 1937, principled opposition to separate electorates, and legal reforms .
- *Scroll.in*, "Meet Begum Qudsia Aizaz Rasul, the only Muslim woman among those who drafted the Indian Constitution" — captures her early life, purdah-breaking decision, and electoral success representing Hardoi in 1937 .
- **Constitution of India website**, member profile—detailed timeline of her legislative roles (U.P. assembly, opposition leader, Constituent Assembly, Rajya Sabha), and key speeches in defense of Hindustani as national language, minority rights, and secularism .
- **Constituent Assembly Pioneer** The sole Muslim woman across 299 members of India's Constituent Assembly (1946–50). Represented United Provinces and was a key member of the Minority Rights Drafting Committee Wikipedia.
- **Bold Constitutional Voice** Famously opposed separate electorates and minority reservations, calling them *"self-destructive"— advocating instead joint electorates as essential to secular unity dvda.in+2The Indian Express+2Wikipedia+2.
- **Grassroots Socialist Feminism** Elected to the U.P. Legislative Assembly from a general (nonreserved) seat in 1937, she also became Deputy President of Council (1937–40), Leader of the Opposition (1950–52), and later served in the Rajya Sabha The Indian Express+4Wikipedia+4dvda.in+4.

44. **Bina Das** (24 August 1911 – 26 December 1986)
- **Bina Das**, *Shrinkhal Jhankar* (Bengali memoir; translated as ***Bina Das: A Memoir*** by Dhira Dhar, Zubaan 2005/2010). In her account, she narrates the assassination attempt on Governor Stanley Jackson at Calcutta University in 1932, her prison experiences, and ideological journey.Taylor & Francis Online+15Zubaan+15Wikipedia+15
- **Veethi.com / Chakra Foundation**, "Bina Das: Profile & Biography" — concise life history, family background, revolutionary involvement with **Chhatri Sangha**, and later political engagement as an MLA and social activist.Wikipedia on IPFS+8Veethi+8ChakraFoundation.Org+8
- **The Indian Express**, "Bina Das: 21yearold who shot Bengal Governor got Padma Shri, but died in penury" (March 2020) — details her convocation gunshots, 9year jail term, Padma Shri (1960), and tragic final years in obscurity.India Today+2The Indian Express+2Wikipedia+2
- **Animesh Bag**, "Revolutionary women, body, and the limits of nationalist ideology in colonial Bengal..." (*Journal for Cultural Research*, Aug 2024) — analyzes Bina Das's and Kamala Das Gupta's memoirs to examine the gendered rhetoric of nationalism and political subjectivity. Sahapedia+9Taylor & Francis Online+9Wikipedia+9
- **Sahapedia**, "Bina Das, the Freedom Fighter Who Shot at the Bengal Governor" — provides an edited memoir excerpt and historical context of the 1932 shooting incident. Wikipedia+13Sahapedia+13India Today+13
- **India Today**, "Meet Bina Das, the young revolutionary who shot the Bengal Governor at 21" (Aug 2024) — commemorates her revolutionary act and life under anonymity in later years. Zubaan+4India Today+4The Indian Express+4
- **Wikipedia**, entry "Bina Das" — detailed overview of her birth, education at Bethune College,

Chhatri Sangha activism, political career as MLA, marriage to Jatish Chandra Bhaumik, Padma Shri award, and tragic demise.Wikipedia+8Wikipedia+8Wikipedia on IPFS+8
- **Revolutionary Feminism in Action**: Member of the semi-revolutionary **Chhatri Sangha**, Bina Das fired five shots at Governor Stanley Jackson on 6 February 1932—her courageous act rebuked colonial authority and inspired student revolutionary activism.Zubaan+11Wikipedia+11wikilifestory.in+11
- **Imprisonment & Political Evolution**: Sentenced to 9 years' rigorous imprisonment in 1932 (under Section 307 IPC), released in 1939. Continued activism during the Quit India Movement (1942–45), leading to further incarceration.Wikipedia
- **Post-Independence Civic Life**: Elected to Bengal Provincial and West Bengal Legislative Assemblies, engaged deeply in refugee rehabilitation. Honored with the **Padma Shri** in 1960 for social service.India Study Channel
- **Erasure & Rediscovery**: Despite her early fame, she lived and died in obscurity—passing away in Rishikesh while destitute in 1986. Her academic degree was conferred posthumously by Calcutta University only in 2012, recognizing her deferred graduation from 1932. Wikipedia+1India Today+1
- **Literary and Political Memoir**: Her memoir—born from introspection in prison—offers rare insight into the subjective experience of female revolutionaries: their emotional resolve, rejection of conventional femininity, and political subjectivity.ZubaanThe Caravan

45. Dr. Kamala Sohonie (18 June 1911 – 28 June 1998)
- **K. Bhagvat & K. Sohonie**, "The NonProteinNitrogen of Pulses," *Biochemical Journal* 29 (1935): 909–913 — pioneering study of pulse proteins and essential amino acid content Reddit+15S & T Digital+15Wikipedia+15.
- **K. Bhagvat & R. Hill**, "Cytochrome Oxidase in Flowering Plants," *Nature* 143 (1939): 726 — identification of cytochrome C in plant tissues, a key cellular respiration enzyme S & T Digital.
  o "Kamala Sohonie." *Wikipedia*, 2025. https://en.wikipedia.org/wiki/Kamala_Sohonie.
  o "Kamala Sohonie." *Asia Research News*, 2022. https://www.asiaresearchnews.com/content/kamala-sohonie.Asia Research News
- "Dr. Kamala Sohonie: Discoverer of an Enzyme and a Malnutrition Fighter." *STEM Pioneers*, 2023. https://idaho.pressbooks.pub/stempioneers/chapter/dr-kamala-sohonie-discoverer-of-cytochrome-c-enzyme-and-using-neera-to-fight-malnutrition/
- **M. N. Guttikar & K. Sohonie**, "Stability of Vitamin C in Neera from Dattagupta Palm…" *Current Science* 21 (1952):137–138 — analysis of nutrients in neera and its resilience during concentration Wikipedia+6S & T Digital+6Wikipedia+6.
- **The Hindu**, "Google Doodle Celebrates Indian Biochemist Kamala Sohonie's 112th Birthday" (June 2023) — overview of her struggle at IISc, PhD achievement, and neera studies Wikipedia+15The Hindu+15The Times of India+15.
- **The Indian Express**, "Meet Kamala Sohonie, the Indian Scientist Being Honoured…" (June 2023) — highlights her biography, cytochrome C discovery, Rashtrapati Award, and leadership at the Royal Institute of Science Wikipedia+10The Indian Express+10m.economictimes.com+10.
- **Outlook India**, "How Kamala Sohonie Opened the Door for Indian Women in Scientific Research" (Women's Day 2025) — personal narrative on her IISc protest, research at IISc, Cambridge, and nutritional mission Outlook India.
- **Feminism in India**, "Kamala Sohonie: First Indian Woman to Get a PhD in Science" (Dec 2017) — detailed recounting of her IISc admission struggle and academic milestones The Indian Express+6Feminism in India+6Wikipedia+6.
- **Asia Research News**, "The Biochemist Who Paved the Way for India's Female Researchers"

(2023) — concise life sketch and impact analysis Asia Research News+1Asia Research News+1.

46. **Dakshayani Velayudhan** (4 July 1912 – 20 July 1978)
- **Dakshayani Velayudhan**, *Sea Has No Caste* (autobiography in outline; unpublished draft) — her daughter Meera Velayudhan shared that by 1976 Dakshayani had planned 59 chapters of her memoir; though unfinished at her death in 1978, the outline and summaries survive and are to be published by LeftWord Books Wikipedia+15Wikipedia+15Constitution of India+15The Times of India.
- **Constitution of India website**, member profile — detailed biography covering her background, education, nomination to Cochin Legislative Council (1945), election to Constituent Assembly (Madras State) in 1946 (she was the only Dalit woman), key interventions in constitutional debates, and her later founding of Mahila Jagriti Parishad in Delhi (1977) socialstudiesfoundation.org+7Constitution of India+7The Indian Express+7.
- **Dakshayani Velayudhan Digital Archive (DVDA)** — collects her speeches, Constituent Assembly interventions (Objective Resolution debate, Article 17, Article 11, federalism and decentralisation) and biographical essays; includes quote "the sea has no caste" and reflections on moral safeguards and education as tools of emancipation dvda.in+1Constitution of India+1.
- **J. S. Balan**, "Remembering Dakshayani Velayudhan, the lone Dalit woman in the Constituent Assembly," *The NewsMinute* (2018) — profiles her journey, legislative contributions, and under-recognition in Kerala's historical memory .
- **Cherai Ramadas**, *Kala Sasanakalkku Keezhadangatha Dakshayani Velayudhan* (in Malayalam, 2023) — collection of her life sketches and Constituent Assembly debates, launched at Maharaja's College, her alma mater .
- **The Better India**, "Dakshayani Velayudhan: Only Dalit woman in Constituent Assembly" (2023) — recounts her educational milestones (first Dalit woman science graduate and first to wear upper cloth), activism in Kerala and in parliament, and her views on caste and national unity .
- **Mathrubhumi English**, "Remembering Dakshayani Velayudhan: A Malayali we consign to oblivion" (July 2023) — highlights her as Kerala's first Pulaya woman graduate, her struggles to complete laboratory work, and the broader pushoff from historical narratives .
- **Political & Social Reformer** After membership in Cochin Legislative Council (1945), she continued work in the Provisional Parliament and later founded **Mahila Jagriti Parishad** in Delhi (1977), focusing on Dalit and women empowerment. She and her husband R. Velayudhan were among first Dalit political couples, their marriage at Sevagram officiated by a leper and witnessed by Gandhi and Kasturba Wikipedia+1Reddit+1socialstudiesfoundation.org+7Constitution of India+7Wikipedia+7.
- **Forgotten Legacy & Rediscovery** Despite her pivotal role, she remained marginalized in mainstream historiography of Kerala—even local colleges included her in curricula only recently. In 2019 the Government of Kerala instituted the **Dakshayani Velayudhan Award** for women empowerment in her honor Constitution of India+2Wikipedia+2dvda.in+2.

47. **Amrita SherGil** (30 January 1913 – 5 December 1941)
- **SherGil, Amrita**, *Evolution of My Art*, included in *Amrita SherGil: Painter Par Excellence – The Unfolding of Art* edited by N. Iqbal Singh et al. (Oxford University Press, 2013) — SherGil's own reflections on how influences such as Ajanta cave frescoes and Gauguin shaped her evolving style Wikipedia+15OUP India+15Reddit+15.
- **Dalmia, Yashodhara**, *Amrita SherGil: A Life* (Penguin, 2013) — the leading modern biography, richly illustrated and praised for its depth, insight into SherGil's Indian/Hungarian identity and artistic shifts Amazon India+4Wikipedia+4Wikipedia+4.

- **Sundaram, Vivan** (ed.), *Amrita SherGil: A SelfPortrait in Letters & Writings* (Tulika Books, 2010) — a curated collection of SherGil's letters, essays, and archival documents alongside critical commentary by Sundaram dagworld.com+3Wikipedia+3Wikipedia+3.
- **Ananth, Deepak** (ed.), *Amrita SherGil: An Indian Artist Family of the Twentieth Century* (Schirmer/Mosel, 1965; reprinted 2013) — includes essays by Karl Khandalavala, K. G. Subramanyan, Tillotson, and others on SherGil's aesthetic evolution Reddit+15Wikipedia+15OUP India+15.
- **Britannica Editors**, *Amrita SherGil* (2025 biography) — concise overview summarizing her life trajectory, artistic innovation, and posthumous national stature as a modernist pioneer in Indian art britannica.com.
- **Hindustan Times**, "Amrita SherGil: An Artist Who Defied Norms" — highlights her Paris training, her south India trilogy (Bride's Toilet, Village Scene), and her sudden death just before her Lahore exhibition culturalindia.net+2Hindustan Times+2Wikipedia+2.
- **Map Academy**, article on SherGil's development — traces her evolution from Parisian nude studies to deeply observing Indian life and landscapes after returning in 1934, noting her signature palette shift post-Ajanta & Ajanta/mural influences MAP Academy.

48. **Rani Gaidinliu Pamei** (26 January 1915 – 17 February 1993)
- Sadly, there is **no known autobiography** published under her own name. However, her life and ideology are traced through numerous memoirs, recollections, and archival sources such as the *Dakshayani Velayudhan Digital Archive* (DVDA) and various biographies.
- **Som Kamei**, *Rani Gaidinliu: Legendary Freedom Fighter from the North East* (Niyogi Books, 2022) — a full-length English biography tracing her leadership of the Heraka movement, imprisonment, post-independence advocacy for Zeliangrong identity, and cultural legacy Wikipedia+15IBP Books+15Niyogi Books India+15.
- **Neiba Ndang & N. Haisoyi Ndang**, *Media's Projection on Rani Gaidinliu & Her Memorabilia* (Kenz & Sons Co., 2025) — explores contested representations of her life, colonial seizure of her belongings, and efforts to repatriate artifacts held in British institutions MorungExpress+1Mokokchung Times+1.
- **Yimkumla Longkumer & Saumya Sharma**, "Rani Gaidinliu, 'daughter of the hills' who spent 14 years in jail…" (*ThePrint*, 2024) — comprehensive profile of her early activism, British repression, jail years, Nehru's recognition, and later social work for Zeliangrong unity Chronicle India+4ThePrint+4Wikipedia+4.
- **Shahima Sherin**, "Rani Gaidinliu: A Visionary Freedom Fighter and Custodian of Indigenous Identity" (*Legal Service India*, 2025) — interpretive essay linking her resistance to preservation of tribal cultural heritage alongside panIndian nationalist movements Wikipedia+15Legal Service India+15Reddit+15.
- **Encyclopedia.com**, entry "Gaidinliu, Rani (1915–)" from *Women in World History: A Biographical Encyclopedia* — succinct life summary, activism, imprisonment, and postindependence role as community leader Encyclopedia.com+1veethi.com+1.
- **Wikipedia**, "Rani Gaidinliu" — updated life history, movement involvements, honors (Padma Bhushan 1982; Tamrapatra 1972), and her spiritual-political leadership ThePrint+5Wikipedia+5veethi.com+5.
- **Veethi.com / Veethi-media profile** — concise biography featuring birth, Heraka affiliation, arrest at age 16, Nehru's title conferral ("Rani"), release in 1947, and post-independence social service Wikipedia+2veethi.com+2Reddit+2.

49. **Ismat Chughtai** (21 August 1911 – 24 October 1991)
- **Chughtai, Ismat**. *Kaghazi Hai Pairahan* (Unfinished autobiography, published 1998) — serialized life essays reflecting on schooling, family, her infamous *"Lihaaf"* trial, feminist

awakening, and adolescence Wikipedia+15Goodreads+15Encyclopedia Britannica+15Reddit+9Sahapedia+9Wikipedia+9.
- **Chughtai, Ismat**. *A Life in Words: Memoirs* (English translation of *Kaghazi Hai Pairahan*, trans. M. Asaduddin, Penguin 2012) — a lyrical translation of her life reflections Wikipedia+3Sahapedia+3Goodreads+3.
- *"Ismat Chughtai."* **Encyclopædia Britannica**, Encyclopædia Britannica, 2025, www.britannica.com/biography/Ismat-Chughtai. (Overview of Ismat Chughtai (1915–1991), trailblazing Urdu writer and feminist, noting her famous short story *"Lihaaf"* (1942) which led to an obscenity trial that she wonbritannica.com.)
- Express Web Desk. *"Who was Ismat Chughtai?"* **The Indian Express**, 21 Aug. 2018, indianexpress.com/article/who-is-ismat-chughtai-writer-feminist-5316847/. (Brief biography highlighting Chughtai's role in the Progressive Writers' Movement alongside Saadat Hasan Manto and others, her exploration of female sexuality in *Lihaaf*, and her legacy in Urdu literature.)
- *Kaliyan* (1941), *Choten* (1942), *Ek Baat* (1945), *Chui Mui* (1952; includes story *Touch Me Not* on motherhood), *Do Haath* (1955), *Badan ki Khushboo*, *Amarbel*, *Thori Si Paagal*, *Aadhi Aurat Aadha Khwaab* (1979/1986) — major Urdu story collections showcasing her evolving feminist sensibility and social critique Wikipedia+1The Indian Express+1.

50. **Chonira Belliappa Muthamma** (24 January 1924 – 14 October 2009)
- **Muthamma, C. B.**, *Slain by the System: India's Real Crisis* (Viveka Foundation, 2003) — a collection of personal essays and reflections critiquing institutional sexism, especially her battles against discriminatory rules in the Indian Foreign Service The CSR Journal+12Wikipedia+12The Logical Indian+12.
- **Wikipedia**, entry *C. B. Muthamma* — detailed biography covering her pioneering career, education, diplomatic postings (Paris, Rangoon, London, Ghana, Netherlands), and landmark Supreme Court case against discriminatory rules in IFS Wikipedia+1Feminism in India+1.
- **The Better India**, "The Untold Story of C. B. Muthamma, India's First Female IFS Officer and Ambassador" — richly contextual profile of her education, career challenges, legal crusade, and postings as India's first woman ambassador The Better India+1kodagufirst.in+1.
- **The Hindu**, "India's first woman career diplomat dead" (14 Oct 2009) — obituary outlining her life, service history, and legacy in breaking formal gender barriers kodagufirst.in+4The Hindu+4kodagufirst.in+4.
- Chandra, Divyanshi. *"How Chonira Belliappa Muthamma, India's 1st Woman Career Diplomat, Took on a Male-Dominated System."* **The Print**, 24 June 2023, theprint.in/india/how-chonira-belliappa-muthamma-indias-1st-woman-career-diplomat-took-on-a-male-dominated-system/1640409/. (Profiles C.B. Muthamma, the first woman to clear the Indian Civil Services exam (1948) and to join the Indian Foreign Service in 1949, and her fight for gender equality in the diplomatic corps.)
- **Feminism in India**, "C. B. Muthamma: India's Women in History" — profile emphasizes her Supreme Court case against Rule 8(2) and Rule 18(4) of the IFS conduct rules and her fight for Articles 14 & 16 equality in civil services kodagufirst.in+12Feminism in India+12Jagranjosh.com+12.
- **Reddit discussion**, highlighting her *Slain by the System* essays and references to Justice V. R. Krishna Iyer's judgement that questioned whether Articles 14 and 16 were myth or reality for women like Muthamma The Better India+5Reddit+5Feminism in India+5.

51. **Kanaklata Barua** (22 December 1924 – 20 September 1942)
- **Barua, Kanaklata**, personal letters and eyewitness testimonies appear in *ICHR volume 4* as part of primary archival files (e.g. PHA Files F. Nos. 11, 76/14, 287, 325) — detailed

in government records describing her final stand and martyrdom.Wikipedia+15cmsadmin. amritmahotsav.nic.in+15assaminfo.com+15
- *Pathak, Guptajit, Assamese Women in Indian Independence Movement: With a Special Emphasis on Kanaklata Barua* (Mittal Publications) — a focused study profiling her life, allegiance to the Mrityu Bahini, and lasting legacy.The Better India+7Wikipedia+7Wikipedia+7
- **The Sentinel Assam**, *"Kanaklata Barua: A True Brave Heart…"* — overview of her birth, orphaned childhood, decision to join the Mrityu Bahini, leadership in the procession, and Holocaust-style martyrdom at age 17.India Today NE+3The Sentinel+3The Sentinel+3
- **The Better India**, *"At 17, Assam's Forgotten Freedom Fighter…"* (April 2023) — recounts her tragic death during a symbolic flaghoisting mission, the symbolic weight of her courage, and ongoing institutional acknowledgement including INS Kanaklata Barua.assamtribune.com+15The Better India+15assaminfo.com+15
- **Assams.info**, *"Shaheed Kanaklata Barua – The Icon of Assam's Freedom Struggle"* — detailed life narrative and recognition as the "Rani Lakshmibai of Assam."assaminfo.com+1assams.info+1
- **The Indian Express**, *"Who was Kanaklata Barua…"* — analysis of her impact as a teenage martyr, unique exception to age restrictions in Mrityu Bahini, and symbolic defiance on the eve of independence.assams.info+8The Indian Express+8The Indian Express+8
- Local gazetteers and Freedom Fighter memorial lists in Assam (e.g. *ICHR vol. 4, Assam Tribune archives*) — include her obituary and references to other local martyrs who fell that day.cmsadmin.amritmahotsav.nic.inassamtribune.com

52. **Anna Rajam Malhotra** (née Anna Rajam George; 17 July 1927 – 17 September 2018)
- **"The Untold Story of Anna Rajam Malhotra, India's First Female IAS Officer"**, *The Better India* (2017) — a richly detailed narrative of her early life in Kerala, her resolve to join the IAS despite prevailing gender norms, and her trailblazing administrative career Wikipedia+13The Better India+13Wikipedia+13.
- **News18**, *"Meet Anna Rajam Malhotra, India's First Woman IAS Officer"* (2023) — concise career overview including her selection in 1951, challenging gendered advice around suitable roles, and her work across seven chief ministers in Madras State Testbook+5News18+5Wikipedia+5.
- **Jagran Josh**, *"First Woman IAS Officer of India"* (2025) — provides early life, education, service selection, cadre choice, major projects (Asian Games, port building), and Padma Bhushan recognition Testbook+3Jagranjosh.com+3Jagranjosh.com+3.
- **Onmanorama**, *"Keralite Anna Malhotra, India's First Woman IAS Official, Dies"* — obituary recounting her educational path, marriage to R.N. Malhotra (former RBI Governor), key service landmarks, and public memory of her legacy Jagranjosh.com+6Onmanorama+6The Hindu+6.
- **The Hindu**, *"India's first woman IAS officer dead"* (18 Sep 2018) — obituary highlighting her early postings (e.g. SubCollector of Hosur), her resistance to gendered bias from C. Rajagopalachari, and her leadership in India's first computerized port at Nhava Sheva Jagranjosh.com+7The Hindu+7Onmanorama+7.
- **NDTV**, *"India's First Woman IAS Officer After Independence Dies At 91"* — tribute to her illustrious multidecade tenure, major project contributions, and dignified public service until retirement www.ndtv.com.
- **Wikipedia**, *Anna Rajam Malhotra* (2025 edition) — provides comprehensive details of her early life in Kerala, education (Madras University), civil service induction in 1951, cadre difficulties, partnership with Indira–Rajiv Gandhi administrations, and her Padma Bhushan award in 1989 Wikipedia+13Wikipedia+13Jagranjosh.com+13.

- Acyuta Yājñika; Suchitra Sheth (2005). The Shaping of Modern Gujarat: Plurality, Hindutva, and Beyond. Penguin Books India. pp. 152–. ISBN 978-0-14-400038-8.
- Ahmad, Moin-ud-din (1924). The Taj and Its Environments: With 8 Illus. from Photos., 1 Map, and 4 Plans. R. G. Bansal. p. 101.
- Altekar, A S (1960). Yazdani, Ghulam (ed.). The Early History of the Deccan. Oxford University Press. pp. 178–179.
- Altekar, A S (2007). Majumdar, R.C.; Altekar, A.S. (eds.). The Vakataka-Gupta Age. Motilal Banarsi Dass. p. 104. ISBN 9788120800434.
- Amin, Sonia (2012). "Hazra, Matangini". In Islam, Sirajul; Jamal, Ahmed A. (eds.). Banglapedia: National Encyclopedia of Bangladesh (Second ed.). Asiatic Society of Bangladesh.
- Anagol-Mcginn, Padma (1992). "The Age of Consent Act (1891) Reconsidered: Women's Perspectives and Participation in the Child-Marriage Controversy in India". South Asia Research. **12** (2): 100–118. doi:10.1177/026272809201200202. S2CID 144336522.
- Anantha Raman, Sita (2009). Women in India: a Social and Cultural History. Santa Barbara: Praeger. pp. 16 (vol. 2).
- Antoinette, Burton (1 October 1998). "From Child Bride to "Hindoo Lady": Rukhmabai and the Debate on Sexual Respectability in Imperial Britain". The American Historical Review. 103 (4). doi:10.1086/ahr/103.4.1119. ISSN 0002-8762.
- Apurva, Ankita (26 January 2021). "Why Do Caste Gatekeepers Not Tell Us About Fatima Sheikh?". LiveWire, The Wire. Archived from the original on 25 February 2024.
- Arvind Sharma (2000). Women saints in world religions. SUNY Press. p. 169. ISBN 0-7914-4619-0.
- Asher, Catherine; Asher, Catherine Ella Blanshard; Asher, Catherine Blanshard; Asher, Catherine B. (1992). Architecture of Mughal India. Cambridge University Press. p. 265. ISBN 9780521267281.
- Asiatic Journal Vol.3 (1830). The Occurrences at Kittur in 1824. London: Parbury, Allen, and Co. pp. 218–222.
- Atwal, Priya (2020). Royals and Rebels:The Rise and Fall of the Sikh Empire. London: C. Hurst (Publishers) Limited. ISBN 9781787383081.
- Azizan Bai – Contribution of a beauty to the struggle of 1857. https://tornosindia.com/azizan-bai-contribution-of-a-beauty-to-the-struggle-of-1857
- B. Satyanarayana Singh (1999). The Art and Architecture of the Kākatīyas. Bharatiya Kala Prakashan. ISBN 978-81-86050-34-7.
- Bakker, Hans (1997). The Vakatakas: An Essay in Hindu Iconology. Groningen: Egbert Forsten. p. 170. ISBN 9069801000.
- Bamzai, P.N.K. (1994). Culture and Political History of Kashmir: Volume 1. M.D. Publications. pp. 139–140.
- Banerjee, Rita (2021), "Women in India: The "Sati" and the Harem", India in Early Modern English Travel Writings, Brill, pp. 173–208, ISBN 978-90-04-44826-1, retrieved 12 February 2024
- Bano, Shadab (2013). "Piety and Pricess Jahanara's Role in the Public Domain". Proceedings of the Indian History Congress. 74: 245–250. ISSN 2249-1937. JSTOR 44158822.
- Barbara N. Ramusack (1999). "Women in South Asia". In Barbara N. Ramusack; Sharon L. Sievers (eds.). Women in Asia: Restoring Women to History. Indiana University Press. ISBN 978-0-25321-267-2.
- Bates, Crispin; Carter, Marina (2017). Mutiny at the Margins: New Perspectives on the Indian Uprising of 1857: Documents of the Indian Uprising. SAGE Publications India. ISBN 9789385985751. Archived from the original on 9 October 2017.
- Begum, Dr. Shameemunnisa. "Iqbalunnisa Hussain's Purdah and Polygamy: Life in an

- Indian Muslim Household: A Study". EPRA International Journal of Multidisciplinary Research. 7 (5): 281–285. doi:10.36713/epra2013. eISSN 2455-3662.
- Begum, Gulbadan (1902). The History of Humayun (Humayun-Nama). Royal Asiatic Society. ISBN 8187570997
- Begum, Gulbadan; (tr. by Annette S. Beveridge) (1902). Humayun-nama :The history of Humayun. Royal Asiatic Society.
- Begums Of Bhopal - Saris and a scabbard". The Telegraph. 16 May 2010
- Bergunder, Michael (2008). The South Indian Pentecostal Movement in the Twentieth Century. William B. Eerdmans Publishing Company.
- Beveridge H. (1952). "The Maathir-ul-umara – Volume 2". Internet Archive. p. 653. Retrieved 31 October 2021.
- Bhabha, Homi K. (2004). "The Black Savant and the Dark Princess". ESQ. **50** (1st – 3rd): 142–143. doi:10.1353/esq.2004.0014. S2CID 162273702.
- Bhagavan, M. (2013). India and the Quest for One World: The Peacemakers. Palgrave Macmillan Transnational History Series. Palgrave Macmillan UK. p. 14. ISBN 978-1-137-34983-5.
- Bhola 'Yamini', Rachna (1 January 2016). The Life and Times of Madam Bhikaji Cama: The Life and Times of Madam Bhikaji Cama by Rachna Bhola 'Yamini': Exploring the Life of a Freedom Fighter. Prabhat Prakashan. p. 19. ISBN 978-81-8430-366-7.
- Bhura, Sneha (18 February 2020). "The story behind the library at Shaheen Bagh". The Week. Archived from the original on 9 December 2024.
- Bilkees I. Latif (2010). Forgotten. Penguin Books India. p. 50. ISBN 978-0-14-306454-1.
- Bose, Purnima (1 January 2008), "Cama, Madame Bhikaji", The Oxford Encyclopedia Women in World History, Oxford University Press, doi:10.1093/acref/ 9780195148909. 001.0001, ISBN 978-0-19-514890-9
- BR, PurushottamShamsher (2007). Ranakalin Pramukh Atihasik Darbarharu [Chief Historical Palaces of the Rana Era] (in Nepali). Vidarthi Pustak Bhandar. ISBN 978-9994611027.
- Burton, Antoinette (1999). "Conjugality on Trial: The Rukhmabai Case and the Debate on Indian Child-Marriage in Late-Victorian Britain". Disorder in the Court. Palgrave Macmillan, London. pp. 33–56. doi:10.1057/9781403934314_3. ISBN 9781349405732.
- Burton, Antoinette (2011). Empire in Question: Reading, Writing, and Teaching British Imperialism. Duke University Press. pp. 199–201.
- Burton, Antoinette (30 March 1998). At the Heart of the Empire: Indians and the Colonial Encounter in Late-Victorian Britain. University of California Press.ISBN 978-0-520-91945-7.
- Chakrabarty, Bidyut (1997). Local Politics and Indian Nationalism: Midnapur (1919-1944). New Delhi: Manohar.
- Chakravarti, Uma and Gill, Preeti (eds). Shadow Lives: Writings on Widowhood. Kali for Women, Delhi.
- Chandra, Satish (2006). Medieval India: From Sultanat to the Mughals-Delhi Sultanat (1206–1526) Part 1. Har-Anand Publication Pvt Ltd.
- Chandra, Sudhir (1992). "Whose laws?: Notes on a legitimising myth of the colonial Indian state". Studies in History. 8 (2): 187–211. doi:10.1177/025764309200800203. S2CID 159894938.
- Chandra, Sudhir (1996). "Rukhmabai: Debate over Woman's Right to Her Person". Economic and Political Weekly. **31** (44): 2937–2947. JSTOR 4404742.
- Chandra, Sudhir (2008). "Rukhmabai and Her Case". In Chandra, Sudhir (ed.). Enslaved Daughters. Oxford University Press. pp. 15–41. doi:10.1093/acprof:oso/9780195695731. 003.0001. ISBN 9780195695731.
- Chandra, Sudhir (2008). Enslaved Daughters: Colonialism, Law and Women's Rights. Oxford University Press. doi:10.1093/acprof:oso/9780195695731.001.0001. ISBN 978-0-19-569573-1.

- Chattopadhyay, Anjana (2018). Women Scientists in India: Lives, Struggles & Achievements (PDF). National Book Trust, India. ISBN 978-81-237-8144-0.
- Chitre, Dilip. "Muktabai." In The Oxford Encyclopedia Women in World History : Oxford University Press, 2008. https://www.oxfordreference.com/view/10.1093/acref/9780195148909. 001.0001/ acref-9780195148909-e-732 .
- Chopra, R. M., "Eminent Poetesses of Persian ", Iran Society, Kolkata, 2010.
- Constable, Archibald, ed. (1916), "Begum Saheb", Travels in Mogul India, Oxford University Press, p. 11
- Cunningham, Lieutenant A.; Engineers, Bengal (1843), "The Ancient Coinage of Kashmir. With Chronological and Historical Notes, from the Commencement of the Christian Era to the Conquest of the Country by the Moguls", The Numismatic Chronicle and Journal of the Numismatic Society, **6**: 1–38, JSTOR 42720623
- Cynthia Talbot (2001). Precolonial India in Practice: Society, Region, and Identity in Medieval Andhra. Oxford University Press. ISBN 0195136616.
- Cynthia Talbot (2008). "Rudrama-devi, Queen of Kakatiya dynasty (r. 1262–1289)". In Bonnie G. Smith (ed.). The Oxford Encyclopedia of Women in World History. Vol. 3. Oxford University Press. doi:10.1093/acref/9780195148909.001.0001. ISBN 9780195148909.
- D.C. Sircar (1997). Majumdar, R.C. (ed.). The Classical Age (Fifth ed.). Bharatiya Vidya Bhavan. pp. 180–181.
- Damodaran, Vinita (2013). "Gender, Race and Science in Twentieth-Century India: E. K. Janaki Ammal and the History of Science". History of Science. **51** (3): 283–307.
- Darukhanawala, Hormusji Dhunjishaw, ed. (1963), Parsi lustre on Indian soil, vol. 2, Bombay: G. Claridge.
- David Gilmartin (2014). "Chapter 5: The paradox of patronage and the people's sovereignty". In Anastasia Pivliavsky (ed.). Patronage as Politics in South Asia. Cambridge University Press. pp. 151–152. ISBN 978-1-107-05608-4.
- Devika, VR (2022). Muthulakshmi Reddy: A Trailblazer in Surgery and Women's Rights (1st ed.). New Delhi, India: Niyogi Books India Pvt Ltd. ISBN 9789391125677.
- Diamond Maharashtra Sankritikosh", Durga Dixit, Pune, India, Diamond Publications, 2009, p. 40. ISBN 978-81-8483-080-4.
- Dinkar, DC (2007). Swatantrata Sangram Mei Achhuto Ka Yogdan (in Hindi) (1st, 2nd, 3rd, 4th ed.). Delhi, India: Gautam Book Center. p. 51. ISBN 978-8187733720. Uda Devi Revolution
- Disturbances at Kittur and the death of Mr. Thackeray. London: Parbury, Allen, and Company. 1825. pp. 474–5.
- Edwards, Michael (1960). The Orchid House: Splendours and Miseries of the Kingdom of Oudh, 1827-1857. Cassell. p. 7.
- Eraly, Abraham (2004). The Mughal throne: the saga of India's great emperors. London: Phoenix. p. 308. ISBN 978-0-7538-1758-2.
- Eraly, Abraham (2004). The Mughal throne: the saga of India's great emperors. London: Phoenix. p. 301. ISBN 978-0-7538-1758-2.
- Eraly, Abraham (2007). Emperors of the Peacock Throne, The Saga of the Great Mughals. Penguin Books India. p. 299.
- Fanshawe, H.C. (1902). Delhi Past and Present. J. Murray. p. 52. Retrieved 6 March 2015.
- Fatima, Masrath (2023). "AP: Statue of 1st 'Muslim woman teacher' Fatima Sheikh unveiled". The Siasat Daily. Archived from the original on 24 January 2025.
- Feminism in India (2017). Kamala Sohonie: First Indian Woman To Get A PhD In Science | #IndianWomenInHistory". Feminism in India. 25 December
- Forbes, G., 1988. The politics of respectability: Indian women and the Indian National Congress. In The Indian National Congress: Centenary Hindsights (pp. 65). New Delhi: Oxford University Press.

- Forbes, Geraldine (1999), Women in Modern India, Cambridge: Cambridge University Press, p. 100, ISBN 0-521-65377-0
- Forbes, Geraldine Hancock (2005). Women in Colonial India: Essays on Politics, Medicine, and Historiography. Orient Blackswan. p. 146. ISBN 978-81-8028-017-7.
- Frykenberg, Robert Eric; Young, Richard Fox (2009). India and the Indianness of Christianity. Wm. B. Eerdmans Publishing. p. 225. ISBN 978-0-8028-6392-8.
- Gail Omvedt. 1995. Dalit Vision, Orient Longman
- Ganguly, Dilip Kumar (1979), Aspects of ancient Indian administration, Abhinav Publications, ISBN 978-81-7017-098-3
- Garodia Gupta, Archana (January 2019). The women who ruled India : leaders, warriors, icons. Hachette Books. p. 312. ISBN 9789351951520.
- Gascoigne, Bamber (1971). The Great Mughals. New Delhi: Time Books International. p. 165.
- George, Christina (14 February 2018). "Begum Aizaz Rasul: The only Muslim woman to oppose minority reservations in the Constituent Assembly". The Indian Express. Retrieved 26 February 2020.
- Ghosh, Durba (2013). "Revolutionary Women and Nationalist Heroes in Bengal, 1930 to the 1980s". Gender & History. 25 (2): 355–375. doi:10.1111/1468-0424.12017. S2CID 143325110.
- Gill, M. S. (2007). Trials that Changed History: From Socrates to Saddam Hussein. Sarup & Sons. ISBN 9788176257978.
- Gopalakrishnan, Subramanian (Ed.) (2007). The South Indian rebellions : before and after 1800 (1st ed.). Chennai: Palaniappa Brothers. pp. 102–103. ISBN 9788183795005.
- Grey, Mary (2016). "Opposition to Untouchability: Gandhi and Ambedkar". A Cry for Dignity: Religion, Violence and the Struggle of Dalit Women in India. Taylor & Francis. pp. 117–118. ISBN 978-1315478401.
- Grover, V.; Arora, R. (1993). Great Women of Modern India: Vija ya Lakshmi Pandit (in Indonesian). Deep & Deep Publications. p. 185. ISBN 978-81-7100-458-4.
- Guida M. Jackson (2009). Women Leaders of Africa, Asia, Middle East, and Pacific: A Biographical Reference. Xlibris Corporation. p. 327. ISBN 978-1-4691-1353-1.
- Guida M. Jackson; Guida Myrl Jackson-Laufer; Lecturer in English Foundations Department Guida M Jackson (1999). Women Rulers Throughout the Ages: An Illustrated Guide. ABC-CLIO. p. 468. ISBN 978-1-57607-091-8.
- Gupta, Anamni (2020). "In Shaheen Bagh, turning a new page of protest". The Indian Express. Archived from the original on 1 October 2023. Retrieved 27 May 2025. It was January 17, the death anniversary of Rohith Vemula, when the organisers, including Satya, Asif, Noor, brought in their own books — a bunch of 30-35 — and placed them on display at the Shaheen Bagh bus stand under the banner of Fatima Sheikh-Savitri Bai Phule Library.
- Gupta, Charu (2016). The Gender of Caste: Representing Dalits in Print. University of Washington Press. ISBN 9780295806563. Archived from the original on 9 October 2017.
- Gupta, Charu (2007). "Dalit 'Viranganas' and Reinvention of 1857". Economic and Political Weekly. 42 (19): 1739–1745. JSTOR 4419579.
- Gupta, K. R. Gupta & Amita (2006). Concise Encyclopaedia of India. Atlantic Publishers & Dist. pp. 1013–1015. ISBN 978-81-269-0639-0.
- Hari Ram Gupta, ed. (1961). Marathas and Panipat. Panjab University. p. 24.
- Haryana (India) (1983). Haryana District Gazetteers: Sirsa. Haryana Gazetteers Organization. p.46.
- Hasrat, Bikrama Jit (1982). Dārā Shikūh: Life and Works (second ed.). New Delhi: Munshiram Manoharlal. p. 64.
- Hayat-i-Shahjehani: Life of Her Highness the late Nawab Shahjehan Begum of Bhopal; translated by B. Ghosal. Bombay : Times Press, 1926.

- Helminski, Camille Adams (2003). Women of Sufism: A Hidden Treasure. Boston: Shambhala. p. 129. ISBN 1-57062-967-6.
- Hodes, Joseph R. "Golda Meir, Sarojini Naidu, and the Rise of Female Political Leaders in British India and British Mandate Palestine." In Jews and Gender, edited by Leonard J. Greenspoon. (Purdue University Press, 2021), 185.
- Humayun-Nama : The History of Humayun by Gul-Badan Begam. Translated by Annette S. Beveridge. New Delhi, Goodword, 2001, ISBN 81-87570-99-7.
- Humayun-Nama : The History of Humayun by Gulbadan Begum, Tr. by Annette S. Beveridge (1902). New Delhi, Goodword, 2001. ISBN 81-87570-99-7.E-book at Packard Institute Excerpts at Columbia Univ.
- India Post (1962), Bhikaiji Cama, Indian Post Commemorative Stamps, New Delhi
- Irvine, William (trans.) (1907). Storia Do Mogor or Mogul India 1653–1708 by Niccolao Manucci Venetian. London: Murray. pp. 219 (vol. 1) – via Internet Archive.
- Irvine, William, ed. (1907), "Begum Saheb", Storia Do Mogor Vol 1, Oxford University press, pp. 216–217
- Iyer, N Sharada (1964). Musings on Indian Writing in English: Poetry. Sarup & Sons. p. 135. ISBN 9788176255745.
- Jafar, Mahmud Syed; Mahmud, Sayed Jafar (1994). Pillars of Modern India, 1757-1947. APH Publishing. p. 67. ISBN 978-81-7024-586-5.
- Jalali, Ghulam Reza (2008). Dignitaries Buried in the Holy Shrine of Imam al-Rida] (in Persian). Mashhad, Iran: Islamic Research Foundation, Astan Quds Razavi. p. 113. ISBN 9789649712390.
- Jayawardena, Kamari (2014). White Women's Other Burden: Western Women and South Asia during British Rule. Routledge.
- Jayawardena, Kumari (1986). Feminism and Nationalism in the Third World. Zed Books. pp. 103–104. ISBN 978-0-86232-264-9.
- JBR, Purushottam Shamsher (2007). Ranakalin Pramukh Atihasik Darbarharu [Chief Historical Palaces of the Rana Era] (in Nepali). Vidarthi Pustak Bhandar. ISBN 978-9994611027.
- John R. Hinnells (28 April 2005). The Zoroastrian Diaspora : Religion and Migration: Religion and Migration. OUP Oxford. p. 407. ISBN 978-0-19-151350-3. Retrieved 19 August 2013.
- Johnson, R.B., 2008. The Biblical Theological Contribution of Pandita Ramabai: A Neglected Pioneer Indian Christian Feminist Theologian. Ex Auditu-Volume 23: An International Journal for the Theological Interpretation of Scripture, 23, p.111.[1]
- Joseph, Chandrasekaran (1978). "Janakia arayalpathra, A new genus and species of Periplocaceae from Kerala, South India". Pascal and Francis Bibliographic Databases. ISSN 0971-751X
- Jovita Aranha (31 August 2017). "The Phenomenal Story of Kadambini: One of India's First Women Graduates & Doctors". Retrieved 22 November 2017.
- K. Sanjiva Prabhu (1977). Special Study Report on Bhuta Cult in South Kanara District. Controller of Publications, 1977. pp. 9–12.
- Kalia, Ravi (1994), Bhubaneswar: From a Temple Town to a Capital City, Southern Illinois University Press, ISBN 978-0-8093-1876-6
- Kandukuri, Divya (2019). "The life and times of Savitribai Phule". Mint Lounge. Archived from the original on 6 January 2023. Retrieved 22 January 2025.
- Karlekar, Malavika (2012). "Anatomy of a Change: Early Women Doctors". India International Centre Quarterly. 39 (3/4): 95–106. JSTOR 24394278.
- Kaw, M. K. (2004), Kashmir and its people: studies in the evolution of Kashmiri society, APH Publishing, ISBN 978-81-7648-537-1
- Khan, Aisha (2018). "Overlooked No More: Pandita Ramabai, Indian Scholar, Feminist and Educator". The New York Times. Retrieved 14 October 2024.
- Khan, Aqsa Khan (22 January 2017). "Remembering Fatima Sheikh: A Woman Lost In

History - #IndianWomenInHistory". Feminism in India. Archived from the original on 7 December 2024.
- Khandekar, Nivedita (2012). "Landmark building with uncertain fate". Hindustan Times. New Delhi. Archived from the original on 12 December 2012. Retrieved 4 October 2018.
- Kopf, David (1979). The Brahmo Samaj and the Shaping of the Modern Indian Mind. Princeton University Press. p. 125. ISBN 978-0-691-03125-5.
- Kosambi, Meera (2000). Intersections : socio-cultural trends in Maharashtra. New Delhi: Orient Longman. p. 101. ISBN 9788125018780
- Kosambi, Meera (2016). Pandita Ramabai: Life and Landmark Writings. New York: Routledge. p. 121. ISBN 978-1138962453.
- Kosambi, Meera. "Indian Response to Christianity, Church and Colonialism: Case of Pandita Ramabai." Economic and Political Weekly 27, no. 43/44 (1992): WS61–71. JSTOR 399059
- Kosambi, Meera. "Indian Response to Christianity, Church and Colonialism: Case of Pandita Ramabai." Economic and Political Weekly, vol. 27, no. 43/44, 1992, pp. WS61–WS71. JSTOR, www.jstor.org/stable/4399059.
- Kosambi, Meera; Feldhaus, Ann (Editor) (2000). Intersections : socio-cultural trends in Maharashtra. New Delhi: Orient Longman. p. 139. ISBN 9788125018780.
- Krishna Prakash Agarwal (1979). British Take-over of India: Modus Operandi : an Original Study of the Policies and Methods Adopted by the British While Taking Over India, Based on Treaties and Other Official Documents, Volume 2. Oriental Publishers & Distributors. p. 144.
- Kshirsagar, R K (1994). Dalit Movement in India and Its Leaders, 1857-1956. New Delhi: MD Publications. p. 362. ISBN 9788185880433.
- Kudva, Venkataraya Narayan (1972). History of the Dakshinatya Saraswats. Madras: Samyukta Gowda Saraswata Sabha. pp. 107–110.
- Kulke, Hermann; Rothermund, Dietmar (2004). A History of India (Fourth ed.). Routledge. p. 91. ISBN 9780415329200.
- Kumar, Radha (2014). The History of Doing: An Illustrated Account of Movements for Women's Rights and Feminism in India, 1800-1990. Zubaan. ISBN 978-93-83074-81-5.
- Kumar, Ravindra (1992). Selected Works Of Maulana Abul Kalam Azad : Volume 7. New Delhi: Atlantic Publishers. pp. 49–51.
- Kumari, Savita. Udham Bai: A Glimpse into the Aplendid Life of a Later Mughal Queen. p. 51.
- Lahiri, Shompa (18 October 2013). Indians in Britain: Anglo-Indian Encounters, Race and Identity, 1880-1930. Routledge. pp. 13–. ISBN 9781135264468. Retrieved 4 March 2014.
- Lal, K.S. (1988). The Mughal harem. New Delhi: Aditya Prakashan. p. 90. ISBN 9788185179032.
- Lal, Kishori Saran, ed. (1988), "The Charge of Incest", The Mughal Harem, Adithya Prakashan, pp. 93–94
- Lal, Muni (1986). Shah Jahan. New Delhi: Vikas Publishing House. p. 318.
- Lamb, Harold (1935). Nur Mahal. Doubleday, Doran & Co. ISBN 978-1299983229.
- Lambert-Hurley, Siobhan (2022). Three Centuries of Travel Writing By Muslim Women. Bloomington: Indiana University Press.
- Lambert-Hurley, Siobhan (24 January 2007). Muslim Women, Reform and Princely Patronage: Nawab Sultan Jahan Begam of Bhopal. Routledge. p. 158. ISBN 978-1-134-14347-4.
- Lawrence, Sir Walter Roper (2005). The Valley of Kashmir. Asian Educational Services. p. 175. ISBN 9788120616301.
- Loomba, Ania (24 July 2018). Revolutionary Desires: Women, Communism, and Feminism in India. Routledge. ISBN 978-1-351-20969-4.
- Mahotsav, Amrit. "Battalion named after Uda Devi". Azadi Ka Amrit Mahotsav, Ministry of Culture, Government of India.
- Mahotsav, Amrit. "Uda Devi: Dalit Verrangna". amritmahotsav.nic.in. Bit about early life

- Majumdar, Maya (2005). Encyclopaedia of Gender Equality Through Women Empowerment. Sarup & Sons. p. 231. ISBN 978-81-7625-548-6.
- Majumdar, RC; Raychaudhuri, HC; Datta, Kalikinkar (1990). An Advanced History of India. MacMillan India Limited. ISBN 0-333-90298-X.
- Malabari, Behramji M. (1888). ""A Hindu Lady"- and her woes". In Giduma, Dayaram (ed.). The Life and Life-work of Behramji M. Malabari. Bombay: Education Society. pp. 113–117.
- Malabari, Behramji M. (1888). "Rukhmabai and Damayanti". In Giduma, Dayaram (ed.). The Life and Life-work of Behramji M. Malabari. Bombay: Education Society. pp. 132–134, 222–248.
- Malik, Malti (2009). History of India - Main Aspects and Themes. New Delhi: Saraswati House. p. 350. ISBN 9788173354984.
- Mandakranta Bose (2000). Faces of the feminine in ancient, medieval, and modern India. Oxford University Press US. p. 192. ISBN 0-19-512229-1.
- Mansingh, Surjit (9 May 2006). Historical Dictionary of India. Scarecrow Press. p. 130. ISBN 978-0-8108-6502-0.
- Manuel, Paul Christopher; Lyon, Alynna; Wilcox, Clyde, eds. (2012). Religion and Politics in a Global Society Comparative Perspectives from the Portuguese-Speaking World. Lanham: Lexington Books. p. 68. ISBN 9780739176818.
- Manzar, Nishat (31 March 2023), "Looking Through European Eyes: Mughal State and Religious Freedom as Gleaned from The European Travellers' Accounts of the Seventeenth Century", Islam in India, London: Routledge, pp. 121–132, doi:10.4324/9781003400202-9, ISBN 978-1-003-40020-2, retrieved 12 February 2024
- Martin, Robert Montgomery (2012). The History, Antiquities, Topography, and Statistics of Eastern India: In Relation to Their Geology, Mineralogy, Botany, Agriculture, Commerce, Manufactures, Fine Arts, Population, Religion, Education, Statistics, Etc. Cambridge University Press. ISBN 9781108046503.
- Marx, Edward. "Everybody's Anima: Sarojini Naidu as Nightingale and Nationalist." In The Idea of a Colony: Cross-Culturalism in Modern Poetry. (University of Toronto Press, 2004), 57.
- McGee, Gary B. (1999). ""Latter Rain" Falling in the East: Early-Twentieth-Century Pentecostalism in India and the Debate over Speaking in Tongues". Church History. 68 (3): 648–665. doi:10.2307/3170042. JSTOR 3170042. S2CID 162798722.
- Mehta, J. L. (1986). Advanced study in the history of medieval India. New Delhi: Sterling Publishers. ISBN 81-207-0298-0. OCLC 1007201916.
- Menon, Vandana (10 January 2025). "Finding Fatima Sheikh: Scholars point to Phule's letter, photo negative & British-era document". ThePrint. Archived from the original on 14 January 2025. Retrieved 11 January 2025.
- Menon, Vandana (9 January 2018). "Fatima Sheikh: The woman who reshaped Indian education with Savitribai Phule". ThePrint. Archived from the original on 8 December 2024.
- Misra, Rekha (1967). Women of Mughal India. Munshiram Manoharlal.
- Mody, Nawaz B., ed. (1998), The Parsis in western India, 1818 to 1920 (conference proceedings), Bombay: Allied Publishers, ISBN 81-7023-894-3
- Mohammad Shujauddin, Razia Shujauddin (1967). The Life and Times of Noor Jahan. Caravan Book House. p. 25.
- Mohapatra, Padmalaya (2002). Elite Women of India. APH Publishing. pp. 65–66. ISBN 978-81-7648-339-1.
- Mokashi, Digambar Balkrishna (1987), Palkhi: An Indian Pilgrimage, SUNY Press, p. 39, ISBN 978-0-88706-461-6
- Moosvi, Shireen (2008). People, Taxation, and Trade in Mughal India. Oxford University Press. p. 264. ISBN 978-0-19-569315-7.

- Muhammad Umar (1998). Muslim Society in Northern India During the Eighteenth Century. Available with the author. p. 215. ISBN 9788121508308.
- Mukherjee (2001, p. 128)
- Mukherjee, Rudrangshu (2021). A Begum and a Rani: Hazrat Mahal and Lakshmibai in 1857. Gurugram: Penguin/Allen Lane, an imprint of Penguin Random House. ISBN 9780670090662.
- Mukherjee, Soma (2001). Royal Mughal ladies and their contributions. New Delhi: Gyan Pub. House. p. 128. ISBN 81-212-0760-6. OCLC 49618757.
- Mukherjee, Sujata (5 January 2017). Gender, Medicine, and Society in Colonial India: Women's Health Care in Nineteenth- and Early Twentieth-Century Bengal. Oxford University Press. doi:10.1093/acprof:oso/9780199468225.001.0001. ISBN 978-0-19-946822-5.
- Mukhia, Harbans (2004). The Mughals of India. Malden, MA: Wiley-Blackwell. ISBN 9780631185550.
- Murshid, Ghulam (2012). "Ganguly, Kadambini". In Islam, Sirajul; Jamal, Ahmed A. (eds.). Banglapedia: National Encyclopedia of Bangladesh (Second ed.). Asiatic Society of Bangladesh.
- N. Venkataramanayya; M. Somasekhara Sarma (1960). "The Kakatiyas of Warangal". In Ghulam Yazdani (ed.). The Early History of the Deccan Parts VII - XI. Vol. IX: The Kākatīyas of Warangal. Oxford University Press. ISBN 9788170691259. OCLC 59001459.
- N. Venkataramanayya; P.V.P. Sastry (1957). "The Kākatīyas". In R.S. Sharma (ed.). A Comprehensive history of India: A.D. 985-1206. Vol. 4 (Part 1) (1987 reprint ed.). Indian History Congress / People's Publishing House. ISBN 978-81-7007-121-1.
- Nadkarni, Asha. "Regenerating Feminism: Sarojini Naidu's Eugenic Feminist Renaissance." In Eugenic Feminism: Reproductive Nationalism in the United States of America and India. (University of Minnesota Press, 2014), 73.
- Nadkarni, Asha. "Regenerating Feminism: Sarojini Naidu's Eugenic Feminist Renaissance." In Eugenic Feminism: Reproductive Nationalism in the United States and India. (University of Minnesota Press, 2014), 72.
- Naidu, Sarojini (1905). The golden threstold. London: Heineman.
- Naidu, Sarojini (1912). Gosse, Edmund (ed.). The bird of time; songs of life, death & the spring. New York, London: John Lane company; W. Heinemann.
- Naidu, Sarojini (1925). Speeches and writings of Sarojini Naidu (3rd ed.). Madras: G.A. Natesan & co.
- Narayan, Badri (2006). Women Heroes and Dalit Assertion in North India: culture, identity and politics. Sage. ISBN 978-0-7619-3537-7.
- Narayan, Badri (2006). Women Heroes and Dalit Assertion in North India: Culture, Identity and Politics. SAGE Publications India. ISBN 9788132102809.
- Narayan, Badri (2006). Women Heroes and Dalit Assertion in North India: Culture, Identity and Politics. SAGE Publications. ISBN 978-0-7619-3537-7.
- Narayan, Badri (2006). Women Heroes and Dalit Assertion in North India: Culture, Identity and Politics. SAGE Publications India. ISBN 9788132102809. Archived from the original on 9 October 2017.
- Nath, Renuka (1990). Notable Mughal and Hindu Women in the 16th and 17 Centuries A.D. New Delhi: Inter-India Publications. p. 129. ISBN 81-210-0241-9.
- Nath, Renuka (1990). Notable Mughal and Hindu Women in the 16th and 17th Centuries A.D. New Delhi: Inter-India Publications. pp. 120–121. ISBN 81-210-0241-9.
- Nath, Renuka (1990). Notable Mughal and Hindu women in the 16th and 17th centuries A.D. New Delhi: Inter-India Publications. pp. 124–125. ISBN 81-210-0241-9.
- Nath, Renuki (1990). Notable Mughal and Hindu Women in the 16th and 17th Centuries A.D. New Delhi: Inter-India Publications. p. 136. ISBN 81-210-0241-9.

- Nehru, Jawaharlal (1989). The Discovery of India. Oxford University Press. ISBN 0-19-561322-8.
- Nehru, Krishna (1945). With No Regrets: An Autobiography. New York: The John Day Company.
- Neth, Renuka (1990). Notable Mughal and Hindi Women in the 16th and 17th Centuries A.D. New Delhi: Inter-India Publications. p. 125. ISBN 81-210-0241-9.
- Nicoll, Fergus (2009). Shah Jahan. London: Haus Publishing. p. 201. ISBN 978-1-906598-18-1.
- O'Brien, Jo9167 (2009). "Naidu, Sarojini (1879-1949)". Encyclopedia of Gender and Society. SAGE Publications Inc.
- O'Hanlon, Rosalind (2022). "What a photograph tells us about Fatima Sheikh". The Indian Express. Archived from the original on 16 February 2022.
- O'Hanlon, Rosalind. 1991. Issues of Widowhood: Gender and Resistance in Colonial Western India , in Douglas Haynes and Gyan Prakash (eds) "Contesting Power. Resistance and Everyday Social Relations in South Asia", Oxford University Press, New Delhi.
- O'Hanlon, Rosalind. 1994. For the Honour of My Sister Countrywomen: Tarabai Shinde and the Critique of Gender Relations in Colonial India, Oxford University Press, Oxford.
- O'Hanlon, Rosalind. 2000. A Comparison Between Women and Men : Tarabai Shinde and the Critique of Gender Relations in Colonial India. Delhi, Oxford University Press, 2000, 144 p., ISBN 0-19-564736-X.
- O'Malley, Lewis Sydney Steward (1985). Indian civil service, 1601–1930. London: Frank Cass. p. 76. ISBN 9780714620237.
- P.V.P. Sastry (1978). N. Ramesan (ed.). The Kākatiyas of Warangal. Hyderabad: Government of Andhra Pradesh. OCLC 252341228.
- Pal, Sanchari (2016). "The Untold Story of Bhikaji Cama". The Better India.
- Pandit, Vijaya Lakshmi (1939). "First Person, Singular". So I became a Minister. Allahabad: Kitabistan. pp. 141–143.
- Pandit, Vijaya Lakshmi (1979). "Interim Government". The Scope of Happiness: A Personal Memoir. New York: Crown Publishers Inc. p. 225. ISBN 0-517-53688-9.
- Pandit, Vijaya Lakshmi (1979). "Interim Government". The Scope of Happiness: A Personal Memoir. New York: Crown Publishers Inc. pp. 200–201, 203, 204–205. ISBN 0-517-53688-9.
- Paranjape, Makarand R. (2012). Making India: Colonialism, National Culture, and the Afterlife of Indian English Authority. Springer Science & Business Media. ISBN 978-94-007-4661-9.
- Pasricha, Ashu (2009). The political thought of Annie Besant. New Delhi: Concept Pub. Co. p. 24. ISBN 978-81-8069-585-8.
- Paswan, Sanjay (2004). Encyclopaedia of Dalits in India: Leaders, Volume 4. New Delhi: Kalpaz Publications. p. 285. ISBN 9788178350332.
- Patnaik, Santosh (2022). "AP introduces lesson in schools on Fatima Sheikh, India's first woman Muslim teacher". The Siasat Daily. Archived from the original on 11 January 2023.
- Pinaki Biswas (2021). Rabindranath Hatya Shorojantra (Bengali). Kolkata: Lalmati Prakashan. p. 22. ISBN 978-81-953129-3-1.
- Ponvannan, Gayathri (2019). Unstoppable : 75 stories of trailblazing Indian women. Hachette Book Publishing India Pvt Ltd. p. 272. ISBN 9789388322003.
- Prasad, Madhu (2019). "A strategy for exclusion". In Raina, Jyoti (ed.). Elementary Education in India: Policy Shifts, Issues and Challenges. Taylor & Francis. p. 166. ISBN 978-1000586954.
- Professor R. Nath; Ajay Nath (2020). Monuments of Delhi: Architectural & Historical. Ajay Nath, The Heritage Ajmer/Jaipur, India. p. 97.

- Rajadhyaksha, Ashish; Willemen, Paul (1999). Encyclopaedia of Indian cinema. British Film Institute. ISBN 9780851706696. Retrieved 12 August 2012.
- Rakesh Ankit, "Between Vanity and Sensitiveness: Indo–British Relations During Vijayalakshmi Pandit's High-Commissioner (1954–61)." Contemporary British History 30.1 (2016): 20–39.
- Ramabai Sarasvati (Pandita); Pandita Ramabai (2003). Pandita Ramabai's American Encounter: The Peoples of the United States (1889). Indiana University Press. pp. 29–30. ISBN 0-253-21571-4.
- Raman, Sita Anantha (2006). "Naidu, Sarojini". In Wolpert, Stanley (ed.). Encyclopedia of India. Vol. 3. Charles Scribner's Sons. pp. 212–213.
- Rappaport, Helen (2001). Encyclopedia of Women Social Reformers. ABC-CLIO. p. 507. ISBN 978-1-57607-101-4.
- Rappaport, Helen (2003). Queen Victoria: A Biographical Companion. ABC-CLIO. p. 429. ISBN 9781851093557.
- Rebecca Ruth Gould "How Gulbadan Remembered: The Book of Humāyūn as an Act of Representation," Early Modern Women, Vol. 6, pp. 121–127, 2011
- Richard M. Eaton (2005). A Social History of the Deccan, 1300-1761: Eight Indian Lives. Cambridge University Press. ISBN 9780521254847.
- Rizvi, Saiyid Athar Abbas (1983). A History of Sufism in India. Vol. 2. New Delhi: Mushiram Manoharlal. p. 481. ISBN 81-215-0038-9.
- Robb, George; Erber, Nancy (1999). Disorder in the Court: Trials and Sexual Conflict at the Turn of the Century. Springer. pp. 42–44.
- S K Sharma (2004), Eminent Indian Freedom Fighters, Anmol Publications PVT. LTD., p. 560, ISBN 978-81-261-1890-8
- Safvi, Rana (2016). "The Forgotten Women of 1857". The Wire-GB. Archived from the original on 11 August 2016. Retrieved 19 June 2016.
- Sahu, Skylab (2023). Unfolding Feminism in India: Women, Power and Politics. Taylor & Francis. p. 181. ISBN 978-1-000-84972-1.
- Sarala, Srikrishna (1999). Indian Revolutionaries: a comprehensive study, 1757–1961. Vol. I. Prabhat Prakashan. ISBN 978-81-87100-16-4.
- Sarasvati (Pandita), Ramabai (1946). A Testimony: The Life Story of Pandita Ramabai, Founder of the Mukti Mission to the Child-widows and Orphans of India, Kedgaon, Poona District. Franklin Press.
- Sarkar, Amar Nath; Prasad, Bithika, eds. (2008). Critical response to Indian poetry in English. New Delhi: Sarup & Sons. p. 11. ISBN 978-81-7625-825-8.
- Sarkar, Jadunath (1989). Studies in Aurangzeb's Reign. London: Sangam Books Ltd. p. 107.
- Sarkar, Jadunath (1997). Fall of the Mughal Empire (4th ed.). Hyderabad: Orient Longman. p. 169. ISBN 9788125011491.
- Sarkar, Sumit; Sarkar, Tanika (2008). Women and Social Reform in Modern India: A Reader – Sumit Sarkar, Tanika Sarkar – Google Books. Indiana University Press. ISBN 9780253352699.
- Sarker, Kobita (2007). Shah Jahan and his paradise on earth : the story of Shah Jahan's creations in Agra and Shahjahanabad in the golden days of the Mughals. Kolkata: K.P. Bagchi & Co. p. 187. ISBN 978-81-7074-300-2. OCLC 176865104.
- Sarojini Shintri, Kurukundi Raghavendra Rao (1983). Women freedom fighters in Karnataka. Dharwad: Prasaranga, Karnatak University. pp. 13, 14.
- Sauquet, Michel (2004). L'idiot du village mondial: Les citoyens de la planète face à l'explosion des outils de communication: subir ou maîtriser (in French). ECLM. ISBN 978-2-84377-094-4.
- Schimmel, Annemarie (2004). The Empire of the great Mughals: history, art and culture. London: Reaktion Books. pp. 266. ISBN 1-86189-185-7.

- Schimmel, Annemarie (1997). My Soul Is a Woman: The Feminine in Islam. New York: Continuum. p. 50. ISBN 0-8264-1014-6.
- Schimmel, Annemarie (1997). My Soul Is a Woman: The Feminine in Islam. New York: Continuum. p. 51. ISBN 0-8264-1014-6.
- Sen, Indrani (2012). "Resisting Patriarchy: Complexities and Conflicts in the Memoir of Haimabati Sen". Economic and Political Weekly. 47 (12): 55–62, quotes from pages 55 and 57. ISSN 0012-9976. JSTOR 23214502.
- Sen, Sailendra (2013). A Textbook of Medieval Indian History. Primus Books. pp. 118–119. ISBN 978-9-38060-734-4.
- Sen, Sailendra Nath (1999). Ancient Indian History and Civilization. New Age International. p. 296. ISBN 9788122411980.
- Sengupta, Arjun (10 January 2023). "Who was Fatima Sheikh: India's oft-forgotten feminist icon". The Indian Express.
- Sengupta, Padmini (1970). Pandita Ramabai Saraswati: Her Life and Work. Asia Publishing House. ISBN 978-0-210-22611-7.
- Sengupta, Padmini. "Sarojini Naidu: A Biography" (Bombay: Asia Publishing House, 1966), 157.
- Sengupta, Subodh Chandra and Anjali Basu (ed.) (1988) Sansad Bangali Charitabhidhan (in Bengali), Kolkata: Sahitya Sansad, p.663
- Sengupta, Subodh; Basu, Anjali (2016). Sansad Bangali Charitavidhan (Bengali). Vol. 1. Kolkata: Sahitya Sansad. ISBN 978-81-7955-135-6.
- Sharma, Sudha (21 March 2016). The Status of Muslim Women in Medieval India. SAGE Publications India. ISBN 9789351505679.
- Shastri, Ajay Mitra (1997). Vakatakas: Sources and History. Aryan Books International. p. 182. ISBN 9788173051234.
- Shinde, Tarabai. 1882. Stri purush tulana. (Translated by Maya Pandit). In S. Tharu and K. Lalita (Eds.) "Women writing in India. 600 B.C. to the present. Volume I: 600 B.C. to the early 20th century". The City University of New York City: The Feminist Press.
- Shujauddin, Mohammad; Shujauddin, Razia (1967). The Life and Times of Noor Jahan. Caravan Book House. p. 1.
- Siddha Mohana Mitra (1909). Moslem-Hindu Entente Cordiale: With Special Reference to Lord Morley's Indian Reforms, Part 13. Publishing Department, Oriental Institute. p. 5.
- Simlandy, Sagar; Mandal, Ganesh Kr (2021). History of India & Abroad. BFC Publications. p. 169. ISBN 978-93-90880-20-1.
- Singh, Pratikshit (9 January 2023). "Fatima Sheikh: Coming out of the shadows of Savitri Bai Phule". The Mooknayak. Archived from the original on 21 March 2023.
- Singh, Satnam (2013). Swatantrata Sangram Mei Achhut Jatiyon Ka Yogdan (in Hindi) (1st, 2nd ed.). Delhi, India: Samyak Prakashan. p. 38. ISBN 9789391503079. Veerangna Uda Devi Pasi
- Singh, Upinder (2009). A history of ancient and early medieval India: from the Stone Age to the 12th century. New Delhi: Pearson Longman. p. 482. ISBN 978-81-317-1677-9.
- Siobhan Lambert-Hurley Muslim Women, Reform and Princely Patronage: Nawab Sultan Jahan Begam of Bhopal. Routledge, 2007. ISBN 0-415-40192-5.
- Smith, B.G. (2008). The Oxford Encyclopedia of Women in World History. Oxford University Press. p. 2-PA406. ISBN 978-0-19-514890-9.
- Stein, Mark Aurel (1900), Kalhana's Rajatarangini: a chronicle of the kings of Kasmir, Volume 2 (Reprinted ed.), Motilal Banarsidass, ISBN 978-81-208-0370-1
- Stein, Mark Aurel (1989a) (1900), Kalhana's Rajatarangini: a chronicle of the kings of Kasmir, Volume 1 (Reprinted ed.), Motilal Banarsidass, ISBN 978-81-208-0369-5
- Subhash Parihar, Some Aspects of Indo-Islamic Architecture (1999), p. 149

- Subodh Kumar Sengupta & Anjali Bose (2016). Sansad Bengali Charitabhidhan Vol.I. Sahitya Sansad,Kolkata. p. 883. ISBN 978-81-7955-135-6.
- Swami Ghanananda; John Stewart-Wallace (1979). Women Saints of East and West. Vedanta Press. p. 60. ISBN 0-87481-036-1.
- Taher, Mohamed, ed. (1997). Mughal India. Delhi: Anmoi. p. 53.
- Taraporevala, Sooni (2004), Parsis: The Zoroastrians of India: A Photographic Journey, New York City: Overlook Press, ISBN 1-58567-593-8
- Thackeray, Frank W.; Findling, John E. (2012). Events that formed the modern world: from the European Renaissance through the War on Terror. Santa Barbara, Calif.: ABC-CLIO. p. 254. ISBN 978-1-59884-902-8. OCLC 828682002.
- Thakur, Harinarayan (2009). Dalit Sahitya Ka Samajshastra (in Hindi). Bhartiya Jnanpith. ISBN 978-81-263-1734-9.
- Thapar, Romila. A History of India, vol. 1. London: Penguin Books, 1987. pp. 225–226.
- Tharu, Susie J.; Lalita, K. (1991). Women Writing in India: 600 B.C. to the early twentieth century. Feminist Press at CUNY. p. 162. ISBN 978-1-55861-027-9.
- Thilagavathi, L.; Chandrababu, B.S. (2009). Woman, her history and her struggle for emancipation. Chennai: Bharathi Puthakalayam. p. 312. ISBN 9788189909970.
- Thomas William Beale (1894). Henry George Keene (ed.). An Oriental Biographical Dictionary. W.H. Allen. p. 42. ISBN 978-1-4047-0648-4.
- Thombre P.v. (2007). Life and Life's-Work of Shree Devi Ahilya Bai Holkar. Holkar State History Vol. 5 pp. 23–24.
- Three Memoirs of Homayun. Volume One: Humáyunnáma and Tadhkiratu'l-wáqiát; Volume Two: Táríkh-i Humáyún, translated from the Persian by Wheeler Thackston. Bibliotheca Iranica/Intellectual Traditions Series, Hossein Ziai, Editor-in-Chief. Bilingual Edition, No. 11 (15 March 2009)
- Tillotson, Giles (2008). Taj Mahal. Cambridge, Mass.: Harvard University Press. p. 22. ISBN 9780674063655.
- Treasure Trove: A Collection of ICSE Poems and Short Stories. New Delhi: Evergreen Publications (INDIA) Ltd. 2020. p. 13. ISBN 9789350637005.
- Tschurenev, Jana (2019). "Civil Society, Government, and Educational Institution-Building, Bombay Presidency, 1819–1882". Empire, Civil Society, and the Beginnings of Colonial Education in India. Cambridge University Press. pp. 276–279. ISBN 978-1108656269.
- Ungalwalla, P.N. (1966). "Review of Sarojini Naidu, a Biography by Padmini Sengupta". Indian Literature. 9 (2): 101–103. JSTOR 23329487
- Usha Thakkar, Jayshree Mehta (2011). Understanding Gandhi: Gandhians in Conversation with Fred J Blum. SAGE Publications. pp. 409–410. ISBN 978-81-321-0557-2.
- Vallée, Gérard, ed. (2007). Florence Nightingale on Social Change in India: Collected Works of Florence Nightingale, Volume 10. Wilfrid Laurier University Press. pp. 775–776.
- Varma, Vrindavanlala; Sahaya, Amita (2001). Lakshmi Bai, the rani of Jhansi. Prabhat Prakashan. ISBN 978-81-87100-54-6.
- Verinder Grover (1993). Great Women of Modern India. Vol. 5: Raj Kumari Amrit Kaur. Deep & Deep. ISBN 9788171004591.
- Verma, R.D (1996). Virangana Uda Devi. Mahindra Printing Press.
- Vishwakarma, Sanjeev Kumar. Feminism and Literature: Text and Context. Allahabad (India): Takhtotaaz. pp. 132–139. ISBN 978-81-922645-6-1.
- Yecurī, Sītārāma (2008). The great revolt, a left appraisal. People's Democracy. ISBN 9788190621809.

About the author

Dr. Iti Samanta, a well-known creative writer, novelist, researcher, eminent editor of the famous family magazine 'The Kadambini', national award-winning film producer and social entrepreneur occupies a significant position in contemporary Odisha. Despite being brought up by her mother single-handedly in abject poverty she successfully overthrew the obstacles in pursuing higher studies and carrying forward her efforts in shaping her life to a successful one. Her life is itself an example of woman empowerment. Starting her life struggling to have two times meal a day to a multifaceted personality now and be able to feed many families and securing their futures by providing job opportunities in her multi setup organisations. She is a popular household name today for her continuous scintillating efforts in revamping Odisha's language, literature, culture, and arts through her conglomerate foundations. All her works dignify women and strive to give them their rights which are often infringed by the arbitrary practices that exist in the society by becoming their voices.

Since 2000 'The Kadambini' has been flourishing and has set a new era in the history of Odia magazine for its regularity, new dimension, colourful illustration and reader centred approach. The entire success of this journal depends on the passion and perception, dedication and determination of its celebrated editor Dr. Iti Samanta. She has been continuously writing her editorials in 'The Kadambini', the most popular family magazine in Odisha on different women related issues, women empowerment and current social problems above two decades. She rediscovered various facets of characters portrayed in the great epics of 'Ramayan' and 'Mahabharat'. One definitely finds a sustained effort by her to draw the contours of modernity which accommodates strong female characters of our ancient society. Above all from history also Dr. Samanta's continued popularity amongst innumerable readers hinges on her series of editorials. 'The Kunikatha', another interesting and educative magazine for young children is also edited and published by Dr. Iti Samanta. She flourished as a writer, braving many distractions that came in her life. Her first book 'Tathaapi' is a collection of short stories came out in the year 2001. Since then, she never looked back.

To promote literature, she has started Kadambini Patrika Haata, Kadambini Literary Festival and Nilimarani Sahitya Samman. She is well known for her social work. Inspired by her brother great educationist and philanthropist Dr. Achyuta Samanta, she has been actively involved in reforming their native village Kalarabank to a Smart Model Village. Presently, there are two schools Kalinga English Medium School and Kalarabank High School, temple complex, rural hospital, library and community centre in her village for sustainable development and women empowerment. She has been motivating the women folk of the rural area to enhance their social and economic standard and by constituting self-help groups. She is imparting holistic education keeping in mind the students be accustomed with the new technological advancement and inherit our cultural values. And most of her works are for the women, realising their problems at every stage she not only brings them to the mainstream society but also gives her efforts in sorting their problems out.

In addition to revamping Odia Language and literature she is working to preserve and promote our state's insignia for rich handloom textile through her luxury designer house 'Shephalee'. She has simultaneously managed to build a varied portfolio of work that spans the entire Art and culture domain. She has a distinct taste in apparel and is an avid connoisseur of hand-crafted Sarees. She has been designing her own Sarees for a long time and has exclusively designed all the creations out of hand weaved fabrics with each being a unique piece at 'Shephalee'.

As a step towards fulfilling Kadambini Media's commitment for literature, it has published / is publishing books with high literary value authored by eminent as well as young writers. As a part of its endeavour, Media has also ventured into the audio-visual medium. So far it has produced several music albums and Video CDs of popular songs. Kadambini Media also has marked its debut in films with its maiden production 'Kathantara' (Another Story), a film with 1999 Super-cyclone as its backdrop. 'Kathantara' went on to bag 8 awards in the 18th Odisha State Film Awards-2005 and Silver Lotus for the Best Odia Feature Film- 2006 in the 53rd National Film Awards. It also participated and received critical acclaims in several National and International Film Festivals. Media's second feature film 'Krantidhara' (Coup de grace) is based on the struggle of women in grass root politics which has been highly acclaimed by critics and audiences in various national and international film festivals and owned 3 Awards in the Odisha State Film Awards-2014. She has produced short film 'Kahani Nuhen', non-feature/documentary film 'The Sea & Seven Villages', 'Kahe Ballav...', telefilm 'Tapoi', educational film 'Chithi', 'Kanya Ratna' & many more. Apart from these she has been consistently involved in television programmes. Her show 'Iti nka Alapa' has generated many conversations with the people who have impacted society with their ideas, determination and struggle. These people have spread Odia language in various platforms over the decades and are testimonial to our depth and gravitas. Her aim through these conversations is to bring to the people the stalwarts of our art and culture. Her conversational show 'Iti nka Alapa' has received overwhelming and tremendous response from all viewers.

Though she had a B.Tech degree in Electronics and Tele Communication Engineering she was attracted to literature and with the inner feeling and passion for creativity, she did her M.A in Odia literature and Master's Degree in Mass Communication and finally achieved PhD in Literature from Visva Bharti, Santiniketan. As a sincere and serious scholar she was awarded Junior and Senior Fellowship from Ministry of Culture, Govt. of India. Her research project to that effect was innovative and influential.

Before Joining the Master's programme in journalism, Dr. Iti Samanta had been practising journalism as the Editor of 'The Kadambini' (a monthly feature magazine).She used to write features on various social, literal, cultural, and socio-political issues. Some of her features were also published in different newspapers and magazines of the state. She has got the art of interviewing people and bringing out different facets of their personalities. Since the beginning of her journalistic career, she has covered hundreds of people from different spheres and has conducted many television shows as a programme producer, content designer, interviewer, and moderator. Besides these, her great ideas have taken the form of books and novels. She has written more than 30 books varying from fiction to factual educational, informational, and eye-opener for society.

Dr. Iti Samanta has been holding several important positions in public and private bodies like CBFC, Govt. of India; Postal Dept., Odisha State Film Award committee, Taranga Cine Award committee, Feature Film Jury Member, 54th International Film Festival of India (IFFI), Indian Panorama etc.

All these activities reflect her unique personality enriched with simplicity, magnanimity, sincerity and dedication.

It seems unbelievable how a person who barely managed to eat ample food a day has become a successful personality with her strong determination to overcome the adverse situations and now has taken responsibility of an overall growth of the ecosystem she is the part of.

Above all she is a self-made woman who has dedicated her whole life for upliftment of women, language, literature, art, culture and social issues.

EARLY LIFE

Dr. Iti Samanta was born in 1970 in a non-descript village Kalarabanka a rural hinterland in Cuttack district in the state of Odisha.

She is the youngest of seven siblings of Nilimarani Samanta and Anadi Charan Samanta. She was neither fortunate to grow up with her father, who passed away while she was only two months old nor had a family income to support her early education and was brought up by her mother amidst abject poverty and sticky social challenges.

Dwelling on margins the lives of herself and her six siblings could be hardly described as decent. The cemented reality of poverty in her life never deterred her from getting an education. With her academic excellence and daily errands or petty activities to augment her family's income she stubbornly faced poverty at unimaginable lengths. It was her grit and firm passion of education that drove her through unchartered paths of economic deprivation to finally complete her engineering. As life had it, her passion of writing and reading in her early years culminated later in her becoming a writer.

EDUCATION

Dr. Iti Samanta pursued her primary education in her village school at Kalarabanka and after that shifted to Cuttack and passed High School Certificate Examination from Khan Nagar High School. After her High School education she took admission in Ramadevi Women's College, Bhubaneswar for pursuing Higher Secondary education in science. Soon after the completion of +2 science she joined **Electronics & Tele-communication Engineering** course to financially support her family. But she had a strong desire since her School days to become a writer, so her literary calling passion gained over her and after completion of engineering degree again she changed her academic pursuit to literature which brought her a meritorious **Post Graduate Degree in Odia Literature** and a lambent **Masters Degree in Mass Communications and Advanced Journalism from Utkal University**, Odisha. Later, she did her **Ph.D in literature from Visva-Bharati**, Santiniketan. She was also awarded **Junior and** prestigious **Senior Fellowship of the Ministry of Culture, Govt. of India**.

CAREER AS SOCIAL ENTREPRENEUR

While **Dr. Iti Samanta** climbed the scholarly career in literature and communication studies, the inner calling of the creative desire, forced her to dedicate herself for promotion of literature, art, culture and heritage of Odisha. The result of this alchemy of creative spirit and literary entrepreneurship led to the establishment of **Kadambini Media Pvt. Ltd.** with the sole objective of promoting art, culture, literature, language and cinema in Odisha and India as well.

The journey of Dr. Samanta in setting up one of the premier media conglomerates is highly inspirational. In its odyssey of Twenty six years 'The Kadambini' has been propagating the empowerment of women as it's nuclei along with overall development of the society and a change in certain perspectives. The monthly magazine is a torchbearer of Odia language, literature, art and culture at the global podium. With the highest readership of any Odia magazine; around a million 'The Kadambini's impact is staggering for propelling an equal, liberal, culturally acknowledged and sophisticated society. Apart from helming the editorial part of 'The Kadambini' she also looks after the marketing of the magazine, so that Odia literature gains enormous readership in popular paradigm. She also works on the advertising as sustaining a magazine is a highly tedious job. 'The Kadambini' turned twenty six years pursuing its service to Odia literature. Through the Kadambini, Dr. Samanta has not only thrown light on elegant prose and poetry but also on socially contentious topics which have enlightened the masses about the downtrodden and marginalised sections amply. 'The Kadambini's acceptance amongst lakhs portrays her popularity and the acceptance of her writings.

Dr. Iti Samanta has proved herself as a successful social entrepreneur in the field of language, literature, education, art, culture and film production. She has received the women entrepreneurship award. A recipient of numerous prestigious awards, Dr. Iti Samanta is not merely a writer or filmmaker - she is a cultural torchbearer, social reformer, and a visionary devoted to the evolution of Odisha's identity across platforms.

□

Black Eagle Books

www.blackeaglebooks.org
info@blackeaglebooks.org

Black Eagle Books, an independent publisher, was founded as a nonprofit organization in April, 2019. It is our mission to connect and engage the Indian diaspora and the world at large with the best of works of world literature published on a collaborative platform, with special emphasis on foregrounding Contemporary Classics and New Writing.

www.ingramcontent.com/pod-product-compliance
Lightning Source LLC
Chambersburg PA
CBHW080321080526
44585CB00021B/2424